GW00570011

Agent
Michael Trotobas

'No villain need be! Passions spin the plot:
We are betrayed by what is false within.'
George Meredith

Agent
Michael Trotobas

And SOE in Northern France

Stewart Kent
and Nick Nicholas

Pen & Sword
MILITARY

First published in Great Britain in 2015 by
PEN AND SWORD MILITARY
an imprint of
Pen and Sword Books Ltd
47 Church Street
Barnsley
South Yorkshire S70 2AS

ISBN 978 1 47385 163 4

Printed and bound in England by
CPI Group (UK) Ltd, Croydon, CR0 4YY

Typeset in Times by CHIC GRAPHICS

Pen & Sword Books Ltd incorporates the imprints of
Archaeology, Atlas, Aviation, Battleground, Discovery,
Family History, History, Maritime, Military, Naval, Politics,
Railways, Select, Social History, Transport, True Crime,
Claymore Press, Frontline Books, Leo Cooper, Praetorian Press,
Remember When, Seaforth Publishing and Wharncliffe.

For a complete list of Pen and Sword titles please contact
Pen and Sword Books Limited
47 Church Street, Barnsley, South Yorkshire, S70 2AS, England
E-mail: enquiries@pen-and-sword.co.uk
Website: www.pen-and-sword.co.uk

Contents

Foreword
by Mark Seaman

The Special Operations Executive (SOE), a dynamic wartime British secret service created in 1940, attracted a remarkable collection of men and women into its ranks. Hardly surprisingly, the agents that it sent behind enemy lines on hazardous missions have attracted great attention from writers and historians and the members of its F (Independent French) Section have been the most closely scrutinised. The Section was formed to help foment resistance in both Vichy-controlled and German-occupied France so that the patriots' efforts could support Allied strategic priorities rather than become enmeshed in (and perhaps neutralised by) French internal politics. To this end the Section relied heavily upon bi-lingual British citizens for its agent pool. These men and women were a very mixed bunch including amongst its number an artist, a teacher, a widow, a grandmother, a lawyer and even a female American journalist with an artificial foot. Apart from a fluency in the French language (and even this was by no means uniform) there was little that the agents had in common other than the special training they received from SOE and their outstanding courage in volunteering for perilous operations launched into the heart of Nazi-occupied Europe.

Many books have been written by and about the F Section agents. Regrettably, all too few have done their subjects justice and authors, publishers and even readers have seemed to favour a good yarn or even a hagiography rather than accurate, factual accounts of these brave men and women. Given that some of these personalities have been the subject of several published works, it is perhaps surprising that it has taken so long for a biography of Michael Trotobas, one of F Section's most daring and resourceful agents, to be written. Even amongst this diverse bunch of heroes and heroines, he emerges as singularly unique; not only had he experienced a tough, working class upbringing but by the outbreak of war he was a non-commissioned officer in the Middlesex Regiment having served seven years with the colours. Unlike most of his fellow SOE agents, he saw action during the battle of France, experiencing great physical danger and being wounded in combat. Trotobas had received an officer's commission before joining F Section in 1941 but there is no doubt that he retained the common touch. While several of his agent contemporaries in France chose to use their ample SOE operational funds to live in comfort in Paris or on the Côte d'Azur, Trotobas made the decision to inhabit the *demi-monde* of *estaminets*, race tracks and smugglers' haunts around Lille, one of the most heavily industrialised regions of the country. Here, in this milieu he found committed, patriotic Frenchmen and women who sought to offer resistance to the German occupation of their country. However, as time went by, no small amount of his followers' motivation was derived from strong personal loyalty to Trotobas himself.

In spite of this pronounced undercurrent of personal affiliation to a charismatic leader, Trotobas's story contains, regrettably, strong strands of weakness and betrayal. Not only did locally recruited members of his FARMER network prove fallible but at least two of his fellow SOE agents were found wanting. We should not be surprised that it has taken a long time for these less savoury aspects of SOE's history to come to the fore. The closure of official SOE records until the 1990s and a desire to protect veterans from (true and false) accusations concerning their behaviour during the war had the effect of largely muting critical analysis. This volume now sets the record straight. Sensibly, the authors have not launched a witch hunt to pillory those responsible for Trotobas's death and their assessments are both fair and grounded on a rigorous examination of all available evidence. Their conclusions that individuals made mistakes and failed to meet the high standards expected of them constitute the sort of assessment historians must surely be permitted to make some seventy years after the events took place. By failing to concede that not everyone performed in an exemplary manner, we inevitably undermine the essential recognition of those who did. But these words of introduction should not conclude by focusing upon those colleagues who failed to attain Trotobas's own exacting standards of duty, bravery and sacrifice. Rather, we should welcome this biography of a complex, sometimes 'difficult' and, like all of us, flawed individual. But what emerges is a rounded character who found his true *metier* commanding a resistance group. Trotobas was an accomplished organiser, an audacious saboteur and an inspirational leader – this book is a fine testament to his life and confirms his real status as a true Anglo-French hero of the Second World War.

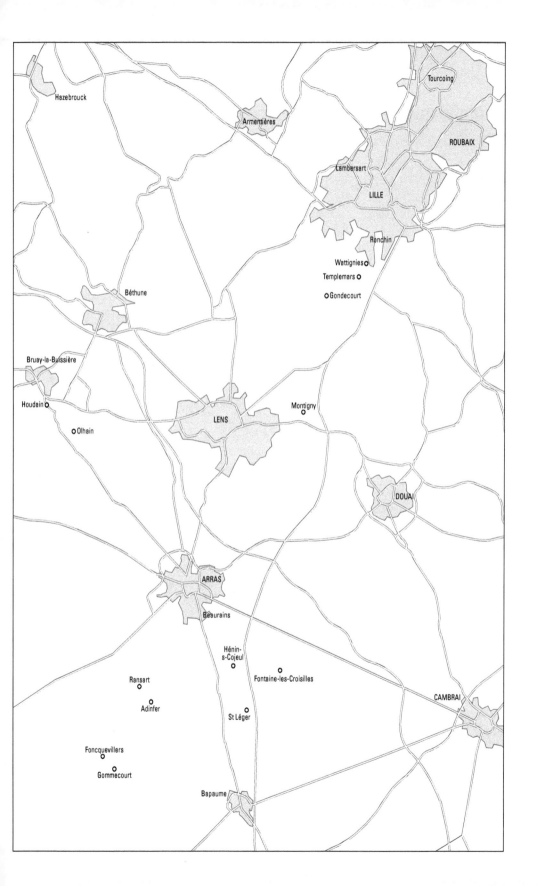

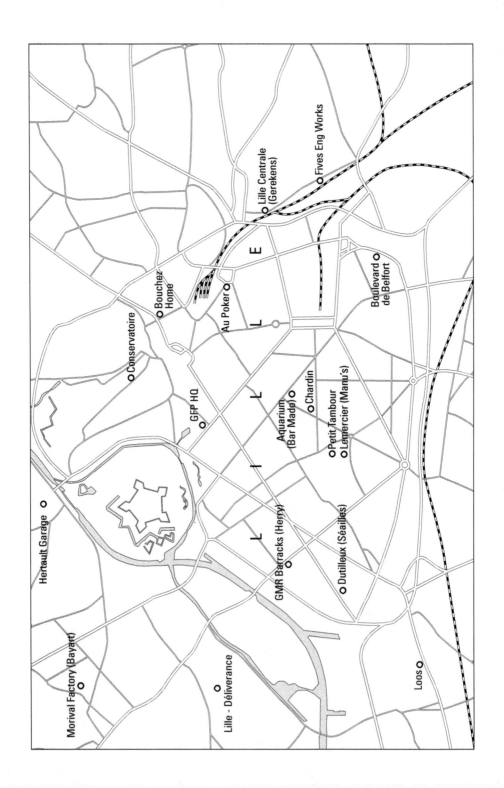

Hertault Garage

Morival Factory (Bayart)

Lille - Déliverance

Conservatoire

GFP HQ

GMR Barracks (Herry)

Aquarium (Bar Made)

Chardin

Petit Tambour
Lemercier (Manu's)

Dutilleux (Séailles)

Loos

Bouchez Home

Au Poker

LILLE

Lille Centrale (Gerekens)

Fives Eng Works

Boulevard de Belfort

Introduction
by Stewart Kent

The exciting and intriguing story of Michael Trotobas has never been published in England and the actions of the resistance groups in the north of France are largely unknown. They have been lost among the more high profile activities around Paris and the glamorous concept of the thousands of members of the *Maquis* who rose out of the hills and woods to play their part in the liberation of France following the Allied invasion in June 1944. Among the scores of post-war publications dedicated to the history of the SOE and the heroism of individual agents there is not one that presents a whole year in the life of one resistance circuit.

When I embarked on my research for this book in 1994 I had no idea that it would take me twenty years to see it come to fruition. There were huge chunks of inactivity during this time due to family and business commitments. It was only a move to Cornwall from London that allowed me to start pulling all my research together. It was already more than fifty years after the events themselves, when even the youngest of the surviving participants was already in their seventies.

My early research took me to the Imperial War Museum in London and to Mark Seaman, then its specialist historian and adviser on SOE. Over a cup of coffee and an hour of outlining the reason behind my research, I was encouraged to commit the story to paper. Mark was as enthralled and captivated by the story as I had been from the very beginning. We both realized that the book would not only serve as a vehicle for personal stories of great interest, but provide an opportunity to give long overdue credit and recognition to the deeds of members of the resistance in the Nord and Pas de Calais regions of France, and in the Arras sector in particular. These have not before been chronicled in any British text. I should like to stress that I do not claim this to be a history of SOE, nor a history of SOE in France, nor yet of SOE as a whole in northern France and the Pas de Calais. It is a reconstructed, selective story of one sector of the resistance in those areas, focusing on the interactions between the people in response to the events that befell them rather than on the historical backcloth against which they were played out.

Mark soon introduced me to Professor M.R.D. Foot, the official author of *SOE in France*. Published in 1966, his book was to be my bible on the subject. At around the same time Mark also introduced me to Gervase Cowell, then custodian of the SOE archives. Gervase was the SOE Adviser to the Foreign and Commonwealth Office. All three – Mark, Professor Foot and Gervase Cowell – agreed that it would be highly improbable that I would still find anyone alive who knew or had met Michael. However, I managed to find and interview no fewer than sixteen people who had known or worked with him. As I write, in March 2015, only three of these people, including my mother, are still alive. The other two are Stephen Grady MBE, who met Michael three times, and Marcelle Arlington of Chemy who was an early resistant and friend of my mother and grandmother.

My research included many years of work, primarily at the Public Records Office (PRO) in Kew, the Imperial War Museum, and London's National Army Museum and has taken me to Ireland, France, Belgium and Greece to interview individuals that included a number of authors. During this time I compiled hundreds of hours of face-to-face interviews, tape recordings, notes and correspondence with contemporaries of Michael such as Pierre Séailles, Arthur Staggs, Eliane Lemercier, Désiré De Becker, René Binot and Stephen Grady as well as many others listed later under 'Acknowledgements'. And, of course, there have been countless conversations with my mother, Yvonne Baudet, née Pachy, who lived through those times and came to know Michael well. I was also privileged to have been given access to much material from the SOE archives, years before their eventual release to the PRO.

I have benefited enormously from the research of two great French writers and historians, who gave generously of their time and materials: Danièle Lheureux and André Coilliot. Danièle kindly presented me with copies of her two major works on the subject, as well as allowing me unlimited access to thousands of documents in her extensive collection. These include contributions from hundreds of contemporary witnesses, participants and their families. In particular there are the testimonies and archives of Pierre Séailles, Arthur Malfait, Julian Gerekens, Jean Chieux and those confided to her by the families and friends of Georges Bayart, Marcel Fertein, Adolphe Herry and Pierre Duval, all of whom were key lieutenants of Michael. André donated the priceless, original diary of Arthur Malfait for me to copy. It was never my intention to attempt to improve on their compelling narratives. Many of the events portrayed in this book have been reproduced faithfully from the results of their research and their diligent scholarship, interwoven with extracts from historic documents, official records and my own personal files, which supplement and add detail to an already unsurpassable tale.

Due acknowledgment is given to many others who helped me, in one form or another, along the way: most notably Duncan Stuart, the last SOE Adviser, and especially my co-author Nick Nicholas, without whose help this book may never have seen the light of day. Comfortable in translating both French and German, Nick has pulled together all of the threads of the story from my research and notes, French documents and books, as well as conducting his own research on the subject from time to time. He has done this in an organized and steadfast manner, never complaining, while at times having to prod me to keep up with him and his writing! I shall be forever indebted to Nick for his hard work and dedication. As with me, his has been an act of reverence for the story without any thought of monetary reward at any stage. Our research trips to France together in recent years were interesting and eventful, to say the least.

For more than any other reason I wanted to write this book for two people – my grandmother, Jeanne Pachy (née Oliger) and Michael Trotobas himself – unsung heroes in the true sense of the term, of whom most people had and have never heard. Both of them sacrificed their own lives so that future generations like mine, and those of my children and grandchildren, would not spend their lives beneath the heel of Nazi tyranny.

From the outset I was in awe of two very significant and poignant facts. First, how young some of the participants were when they died: 29 in the case of Michael, and 49 in the case of my grandmother. Second, that these two people had a say in where their life would take them. No-one forced them to do anything: it was their choice. But what brave and risky choices they made. At a time when the average worklife expectancy of an organizer or wireless operator in occupied France was expected to be between three and six months at most, Michael was a full year into his second secret mission. He knew that the German security forces were closing in on him, but he chose not to extricate himself from France by air, or by train and on foot through Spain, but to stand and fight to the death, and not to abandon the French patriots who themselves had remained loyal from the very beginning.

Likewise, my grandmother, 43 at the start of the war and a widow with two young children to support, took enormous risks to shelter frightened, hungry, and sometimes wounded young soldiers and airmen in her home, hide them from the enemy, and pass them down the line through the early escape lines. In 1940 and 1941 she was not part of any recognized resistance group, but just one of many brave women who made a choice to help others in dire need. Many in France at the time – perhaps understandably to the weaker of us – chose to keep their heads down and not get involved, to simply survive, or in some cases to thrive and even collaborate, as illustrated by my family's betrayal by a Frenchwoman.

It has been written that only four per cent of the population of France was actively involved in the resistance, which, in the post-war years, took on an air of magnificent glory in the eyes of many authors, historians, and film and television producers. My mother's estimate of this direct action or activity is put at less than one per cent.

The courage and work of Michael was recognized by France, but not by Britain, while, conversely, that of my grandmother, who would eventually perish in Ravensbruck concentration camp north of Berlin, went unrecognized by France but was formally acknowledged by Britain. So each was honoured by their alternate authorities but not by their own. The RAF Escaping Society had no record of her, while at least a representative of MI9 (my late father from 458 Squadron RAAF) was to convey in 1945 a 'certificate of thanks' from Air Chief Marshal Tedder and a cheque for £25.00 to her orphaned daughter. Twenty-five pounds for a life lost does not seem a great deal to me, either then or now.

So it was for these reasons that I embarked on a long journey that was sometimes very sad, and at other times very happy and rewarding. As will be seen, some truly amazing things emerged from my research along the way. Above all else, the main reason for writing this book was so that two wonderful and courageous people, one a citizen of Great Britain, the other of France, will be read about and, I sincerely hope, remembered by future generations.

Stewart Kent
Penzance, 2015

Prologue

'Faith has need of the whole truth.'
Pierre Teilhard de Chardin

In January of 1946 a Royal Air Force warrant officer from MI9, the escape and evasion branch of the War Office, knocks on the door of a little house in the village of Gondecourt, south of Lille. A fluent French speaker, he has been assigned to make contact with French patriots who had assisted Allied servicemen during the war. The door is opened by a vivacious dark-haired young woman of 22, who invites him into the tiny lounge. He listens to her story and hands over a cheque and a certificate from the British government, formal recognition of her family's help and sacrifice. He becomes attracted to her, and she to him. Within a month they are married at the *Hôtel de Ville* in Gondecourt and he takes her back to England. In mid-November a son is born.

Some years later the boy comes across a photograph of a young man sleeping. He has an enquiring mind and, as he often did, asks his mother for more details – in this case, who it is and why he is sleeping? This time she does not answer but gently takes the print from him and puts it back in its box. Disappointed, he asks why. She tells him he is too young to understand. Every so often he asks her again and receives the same answer. As he grows up he forgets about it.

In August 1988, now a successful businessman, he is hurrying through Heathrow's Terminal Three to catch a plane to Cairo. Fleetingly he glances at his watch: does he have time to find something to read during his three hour flight? He decides that he does – just. Moving rapidly into WH Smith, he scans the new releases: nothing there. He crosses to the non-fiction section but sees only the old familiar titles. He turns to leave and as he does his eye is drawn to *Turncoat*, a slim volume written by Brendan Murphy, with an attention grabbing subtitle: *The Worst Traitor of the War*. It is very much his subject, and the enormity of the claim intrigues him. He pays, stuffs the book into his travel bag, and makes his way to the departure gate. After boarding the aircraft he begins to read, remaining absorbed through take off, drinks, and the inflight meal. Over the Mediterranean his eyes begin to close and reluctantly he tears himself away from the pursuit of alleged traitors in occupied France. He fingers the corner of page 143 to mark his place. As he does so a sentence leaps out at him, so startling that he sits bolt upright in his seat, his tiredness replaced by surging adrenaline. He reads the fifteen words once more – slowly. He reads them again – and again. *'She introduced Verloop to a woman named Pachy in Gondecourt who was harbouring British escapees'*. He is dumbfounded, for Madame Pachy was his grandmother.

The adrenaline stays with him right up to his checking into the Nile Hilton in Cairo, from where, without even considering the time difference, he immediately telephones his mother, who has remarried and is now living in France, to tell her about his discovery. Her response is one of utter astonishment because she has never heard of the family name, let alone that of her own mother, ever being mentioned in any publication. When he returns he visits her, and they talk about his grandmother. In a sudden flash of recall he asks her if what she did is somehow connected with the mysterious photograph of the sleeping man. This time she answers and what she tells him launches him into a personal odyssey to find out more.

After ten years of extensive travel and research he is once again surrounded by photographs. This time they are not all family treasures: some are of buildings, some of artefacts, but mostly they are of men and women, of whom a great number have passed away. Some died peacefully and naturally: some died in great pain and suffering. Some died a brave and violent end: others died ignominiously and shamefully. In addition to the photographs, he has accumulated a wealth of documents – books, periodicals, testimonials, and notes he has taken after scores of conversations in many countries, all meticulously indexed and catalogued. Those he treasures most are letters painstakingly written by old, shaking hands as fading memories desperately sought to pass on to him scraps of personal knowledge and remembrance – first-hand accounts of people and events that are not to be found in official histories; precious fragments of a story they want him to tell.

It is a story of courage, bravery and sacrifice. Its compass is not vast, just a few months of time in one small region of occupied France, its cast a mere handful of players. There are many heroes and heroines, and there are villains. The villains are not always distinguishable by their uniform or by the colour of their flag, for it is also a story of treachery, of men and women betrayed not only by dedicated enemies and pursuers but also by people they trusted and by the very organizations whose cause they sought unselfishly to serve. For the central character, a British Army officer, the ultimate betrayal was by his own country. In France he became a legend. His deeds are remembered and celebrated by a fine memorial; a medal was struck in his honour. The British awarded him no decorations other than the usual service medals, even though he was recommended by his commanding officer for the Victoria Cross. In England there is only sparse information, short on detail and peppered with inaccuracies.

Chapter 1

Beginnings

'It is good for a man that he bear the yoke in his youth.'
Lamentations 3:27

When Captain Michael Trotobas launched himself into the night sky in November 1943 he would have felt a deep sense of relief. Relief that the waiting was at last over; relief that he had been given the chance to redeem himself for what he saw as the failure of his first mission; and relief that he was returning to his spiritual home. Below him in the darkness France slept its troubled sleep.

His father, Henri, came from a small village in the Var region of Provence, stronghold of the Society of Mary, a Roman Catholic religious congregation founded in 1836, where he was brought up in the Marist faith. At the age of nineteen, weary of the religious disciplines and bored with the quiet rural existence, he set out with a friend to fulfil a long-held dream of working a passage to America on one of the majestic ocean liners that sailed regularly from England. They arrived safely in London, but in the smoke, noise, bustle and confusion of Waterloo station they boarded the wrong train, and the vessel left Southampton without them. Fate had intervened to shape the destiny of the as yet unborn Michael, for the year was 1912 and their intended sailing was the maiden voyage of RMS *Titanic*.[1]

While his disappointed companion went back to France, Henri rejected the thought of going home with his tail between his legs, and decided instead to stay and try his luck in England. He found his way to Brighton, where jobs in the flourishing hotel industry were plentiful. Starting as a kitchen porter, he quickly became a sous-chef and moved on to a larger hotel on the seafront, where he met a kindred spirit in Agnes Whelan, a pretty Irish girl who had left her overcrowded home near Dublin to search for a better life in England. They were an ideal match in their pride and their will to succeed; his quiet resolution and determination the perfect foil to her fiery Irish temper and impatience. They married in October 1913, when he was 20 and she was 22, and set up home at 1, North Place, Brighton, which subsequent residents have described as a narrow terraced house, consisting of a basement with a small area for cooking and eating, and three floors above it. On the ground floor there was a large sitting room, and the first floor consisted of a single bedroom, with a toilet at the head of the landing. The top floor was divided into two small bedrooms. As was the case with all the other houses in the street, there was no bathroom: residents either bathed in a tin bath or went to the local baths. There was electric lighting throughout but only one power point, which was located in the kitchen. Coal was supplied through an outside chute to a cellar under the pavement. [2]

It was there that Agnes gave birth to Michael on 20 May 1914, and, when Europe went to war four months later, Henri returned to France to enlist, leaving Agnes to bring up their child alone. With hardly any money and no relatives on hand to support her, she would have found life a struggle, both mentally and physically. The daily chore of carrying heavy buckets of coal up two flights of stairs from the basement to feed the open fires in the living room and bedrooms – their only source of heat – would take its toll. Four years passed with no news of Henri, during which time his son grew into a sturdy child whose entire universe centred on his mother. Their Spartan life instilled in him toughness and a sense of responsibility. His pleasures were few and simple – laughter in the tin bathtub in front of the fire, his mother reading to him, telling him stories of her own childhood, and walking him along the promenade.

When Henri returned, after three years in a prison camp in Germany, he was desperate to ensure a warm and secure future for his family. During the war years many French men had brought their families across the Channel to the south coast of England, and Brighton had a thriving expatriate community that made him welcome. These contacts, and pre-war references from his previous employers, enabled him to find a position as chef in a medium-sized hotel, where the ambitious owners aspired to offer their guests a genuine French cuisine. He worked long hours with only irregular half days off, but he was able to feed his family well. Although the pay was poor he was allowed to bring home substantial quantities of unused and leftover meat, fish, vegetables and pastries.

On Michael's fifth birthday Henri gave him a box of tin soldiers. In later years he received a bicycle and a carved chess set, but it was the soldiers that gripped young Michael. Curiously, they prompted Henri to talk for the first time about his war experiences, causing Michael to weep as he heard about the harsh and demeaning treatment his father had received at the hands of the Germans. Although suffering from wounds, he had been put to hard, physical work by his captors, fed only one bowl of thin watery soup each day, and beaten regularly. As a vanquished Frenchman he was held in contempt by military and civilians alike, each Sunday being forced to march in shackles through the streets of the nearby village, mocked and insulted by the local people. Too young to understand that these sufferings were common to many French prisoners in Germany, Michael took his father's humiliation personally, and the memory stayed with him. But his father had come home, and the family was together again.[3]

For the next few years Michael appears to have spent a normal childhood – playing with his toy soldiers, cycling into the countryside, and swimming in the nearby public baths and the sea, a pastime in which he became proficient. Racing against other boys from school gave him a hard, competitive streak and introduced him to the intoxication of winning. He became incensed when he felt that he had been cheated; up would come the fists, even against boys much older and bigger, and he frequently came home battered, bruised and bleeding, much to his mother's distress. Yet, far from trying to make him give up, she urged him to get his blows in first and use every means at his disposal to inflict maximum damage on his opponents, including kicking, biting and scratching. As a result he won more fights but lost his friends, who simply refused to let him join in their games, forcing Michael back into himself once more. Never one for books, he spent hours in his room brooding.

Urged to do something by his wife, Henri stepped in. He called in a favour from a trainer at a backstreet gymnasium on the other side of town, where they took on boys from the age of seven and taught them to box. Matching youngsters with partners of similar height and weight, the instructors encouraged them to put their lessons into practice at the end of each session by setting them against each other for two rounds in a miniature ring. Supervision was strict, and points were deducted for unfair play, as a result of which Michael was penalized over and over again until he finally saw sense. Thereafter he began to win regularly, but his satisfaction and delight at each victory were short lived, as he was immediately given heavier and more skilful opponents, which led, inevitably, to more defeats. Nevertheless, he thrived on the activity and physical training and came back home after the twice-weekly sessions tired but happy.

This period of domestic stability did not last, as Agnes's health deteriorated rapidly, culminating in her contracting tuberculosis. She died in 1923 at the age of just 30, and Michael was devastated: his mother had always been there for him, and he adored her. His father now became a remote and austere figure. The death of his wife so soon after his return from war hit Henri hard, driving him into himself and his work. Like most men of his generation, he loved his son and played with him, but he knew little about his inner needs. He did his best, but the demands of his job as a chef were great; the hours were long and although there was ample food, the pay itself was poor. Realizing that he could not continue to work eighteen hours a day and look after a growing boy, Henri recognized that he had to make a difficult choice. He could not employ someone to care for his son, and at a time when millions were unemployed he reasoned that it would be folly to sacrifice his job. He calculated that with careful management he could stretch his income to cover his own modest needs and at the same time allow him to provide for his son's welfare and education, even though it meant that they would be separated. Reluctantly, Henri arranged for the 10-year-old to go to his own home region of Var, in Provence, to live with his sister Marie-Louise, a teacher at the School of the Seine in Cuers.

This was not such a hardship for Michael, because from the moment Henri had walked back into the house he had started to teach his son to speak French. They began with simple words and the names of everyday objects: whenever Michael spoke to Henri he had to give both the English and the French words. If he did not know the word he was to ask, and in this way he built up his vocabulary. They soon progressed to familiar phrases, at which point Henri arranged for a French schoolteacher friend to come three times a week, rewarding her with food and other bartered goods. In France, Michael entered the Marist school at St Cyr, where he flourished under the dutiful attention of his aunt and his teachers. His French developed rapidly, the formal language and grammar of the priests mingling with the local patois and the rough, crude *argot* of the children. He came to love the French way of life, relishing the peaceful countryside and open spaces that were so different from the austerity of post-war England. He formed a very close relationship with his aunt, whom he regarded as a second mother.

The Marist schools were recognized as fertile grounds for a vocation to priesthood, and it might have been this that Henri had in mind for his son, for in 1926 he arranged for him to broaden his education and moved him to the Catholic University School in Dublin. It had been founded by the Marists in 1867 to give young Irish boys a sound Catholic education with a view to their entering the Catholic University. It also offered a curriculum that provided a good foundation for mercantile and professional careers. Here Michael was to benefit once more from his family's generosity and he was able to live with relatives of his mother while attending school by day. [4]

Instruction did not end when he left school in the evening, for the Marists attached great importance to the ability of pupils to develop by learning to work on their own without the supervision of a teacher. Parents were to see that their boys were provided with the necessary facilities and time for study at home – at least two hours were required, and this increased according to the boy's position in the school. Great store was set by punctuality and good timekeeping, and failure to arrive in time for the first lesson of the day was a disciplinary offence with written explanations required in the event of absence. Reports of work were sent to the boy's home each week, as were detailed summaries of progress and examination results at the end of each term. The Marists recognized the importance of developing the body as well as the mind, and the school was equipped with a gymnasium and playing fields within easy reach, providing excellent facilities for football, hurling, cricket, tennis and boxing. There were regular organized walks and bicycle rides to local beauty spots and country houses, and there was a flourishing debating society. Michael relished the life and established a reputation as a keen all-round sportsman and chorister.

After two happy years in Dublin, Michael returned to France to complete his education and perfect his French at the Marist School in Toulon, from where in 1930, at the age of sixteen, his sense of duty and a desire to repay his father's sacrifice saw him return to England. There he followed in Henri's footsteps and became a cook, taking work wherever he could find it.

The legacy of a lack of permanence in his life began to tell, and an impatient and impulsive nature came to the fore. He never felt settled and was dogged by restlessness and an urge to move on. This urge took him back to France after only four months. For the next eighteen months he lived in Paris, working first as a sous-chef, then as an apprentice electrician. He quickly assimilated the tough urban culture and working man's slang. He learned to stand up for himself by using his fists when necessary and living by his wits. He took to gambling at the tables each night, often with moderate success, but his impulsive nature and a profound belief in his own invincibility led him to chase each success with a string of reckless bets that left him back where he had started.

Eventually, his debts forced him to leave Paris in a hurry, and he returned to St Cyr, where he threw himself on his aunt's mercy. She wrote straight away to tell Henri of his son's arrival and received a swift reply, enjoining her to make sure he spent his time usefully, and promising to send a small sum of money each month towards his upkeep. Consequently Michael did very little except live largely off his aunt's goodwill, and, by way of recognition, accompany her on countless visits to his father's many relatives and friends along the length of the Côte d'Azur.

Inevitably, boredom set in. After his time in Paris and eight months in Provence he was by now bilingual, and he considered himself to be more French than English. However, when he received a letter from his father telling him that he had remarried, sold the Brighton house and moved to London, inviting his son to come and see them and enclosing money for his fare, he decided it was time to move back to England. His first meeting with Antoinette, his stepmother, was a disaster, she making it clear that she wanted no part of him, and he resentful and angry that she had usurped his mother in Henri's thoughts. He left after half an hour. Not wishing to live with the couple he was once more thrown back on his own resources, working as a production hand in a canning factory while renting a dingy room near Victoria station. [5]

Now nineteen – the same age his father had been when he set out to make his way in a different world – Michael was a young man who had already been through and seen a great deal. From the age of nine, when his mother had died, he had taken on a tough mantle of independence. A keen rugby player and a boxer of considerable skill, his travel between France, England and Ireland and a multitude of jobs had given him a love for physical activity, adventure and the unforeseen. Already worldly wise, he understood that he was unlikely to find the variety and challenge he sought in England's struggling civilian economy, so in April 1933, disillusioned with job prospects, he had a long chat with his father and, on his advice, joined the Regular Army. A new phase of his life was about to begin.

Chapter notes

1   For the information about Michael's pre-Army days I am indebted to historian Dr John Laffin and his article *A 'Die-hard' in the Resistance: Le Capitaine Michel*, published in the British Army Review of August 1981. Dr Laffin met and interviewed Henri, and kindly sent me a copy of his article in June 1996.

2   Mr W. Martin, a later resident of Michael's Brighton home, and his neighbour, Mr H. Heal, kindly wrote to me in 1999 giving me a detailed description of the house and life in the area.

3   My mother (who is referred to as Yvonne Pachy) had countless conversations with Michael, both in his British Expeditionary Force days and during his time in Lille. He could not talk about his work, but he could and did spend hours telling her about his childhood and his father. In this and in subsequent chapters I cannot vouch for the accuracy of what he told her, but I have no reason to doubt the clarity and precision of her recollections I recorded in more than three hours of tapes during 1997 and in more than a dozen notebooks subsequently. The citations that appear later are from Nick's meticulous transcripts of his conversations with her in 2008 to 2010.

4   In February 2003 I visited the Catholic University School in Lower Leeson Street, Dublin, where Vice-Principal Kevin Jennings and his staff gave me a warm welcome and access to their records of Michael's years there.

5   In March 2002 I met Mr Eric Taylor, who moved in next door to Henri and Antoinette in 1964. He provided many interesting details about his neighbours. He said that Henri did not talk a lot about his son, but he kept his back bedroom as a shrine, with pictures and newspaper cuttings on the walls.

Chapter 2

The Diehard

'The path of duty was the way to glory.'
Alfred Lord Tennyson

When he enlisted with the Middlesex Regiment at Inglis Barracks in Mill Hill, Michael joined one of the most prestigious London-based regiments, which had a tradition that matched his own spirited and adventurous temperament. It had gained its 'Diehards' nickname from the Peninsular War when, in 1811, the commander of the 57th Regiment of Foot serving in Wellington's army at Albuera, had his horse shot from under him. Severely wounded, and outnumbered by the French, he called to his men '*Die hard, 57th. Die hard!*' [1]

In Dr John Laffin's article for the British Army Review [see Chapter 1 notes] he records that enlisting at the same time was Alf Thomas – like Michael a non-Londoner – from Stockton-on-Tees. They became close friends and were placed together in Badajos Squad under Sergeant Dick Smith [later Major R.W. Smith MBE] in the Middlesex Regiment's 2nd Battalion. Thomas saw early on that Michael was a natural leader, albeit with '*a sometimes worrying devil-may-care attitude'*. This belief was vindicated in April 1934 when Michael was made acting lance corporal, a temporary, probationary rank intended to provide a platform for future non-commissioned officers (NCOs) to demonstrate their potential. He also found time to become a proficient boxer.

He performed well, and in June 1935 he was confirmed in the rank and posted to B Company, 2nd Battalion at Colchester, where he continued to make good progress. He was promoted to corporal in August 1936, becoming a section leader under Lieutenant Aylmar Clayton [later Colonel A.S.J.dS. Clayton OBE], who remembered Michael as '*a brilliant boxer and a splendid rugby player'* and made sure that when he came to run the rugby club he had him as his rugby NCO.

In November of that year the battalion moved to Victoria Barracks in Portsmouth, where Michael learned that the Middlesex was one of thirteen infantry regiments selected for conversion to machine guns. The battalion's new role as a support unit meant that training became focused on inter-unit cooperation in the field with rifle battalions. Individual squads had to acquire the flexibility and instant readiness for detachment in various roles, frequently coming under the command of another battalion or company. The machine gun units were constantly in demand for one exercise or another, and as a consequence the time available for traditional regimental ceremonials and formal manoeuvres diminished considerably. In December 1937 the regiment moved again, this time the short distance to Gosport, where the hard-pressed battalion underwent further reorganization. The anti-tank company was replaced by a fourth machine gun company, and Michael was assigned to the instructing team charged with bringing it to the same state of efficiency as the other three companies in as short a time as possible.

The following year the battalion took part in a large-scale combined operations exercise in the Portsmouth area. The object of this was to investigate the tactical and mechanical aspects of an approach from seawards, including landing a force on a defended coast with sea and air cooperation. The actual landing was made in Start Bay, where Michael waded ashore in the early morning as one of the troops supporting the covering force, helping, encouraging and cajoling the many young soldiers who were in the initial stages of their Army training. Although the form of the exercise was unfamiliar, the operation was an outstanding success, and the battalion was warmly complimented on its performance.

As his official service record shows, Michael continued to impress his superiors. He took easily to the use of arms and became an accurate marksman, eventually achieving instructor certificates in all the infantry weapons, including the machine gun. He was comfortable driving any kind of motorised vehicle. A keen swimmer, he held a lifeguard certificate from the Royal Life Saving Society, and, with Thomas as his second, fought his way through platoon and company championships to become the regiment's light-heavyweight boxing champion. He enjoyed his sport but work was his passion. Although never a bookworm he now sought out every publication he could find on machine guns, badgering the manufacturers for their latest technical sheets and brochures. Tactics, too, obsessed him, and he spent hours working out how to make the most effective use of his platoons in a wide variety of scenarios.

It came as no surprise to anyone when his all-round abilities and proficiency saw him promoted to lance sergeant in October 1938. It coincided with orders for the regiment to step up its training in preparation for the war with Germany that seemed inevitable. The 2nd Battalion had to be brought up to the highest standard of readiness for all possible roles, including that of an independent machine gun battalion, and Michael was kept busy rehearsing tactical moves to operational areas 2- 300 miles away. As Major Smith was later to comment to Laffin, he was *'a man who got things done, even if not always by the book, and one who always wanted to be that little bit better at everything'.* [2]

The months of 1939 raced past, each bringing with it a new tension and a gradual darkening of the European sky, until, as August faded into September, the Germans struck at Poland, and once again Great Britain was at war with the old enemy of 1914. Fate had placed Michael in exactly the right place and at the right time for him to satisfy his restless, combative nature and thirst for adventure. So, for the second time in the century, a Trotobas was to set off for France and war. The 'Die Hard' call would be heard once more and would be answered.

British military planning called for the immediate mobilization of a substantial British Expeditionary Force (BEF), to be sent to the Franco-Belgian border as soon as war was declared. When the order to mobilize was received on 1 September, 1939, 2nd Battalion was still at Gosport. Trained, fit, and efficient, it was ready for the tasks that lay ahead, but with the ranks now swollen by new recruits there was an urgent need for competent leaders. Michael was well placed as an established professional NCO to assume greater responsibility, and on 5 September he was appointed to acting warrant officer. Mobilization, except for a few articles of war equipment, was completed on 10 September, and there was time for a brief exercise with the division in the Dorchester area. Sand-model lectures and exercises were laid on to give companies and platoons some idea of what they might expect in action, but most of Michael's time was spent organizing the forthcoming move and preparing the necessary loading tables and orders.

In spite of the early notice and extensive preparations the departure from Gosport was beset with false starts, and it was not until 28 September that 2nd Battalion set off. In the meantime, Michael had been confirmed as substantive platoon sergeant major, a new rank equating to warrant officer III class, that had been recently created to give experienced NCOs command of units formerly reserved for commissioned officers. He was tasked with leading B Company's 7, 8 and 9 Platoons.

In his 7 Platoon was Private Tom Roberts, who often acted as sparring partner. He recalled that Michael fought and won his last fight in the Gosport gymnasium before leaving for France.

> 'He was a good sergeant, well liked and respected, and could take good care of himself. A natural leader, he gave everyone confidence. We had no idea that he could speak a word of French and were flabbergasted when, following the pre-move pep talk, the brigadier said Sergeant Trotobas would give us a rendition of the Marseillaise. It was not a bad performance, and I remember that he could not quite reach top note and broke off, saying that "it was a good song anyway"'.[3]

On 29 September the division disembarked at Cherbourg, from where it left by train for its concentration area in the plains of the manufacturing areas south of Lille. Its sector was at Gondecourt, a village to the south-west of the industrial city of Lille and close to the frontier with Belgium, located in undulating farming terrain and surrounded by various light mills and factories in nearby Seclin. B Company was attached to 8th Infantry in the forward area south of Lille, holding the line of the River Marcq, where for the next two weeks the time was spent digging gun positions for the defence of the divisional area. Excellent progress was made in spite of very bad weather, and at the end of the month exercises were held to test the strength of the defences. In the first week of November, 2nd Battalion moved from Gondecourt to Roubaix, where the presence of an occasional enemy reconnaissance aircraft over their positions suggested that a German invasion of Belgium might be imminent. Michael and his fellow NCOs seized the opportunity to carry out endless practices and demonstrations for the benefit of reserve officers and other ranks whose training with the machine gun had been incomplete. But the month ended in disappointment and anticlimax when orders were received to move back to Gondecourt.

There in the tranquil French countryside the illusion of a 'phoney war' took hold, with little to distinguish the wartime activities of the BEF from its peacetime manoeuvres. Soldiers went home on the regular Friday leave-boats from Cherbourg, attended training courses, and played football against village teams. Sports provided the only recreational facilities, which would have suited Michael admirably as he enhanced his growing reputation on the field and in the ring. Militarily, he was stretched to find things for his men to do. A general instruction was issued that they should be kept busy, as a consequence of which the days were spent in mundane activities, as Roberts recalled:

'The divisional commander paid frequent visits to inspect the progress of the defence work, and we were all thoroughly fed up digging trenches, servicing vehicles and carrying out other mundane tasks. We were, after all, machine gunners, and I remember that at one point, out of total frustration, we ended up in a fight with members of the Royal Artillery!'

Shortly after the battalion's return to Gondecourt word had gone out for French speakers to come forward to form a Community Liaison Committee, whose job it would be to arrange social events and negotiate deals with local farmers and tradespeople for fresh meat and produce. Michael had been 'volunteered' by his platoon commander, and had effectively taken on the role of chief negotiator and spokesman, since his French was far superior to that of anyone else on the committee and his bargaining skills greatly exceeded those of the officer in charge. He soon got to know and become friends with many people in the neighbourhood. His familiarity with French ways, and his ability to come up with little extras for his men, made life infinitely more interesting for his platoons; they were proud of his knowledge of the language and impressed by his passion for the French people, of whom he was openly protective. He tolerated no criticism or mockery of local customs, their slow way of life, or their stolid indifference to the presence of the troops, many of whom felt that they were there to protect the French and were consequently entitled to expect favours from them. Inevitably, competition was fierce for the attention of local girls, and matters frequently got out of hand. Michael stepped in on more than one occasion, his fierce glare, clenched fists and growing reputation as a fighter usually sufficing to give the offender second thoughts and make him back away. However, his frustration with the inactivity and lack of opportunity to get at the Germans boiled over one evening when he came across another NCO who had gone too far and interfered with a local girl. Roberts again:

> *'He grabbed the man – a corporal – swung him round and let him have one of his best punches. The corporal went down like a sack of spuds.'*

The presence of nearly two thousand troops impacted on the community in many ways, but the British forces brought welcome additional income to local businesses, one of which was a little boutique in Gondecourt that sold fine lace, postcards and other bric-a-brac. It was owned by the Pachy family and run by Madame Jeanne Pachy and her young daughter, Yvonne. It became a popular destination for soldiers wanting to buy souvenirs and trinkets to send or take home, and they were always warmly welcomed, some more than others. Conscious of the bitterly cold conditions of that harsh winter, Jeanne took to inviting selected parties to relax in the comfort of her home in the evenings. Impromptu dance sessions would often take place, and to the impressionable 16-year-old Yvonne these evenings were particularly exciting, providing as they did a break from the repetitious customs and routines of country life and offering a glimpse of another, altogether more glamorous world. As she recalled:

> *'They only came in the evenings, of course, and during weekends when they were not on exercises. In return for our hospitality, the men would often bring back small souvenirs from England, including the latest records from America, which they played over and over again on our wind-up gramophone, the big-band swing of Glenn Miller being a regular choice. We kept no alcohol in the house, but when officers came they usually brought hip flasks, and the men*

sometimes brought beer or wine. I thought it was strange how the officers always sat in the front parlour, drinking and talking, while the normal soldiers had to stay in the back room. We only had one small bathroom, of course, and I thought it very odd when a soldier passing an officer on his way to it had to salute formally or be reprimanded.'

As well as the welcome boost to the little shop's income, the British troops were able to provide much-needed basic commodities:

'For reasons we could never understand, before the war things like tobacco and matches were in very short supply in France, difficult to obtain, and expensive. Yet in Belgium they were plentiful and cheap. My mother and I regularly used to cycle the 150km or so across the border and back. We had friends there who lived just near Ypres, and we got to know all of the border guards and customs men, who turned a blind eye to our bulging coats and overfull panniers. When the soldiers came they seemed to have enormous quantities of everything and were very generous with cigarettes and other items, which to them were everyday basics in plentiful supply but to us were near luxuries.'

Michael was a regular visitor. Initially he was invited because of his excellent French, but he soon became a favourite of the family with his easy manner, his range of stories and exotic recollections of his days in Provence, a region as remote and foreign to the Pachy family as England itself. Yvonne felt he was somehow special and different from the others.

'He was definitely my favourite, and usually came with Sidney Coleman, Leslie Chapman or Alf Thomas. He was so good looking, with dark, sparkling eyes and a slightly crooked smile. I remember he bought and presented to me one evening a record of the Ink Spots singing My Prayer, *because he knew I loved the tune, which in French was the song* Avant de Mourir. *It was a lovely gift.'*

While Michael's relationship with Yvonne was akin to that of an elder brother, the same could not be said of his romantic attachment to her close friend, 18-year-old Marie-Jeanne Bouchez, who lived with her wealthy parents in Lille and came to Gondecourt frequently. Strikingly attractive, and always beautifully dressed, she drove around in an open-top sports car, constantly besieged by a crowd of local admirers, with whom she was happy to flirt; but she generally found them boring, and kept them at arm's length.

Michael was something different and exciting, and the two of them hit it off immediately, as Yvonne recalled:

> *'Michael was very taken with my friend and doted on her, although she never felt quite the same about him. I think he had hopes of marrying her when the war was over. He even borrowed money from my mother to buy Marie-Jeanne a beautiful ring, mounted with a small sapphire, which he gave her. Marie-Jeanne showed it to me later. I don't think Michael ever repaid the loan to my mother.'*

Michael was not well received by Marie-Jeanne's parents. Understandably, her father was very protective of her and felt that he was nowhere near good enough for his only daughter, whom he had earmarked for greater things than life with an NCO. He was also pro-German and anti-English, and would probably have taken steps to bring the relationship to an end himself, if Michael had not moved on to Belgium shortly after he and Marie-Jeanne began to see each other regularly. Yvonne again:

> *'It was almost certainly this experience that prompted the long discussions Michael would have with my mother about the loyalties of the French people. My mother, whose maiden name was Oliger, had met and married my father when he was a cavalry officer during the first war. He had seen a lot of the Germans and disliked them intensely, so our family was naturally very pro-British. But even in Gondecourt there were those who would take the side of the Germans, and some who believed that communism was the right path. Although I didn't take part, I remember hearing very clearly my mother telling him who she thought might be on the side of the British when war came.'*

Meanwhile, the Middlesex Regiment continued to prepare for the fight it knew was inevitable. In December Michael led his platoons in a three-day divisional exercise, throughout which the weather turned extremely cold, with hard frosts night and day. It was repeated three days later, again in the most spartan conditions. Christmas passed quietly and Michael spent the remainder of the year assisting with the selection of sites for pill-boxes on the divisional front.

The year 1940 opened with another long spell of extreme cold and Michael found himself deployed on a roving patrol in front of the Maginot Line, from where the gap to the sea along the Belgian frontier, held mainly by the BEF, was being strengthened by as many fixed gun positions as possible. This kept the battalion busy in its sector round Lille as winter turned to spring.

Although there was as yet no indication of any activity on the part of the enemy, the sands were running out: German divisions were massing behind the Dutch border in the wooded 'impassable' area of the Ardennes forest. The first intimation that anything unusual was afoot came, with startling suddenness, from the BBC's seven o'clock news bulletin on 10 May – Germany had invaded Holland and Belgium. The news spread quickly through the battalion, and, without waiting for confirmation from divisional headquarters, transport was loaded with the necessary equipment and stores for the pre-planned move forward to Louvain.

After taking up their allotted positions, the platoons were quickly withdrawn west of the town when it was discovered that Belgian troops were in position on the line of the River Dyle through Louvain. Michael posted his machine gunners around the railway station, and sent two men with anti-tank rifles to the other side of the tracks, with orders to fire on German tanks, and if possible, block the road. After German aircraft repeatedly strafed his positions, he ordered a gun to be mounted on a vehicle. When the planes returned in the afternoon, they received a warm welcome, the gunners claiming one aircraft shot down. The four companies of 2nd Battalion were ordered to make their way forward to occupy the positions they had vacated only hours before and were now well ahead of the rest of the division; their orders were to 'stop the German Army' while the remainder of the division dug in on the high ground west of Louvain.

Here, in the first of the many bizarre and colourful accounts of Michael in action that will punctuate this story, Thomas told how he took him on a raid into the outskirts of Louvain, armed with a longbow and arrows he had found, in addition to Thomas's rifle and Michael's revolver. Thomas claimed that Michael fired three arrows at a German patrol and that they *'heard a grunt and a thud as of a body falling'*. There was more to come, as Michael requisitioned an abandoned car, knocked out the rear window and mounted a machine gun in the back, assigning a young private to drive it and causing Thomas to comment *'Trotobas, unconventional himself, did not object when* [the private] *gave himself a gangster outfit of fur coat and a bowler hat.'* He did not say what happened subsequently.

Despite the division's best efforts it was forced slowly back, and the machine gunners were in constant action, fighting a running rearguard action to hold bridges, crossroads and other key locations as the long columns of men and machinery passed through. Michael would have spent his twenty-sixth birthday catching up on lost sleep. The night was quiet and no incidents were reported, although intermittent small arms and artillery fire could be heard as the enemy's advance units made their way along the east bank. Early next morning Michael ordered 9 Platoon to engage a small party of Germans attempting to bring up mortars close to the river in the

Warcoing area. Four mortar tractors were hit, but that was the extent of the action. During the night of 23 May, after another withdrawal, this time to Wattrelos, Michael led 7 and 9 platoons to give cover for 8th Infantry Brigade as it advanced to the line of a railway, about 1,000m [metres] in front of the forward positions. There it ran into heavy fire from artillery, mortars, machine guns, and anti-tank guns. The two platoons did what they could but, gallantly as they fought, they could not silence the opposition. One gun of 7 Platoon received a direct hit, causing a few casualties, but the remainder continued to fire until the advance was called off.

It was in Wattrelos that an incident occurred which Laffin recorded in his 1984 book *The Man the Nazis Couldn't Catch*, the story of Leonard Arlington, a private in C Company who spent the war in hiding in France after being captured at Dunkirk and escaping. Laffin recounts how Arlington saw Michael called upon to intervene when a French civilian was suspected of giving away the location of two machine gun sections in Wattrelos. The man had been ostentatiously washing down the pavement outside the houses in which they were stationed, immediately after which the buildings were quickly strafed by two German fighters. The lieutenant in command

> *'spotted the pavement-washing Frenchman who had taken cover, ordered the sergeant to bring him in, and sent for Platoon Sergeant Major Michael Trotobas. With his fluent French Trotobas found out that the man was no spy but a good neighbour who washed the pavement every Saturday morning. With the spy scare at its height, the Frenchman was lucky not to have been shot.'*

Shortly afterwards the Belgian front in the north collapsed, and Belgium's unconditional surrender exposed the BEF's left flank. There was now only one course possible: a further quick withdrawal to the coast and the holding of a perimeter long enough for the Army, or as much of it as possible, to embark. With the situation changing almost hourly, the machine gunners fought their way to the beaches, first at Poperinge, then at Fumes, where Michael set up 8 and 9 platoons in positions around an old farmhouse. Thomas had vivid memories of this period.

> *'We kept moving back towards the beaches and took up positions in an old farmhouse north of Fumes. Hundreds of planes passed overhead to bomb Lille, and it was then that Michael became angry. He ordered me to act as observer while he personally took over a machine gun. About 1000 yards away was a German-held village and Michael shot at everything in sight. He must have created havoc, because later we took a terrific beating from enemy mortars, and the position became untenable.'*

With some difficulty Michael managed to extricate his men and rejoin his company on a beach near Dunkirk. Here he was wounded by strafing enemy fighters and separated from his platoons. Roberts took up the story.

'When we last saw him it was during a battle as we were making for Dunkirk and the coast after being pushed back from the outside of Brussels. We were in a big push in a small pocket and within yards of the enemy. Alf Thomas and I were struggling to get our machine guns on to the lorries to fall back. At no time during our retreat was the line broken as when this looked likely another battalion plugged the gap. Michael was a PSM [platoon sergeant major] *which was a new rank at the time and he was involved with 3 platoons in B Company, 7, 8, and 9. He was tough and very good in action. Alf and I were in 7 Platoon. During the battle we saw no more of him as he would have been occupied with his other platoons, using them possibly for plugging the gaps as we pushed along in zig-zag fashion.'*

Thomas and Roberts were among the last to leave the beaches as the evacuation resolved itself into individual exploits and incidents. Roberts added a final note:

'I was one of the last to leave on 5/6 June, and had to save my brother-in-law who couldn't swim. We boarded the Skipjack, *a small fishing boat, which was promptly sunk by Stukas. We were then picked up again and got back to the UK. I understood Michael Trotobas to have been slightly wounded. When we got back to England I was sent home for a couple of days and then told to report to the nearest depot or police station where I would be given a warrant to join my unit that they were reforming. The idea was that checks could be made on who had got back and who was still missing. Michael never reported back so we could only presume that he had either been killed, taken prisoner or wounded.'*

Chapter notes

1   For information about the organization and movements of Michael's unit before mobilization and up to Dunkirk I was able to refer to *The Middlesex Regiment (D.C.O) – Chapter IV: 2nd Battalion 1939-1945* from the National Army Museum collection, and to *The Die-Hards The Middlesex Regiment by* Wolmer White. For his service records I have been able to refer to his Army personal file.

2   For the more personal insights into Michael's time with 2nd Battalion I have again drawn on John Laffin's article and my mother's recollections.

3   I am grateful to Tom Roberts for his memories. I talked with him at length in the summer of 1997, and we subsequently corresponded.

Chapter 3

SOE

'War is much too serious a thing to be left to military men.'
Charles Maurice Talleyrand

In fact, Michael did make it back. On his return from France he spent six weeks in hospital recovering from a head wound, and then went to Mill Hill for two months. Mentioned in despatches for his bravery and leadership during the retreat to Dunkirk, he was recommended for a commission, and at the end of September 1940 he was sent to the 170th Officer Cadet Training Unit. It was customary for officers commissioned from the ranks to be assigned to regiments other than their own, so on 10 January 1941 Michael was appointed to an emergency commission as second lieutenant in the Manchester Regiment and posted to the machine gun training centre at Ladysmill Barracks in Ashton-under-Lyne. But he was to see no further active duty as a Regular Army officer: his destiny lay elsewhere.

His experience and qualifications had caught the attention of the Special Operations Executive (SOE), the secret organization established in 1940 on Prime Minister Winston Churchill's instruction to 'set Europe ablaze'. It had two main roles: to create and foster the spirit of resistance in Nazi-occupied countries, and, once a suitable climate of opinion had been set up, to establish a nucleus of trained men who would assist as a 'fifth column' in the liberation of the country whenever the British were able to invade it. Its agents could perform reconnaissance and sabotage in these countries where otherwise the real situation would have been unknown, particularly in areas that could not be attacked by the Royal Air Force for fear of civilian casualties and heavy German defences.

SOE's operations in France were directed by two London-based country sections: F Section, which was staffed primarily by British personnel, and RF Section, which was linked to General Charles de Gaulle's Free French movement. Considerable rivalry, jealousy and mistrust existed between the two sections, and there was little in the way of mutual cooperation. There were also two smaller sections: EU/P Section, which dealt with the Polish community in France, and the DF Section, which was responsible for establishing escape routes. From November 1941 until the end of the war F Section was headed by Major [subsequently Colonel] Maurice

Buckmaster. It had two main objectives: to promote and build an organization for effective French resistance, and to carry out sabotage. Starting in May 1941 a stream of F Section agents, from all classes and many diverse occupations, was sent into France, where they served in a variety of functions including arms and sabotage instructors, couriers, circuit organizers, liaison officers, and radio operators. No limit was ever set on the number of agents who could be in the field at any one time. Quite simply, the more there were, the greater the damage that could be inflicted on the enemy, and operational difficulties aside, one of SOE's major headaches was finding enough suitable agents.[1]

There were three major obstacles to successful recruitment. First, the job description itself was unlikely to attract a wide and enthusiastic range of candidates. Agents had to survive and continue to operate in a country under a brutal occupying force, with a number of experienced and intensely focused security organizations constantly on the alert and committed to tracking them down. Imprisonment, torture and execution awaited those that were captured, for the German security services considered agents to be terrorists, and operational directives throughout the war dictated that terrorists were to be shot.

Second, the job requirements themselves were exceptional and demanding. Training would be provided to satisfy the physical and technical requirements, but competence alone was not sufficient. The right motivation, along with courage, resourcefulness, steadiness under pressure and the ability to think several moves ahead, were key characteristics required, along with a deep knowledge of the country in which the agent was to operate and fluency in its language. Exiled or escaped members of the armed forces of occupied countries were obvious starting points, and this was particularly so of France. The ideal candidate was one who had extensive local knowledge of a particular region based on long experience of the country and the people. This could only be gained by residence over a number of years, living and working with and speaking the language of the people. Such candidates were few and far between, particularly since the natural inclination of indigenous Frenchmen was to pledge their allegiance to the Free French, rather than to any British-run organization.

Third, the need to maintain absolute secrecy about its organization and activities precluded open recruitment – SOE could not simply place an advertisement in the local paper or post office, and it had therefore to resort to more clandestine and time-consuming methods. A Cabinet decision empowered SOE to draw on officers and men from all three branches of the armed services or from elsewhere, and staff were assigned to trawl through a mountain of service records to seek out, initially, men with an aptitude in a foreign language or a decoration for some distinguished special or unconventional operation overseas.

In mid-March 1941 Michael was instructed to present himself for interview at the War Office for 'special duties', unaware that enquiries were being made about him with MI5 to establish his bona fides and loyalty. A memorandum from SOE's Section SO2, signed FG and dated 1 April 1941, requested any available information about:

> 'Trotobas, Michael Alfred, currently serving as Lieutenant in the Manchester Regiment; this man is under consideration for employment by this section as a prospective organizer.'

MI5 replied by phone the same day indicating that he was not on record with them, and he was duly called to London. He was directed to a hotel in Northumberland Street, where he underwent two rigorous interviews with a man who did not introduce himself. During these, Michael's mastery and control of French was tested, questions were asked of his experiences in France, his feelings towards the Germans and his commitment to fighting them, his attitude to civilians and many other issues. All of this might well have been asked to establish his competence to fight in France. However, during the second interview the true nature of his future role – as an organizer of a resistance group – was explained to him. Given the chance to decline the opportunity and return to his unit, he waved it away, but was told to think about it overnight.

The following day he gave his decision and effectively terminated his career as a frontline soldier. He was handed a sealed envelope to give to his adjutant, containing instructions regarding further arrangements. He was ordered not to discuss the interview with anyone at all, including his commanding officer; this too was explained in the envelope. His interviewer told him that they would not meet again and that the next Michael would hear would be an invitation to join a specialized training course. Wheels were set in motion to obtain his release from his unit, and on 6 April a memo accompanied by requisition form A2 was sent to the Army's Department of Personnel:

> 'We recently interviewed Lt. M.A. Trotobas, Manchester Regt., now stationed at Ladysmill Barracks, Ashton-under-Lyne. Could you please arrange for this officer to be made available for a fortnight's course beginning 21 April? He possesses unusually good French and knows France well and if his work on the course is satisfactory, we shall be asking for his transfer with a view to making use of these qualifications.'

A handwritten note on the bottom of the memo added:

> *'We should like him to report at 055A War Office at 1000 hours on 21-4-41.'*

The 'FG' personal file was now opened. It recorded the transfer request, adding:

> *'It is intended to employ him when trained as an agent in 27-land'.* [2]

A further note showed Lieutenant Trotobas as:

> *'Proceeding to STS 5 14.4.41'.*

STS 5 was SOE's Special Training School at Wanborough Manor in Surrey.

Chapter notes
1   For information about the establishment and organization of SOE I refer the reader to Professor M.R.D. Foot's *SOE in France: Chapter I: The Origins of SOE.* For this information and other details about SOE I am indebted to Professor Michael Foot, who kindly sent me a signed copy of his book and invited me to draw on this definitive work.
2   FG was the cover used by Selwyn Jepson, SOE's principal recruiter, and 27 (or 27-land) refers to France.

Chapter 4

Training

'*Training is everything.*'
Mark Twain

The adapted country estate at Wanborough Manor near Guildford was one
of the first of SOE's Special Training Schools, of which by the end of 1944
there were more than fifty. Much has been written in post-war publications,
both fact and fiction, about the schools and the training methods, and the
subject is covered thoroughly in Professor Foot's book *SOE in France*.
Michael's training followed the well-documented path of basic military and
physical training at Wanborough, a stiffer paramilitary course at one of the
Group A schools around Arisaig in Scotland, parachute training at
Manchester's Ringway airfield, and instruction in clandestine techniques
and security, coding and ciphering at one of the Group B schools around
Beaulieu in the New Forest. At the end of the final course he would have
been put through a four-day scheme that included reconnaissance of a target,
contact by prearranged password with other agents, and transporting,
securing and activating explosive devices on railways, canals and military
hardware. [1]

As time went on, a clear syllabus was established for each phase of
training, and procedures, techniques and drawings were incorporated into
training manuals. But, when Michael and the other nineteen potential agents
in the very first group were sent for training in the spring of 1941, there was
very little precedent, and no manual. The planners could only work with
the resources and experience available to them, and they were handicapped
in the early days by the absence of anyone who had actually been in the
field and returned. A further difficulty existed in the need to keep secret the
very idea that agents were being trained in large numbers to infiltrate
occupied countries, a necessary precaution that extended to both trainees
and instructors.

In 1941 no attempt was made to stream trainees into groups
commensurate with their skills and backgrounds: everyone started on the
same level and was treated identically. This was an aspect that led to
considerable resentment among the ex-military personnel, many of whom,
like Michael, had seen and been involved in direct frontline action against

the German fighting machine. The programme was largely improvised, and none of the instructors had any experience of undercover work in occupied France during the present conflict.

Similarly, many of the agents were amateurs at the business of war when they entered SOE, and few had experience of subversion and sabotage. By the time Michael arrived at Wanborough he had seven years military training and experience behind him, and had earned a mention in despatches during the retreat to Dunkirk. He disliked being grouped with novices, and having to endure the most basic of instruction in skills which, in his opinion, he had long since mastered. Moreover, perhaps as many as three quarters of the trainee agents came from a civilian background, and Michael had no time for civilians in war – they could never hope to match his training, experience and instinct for survival. They were, he felt, likely to be a liability, and he certainly did not want to be forced into a situation where his life was in their hands at any point – a view he did not hesitate to make known throughout the courses. He did everything possible to avoid being paired with civilians during exercises and, when forced to comply, he simply ignored his partners and went about things in his own way, frequently – particularly during night exercises – disappearing and leaving them to fend for themselves. This attitude inevitably caused resentment in his fellow trainees and dismay and frustration in his instructors. Basically, he doubted that the training courses would teach him much he did not already know – what little there was he was prepared to take on board quickly and move on.

In such a large group of highly active men, of mixed backgrounds and temperaments, tensions were bound to arise, minor irritations would be blown out of proportion, and tempers would become frayed. And there would be prima donnas. Michael was one, and another was George Langelaan, a former journalist with the *New York Times* who had been born in Paris and was living there with his mother when war broke out. He enlisted in the British Army and became a field security policeman with the 9th Field Security Section, which was responsible for general military security within the BEF. He was posted to the north of France, and when the Germans overran the country he was well placed to escape to England from Dunkirk. When he arrived, he wrote a long report about the situation in France, which in time found its way to SOE, who promptly recruited him.

Like Michael, Langelaan was strong willed, with a high opinion of his own capabilities and a generally low opinion of others on the course. The exact causes of their mutual animosity are not known, but they were both volatile and impulsive characters, and it is likely that each soon recognized in the other a threat to his own perceived superiority. Their hostility was noticed by the instructors and referred to in one of Michael's assessment reports. Yet, although Langelaan was to write in great detail about his training in his 1959 book *Knights of the Floating Silk*, he makes no mention of Michael or of any disagreement with him at this time, while making numerous generous references later in the book to Michael's subsequent exploits. It seems that the only thing they had in common was a determination not to end up as radio operators, and they steadfastly refused to demonstrate any degree of competence, interest or technical awareness in this area.

Little wonder then that some of Michael's reports were less than favourable, and, given that judgments on an agent's ability were made in a very short space of time – in many cases within seven days of initial training – the odds would appear to have been heavily stacked against his finishing the courses. It was probably only his outstanding skills and military professionalism that saved him. In terms of his general and physical training he passed, as might be expected, with flying colours, but uncertainty about his temperament and personal character surfaced time and time again.

Even when supposedly relaxing, the trainees remained under scrutiny, often unknowingly, as instructors mixed with them in pubs and social areas, eavesdropped on conversations, and themselves acted as *agents provocateurs*. They bought them drinks and made personal remarks or controversial statements about government policies, politics, religion, women, pacifism or simply the progress of the war – all designed to test agents' ability to keep their feelings and thoughts to themselves, control their emotions and keep within their individual limits of alcohol influence. The potential agents on each course had a conducting officer with them, usually a subaltern or captain sent by the controlling country section. These officers would accompany the agent throughout his training, sharing the dangers and discomforts and taking as their principal task the sustaining of morale, and, in F section, providing weekly progress reports on their charges. They were also useful as judges of character, for their longer spells with individual agents gave them better chances to assess them than were open to instructors at the schools.

Michael's conducting officer was Lance Corporal [later Captain] Searle, and he was the first to comment on him at Wanborough. His initial confidential report on 30 April was encouraging:

> *'Trotobas is particularly well trained and keen, although he has periods of dejection when he feels his special qualities remain unutilized. He is very keen to have real work to do. Swift thinking and quick to sum up a situation and quick to react. He is athletic and would probably be better employed leading a party than working alone. Good natured and a good mixer.'*[2]

In a second report, written a week later on 6 May, Searle, probably unaware that Michael's leadership under fire had already been well-proven and recognized, was to write:

'Lieutenant Trotobas, although disturbed in some degree by the feelings of Lieutenant Langelaan, is more suited to the work for which this course primarily caters. Although he speaks and understands French well he would have difficulty in passing for a Frenchman, over a period. As leader of a raiding party, he would be at a disadvantage. He likes to make his own rapid decisions, knows his job, has an inventive brain, and is full of enthusiasm. Perhaps he is inclined to take too much on his own shoulders but he is very capable and, once he has learnt to appreciate the qualities of the men he has to lead, he should lead them very successfully.'

Given what we know of Michael's early life, Searle's critical judgment of his ability in French is puzzling. Yvonne Pachy later recalled that Michael spoke perfect French, with a slight accent of the south, and that his appearance, mannerisms and language would never have given him away as an Englishman. In its own request for his release from the Army, SOE had referred to his 'unusually good French' and his 'good knowledge of France', and, clearly, this aspect of the report was disregarded and discounted further up the line, otherwise Michael would have gone no further in the face of this apparently damning indictment of his ability in what was a fundamental skill and core requirement of F Section.

A senior officer, Major Larder, wrote on 9 May:

'Trotobas is intelligent and keen. A quick thinker with a good military background, he is extremely keen on getting a job to do. Has initiative and is a good leader.'

But there was a sting in the tail:

'This officer was inclined to be slack owing to the fact that he knew his subjects. He felt that he was wasting his time on this course, and his exam results for map reading and demolitions bear this out.'

Nevertheless, he passed and moved on to Special Training School 25a (STS25) at Garramor House, near Arisaig in Inverness-shire, Scotland. Here the syllabus was much more to his liking. Experts instructed him in unarmed close combat and silent killing, and demolition training took on a much more serious aspect in the surrounding remote countryside. These were skills in which he achieved an eighty-eight per cent pass rate. He was also taught the essentials of personal survival in the wild and how to live off the land. All of this Michael absorbed quickly and well, but his innate restlessness and frustration came to a head in an episode that shows his maverick nature, his blatant disregard for authority or property, and his love of showmanship. Bored, and wanting to relieve his pent-up feelings, he pocketed some explosives, borrowed a motorbike and set off into the hills. One of his instructors, Captain [later Colonel] Ernest van Maurik, found him and recalled:

'Michael Trotobas was in the Army, obviously quite well trained, but from the first moment he was a loner. He came from the south of England, and if I may say it, he looked almost like a spiv, but in fact he was a wonderful man. One night we set them the task of getting ready for an exercise in the mountains the next morning. It was a Saturday night and my commandant, Jimmy Young, and I took advantage of going to the local pub, having a couple of drinks and then driving back. We found the wheels of a motorcycle upside down in a ditch and still turning. We looked down and there was Michael. He exclaimed "It's bloody marvellous". He said there were hundreds of salmon floating all over the place. He had somehow got hold of a small piece of plastic explosive and a detonator. After he'd had one or two too many to drink, he had "borrowed" the staff sergeant's motorcycle and experimented with this little bomb by throwing it into the pool. Jimmy Young was really a very orthodox Scot and the idea of anybody having dynamited the salmon pool was anathema to him. We drove up to the pool. We hoped perhaps they were stunned, but no. Now we knew this would be an awful hoo-ha with the local people. So we tried to fish them out and hide them. But next morning the inhabitants of Morar went up to church and they had to pass this pool and of course there were still a number of dead fish floating around all over the place. The problem was that we could not explain that this young man was under pressure. We heard afterwards that all the local inhabitants had a very good meal of salmon that night. I felt that if they had known of his later achievements they would have forgiven him for blowing up their salmon.' [3]

Searle, in his final report as escorting officer, wrote on 28 May:

'Lieutenant Trotobas will always be inclined to be a little over-eager, but he seems ideally suited as a leader of a raiding party, the members of which are capable of the rapid fulfilment of the plans he

puts into operation. He should not be restrained in his actions. Rather, he should have the men to work with him with the ability to keep up with his speedy execution.'

To this, the senior officer at Arisaig, Lieutenant Colonel Munn, added in his own report on 28 May:

'Trotobas has guts and determination. Moderate intelligence but extremely keen. Has shown slight tendency to be impulsive and has given the impression of being opinionated. Has not shown any marked qualifications for propaganda work and has proved inaccurate in codes and ciphers.'

Captain Young, one of the training officers at STS25, had mixed reservations about Michael, writing on 2 June:

'Inclined to make mistakes in map reading through impetuosity. Very intelligent with a thorough military grounding in which he is most efficient. He is impetuous, as a result of which plans are likely to miscarry. He is quick-tempered and fretful. His general attitude has a bad effect on other members of the party. He ought to be a good leader, but in view of the foregoing I do not consider that he is. He would be useful on a snappy operation. In physical condition and stamina he is excellent and I should say he is very courageous.'

The conflicting wording and emphasis of these reports suggest that the instructors were unaware that some of the trainees on this course might be destined for a clandestine rather than an open operational future, and had little if any awareness of the qualities required of an agent. But these were early days for the training establishments, and it was not until much later that the practical experience of agents who had returned from the field could be utilized. The reports all contain a mixture of positive and negative assessment, but SOE urgently needed agents in the field. Its officers were well aware that the individualism so severely criticized by the instructors might be a key factor in an agent's ability to survive undercover. [4]

In the view of his instructors Michael was a complex character, and the reports highlight this. His ability and enthusiasm to get into the thick of the action as quickly as possible were recognized and lauded, and his determination to succeed was evident. His thirst for action, impatience and impetuosity would certainly have made him unsuited to the traditional role of a spy – the slow, inconspicuous and meticulous gathering of information as practised by the Secret Intelligence Service. However, although they finally earmarked him for leadership, his instructors were uneasy about the perceived flaws in his personality that might constitute a threat to the success of a mission. Among vital qualities unknown to them was his capability to build, train and lead a team to inflict maximum damage to the enemy. In the event their fears were to prove groundless.

There is no report on file of his final test, but two years later he was to describe it to one of his French lieutenants, Arthur Malfait, in the following terms:

'I had to pass a sealed envelope to an agent from whom I would receive a signal, in a café jam-packed with people. My unknown examiners played the part of the Gestapo and had to mark me according to how well I performed. I went into the café, spotted my contact and very quickly identified the "Gestapo agents". I sat down calmly at the counter and had a look around. After determining the lie of the land I offered to buy some refreshments. After chatting for a while about nothing in particular I managed to move so that my contact and the "agents" were all quite close to me. I carried on with my meal and then pretended to look for something I couldn't find. The faces of the examiners showed evident satisfaction at the success of their surveillance, but while they were enjoying this, right under their noses, I knocked over my cup, apologised, used the message to mop up the mess and gave it to the proprietor, who just happened to be my contact. By means of a secret signal I was able to convey to him that the mission was complete. Then, adopting a sheepish manner left the café. Later, the planners met to assess the results. Against my name they put a superb zero but I would love to have seen the faces of my examiners when my accomplice passed them the message and explained my strategy. They had not noticed. Happily, they changed the mark and awarded me the maximum.'

From Arisaig, Michael went to Ringway airfield near Manchester for parachute instruction, but there are no official records to throw light on any subsequent training or on his final assessment. His training period ended in June, and to his disappointment he was assigned not to a commando or sabotage role, but to the role of organizer, responsible for recruiting local agents, establishing and setting up a resistance network, and directing all of its operations. For this task he received only the most basic instruction. How he went about it would be largely up to him and the local conditions in his assigned area. But he was relieved that, finally, his own personal 'phoney war' was over; he was more than ready to return to France and face the enemy. Whether he had been adequately prepared is another matter.

Chapter notes

1   For detailed information about the training schools and methods, see *SOE in France: Chapter III: Recruiting and Training*.
2   Michael's training reports are taken from his SOE personal file.
3   Colonel van Maurik kindly agreed to meet me at the Special Forces Club to talk about Michael, and afterwards sent me a letter containing this interesting and revealing story.
4   It was not only Michael whose reports include doubts as to his potential abilities. As will be seen later, similar reservations were expressed about Arthur Staggs and Francois Reeve.

Chapter 5

Vestige

'Now all roads lead to France and heavy is the tread.'
Edward Thomas

Michael's desire to return to France was matched by SOE's wish to get him there – him and a great many more agents besides. Driven by the political pressure to make something happen, the decision was taken to send in all of the available agents, more or less simultaneously, to the unoccupied zone in the south of France. The reasons for this have never been fully explained, but it might well be that this was considered a relatively safe option for untried men and unproven methods of operation. It could be an excellent proving ground or finishing school for the newly-fledged agents; there were few German soldiers there, everything being administered by the Vichy French authorities and it was a sensible base from which to gather intelligence and gradually explore possibilities in other parts of France. In the absence of German security forces, the risk of capture might have appeared to be minimal, and the consequences for any agents who were arrested likely to be relatively mild in the hands of the Vichy police, as opposed to those of the German *Abwehr* or the Gestapo. Moreover, the USA had an embassy and a consulate there, and, perhaps significantly, SOE already had in place in Lyon with its first resident woman agent, Virginia Hall.

The other side of this particular coin, as Michael might have known from his early days spent there, was that the people in the south were by nature not receptive to change or any ideas that might threaten their relatively placid existence. There was no significant German presence there so they did not feel in any way threatened or repressed; nor were they faced with the invader every day on the streets. Apart from some shortages of essential items, life went on much as before, and it was all the more appreciated and welcome after the horrors of the war and the fear of what the all-conquering Germans might have inflicted on the people of France. But an armistice had been concluded, and the country was now at peace; people moaned about the Vichy government, but they had moaned about all previous governments. The Germans had overrun their country and the British had gunned down their fleet. The general tone was one of apathy, with little if any thought of resistance: a few people carried out minor sabotage acts, and some clandestine leaflets were circulated from time to time.

In a post-war report Colonel Buckmaster outlined the situation within SOE at the beginning of 1941:

'*The Policy of the Section was not clearly defined, the general directive being merely "to foster subversive activities by all means against the enemy". By February 1941 a list of possible helpers, on whose bona fides we could count, was drawn up. It included among other names that of Monsieur Max Hymans, whose property appeared to offer a suitable site for a parachute operation.*

'*In the first three months of 1941 the sources of recruiting available to F Section were carefully studied, and a preliminary party of some ten members were selected for training. These men had, for the most part, acted as liaison officers with British units in 1939-40, and consequently had a background of both French and British military experience. Among them was* George Noble *(now known under his real name of Commandant Bégué, MC). He had already had very great experience as a radio operator, and volunteered to be the first man to be parachuted into France by SOE. He was followed by a series of organizers, who were briefed to investigate and report upon the preparedness of French resistance, and upon its requirements. At that time they were ordered not to engage in any sabotage which could be traced back to deliberate interference, but were to confine their efforts to preaching and carrying out "insaississables" [unattributable] actions and "go slow". It is understood that this limitation was imposed at the request of the Foreign Office. F Section suffered considerably from lack of a clear directive, due no doubt to uncertainty on the part of the authorities as to how far indigenous French resistance could be trusted. It was decided to proceed however with the despatch of British officers, on whom we could rely, in order that they might try out the temper of the local resistants. Each of our early organizers was allotted a zone and was instructed to organize and report on the possibility of general resistance in that zone. One of the earliest organizers to be sent out was* Comte Pierre de Vomécourt, *who was known as* Lucas *in the field.*'[1]

If SOE's strategy was marginally defensible, the same could not be said of its decision to saturate one area, possibly on the tenuous assumption that sheer weight of numbers would ensure that some, at least, would complete their missions. Certainly, the operation seems to have been put together with undue haste and without proper preparation. The first agents were sent in while Michael and his companions were beginning their training, and this had barely been completed when he and most of his fellows were given the task of following up the initial penetration. Michael was just one of seventeen SOE agents – nearly all from that initial course at Wanborough Manor – sent in during the six month period between May and October 1941. This high-risk policy was made even more dangerous as a result of the questionable planning that saw them all given the same contact address in Marseilles and 'cover' papers issued in the agents' real names. No specific operational instructions for the party as a whole have emerged – if indeed they were ever issued – and from subsequent debriefing reports, it seems that the agents had not been instructed as to how to conduct themselves or explain themselves if they were arrested. The most that can be gleaned is that they were briefed to test the water, explore the strength and commitment of resistance in the unoccupied zone, and develop groups where possible. In Michael's case there is a vague reference to his being sent to start a circuit in the south, and he would certainly have been disappointed, if not downright angry, when he learnt of his destination. Far from fulfilling his desire to get back to fighting and, hopefully, killing Germans, he was being sent to where there were no Germans at all. The intensive training he had been given in deception, sabotage and unarmed combat must have appeared completely pointless: he could just as easily have been sent in without wasting time in school.

To understand fully the context and personnel involved, in what turned out to be an ill-fated expedition, it is necessary to go back to the insertion of Georges Bégué who went in on 5 May. He met up with Max Hymans, code-named *Frédéric*, a retired politician and patriot sympathetic to the Allied cause, who in turn introduced Bégué to a local chemist, Renan, and a garage keeper, Marcel Fleuret. These became F Section's first live 'letterboxes' – custodians of secret locations where agents could leave and receive messages. Bégué reported Renan's address back to London on 9 May, and three more agents arrived shortly afterwards. One of these was arrested when he dropped off money for Bégué at Renan's shop, after being denounced to the police by some local peasants who had seen him land. Neither he nor the third agent play any further part in this story, but the first man to land, Pierre de Vomécourt *(Lucas)*, a nobleman and landowner around Limousin, became instantly and effectively active, recruiting his two brothers, both of whom would go on to play important parts in the growth and development of SOE in France. [2]

One of de Vomécourt's first acts was to arrange through Bégué for SOE to drop two containers of weapons and materials near his brother's château at Bas Soleil, ten miles east of Limoges, on the night of 13 June. De Vomécourt and his gardener managed to recover and hide the arms, but the amount of radio traffic generated by Bégué in arranging this alerted the German wireless interception service. It had detected his transmissions almost at once, started to jam them, and advised the Vichy police to keep a sharp look out for strangers in the vicinity of Châteauroux. This, coupled with the fact that Fleuret's garage became a general rendezvous and gossip shop, not only for SOE and local resistance men but also for the general population, drawn to this centre of activity and fascinated by what might be going on, was to have unfortunate consequences for later arrivals.

On 6 August two agents who were to have a significant impact on the missions of Michael and his colleagues – Captain Jacques Vaillant de Guélis (*Jacques*) and Captain G.C.G. Turck (*Christophe*) – dropped blind many miles from their target and lost contact with each other during the landing. Turck fell into a quarry, where he was picked up the following day, injured and unconscious, by two gendarmes. De Guélis made contact with Bégué, and during a short stay had meetings with the de Vomécourts and other self-styled local French leaders. Previously, Turck had been a liaison officer between the French *Deuxième Bureau* and the British intelligence services, and when he recovered from his injuries he spun a yarn to the police about hating England and bribing an RAF pilot to drop him back into France. Whether this unlikely story was believed or not, he was soon released and quickly met up again with de Guélis, to whom he passed on details of a number of contact points, one of which was the Villa des Bois on the outskirts of Marseilles.

De Guélis meanwhile had recruited an old friend, Robert Lyon (*Adrian*), a former colleague in the *Mission Francais de Liaison* in 1940, who was now working as a regional administrator and liaison officer for the American Red Cross. De Guélis told Lyon that he wanted him to establish a circuit in Marseilles, adding that some Englishmen were due to arrive shortly from London. De Guélis wanted Lyon to find a cover for Bégué, who was to be the circuit's radio operator [commonly referred to as W/T or WT – for wireless telegraphist], and put Lyon in touch with Francis Bouguennec (*Garel*), a courier he had recruited earlier. Bégué made contact with Lyon inside two weeks and was told that cover had been arranged for him as an import and export representative with a commercial firm run by one of Lyon's friends. It was a position that allowed him to move around freely and talk to people without arousing suspicion, as indeed could Lyon himself, whose Red Cross activities gave him the use of a car. De Guélis returned to England on 4 September, taking with him valuable information about the situation in the unoccupied zone and local conditions in the Marseilles area, including the list of contact points given to him by Turck.

During the course of the next few weeks fourteen more agents arrived in the area. The first group of six was dropped near Châteauroux on the night of 6 September, four arrived by sea two weeks later, and four more parachuted in on 10 October. All were given details of Fleuret's letterbox and eight of them were given specific and identical instructions to proceed to Marseilles and make contact at the Villa des Bois with Turck (identified in the orders as *Christophe)* who would help them with accommodation. From the reports of interviews of many of these agents on their eventual return to England it is possible to reconstruct subsequent events, understand the mentality of the agents, and note their naivety and lack of preparation for adversity. [3]

Michael was in the first group of six, and so found himself on 6 September, now promoted to captain and assigned the operational name *Vestige,* with the cover name of *Denis,* on board 138 Squadron's Whitley Z6728, piloted by Flight Sergeant Reimer, along with his old protagonist George Langelaan, their earlier differences presumably forgotten. There were four others: Major Ben Cowburn, Lieutenant Comte de Puy, Lieutenant George Bloch, and Victor Gerson, a civilian. The aircraft crossed the English coast near Tangmere at around 2120 hrs, and the French coast in thick cloud somewhere near Caen shortly after 2200 hrs, arriving at the drop zone near Châteauroux, just inside Vichy France, half an hour before midnight. A break in the cloud enabled Reimer to make out the pinpricks of light laid out by the reception committee, and the agents were given the signal to go. The rear gunner reported that he had seen all six parachutes open and the agents land safely. They were met by a reception committee organized by Bégué, after which Cowburn, Bloch and de Puy moved out of the area and play no further part in this account.

In his post-operation report Langelaan recounted what happened next:

> *'Six of us jumped out safely and were heartily welcomed. Contrary to what we had been told we had to move before dawn with no rest of any kind. We were very lucky in no-one being caught since that particular day was the* Ouverture de la Chasse *and all the gendarmes in France and Navarre were out patrolling the roads while hunters were already searching fields and woods for any game. I travelled all that day, arriving at Lyon late that evening.'*

In Lyon he came across a local woman who introduced him to Philippe Liewer, who had been a liaison officer with the British in the early days of the war and was looking for a way of escape to England. After a number of meetings Langelaan decided to recruit him.

> *'Liewer had been a newspaper man in the Agence Radio, where I believe he held the post of Foreign Political Editor. Being an Israelite*

he was no longer employed. After several talks with him, and feeling that he was quite trustworthy, I told him who I was and gave him a vague idea of what I was doing. He was terribly keen. I proposed taking him on, after London approved, as my assistant, and his job would have consisted of visiting certain parts of the country to collect information and opinions in view of future propaganda. I agreed to give him 5,000 francs a month plus expenses.'

At the end of September Langelaan moved to Pau, where he stayed at a hotel run by one of his pre-war friends. In the meantime another agent, Frenchman George Morel, was seized. He had been brought in on the Lysander aircraft that took De Guélis back to England, and his mission was to contact various friends and encourage them to form groups that would support sabotage operations. On 3 October he was arrested by the French police after being betrayed by one of those contacts. This alerted the authorities once more to the possible presence of other agents in the area, and investigations began that led to a series of arrests. First to go was Langelaan:

'Having settled down I sent for Liewer and gave him his first assignment, which was to take a message to Châteauroux for transmission to England. He met Georges [Bégué], *and after a few days returned home with the answer that I was to meet* Georges *in Châteauroux a few days later. I sent him back home and went to Châteauroux on 5 October. I followed out all instructions for contacting* Georges *and on the 6 October was arrested by the French surveillance du territoire at the* Café du Phésant *where I was to meet* Georges. *The six men who arrested me searched me thoroughly and unfortunately found Liewer's address in my pocket book. I was one of the first to be arrested and they had a vague idea that I might be a German spy.'*

He was roughly treated and beaten up several times.

'Some twelve hours after my arrest without anything to drink, no food, and badly disfigured, I owned up that I was a British officer. Their attitude towards me changed completely, they apologized for the rough treatment and assured me that I would very shortly be interned in a British camp. I gave them my real identity since in any case they would get it from Liewer.'

Liewer took up the story:

> *'Captain Langelaan then told me he intended going to Paris and that he believed he'd be away two or three weeks and wouldn't be wanting me for the time. He intended to contact me as soon as he was back in the unoccupied zone. I therefore went back to Antibes, where I was living with my wife, and next thing I knew, the police were there to arrest me, on the morning of 11 October, that is a week after I had last seen Captain Langelaan. I was arrested by a commissaire special from the Nice police force, accompanied by a member of surveillance du territoire, who had come down from Vichy especially for that purpose, and I was then taken down to Nice, with my wife. Incidentally, my wife knew nothing whatsoever of my connections with the service.'*

After negotiating the release of his wife in exchange for information he went on:

> *'But the point the police were most interested in was the whereabouts of* Georges. *They first tried to make me believe they had arrested him, which I didn't swallow. They asked me afterwards for a description of him, and I gave a fairly inaccurate one. They finally admitted having lost his track.'*

Next in the bag was Michael, who had made his way to Marseilles as instructed. In the only known personal statement by him to have survived the war, he told what happened prior to his arrest.

> *'I was dropped in France on 6 Aug* [a margin note corrects this to "Sept"] *1941 and went direct to Marseille, where I made contact with* Christophe, *meeting him in the company of* Georges *and* Frederic [Max Hymans]. *We had various conversations and during this time nothing led me to have any doubts about* Christophe. *He showed me an identity card in the name of Turque* [sic] *and told me he belonged or had belonged to the* Troisième or Cinquième Bureau. *He found a room for me in Marseille through the intermediary of a* bureau de placement. *I saw and talked to* Christophe *on several occasions and came to the conclusion that he seemed very keen on his work, but that he wrote a great deal too much, in fact he seemed to be continually writing. On one of the occasions when I went to see him I met* Frederic *and gave him a message for transmission to London. This was a request for supplies to be sent to a prearranged landing-ground. I asked* Frederic *to arrange for* Georges *to send me a telegram by the 6 October which would be either negative or*

positive, but this did not arrive and I decided to go to see Georges
*personally, as I had not yet found anyone I considered secure enough
to act as courier. About this time, incidentally,* Christophe *informed
me that he was leaving to go to Paris on duty.* '4

When he arrived in Châteauroux on 10 September Michael found that
Bégué was not around, so he went to Fleuret's garage to leave a message,
unaware that Fleuret had been arrested on suspicion of black marketeering
and had spoken about *Georges*. There Michael met Bégué's courier,
Bouguennec, and within minutes both of them had been arrested by a police
surveillance team and locked up overnight. Like Langelaan, Michael
revealed his true identity and was charged with 'activities contrary to the
interests of the state', before being taken to the Prison de Beleyme in
Périgueux.

On the evening of Michael's arrest, four more agents – Jack Hayes,
Clement Jumeau, Jean Le Harivel and Daniel Turberville – were dropped
to a reception committee consisting of local resistance leader and former
socialist deputy, Pierre Bloch, another of de Guélis's recruits; a local doctor
and Albert Rigoulet, owner of a post office and garage in Villamblard.
Hayes's mission was to contact Bloch to organize an area south of the Loire
and west of the Rhône, recruiting locally and instructing in sabotage.
Turberville was to base himself in the Massif Centrale, while Jumeau was
to set up a similar organization in Marseilles, with Le Harivel as his WT
operator. De Guélis had given Jumeau the names of Lyon and Jean
Bardanne, a well-known local journalist. Hayes, who was carrying
2,000,000 francs with him when he landed, explained what happened next:

*'Myself, Jumeau and Le Harivel jumped in that order, and all landed
in woods bordering the landing ground. Owing to this
miscalculation, contact was made with Rigoulet, one of the reception
committee, only after some delay. Rigoulet was the only member of
the reception committee who showed any initiative and cool-
headedness on this occasion. Chutes were got down from tree
branches and hidden with the equipment. The other two members of
the reception committee were then contacted and seemed in a very
nervous state. The money, which we were to deliver, was handed over
to them and they left with Jumeau, while Le Harivel and I remained
behind with Rigoulet to transfer all the material to a hiding place in
a barn some distance away. This operation lasted until six am.
Jumeau eventually joined us in this hideout, not having been able to
find accommodation with the other two members of the committee,
the wife of one refusing to help.*

'The following day we heard that Turberville had been dropped 6km north of our landing ground with the containers, that the containers had been found by the police and Turberville subsequently arrested. Le Harivel intended trying to get in touch with London to report, but we found, on unpacking the WT set dropped with us, that it was neither his set nor a transmitting set and therefore useless.'

Rigoulet brought news of the arrest to the barn the following morning, along with the information that the noise of aircraft during the night was the principal topic of conversation among the locals, some of who swore to having seen parachutes in the sky. Bégué, who had met up with Bloch to agree distribution of the money brought in by Hayes, caught sight of Michael and Bouguennec being led away in handcuffs to the station, but could do nothing. Shortly afterwards, Bloch arrived at the farm and told the waiting men that Bégué's cover had been blown. Hayes continued:

'On hearing of Turbeville's arrest and the discovery of the containers, we decided to leave the district. Acting on instructions that in an emergency we could contact Christophe *in Marseilles, Jumeau and I proceeded to that town: Jumeau to join his post at Marseilles, Le Harivel to proceed to his post and myself to go to Marseilles for a while until the alarm in the Bergerac district had abated. Jumeau and I were taken to Bergerac by Rigoulet where we stayed with some other sympathizers until the departure of the bus for Marmande in the evening. Security on the part of our hosts was alarming, as present at the lunch offered us was the whole family, including wife, children and maid or help, all of whom knew who we were. For one who was to work in the district, the broadcast of his identity was not very helpful. On arrival we contacted Bardanes [sic] and Lyon but could not locate* Christophe's *villa on the first day. Bardanes seemed a very efficient co-operator and gave us to understand that he was very short of cash to continue his activities. It seemed to us that his cooperation could be most valuable. That night was spent at Lyon's home.'*

Lyon provided additional details, stating that Jumeau had proceeded as instructed to the home of Ann Manceaux, a local sympathizer:

'Although she was not there, he was told he could sleep there, which he did, hoping she would return the next day. Hayes, Jumeau and I had a rendezvous the following day, but Jumeau did not appear. Hayes therefore made enquiries and discovered that Ann Manceaux had been arrested and her house was being watched.'

On the afternoon of 16 September Jumeau had put through several telephone calls to *Christophe* as he had been instructed, but there was no reply. The next morning he met Anne Manceaux, who showed him a letter bearing a message that Bouguennec had been arrested in Châteauroux. In his subsequent report Jumeau stated:

> '*I suggested meeting* Christophe *and informing him what had happened. Anne Manson* [sic] *felt rather uneasy about my seeing* Christophe. *She told me she had no confidence whatsoever in him; but I overruled her and proceeded to the Villa des Bois…there was no time to lose. If Bouguennec was to be saved, the necessary demarches would have to be undertaken at once….I was met at his house, the Villa des Bois, by three inspectors of the surveillance du territoire, who insisted on my following them.*'

Hayes continued:

> '*The next day I went to Bardanes to report this matter and he arranged for me to go to the* Hôtel des Palmiers *at St Maxime where I was to stay until he told me to return. In the meantime I had tried to contact Le Harivel by meeting trains at Marseilles station and patrolling the Canebière, as Bardanes had informed me that he needed a WT operator and had a set at our disposal. Le Harivel was not encountered and I proceeded to St Maxime. I stayed a week there and finally returned to Marseilles on Bardanes' instructions. During my stay in St Maxime, Lyon had been endeavouring to contact* Christophe *and on my return informed me that he had arranged a contact at the* Restaurant Mont Venthou *for 1030 hrs on Friday, 24 October.*'

Bardanne then sent a message to Hayes, telling him to come back to Marseilles. Hayes arrived at the restaurant on time, while Lyon turned up half an hour later with Bardanne, who then left. The two of them must have been followed, because almost immediately four members of the *Sûreté* burst in and arrested Hayes and Lyon. The latter had on him a letter with a Châteauroux postmark, which made the police suspicious because of the reported parachutists there.

Le Harivel, meanwhile, had arrived a day earlier than expected and gone straight to the villa to see *Christophe,* where he met a woman who told him that *Christophe* was away and in Paris. He asked when he would be back:

> '*The reply was that* Christophe *would be back in eight days. He was at present in Paris (this was on 17 October). Would I come*

back in eight days? I spent a whole week in Marseilles doing nothing. I knew no-one there. I had no other contacts to make, having been told not to go to Lyon, where I was to operate, before having seen Frederic *and/or* Georges *or* Christophe. *In any case it was no use my going to Lyon without a wireless set.* Christophe *was the person who was going to give me full instructions as to my next move. Through him I hoped to be able to contact a WT operator and send a message to London. After a week had elapsed I returned to the villa, and was told* Christophe *had not come back, but that if I came to the* Café Riche *next morning at 10.30 am, this woman's husband would see me and tell me if it were possible for me to contact* Christophe.'

Jumeau kept the appointment, which proved unsatisfactory, and was arrested by the police shortly after leaving.

The final curtain on this SOE debacle in the unoccupied zone came down with the arrests of Raymond Roche, who had come by sea, and of Georges Bégué. The two had met up in Marseilles by arrangement and Bégué recounted:

'I rang Christophe *personally when I got off the train. He himself answered and told me to come, everything being normal....When we arrived at the Villa des Bois we found the grill closed. I therefore knocked on the door to alert* Christophe. *He came out of the house after half a minute or so and went down the steps to cross the garden, but when he was a few metres from the door he stopped and asked twice: "Who's there?....Is that* Georges?*" and appeared to be waiting for something to happen. Suddenly we were surrounded by half a dozen policemen who let* Christophe *go on his way'.*

From these first-hand reports it appears that none of the captured agents had the slightest suspicion that anything might be wrong, nor took any precautions. Manceaux had tried to warn Jumeau but he had ignored her. The only one to show caution was the civilian Gerson, who had dropped with Michael. He had taken the precaution of observing the comings and goings at the villa, without revealing himself, and had become suspicious. He backed away from any contact, headed for the Pyrenees, and from there made his way back to England.

The extent of the damage to SOE was summarized in a captured German document. Emanating from the office of the *Sicherheitspolizei* commander in France and marked 'Secret' it includes the following:

'British parachutists and agents in the Unoccupied Zone of France.
Please find a summary of what we know so far about the incident
of the British agents dropped in the Unoccupied Zone of France.

On 3 October 1941 a Brigade of the Surveillance du Territoire
in Limoges captured Gerard MOREL, who had been dropped from
an English aeroplane. In the course of further investigations 16 more
persons were seized. The English agents are:

- *Langelaan, Georges*
- *Trotobas, Michael*
- *Jumeau, Clement*
- *Leharivel, Jean*
- *Hayes, John*
- *Dunais, Georgette*
- *Abel, Friedrich*
- *Rosche, Raymond*
- *Bégué, Georges*
  (all dropped by parachute)
- *Married couple Fleuret*
- *Plus Lyon, Robert, and Bloch, Pierre and their wives*

'Based on information from an informant, a safe house in Marseille
was identified, the Villa Desbois, Vallon de la Baidille. Surveillance
of the safe house enabled the capture of those named above. The
prisoner Pierre Bloch, a previous Deputy of the Aisne Department,
was caught in the act handing over 1,150,000 francs to an agent.
Also involved was previous Deputy of the Indre Department, Max
Hymans, who managed to flee to Spain and from there almost
certainly to England. Enquiries into the whereabouts of a certain
"Christa" (codename), leader of the organization, proved fruitless.
The organization, which reported through Christa directly to the
Intelligence Service, was tasked with intelligence gathering and
sabotage in the Occupied Zone.

'On 12 October 1941 the English officer Daniel Turberville was
arrested shortly after his landing near Périgueux. His mission was
to carry out sabotage. Along with him three of the familiar containers
were dropped, containing explosives and arms. The goods were
seized, and Turberville managed to escape while being taken to the
State Court in Lyon.'[5]

Bouguennec, who had had the simple misfortune to go to Fleuret's
letterbox at the precise moment it was being searched, does not appear in

the German report and was clearly not thought to be connected to the agents. The report was distributed to all *Sicherheitsdienst* (SD) and *Sicherheitspolizei* (SiPo) [counter-intelligence and security police] units in France and copied to their general headquarters in Berlin, as well as to numerous other formations and units with an interest in terrorist, espionage or sabotage activities. Worse, full descriptions, photographs and identity details of all the named agents followed, posing a potentially fatal threat to any of them who might return to operations in France after escaping or being repatriated. SOE's decision to issue the agents with papers in their own name, taken in the belief that this might help mitigate their treatment in the event of arrest, thus rebounded badly, as did giving everyone the same contact address. Of the fifteen people listed in the German document, thirteen had been arrested directly or indirectly as a result of following up the clearly compromised contact at the Villa des Bois. One by one and two by two the mice had walked obligingly into the trap set for them. The exceptions were Langelaan and Michael, who had been taken in Châteauroux. Even so, there was an inevitability about events which is encapsulated by Michael in his interrogation report:

> *'The police (Sûrété du Territoire)*[sic] *pointed out that they were in no way connected with the Gestapo, and that I could consequently speak quite freely with them. They said they were working in the interests of France and had the right to know the reason for my presence there. During these conversations I realized that they knew by this time that container operations were to take place in France for the purposes of sabotage. They also spoke of the VILLA des BOIS (CHRISTOPHE's address) as a "souricière"* [mousetrap] *stating that I would eventually have been caught there.'*

The effect on SOE was significant. In Buckmaster's words:

> *'These arrests, bringing others in their train, almost cleaned up our organization in the ZNO* [unoccupied zone]. *The opening of 1942 therefore found us without radio contact with* Lucas [de Vomécourt] *and his groups and with little else in the field, except Miss Virginia Hall, firmly established in Lyon with American consular assistance, and keeping more or less open house for F Section agents.'*

All of the captured men were sent to the serious offenders' prison at Périgueux, where they found themselves in adjoining cells, Michael next to Liewer on one side and Langelaan on the other, the latter sharing his cell with Morel and the ageing Fleuret. Morel made himself deliberately ill and was taken to hospital in Limoges, where he had a major abdominal operation. The night after the stitches were removed he fled the hospital with the help of a nurse, and eventually found his way to Spain. Critically for the future of the group, Gabrielle 'Gaby' Bloch (Pierre's wife) was released, while Bardanne and Rigoulet were still at large, not having been identified.

On the whole the prisoners were not badly treated in terms of violence or abuse, but various methods of intimidation were tried. After a few days they all found themselves sharing the same cell: Michael, Langelaan, Jumeau, Hayes, Le Harivel, Bégué, Roche, Liewer, Fleuret and Bloch, and within the prison they mixed with common criminals. Conditions were poor, with little in the way of food; there was inadequate sanitation, no heating and an infestation of lice and other insects. Consequently morale was very low. They spent the days communally in a large, bleak and filthy room, with one long table and two rows of benches with insufficient space to seat all of the occupants; consequently a fierce scramble for places ensued every time the meagre food allowance was served. By night they were confined to a large attic room strewn with a collection of dirty, lice-infested mattresses allocated on a 'first come, first served' basis. In the middle of the room was a cut-down fuel drum with a plank across which had to do duty as a single latrine for all of them.

In an effort to establish some kind of small economy they created prison money in the form of 10 and 50 franc notes, signed by Bégué as 'President' and Langelaan as 'Treasurer', in anticipation that these bills would later be honoured by SOE. Eventually they were allowed to receive parcels of food from outside, and the Frenchmen pooled everything they received from families and friends. The principal organizer on the outside was Gaby, who had on her nearly all of the money brought in by Hayes when she was arrested; the notes were returned to her when she was released, and she put the SOE funds to good use for bribery and for purchasing small luxuries such as razor blades and packs of cards. Michael was particularly pleased to find a chess set among these comforts and he quickly organized a tournament complete with its own ladder. During the course of these matches he found himself up against a young French officer who was to play an important part in his future.

Pierre Séailles, well-educated and from an upper-class background, had been studying Industrial Art and Design when war brought an abrupt end to his studies. Called up to the Reserve Officers' College in Orléans, where he failed to distinguish himself, a brief military career saw him drifting from one vague assignment to another without once coming into contact with the enemy. When he heard of the German occupation, he set off on 17 June for the coast, in the hope of finding passage to England, but with the roads a seething mass of refugees, he made slow progress. The military police were out in force looking for deserters and they picked Séailles up in Bordeaux and took him to an open prison near Agen, where he spent two months. When the Army was reorganized following the armistice he was kept on and posted to Montrésor to guard the demarcation line along the Cher, before being declared unfit for service and discharged. After spending Christmas of 1941 with his family in Paris he decided try once again to get to England, this time via Spain. Calling at Montrésor he learnt to his surprise that there was a warrant out for him and he was arrested as a deserter. He protested that he had been officially discharged, but it was in vain and the following morning he was taken in handcuffs to Périgueux, where a judge found him guilty of the serious charge of 'desertion in time of war and in the face of the enemy'. He defended himself vigorously and, after advice was taken, 'in the face of the enemy' was struck off the charge. He was awaiting sentence when he met Michael.

In March 1942, thanks to the intervention of the US Consulate, the whole of the SOE group was transferred from Périgueux to an internment camp at Mauzac, to where Séailles, sentenced to one year in prison, was also sent.

Chapter notes

1   This extract is taken from Colonel Buckmaster's informative article *F Section History*, written in 1946.
2   For the material in this chapter I have referred to *SOE in France, Chapter VII: Opening gambits: 1940-1941* for background and dates. More specific detail has been provided by references to operational reports and debriefings of many of the agents concerned. The contents of these reports are consistent with each other.
3   A number of interrogation reports were available in public records, including Langelaan on 11 November 1942, Liewer on 17 September, Hayes on 10 October 1942, 16 November 1942, and later on 18 December 1944 (HS6/572), and Lyon (under his later operational name of Captain Calvert) in March 1945 (HS8/143). In addition, reports were found in the investigation into Turck (from Le Harivel and Bégué (both 21 November 1942). There are no post-operation reports from Michael on file.
4   In 1943 an exhaustive, long-running enquiry was launched into the behaviour of *Christophe*. Many of the agents involved, including Michael, were questioned about him and their contact with him. This extract is from the cover file, *TUNMER/CHRISTOPHE HS/434*.
5   The reference IVE/N.A.15/12 g-, dated Paris 19 August 1942 indicates that this is a Gestapo document. The *Sicherheitspolizei* (SiPo) was the security arm of the German police infrastructure, which was divided into seven main departments: IV was the Gestapo, the political secret police whose functions included spying on enemies of the Nazi regime (imaginary as well as real) and weeding out dissidents and opponents; Department III was the *Sicherheitsdienst* (SD), responsible for foreign and domestic counter-intelligence and espionage.

Chapter 6

Mauzac

'To walk into history is to be free'
Elizabeth Bowen

The Sauveboeuf internment camp at Mauzac was set in open countryside 20km east of Bergerac, and surrounded by barbed wire. Inmates were segregated into barracks according to their social and political categories, which helped the guards to determine those who had influence and were likely to complain about poor treatment. Living conditions at Mauzac were much better than at Périgueux – it was springtime, they had fresh air, washing facilities and their own individual mattresses. They quickly organized themselves into working parties to transform their dismal accommodation into something more habitable and comfortable, and soon had the place spick and span, with even some token decoration. The prison food supplied in the refectory for the two thousand prisoners was poor, but soon British and American Red Cross parcels started to arrive and the men obtained permission to prepare their own food.

The close confinement gave the SOE agents a golden opportunity to get to know the local activists and to establish contacts for the future. Michael was able to resume his friendship with Séailles, who was in the next hut with the Gaullist faction. He told Michael of his determination to get back at the Germans for the humiliation and cruelty he had witnessed in 1940. Michael also got to know Pierre Duval, a cheerful young civilian who had fought his own private war as forager, transporter and procurer of black market and stolen goods, particularly petrol, and had run a fleet of vehicles criss-crossing borders seemingly at will. He had been picked up a number of times but on each occasion had managed to escape or talk his way out, until he finally ended up in Périgueux, where a tribunal had found him guilty of espionage and sent him to Mauzac. Michael informed both Frenchmen that he fully intended to escape, make his way back to England and then return to France to resume his interrupted mission to make life as miserable for the Germans as he possibly could. Both men indicated their willingness to join him and gave him their contact addresses – Séailles in Paris and Duval in Abbeville.

Although Michael would have relished the open air, sunshine and weekly shower, which allowed him to build up his physical and mental strength, he was never much of a socializer and found the enforced confinement and communal life difficult, as Le Harivel was to write:

> '*I remember Trotobas very well...He was not very talkative, but we were good friends and got on well together.*'

And later:

> '*Our days were rather alike. The monotony of prison life is one of the more unpleasant aspects. But we did our best to overcome that by playing bridge every day, and chess sometimes. I became a very good bridge player, because some of my friends were excellent players. Chess was more difficult, but I had an excellent teacher. We played volleyball outside with a homemade ball, and that kept us fit... . It was my job to do the cooking for twelve every day – because the prison food was very mediocre. We had a homemade cooker made out of old vegetable tins, and many chips of wood. Very effective. After a while we received Red Cross parcels and then we made our English breakfast... . I remember an incident when Trotobas (who could be violent) beat up a common-law prisoner, with whom he was very friendly, who made the mistake of stealing his watch. The watch was returned very rapidly. Trotobas was not very effusive. I often had talks with him but he kept apart from us quite often. He was a lone wolf.*' [1]

In transferring the group *en masse* the Vichy authorities had unwittingly replicated the 'all eggs in one basket' folly that had delivered their captives to them in the first place. Whether they were blinded by the light of their success, or simply complacent, they managed to keep together a group of people from a wide range of professional, technical and military backgrounds, many of whom had been trained expressly to be resourceful in subversion, survival and evasion. Others had extensive local knowledge and contacts, all spoke fluent French; everyone was dismayed at their early capture and each was itching to get out and get back. Escape was very much on their minds, and no sooner had they arrived and taken stock of their surroundings than the business of planning and organizing a break-out had begun, under the leadership of Bégué, an ideal man to mastermind the vital networking and liaison with local sources of information, for he had been born in Périgueux and knew the area and its inhabitants intimately.

Frustrated by the daily monotony of prison life, Michael bought into the plan for a mass escape across the mountains to Spain and from there to

England. The details he left to others, but to prepare himself and them for what would be an arduous journey on foot, over rough and inhospitable terrain, he volunteered to take on the responsibility for getting everyone as fit as possible. It was a role that came naturally to him and one for which Army experience had equipped him well, as George Langelaan described in *Knights of the Floating Silk*:

> *'Inside the camp we were leading a very busy Jekyll and Hyde sort of life. Every morning, for well over an hour, Captain Michael Trotobas, an athletic professional army man…would lead us out between the barracks and put us through some fast physical training drill, the idea being that we had to build up our strength again after months of starvation and total inaction in the prison of Béleyme, and thus get us physically fit for any sort of prolonged effort we might have to undergo during or after our escape. In the afternoons we played innumerable games of* pétanque…*which gave us all the opportunities we needed for a close study of the double fence of barbed wire surrounding the camp.'* [2]

Aware of the danger of gathering in large groups and communicating a sense of excitement and anticipation, Bégué encouraged the agents to operate in small cells, each with its own area of responsibility, and to keep others in the dark about what they were doing. All were instructed to appear morose and apathetic during contact with other inmates and, in particular, with the inevitable but small number within their own group who had expressed no desire to do anything but sit out the expected short war in safety and do nothing to antagonize their captors into handing them over to the Germans. The success of this policy led to Hayes commenting in his report of 10 October:

> *'Another point which should be mentioned is that tension was sometimes acute between members of our group though this was probably caused by nervous strain, malnutrition and enforced confinement. The team spirit was nevertheless non-existent throughout our period of confinement, except during the escape.'*

By way of diversion, a visit to the camp was arranged for a local sympathizer – a priest who had lost his legs in the First World War – to come and give a talk. He arrived in a wheelchair, in which he smuggled a small suitcase containing a radio transceiver. It was promptly put to good use, as Langelaan recorded:

*'In no time at all we had it hidden away in the roof of our barrack.
Working at night, Georges was able to tap a line passing just under
the edge of our roof and, in no time, had everything in working order.
Within a week he had made contact with London. Our escape was
now getting really organized and, by means of our transmitter, we
were able to communicate, via London, with the people outside who
were getting everything ready.'*

At the centre of communications was Gerson, who after his return to
London in November had immediately volunteered to go back into the field
in order to set up a safe escape route from the south of France. Along with
his radio operator, Marcel Clech, he was put ashore in the early hours of 21
April from the British submarine HMS *Unbroken*. The two men met up with
Virginia Hall in Lyon, where Gerson established his base and slowly built
up his 'VIC' network. This included George Levin, Lazarus Racheline and
Thérèse Mitrani in Lyon and René Feraggi in Marseilles. He set up a small
subgroup in Perpignan.

Although it was Bégué who was primarily instrumental in initiating the
important and essential contacts outside of the camp, it was Gaby who
carried them out; her regular visits to bring in food and cigarettes providing
ample opportunity for messages and materials to be passed to and fro. Bégué
told her to contact Hall who put Gaby in touch with Gerson and his escape
line, which now included Rigoulet, and they began to make arrangements.
Liewer had an excellent local lawyer, Brissonnière, who during the course
of weekly visits to his client kept the planners up-to-date with the many and
varied regulations and restrictions that were being introduced, as well as
providing vital samples of travel documents and permits.

The first immediate problem for the escapees was to get out of the
barrack hut itself. Its windows were situated at an awkward height and criss-
crossed with barbed wire, which made exit through them impossible,
particularly since a number of the locals were middle-aged and nowhere
near as fit as the SOE agents. Langelaan recounted how this problem was
solved by the ever-resourceful Bégué who crafted a duplicate key from an
impression made in moistened bread shoved into the keyhole:

*'Every night, after a final roll call and inspection, we were locked in
our barrack. Night after night, we held interminable sing-songs in
order to cover the noise Georges Béguet [sic] was making, filing
away at a piece of iron. Béguet, who had been one of our radio
operators and who was quite a good mechanic, was gradually
shaping a key that would, we hoped, open and close the door of the
barrack.'*

The second problem was that every time the door was opened it would be visible under the arc lights and likely to trigger an immediate alert.

'We finally hit on the idea of preparing a false door painted on sack cloth which could be pinned up in a matter of seconds once the real door was opened.'

Last but not least there were the hourly patrols and the watchtowers, where the guards were changed every four hours. Bégué realized that the cooperation of at least one guard was essential. A number were approached tentatively, but only one responded; this was Anton Sevilla, an Andalusian who had come to France for employment and was happy to assist in the escape in return for a place in it and eventual passage to England. He was scheduled for a period of duty at the top of the tower nearest to the SOE barrack from midnight to 0400 hrs in the new moon period of 14 to 19 July, and the decision was made to break out between patrols during this period.

On 8 July Gerson told London that the Mauzac men would leave five nights later, and asked what their identity status should be if they were arrested. London replied that identity papers for the escape had been prepared in false names, but in the last resort they should give the identity and status of British officers. On 10 July Brissonnière told Liewer that preparations for the escape were already well advanced. Liewer gave him a full account of what was needed in the way of tools and materials with which to negotiate the barbed wire, as well as details of the guards' patrol patterns. Liewer had already established from a Gaullist inmate that some of the guards were open to bribery, and his lawyer brought with him on this occasion Lazare Racheline, a member of the escape line and a long-standing friend of the Blochs, who would take care of bribes. Brissonnière came back a fortnight later to give final instructions, and Liewer went over every detail of the operation with him.

To allay suspicion, considerable attention was paid to establishing a routine of innocent activities and an air of apparent resigned acceptance. A fair-sized library provided a wealth of reading material while cards, chess and bridge tournaments became regular features – as did decorating. The more theatrically inclined held their own 'Comic Parliament', while those who had parachuted into France formed an association entitled 'Companions of the Floating Silk' with a particularly English motto of 'shit or bust'. Langelaan again:

'By the way in which we all worked hard at decorating and improving everything in our barrack, anyone might well have thought that we intended living there for the next fifty years.'

A carefully-staged photograph taken in Mauzac shows the men of the SOE contingent, dressed in suits and lounging outside one of the huts, smiling and looking for all the world like a party on a works outing. Whether by accident or design, Gaby, the photographer, had positioned Michael right in the centre of the group, where he stands with hands thrust in trouser pockets, jacket open, legs wide apart staring fixedly at the camera – a self-confident and cocky pose. [3]

The time passed slowly for him, but eventually the eagerly awaited day arrived, just three short months from his arrival in Mauzac – a tribute to the skill and dedication of the planners. On the evening of 14 July the men celebrated Bastille Day, and the *Marseillaise* rang out around the camp. Many of the guards joined in the singing, believing that this was just another demonstration of patriotic normality and of the prisoners coming to terms with their fate: a false sense of security, for the escape was to take place the following night.

Shortly after four o'clock the following afternoon, as the men were preparing tea, they observed an old woman trudge slowly past the camp, accompanied by three children. This was the prearranged signal for the escape, but at the very last minute a complication arose. It had already been agreed that not all of the hut would attempt the escape with some of the local men preferring to wait for their eventual release, which they felt to be only a matter of time. But one of the group refused stubbornly to have anything to do with the plan. Fleuret was over 60 and worried about the possible repercussions on his wife and daughter if he escaped. He also feared that if the rest of the group escaped this would bring further trouble on him and his family, and he threatened to expose the plan to the guards. During dinner that evening he was given a heavy dose of a sleeping drug Langelaan had obtained from a co-operative medical officer in the camp infirmary; this, it was hoped, would keep Fleuret quiet until the following morning and help persuade the authorities that he had no part in the venture.

Pulling on gloves to protect their hands from the barbed wire, and socks over their shoes in order to make as little noise as possible, the men settled down to wait for Sevilla to light his pipe – the signal to move out. Michael had volunteered to lead the way, having carefully studied and memorized the route to the wire. He peered anxiously through the narrow gap in the door, growing ever more frustrated and anxious as the minutes passed slowly by. The others crouched behind him, equally impatient. Doubts began to creep in. What if the duty roster had been changed? What if the guard had betrayed them?

It had been agreed that if the signal had not been given by 0300 hrs, everything would be called off because it would be too close to daylight. But with only minutes to spare it came – a little momentary flicker of light.

Langelaan provided a gripping account of the break-out, corroborated in all essential details by other reports, and described the part played by Michael after Jumeau had opened the curtain, seen that the coast was clear, and dashed into the adjoining alleyway to act as lookout.

> *'Next man out was Michael Trotobas who, with a strip of carpet rolled under his arm, was to open the way. As he crept silently towards the spot we had chosen, he unrolled a ball of string, which was to be a signal-line. One tug was to mean: "All clear, carry on" and three sharp tugs: "Danger, hold everything".*
>
> *'In silence, and for what seemed like hours, we waited for the first all-clear signal. We all jumped when we heard the barbed wires twanging like piano wires, and guessed that Trotobas was hard at it, pulling them out from the wooden stakes. He had a hammer wrapped in an old rag with which he he was going to nail them back again afterwards; so that we should leave no traces on the ground, he had laid out the carpet over which we were to crawl.*
>
> *'My turn came at last, after Pierre Bloch. I found Trotobas standing in the alley running between the two barbed-wire fences, ready to help us through should we get stuck. He had, however, made such a good job of it that he rarely had to intervene… . I was almost through the second fence when a guard, who had come down from yet another mirador* [watchtower] *appeared in the alley.*
>
> *'"Carry on," said Trotobas quietly, "I'll take care of him." His rifle slung over his shoulder, the guard came to within twenty feet of Trotobas, who was getting ready to spring at him.*
>
> *'"Is it the English?" he asked in a loud whisper.*
>
> *'"Yes," answered Trotobas.*
>
> *'"I thought so. Well, don't make so much noise," he said, turning around and walking away.'*

Under cover of almost total darkness the men ran across the adjoining field in twos and threes towards a small shaded light on a van, where Rigoulet was waiting. Michael was the last to leave, having hammered the stakes back into the ground, retrieved the carpet and re-attached the wires. By the time the alarm was raised Rigoulet had taken them to a large disused farm near Bergerac, 35km from Mauzac, where they were safely ensconced in the hayloft, and where materials for making up the papers for their new identities had been stashed some time earlier. [4]

In their wake a massive but unproductive search and enquiry took place back at the camp. The Vichy police arrived in great numbers and within hours all road traffic within 100 miles was being checked, and crossroads, bridges, railway lines and stations were watched and guarded. Gaby was arrested but released, as at the time of the escape she was, by careful pre-arrangement, on her way back from Vichy, where she had contacted numerous important government officials to ask them to help her husband, their old colleague who was languishing in a prison camp. Fleuret, the only man in the camp to sleep peacefully through the night, was interrogated and roughed up a little, but his story was accepted at face value, no harm befalling him or his family.

Although the farm was isolated, the men slept during daylight and only went out for a little exercise at night. Michael, typically, prowled the area around the barn and familiarized landmarks in case they were discovered and forced to leave in a hurry; a precaution that turned out to be unnecessary as arrangements for the next stage of the escape moved smoothly into gear. They stayed there for several days while Gerson arranged their documents, Hall and Thérèse Mitrani acted as couriers to bring their cards, passes and photographs.

Langelaan described one final act of Michael's which sums up his 'derring-do' approach:

> *'We had just climbed back into our loft, one morning, when a gendarme strolled into the yard below us. "Hey! Where are you? Come out!" he shouted. "I know you're there. The woman in red* [cover name for Mitrani] *told me I would find you here!"*
>
> *"'You should have said that sooner," said Trotobas, jumping lightly down to the ground, still holding the copper wire with which he was preparing to lasso and strangle the gendarme, little dreaming that he was a member of the local resistance and had come to bring us our new identity cards.'*

When all their papers were in order they left the farm in ones and twos en route for Lyon. They met up at a hotel in Oullins, before being spread around various families, where Gerson visited them to prepare for the next stage of the journey. Michael was not alone in feeling more and more uneasy, as Hayes was to comment on his return to England:

> *'My impression on arrival in Lyon was of a complete lack of security. A large number of the group had assembled there and were in constant touch with each other, using the same meeting places. Too many of the surrounding populous seemed to be aware of their presence and in some cases their identities! To my mind this was almost a repeat of the situation that prevailed at Châteauroux. There was a seemingly unjustifiable sense of safety indeed reliance on the goodwill of the Vichy authorities.'*

Nevertheless, they survived, and the next phase began.

It might be supposed that SOE was completely in the dark, and that its men would simply turn up in Spain unannounced and unexpected. This was far from the case as before, during and after its implementation, the escape was the subject of a whole series of signals, telegrams and diplomatic notes between Lyon, Barcelona, Madrid, Gibraltar, Berne and London, many details of which have been preserved in the SOE War Diary. They shed interesting light on just how much London knew about the project, on the relationships between SOE, the Foreign Office and the Diplomatic Service, and on the sheer profligacy of valuable and dangerous airtime taken up by communications that had no direct impact on the war effort. The texts also reveal just how much confusion was caused by the need to preserve the agents' identities through the allocation of alternative code names – transmissions referred sometimes to real names, sometimes to the field names given to them before their missions, sometimes to the false identities provided in the escape documents – and the extent to which the men had been sent in unprepared. [5]

On 19 July Gerson had sent a message saying the men were out, but the names were so mutilated by transmission, reception and encoding that only six were recognizable; Gerson added that there were two men whose identity he did not know. Two days later F Section alerted its man in Gibraltar that eleven of its men were out, and gave their correct names. Congratulations were sent to Gerson, and on 30 July London instructed him that the Mauzac men should go direct to the consul at Barcelona and say that they belonged to the 'Clan Cameron', a code which would identify the men as members of SOE and not regular service people using the escape lines.

On 5 August Gerson advised that all of the 'Clan Cameron' party had been safely transferred to Lyon. The agents had been organized in two groups for the departure to Spain and the first group, consisting of Bégué, Jumeau, Le Harivel, Hayes and Roche, would be leaving Lyon the following week. They duly set off on 8 August for the Spanish frontier. Four days later the British Embassy in Madrid cabled that Gerson had said a group of about twelve agents was now on its way to Spain, and asked the Foreign Office to confirm this and to say who they were. Were they the same as the party mentioned in London's telegram of 25 March? London answered that they were but it was understood the men would be arriving at intervals in small groups. The second group, comprising Michael, Liewer, Langelaan, Lyon, Bouguennec and Sevilla, was due to leave on 14 August, but the departure was delayed while the organizers waited for a telegram confirming the safe arrival of the first party. It never came.

On 21 August Madrid cabled that six men claiming to be of 'Clan Cameron' were in prison at Girona, giving a list of names. London confirmed that all of these men were 'Camerons'. The following day the consul general in Barcelona forwarded to the Foreign Office a copy of a telegram he had sent to Madrid, saying that six men had been arrested on a train near Girona about 14 August and were now imprisoned there, having been interviewed by the local consular representative. They had given their names and asked that their fate and present whereabouts should be communicated to a member of the consul's staff, giving his full name and title. The consul promptly protested about this 'amateurish indiscretion', warning that the whole future of the consulate's work in facilitating the return to England of soldiers and airmen was now in jeopardy. He demanded that the next party should be told to prepare a more convincing cover story than the tenuous 'Clan Cameron' tale, adding that the individuals had clearly not been 'properly briefed by their responsible superior authorities before they left London'. On August 29 Madrid reported that all six had been sent to prison camp in Miranda de Ebro.

The previous morning Michael and his party had decided to wait no longer and agreed to move out. Although there is no report from him about the journey, those of Liewer, Langelaan and Lyon who accompanied him provide sufficient information to enable the main points to be established. The group first went to the station, from where they had been instructed to follow Mitrani as far as Narbonne. There they were to contact a man in the station restaurant and follow him, while Mitrani and Gerson returned to Lyon. All went according to plan, and from Narbonne their contact led them to Perpignan, where they took a taxi to the rendezvous with their Spanish guide. There should have been a second guide, but having waited some time, they decided to set off without him.

After a long, tiring journey of one whole day and two nights, during which they wandered around in the clouds for some time with no sense of direction, they eventually reached the other side of the mountains and Spanish territory, where they had to leave Langelaan behind, suffering from exhaustion. His companions had helped him through the mountains, but once he was safely down he told them to go on without him, and promptly lay down and fell asleep. The remainder of the party walked on slowly and painfully, feet bruised and blistered from the poor footwear they had been given for the journey. When they reached the outskirts of Figueras, the guide suggested they sell some of their belongings as they had no money and were without food. They gave their watches to sell, and he disappeared, never to be seen again. After waiting the whole of 30 August for his return, they continued on their own, weak from lack of food.

Skirting Figueras, they set off along the 30km of railway line towards Girona, leaving the track around midnight to avoid possible brushes with sentries and cutting across grassland into an orchard full of fruit trees and

Muscat grapes. Greedily they ate their fill and rested for the remainder of the night and most of the following day, during which Michael and Bouguennec were laid low with severe stomach cramps and intestinal pains that made walking impossible. After a brief discussion they agreed that the other three should go on without them.

On 2 September Madrid cabled that two of the second party had arrived at Barcelona the previous day, three more were expected shortly, and one had been lost during the journey. Michael duly arrived that afternoon and presented himself with the 'Cameron' password at the British Consulate. There he was reunited with Lyon and Liewer, who had arrived a week previously, and with Bouguennec, who had reported in the previous day. Sevilla turned up shortly afterwards and the five swapped stories. Michael learned that the first party had apparently been denounced by their fellow travellers on the express train between Figueras and Girona, arrested, and taken to a detention camp at Miranda del Ebro. Langelaan was now the only member of Michael's party still missing, and on 4 September Madrid informed London that he had been caught and was on his way to Miranda. For the five currently in Barcelona, Madrid planned to send a party of three to Lisbon in the consulate car, and the other two to Gibraltar by smuggling boat. He asked the relative importance of the men, and London answered that the order of importance was, significantly, 'Trotobas, Bouguennec, Lyon, Liewer and Sevilla'.

On 10 September the embassy in Lisbon cabled that a party of three men was expected on the following day at a safe house in the city. They were Michael, Liewer and Bouguennec, all members of 'Clan Cameron'. As Lisbon knew nothing about these men, London was to telegraph to say whether they should be sent by air 'in the usual way for agents' or whether they could be reported to the Portuguese authorities as 'volunteers'. London replied immediately that they should be sent by air if possible.

That evening Michael and his two companions left Barcelona. After their protracted, arduous and problem-filled journey from France into Spain, the next part of their journey was made in considerable comfort and style. They were driven in a diplomatic car to Madrid and taken the following day to Lisbon, where they were arrested and placed in a comfortable cell 'for their own safety', while enquiries were made. On 15 September Lisbon reported that the three men were temporarily in prison but would be released very shortly. The following day London learnt that the men were leaving that night: places had been reserved for them in the names of 'Morgan', 'Trotobas' and 'Walther' on one of the Sunderland flying boats that worked a regular but hazardous shuttle to and from England's west country. They arrived in London early in the morning of 17 September, where Michael took his leave of the companions with whom he had been through so much. All of the other escapees returned to London safely by the end of the year, but Michael never saw any of them again. Many of them would return to France and distinguish themselves.

As a postscript to the Mauzac saga, it is worth noting that the Foreign Office had forwarded copies of all their telegrams to SOE with added comments, asking that the briefing of SOE personnel be looked into, so as to make sure that, in the case of arrest, they told the best possible story. Lieutenant Colonel Sporborg, deputy to SOE Director Gubbins, eventually replied, admitting that the six men had been guilty of 'appalling indiscretion' but pointing out that they had been among the first sent to France, that they had not been given adequate instruction in the case of arrest, and that they had to be briefed on this point by WT through an agent who must have given them additional ill-advised information. He had been notified of the 'catastrophic result' and everything possible had been done to ensure that such indiscretions did not occur again. Sporborg added that SOE had excellent relations with the consul, and was working with him to perfect better arrangements in Barcelona, so that SOE people could be dealt with quite separately and not risk the possibility of interference with escaping prisoners-of-war or compromising the Consulate.

In spite of this, and the difficulties encountered during the operation, F Section could feel with some justification that it had achieved its aims, in as much as the reconnaissance in force had taught it a great deal about the situation in the unoccupied zone. Mistakes had been made, but lessons had been learnt. Their judgement as to the likelihood of agents being treated with leniency had been vindicated. They had got nearly all of their men back, and their reports would provide invaluable information for future training and planning.

Chapter notes

1   I contacted Le Harivel in September 2000 via the Special Forces Club, and received a handsome reply from him at his home in Vallauris, dated Christmas Day. I wrote again in April 2001, and he replied at the end of July.

2   For details of camp life and the escape I have again referred to the reports mentioned in the previous chapter. None of these, however, is comprehensive, but Langelaan, in *Knights of the Floating Silk*, tells the whole story of the break-out in a compelling narrative. The occasional references in the agents' reports corroborate his story.

3   In his letter of 25 December 2000 Le Harivel confirmed my identification of the members of this group, adding that Langelaan and Bouguennec were missing. Two unidentified men he believed to be members of a separate French group.

4   Unknown in Britain, this dramatic and successful escape was dramatized in 1970 in the French TV production *Adieu Mauzac*. It was shown again in July 2010, when my mother watched it. The part of Michael Trotobas was played by Jacques Harden.

5   The history and record of communications that follows is taken from the voluminous 'Clan Cameron' papers *(HS7/244)*, which provide extensive detail on the progress of the escape.

Chapter 7

Farmer

'I am about to take my last voyage, a great leap in the dark.'
Thomas Hobbes

As a putative training ground for organizers, the operation in the south was a failure, since few of the agents were at liberty long enough to learn anything at all about recruiting and setting up a circuit. But the Trotobas that came back from Spain would have been a different person from the young officer who had set off for France almost exactly a year earlier, having matured as a man, learned the value of teamwork and the vital importance of being able to trust and rely on his companions. The courage, determination and resourcefulness of the numerous civilians who had been swept up with the SOE men must have changed his view of the part they had to play in the fight to free their country. This new-found respect and open-mindedness towards the ordinary French people would prove to be of vital importance in the months ahead. As would his appreciation of the coolness and efficiency of the women who had done so much to help with the escape, and of the organization that had brought him from the wires of Mauzac to the pavements of London in the space of just twelve weeks. Awareness of the absolute necessity for efficient and secure escape lines, to enable rapid retreat and repatriation when things went wrong, became an important part of his future thinking. At the same time, no doubt, he was extremely frustrated at having spent the best part of a year in France without firing a shot and without even seeing a German soldier.[1]

Two months were to elapse between his returning from Spain and setting off on his next mission, but there is no information available about how he spent this time. Michael kept no diary, wrote no letters, and there are no reports on file relating to his first mission or his preparation for the next. Based on other histories and accounts of agents returning from the field, it is reasonable to speculate that he would have reported verbally to Buckmaster, undergone a formal debriefing interrogation, taken some leave, returned to one of the training schools for a 'refresher' and an update on conditions in northern France, before being briefed and prepared for his next mission.

No doubt Buckmaster would have congratulated him on his safe return, and listened with great interest to a detailed account of his arrest, imprisonment and escape, while an orderly took notes. It can be assumed that Michael would have emulated other members of the party in expressing concern about the lack of proper preparation, the woefully inadequate identity papers and the poor planning that had sent the men straight into the arms of the police. He would have made these points forcefully and not minced his words. When the question of another mission was raised, he would probably have told Buckmaster that he wanted to go back immediately, this time into the occupied zone, where he could do some real work and frustrate the Germans. Buckmaster never demanded or ordered that an agent should return, so whether Michael volunteered of his own free will or responded to a request is academic, for a second mission there would be.

The only interrogation report on file is that of his interview on 9 October with an unknown officer, as part of the TUNMER/CHRISTOPHE investigation and the sequence of events leading up to Michael's arrest and imprisonment, with particular emphasis on the Villa des Bois and its inhabitants. It is clear from the report [see previous chapter] that he felt embarrassed at the ease with which he and the others had been seized. When pressed for his views about *Christophe*, he felt obliged to say that he had not shared the strong opinions – expressed by many of the others, and debated at great length during their confinement – that Turck had been turned and was working for the French security forces. The police had told him during his interrogation that the Villa des Bois was a trap, into which he would have fallen eventually, and he felt that the arrests were more likely to be the results of effective surveillance rather than betrayal.

As regards to what he might have done on leave, two facts have emerged. First that he went to see his father, a visit that was not a success, as Yvonne Pachy recalled from her conversations with Michael:

'His stepmother was openly hostile to Michael, and she made it clear that she resented his presence as a reminder of her husband's previous marriage. Michael in his turn found little in her to admire or appreciate, but for his father's sake he made every effort to be polite and sociable, only to be rebuffed at every approach. In the small terraced house with just a kitchen and parlour it was impossible to avoid each other, and he could only talk to his father when she went to the shops'.[2]

The second fact is that during this time he reviewed his will, which he had drawn up on 6 August 1941, a month before leaving for Marseilles.

This would not have taken him long, since nothing had happened in the year to cause him to change anything. His residual estate after expenses and disbursements was estimated to be £616 – a substantial amount at that time – and the principal beneficiary was his father, who was to receive four tenths, with the remainder divided between a number of women, one of whom was Marie-Jeanne Bouchez, his old flame from his time in Gondecourt. [3]

Going back to training school would have been an essential part of the preparation for his next mission. Information from returning agents and refugee Frenchmen had by now made it possible to build up a picture of life in the occupied zone and of the many pitfalls to be avoided. The course would have covered the 'dos and don'ts' for an agent there, as well as more thorough contingency planning for capture, interrogation and escape.

An agent needed to be well-briefed or have detailed personal knowledge of his area. An obvious lack of awareness of surroundings could result in his being identified as a suspicious person in one of the many impromptu round-ups that took place almost daily, when a whole street, perhaps containing bars, a cinema or a hotel, would be cordoned off and everyone's papers thoroughly scrutinized. Knowledge and possession of the correct compulsory documents was vital. Valid identity card, ration card, a certificate of lodging signed by the concierge if living in an apartment and, if travelling, a certificate of travel were general basic requirements, but these could be supplemented by other local papers such as those applicable to a particular area of the city, vouchers provided by employers and passes issued by the police.

Similar problems arose when it came to clothing. Agents had to blend in with the locals, and, when kitting out an agent, the experts in England had to be aware of what was customary – and indeed available – in the target zones. For example, good shoes with crepe or rubber soles had not been seen in France since 1940 and would instantly raise suspicion in a watchful eye, as would town suits worn in the country, and navy blue suits were hardly to be seen at all. The only safe wardrobe was one made in France. The faint shadow of labels removed from garments made in England, as well as scratches in shoes made when removing size and other markings, were telltale giveaways, as were traces of English tobacco or jewellery and personal objects not obviously of French origin.

Rail travel, which along with the bicycle was the only viable form of transport, given the shortages and petrol rationing, was fraught with risk, for frequent ticket checks were made throughout the journey. However, unless a special alert was in progress, these tended to be cursory, and the chief hurdle was the barrier at each station, where stricter controls were in place. This was particularly so in large cities and industrialized areas. In the cities, other hazards faced the unwary agent. Many buildings requisitioned by the Germans were surrounded by white lines, which it was forbidden to cross. Anyone infringing the regulation would be stopped and interrogated. Ordering an unfamiliar drink in a bar, or unavailable food in a café, would immediately result in questions being asked, and carrying anything that was not obviously of local origin would arouse suspicion, including everyday items such as briefcases, books, cigarettes and matches. Awareness of regulations concerning the use of bicycles, where and when local curfews were in force, even the accepted manner of addressing policemen and members of the security forces, had to be learned and retained. At least one agent was captured because he and his companion were seen standing on an otherwise deserted station platform waiting for trains that did not run on a Sunday.

Last, but by no means least, was the presence of the security forces, of which the most prevalent were the regular German troops, to be seen at nearly every street corner, railway, bus and Metro station. By the end of 1942 more and more regulars were being transferred to the frontlines and support had to be drafted in from local paramilitary organizations and the civilian police, many of whom were not strongly pro-German and in some cases actively supported the resistance and could be relied upon to turn a blind eye to minor misdemeanours. But it was not the common German soldier or French uniformed policeman that presented the greatest threat. Operating in France were two distinct but overlapping German counter-espionage organizations, one political, the other military. The *SS Sicherheitsdienst* (SD) was a Nazi Party organization, controlled from the *Reichssicherheitshauptamt* (RSHA) in Berlin, with its principal operational branch in all occupied areas being the *Sicherheitspolizei* (SiPo), which was itself divided into the *Kriminalpolizei* (Kripo) and the greatly-feared *Geheime Staatspolizei* (Gestapo), whose Section (Amt) IV was responsible for arrest and detention of enemy agents and saboteurs. The *Abwehr* was the intelligence arm of the German *Wehrmacht*, and in France it had two main branches, both independent of the uniformed *Feldgendarmerie* (Military Police). Its counter-espionage branch was the *Geheime Feldpolizei* (GFP – Secret Field Police), whose principal role was the arrest of security suspects, usually in surprise raids carried out in the dead of night or early hours of the morning. Little was known in England about their techniques and methods of interrogation since no agent captured by them had yet escaped, but their treatment of prisoners was expected to be harsh.

Although no records exist, it is clear from subsequent events that, once Michael had declared himself ready and willing to return to France, Buckmaster told him that his mission would be to establish and run a new circuit in Lille, a great industrial city with a tradition of militant trade unionism and strong communist elements. Professor Foot summed up the mission as:

> '*To set up* FARMER, *a sabotage circuit based in Lille*...[a] *promising area, where most grown men and women remembered how disagreeable German occupation had been twenty-five years before. Thousands of evaders and early escapers from Dunkirk had passed through* FARMER's *neighbourhood; there were plenty of people there with clandestine experience, and plenty more with strong pro-British and anti-German feelings. What had kept SOE from earlier attempts to work up the area was the difficulty of getting close to it by low flying aircraft. There was a big German bomber base at Merville airfield west of Lille, and the concentration of fighter and AA defences was severe. Still, the importance of the district outweighed the awkwardness of the approach; Trotobas was sent to find out how much he could do. We shall shortly see him doing rather a lot.*'[4]

Before the First World War northern France had been one of the most flourishing and productive areas of the country, its metallurgical firms generating more than a million tonnes of steel every year – a quarter of France's total output. Local industries transformed the steel into industrial and consumer goods; prosperous textile, flax and cotton concerns flourished in Lille and the surrounding towns, and a massive rail network grew up to service them. With the whole region generating one sixth of the country's total taxes, occupation of the area and seizure of its mills, factories and communications made it of high strategic importance for the occupying Germans then as now, and they went about its annexure with ruthlessness and brutality. Hardly a family had been left untouched by the cold-blooded imposition of draconian levies and fines, curfews, deportations and executions. These atrocities, coupled with the pillaging and destruction of Lille and its environs, had left a legacy of strong anti-German resentment in the youngsters of the time, who had carried it into their adulthood. The city was a natural and fertile breeding ground for dissent.

In the light of this, and given Buckmaster's awareness of Michael's knowledge of the area and potential contacts, it is possible that he had prioritized his return from Spain for this very reason.

Allocation of the code name FARMER to the circuit followed SOE's normal practice at the time of designating most circuits [*réseaux*] with the names of occupations or professions, and to link this with the designated field name of its leader – in Michael's case *Sylvestre*. The field name would always be used, and the true identity of each agent would be known only to

London. The typical SOE circuit in France came to feature a backbone structure of three people. The first of these was the leader or organizer. The second was the radio operator, who needed to know and understand the functioning of his transmitter/receiver, as well as being fluent in Morse code and able to encode and decode messages. The radio was the organizer's most vital piece of equipment and important asset: without it he would be unable to make direct contact with London. The third key element was the courier, whose job it was to move between individual groups of the circuit and between adjoining circuits, carrying orders from and gathering information to be passed back to the leader.

Buckmaster would have told Michael that his radio operator and his equipment would be inserted with him, but he would need to recruit his own courier or couriers when he arrived in Lille. He would receive a formal briefing that would include a list of priority targets and objectives for eventual destruction. SOE policy at the time was to brief agents that their principal task was not to gain intelligence but to prepare the way for an insurrection of armed and trained saboteurs, who would be able to swing into action at a given signal shortly before the invasion, whenever that came. Arms and other essential materiel would be provided by air, but it would take time to build up, equip and train an organization. Although they were expected to press on with recruitment urgently and immediately, they had to remain patient at all costs and keep in mind the ultimate objective. Michael was therefore to refrain from impulsive or premature activities that might put the organization at risk and prejudice final success. Although targets of opportunity might present themselves, they were not to be attacked without prior clearance from London, and under no circumstances was Michael himself to take part in local actions.

No doubt he confirmed his – possibly reluctant – understanding and Buckmaster wished him luck, before sending him away to attend to the various formalities and logistical tasks that had to be completed, including the issue of false papers in the name of Michael Joseph Rampal. Concerned that photographs and details of all the Mauzac escapers might have been circulated in France, Michael dyed his hair and moustache blond for the photograph to go on his documents. That he was delighted with his assignment was something he made clear to his radio operator when they met a few days later.

Lieutenant Arthur Albert Staggs had a similar background to Michael, each having had a Catholic education and been brought up by fathers who had remarried. Staggs' mother died in 1914, when he was two. Born in France, he spent his childhood at school in England, before, in December 1925, when he was thirteen, his father took him and his new wife back to France, where he worked as an engineer in Roubaix. They stayed there together until war broke out in 1939. His father wanted him to remain in Roubaix and work in the factory, where he would be in a reserved occupation and thus avoid military conscription, but Staggs had other ideas and returned to England. After fourteen years of living and working in France he spoke fluent French, and his attention was caught by a government notice in a Sunday newspaper asking for linguists to come forward. He applied, was interviewed and accepted. He underwent medical and army training at Aldershot and was then posted to the Corps of Military Police (part of the Intelligence Corps) as a field security officer. He had two jobs: reading and advising on detailed maps of the north of France, and interviewing French troops who had escaped at Dunkirk to weed out German infiltrators, of which some half a dozen were exposed. He was then moved to the Intelligence Corps at Winchester, where he was put in charge of stores and supplies. Through the military grapevine he came to the notice of both MI5 and MI6, was interviewed by both, and moved to Oxford, where he was used for verification concerning French roads and towns in the Nord. In due course his name came to the attention of SOE. He was interviewed again, told of the dangers, and eventually recruited as a trainee wireless operator. His training lasted around six months, concluding with thirteen weeks' instruction at Thame Park in radio operation and procedures.

Also being inserted with them was a Canadian officer, Major Gustave *'Guy'* Biéler, whose mission was to place himself at the disposal of CARTE, a French organization based in the south with contacts in the occupied zone, making use of Staggs for his communications when necessary. Born in Beurlay in France, Biéler had emigrated at the age of 20 to Canada, where he settled in Montreal, working first as a school teacher then as an official translator for an insurance company, adopting Canadian citizenship. When war broke out in Europe, Biéler, then 38, was married with two children, but he immediately joined the Canadian Army, where he was commissioned into the *Régiment de Maisonneuve*, part of the Canadian 2nd Division and the first to be pronounced 'war ready' and sent to England, where it formed alliance with the Shropshire Light Infantry. He was given an accelerated promotion to captain, and his familiarity with France and his fluency in French soon brought him to the attention of the SOE, after which he went down the same path that Michael had followed, similarly stepped up in rank on his assignment to F Section.

Staggs recounted how he met the other two for the first time just two days before their departure, at a flat in Orchard Court, where they were given a final briefing by Buckmaster's assistant, Vera Atkins, who instructed them not to move from the building. As she herself was leaving, Atkins wished Staggs a happy birthday – an innocuous and well-intended aside that was to have unfortunate consequences. After establishing that it was in fact Staggs' thirtieth birthday, Michael made a remark to the effect that he would 'carry the old man's baggage into France, if he found it too much for him'. This was coldly received by Staggs, who took exception to what he perceived to be rudeness and arrogance on Michael's part. It set the seeds for an uncomfortable future relationship. [5]

Late in the afternoon of 18 November the party was taken by car to RAF Tempsford in Bedfordshire, home to Special Duties squadrons nos. 138 and 161, which were tasked with inserting SOE agents and supplies into occupied Europe. There Atkins completed the final formalities, making them turn out their pockets, removing all potentially incriminating items, and meticulously scrutinising and inspecting their clothes and suitcases. Finally she checked their identity cards and travel documents – Biéler was 'Maurice Alfred Léger' and Staggs 'Albert Foulon' – after which they were taken to an old farmhouse on the edge of the airfield and told that they would be collected twenty minutes before departure.

The night was dark and damp, and a cold wind found its way through the gaps in the wooden walls, forcing the men to huddle together, smoking, comparing notes and discussing their experiences. Staggs was gratified to hear Michael and Biéler welcoming the fact that they had been allocated a fully-trained radio operator: a professional soldier from the Intelligence Corps who had lived in France, spoke good French and knew the Lille area well. Both men knew that SOE was desperately short of radio operators, and would remain so throughout the war, as Michael would learn to his cost. All the experienced men had long since been sent into Europe, and contact had been lost with many of them already. The German counter-intelligence agencies had stepped up their surveillance, and with each arrest gained more and more experience and knowledge of the procedures the radio men had to follow, and the type of locations they needed for best reception. Consequently, the radio operator was often the first of a cell to be discovered.

They were all relieved when at 1815 hrs they were instructed to board an unmarked, twin-engine Whitley V bomber, BD276 T. At 1830 hrs the pilot, Flight Lieutenant Prior, taxied past the barn and turned on to the end of the main 1,600-yard runway, where he made final adjustments to the engines while waiting for the shaded green light from the control tower away to the left. When it came, Prior rolled down the runway for take-off into the gentle ten-knot south-westerly breeze. The 161 Squadron operations record book shows that he took off at 1840 hrs, with six crew on board plus the three agents with their supplies, as well as two packs of leaflets and ten pigeons for release on the homeward journey. The near-full moon was completely hidden behind a complete overcast, and the weather forecast was for low cloud ahead with visibility of less than two miles. Their destination was a small field sixty-five miles south of Paris, close to the town of Montargis. [6]

They crossed the English coast near Tangmere at 1936 hrs, flying at 2,000 feet towards Cabourg, but strong winds pushed the Whitley eastwards to a landfall over Le Havre. Conscious of a slight loss of power in the starboard engine, Prior turned the aircraft seawards, out of range of the heavy port defences, before crossing the French coast west of Cabourg shortly after 2000 hrs and setting a new course for easily identifiable islands west of Blois, thence to Loire near Mer, before following the railway line to the drop point. There an island and a prominent bend in the river provided a clearly visible navigational reference point. During the flight the three agents kept themselves warm with flasks of coffee and rum and, with conversation impossible over the noise of the engines, they sat in strained silence, each with his own thoughts, which Michael pushed to the back of his mind when Flight Sergeant Ritchie, the dispatcher, signalled that they would be at the drop zone in fifteen minutes. The agents had drawn straws, with the result that Michael jumped through the hatch first, followed by Staggs and then Biéler. The logbook does not record the time of the drop, but Staggs thought it was around 2300 hrs when they landed. Ritchie kicked out two packages for the agents, unaware that there should have been a third, and reported that he had seen all five chutes open safely, whereupon Prior turned the aircraft northwards to return via the same route. [7]

For security reasons, the adopted practice was to start a journey in a remote rural area where checks were likely to be more perfunctory, especially late at night or in the early hours of the morning. There agents could blend into the mass of ordinary people who were constantly on the move visiting relatives or looking for black-market produce in the countryside, to which local police were likely to turn a blind eye, recognizing as they did its absolute necessity for survival. To carry his or her goods almost everyone travelled with a large suitcase, bag or carefully wrapped package, which worked in the agents' favour. Although being stopped for items to be checked could lead to closer inspection of paperwork and belongings, the usual penalty was confiscation of any offending material and a warning. Of course, anyone found to be carrying a radio transmitter or firearms would be arrested on the spot.

Once on the ground the agents faced the prospect of a long trek to catch their train, and immediately found themselves with a problem. Michael and Staggs had come down safely in a freshly ploughed field – the latter expressing relief at having landed on his feet, something he had failed to achieve during his training at Ringway. On landing they had narrowly missed a heavy piece of farm machinery, but Biéler had been less fortunate, first colliding with a tree then falling on stony ground at the edge of a wood, injuring his back badly in the process. After checking to see that he was in no immediate danger, although he was evidently in pain, the other two gathered up their parachutes and equipment, only to find that one suitcase was missing. They scoured the woods for some time without success and discussed the situation. Michael held the opinion that they should continue searching until the suitcase and its parachute were recovered, but his companions were emphatic that this was contrary to everything they had been taught, and that it would be foolish to remain in the locality in case their aircraft or parachutes had been observed and reported to the Germans. [8]

They buried their chutes and jumpsuits along with their knives, revolvers and torches, items that could not be easily explained if they were stopped and searched, and after another brief argument Michael agreed reluctantly that they should move on, However he did insist that they rest for a while: they had a fair distance to cover on foot over muddy fields and in the dark in order to catch an early morning train to Paris. Staggs disagreed, but Biéler sided with Michael, to Staggs' annoyance, and his attitude was so strong that when he was interrogated in 1944 the interviewing officer noted:

> *'From source's* [Staggs] *account of this incident, and many subsequent references throughout the course of his interrogation, it is clear that he adopted a somewhat truculent and possibly unreasoning attitude during the discussion mentioned above, which was held at a time when undoubtedly any agent's nerves are apt to be on edge. This created a very bad impression with* SYLVESTRE, *and it appears that this impression was never overcome, but rather increased during their subsequent association, causing friction and mistrust on both sides.'* [9]

The absence of the third suitcase proved to be a blessing, because Biéler, hobbling on a makeshift crutch, could not have carried it. Michael had the case with his and Staggs' belongings, and Staggs himself had the radio transceiver in his case. At around midnight they set off across country for the small station at Auxy-Juranville. Pulling on old, thick socks over their shoes and trouser bottoms to keep them free of mud – an instant giveaway to an observant policeman – they made their way slowly across ploughed fields and grassy meadows, initially for seven or eight miles in the wrong direction, due no doubt to the fact that, as the interrogation report records, the aircraft had missed the landing ground and was further on than intended. Staggs thought they were a mile or so short, but according to Professor Foot they had been dropped ten miles wide. Realising their mistake, they reversed direction and made steady progress, until at around 0600 hrs they noticed the loom of bright lights ahead. With a gesture to his companions to stay where they were, Michael disappeared into a copse to reconnoitre, leaving Staggs, who thought it unwise to split up, to wait in state of nervous anxiety with Biéler. When he returned after quarter of an hour he reported that the lights were arc lamps from some kind of prison camp, and that he had withdrawn quickly when he heard the sound of dogs barking. He then led them in a wide sweep to avoid the location, during which Biéler indicated that it was almost certainly the internment camp at Beaune-le-Rolande, on which he had been briefed. Originally constructed by the French in 1939 to house future German prisoners of war, it was now being used by the Germans as an internment and transit camp for French deportees.

The presence of the camp was a strong indication that they were nearing their destination, and they soon came upon a signpost that told them they were only three or four miles from their target, where the railway line turned north. Guided by the sound of a whistle from an early train, they sighted the station shortly before 0800 hrs, discarded their oversocks and generally tidied up their appearance. Michael went ahead on his own, in spite of Staggs' protests, and returned with tickets for the 8.37 am train to Paris, after which the three of them made their separate ways at five-minute intervals to the small rural halt, where a solitary gendarme stood at the barrier and made no move to prevent their passage. At the far end of the single platform four German soldiers in field grey were sitting on their bags, playing cards and passing round a metal flask, paying no attention to three more workmen shuffling into the waiting clusters of a score or so of civilians hunched into their coats, their weary, bleary-eyed faces staring vacantly into the distance in the manner of early-morning commuters the world over. Once on the train they made sure to keep plenty of distance between themselves, a common-sense precaution which nevertheless annoyed Staggs, left alone as he was with the incriminating radio set and clearly at the greatest risk. He recalled feeling even more angry with Michael who, in spite of his offer to 'carry the old man's suitcase', had made no move to do so, and had not even taken up a position in the train from which he could see Staggs.

Any concerns they might have had about the integrity of their documents being questioned turned out to be unnecessary. There were no security checks on the train, and it proved to be an uneventful journey into the capital, where they were to meet up with the leader of the PROSPER group, Francis Suttill. Born near Lille in 1910 to a British father and French mother, Suttill had been taken to England for education at Stonyhurst College in Lancashire, after which he returned to Lille to study law at the university. He settled in London, where he was called to the Bar, and in 1935 he married and had two sons. Following the outbreak of war he was commissioned into the East Surrey Regiment, where he was spotted and recruited by SOE in early 1942. Like Michael, he trained for the role of organizer, and had been dropped into France six weeks earlier, with the fieldname *Prosper,* to set up PHYSICIAN, a new Paris-based circuit to take over from the AUTOGIRO circuit, which had been penetrated earlier that year. Assisted by wireless operator Gilbert Norman *(Archambaud)* and courier Andrée Borrel *(Denise)*, he had made rapid progress, taking over the surviving AUTOGIRO contacts and forming new sub-circuits across much of northern France, all of which came loosely under the PROSPER banner.

By ten in the morning the commuter rush had cleared the main concourse at the Gare de Lyon, but it was still sufficiently crowded with soldiers and civilians bustling in all directions for Michael and his party to merge into its anonymity, Biéler's condition passing unnoticed amongst the many wounded and disabled men hobbling along or being supported by relatives.

As emerged during the course of Staggs' second interrogation, he and Michael had been given instructions to proceed to a safe house, where they were to stay for a month before undertaking any further activity. Staggs waited in a café while Michael went to the house and gave the agreed password, and they found themselves in a small flat already occupied by two other people, which made conditions awkward but not downright uncomfortable. Neither Staggs nor Michael could remember when they had last eaten and they wolfed down gratefully the hot soup, bread and wine set out for them by their hosts. Incredible as it seemed, a mere twenty-four hours had elapsed since they boarded the aircraft at Tempsford, during which time they had been continually on the move, and they were both soon fast asleep.

The next morning they were contacted by Christiane Henri de Bizien *(Lesley)*, a volunteer ambulance driver for the French Red Cross and courier for both PROSPER and the escape line run by the *Armée de l'Air*. She informed them that Biéler had been taken to near neighbours Marie-Louise Monnet and her daughter, where a doctor would be calling to examine him, and she gave them details of more permanent accommodation that had been arranged for them. After two nights the agents moved out, Michael to the home of Madame Benech in Rue de Passy, and Staggs to a flat owned by Madame Ponceau in Boulevard Montmorency, just around the corner. De Bizien herself lived close by in Avenue du Colonel Bonnet, and while the Englishmen found her charming, efficient and helpful, they were not to know that in due course she would prepare a scathing report about their arrival and their subsequent activities.

Chapter notes

1   The reason there is so much speculation in this chapter is the absence of reports from Michael or anyone else. As we have seen, this was not the case with many of his companions on his first operation.

2   My mother told me that Michael became very emotional when talking about his father, and that he blamed his stepmother entirely for the estrangement.

3   The Executor's Statement dated 12 September 1945 lists the names, but not the addresses, of the five women. Obviously intrigued, I tried to trace them to find out more, but, with the exception of Marie-Jeanne Bouchez, I was unsuccessful.

4   For SOE background and dates in this and subsequent chapters I have referred generally to *SOE in France, Chapter VIII: Development 1942* and *Chapter IX: Middle Game 1943*.

5   I conducted many interviews and engaged in much correspondence with Arthur Staggs in the late 1990s and early 2000s, accumulating over 20 hours of tapes. These have enabled me to reconstruct personal events of the insertion flight and subsequent activities. More than fifty years later the incident of the 'happy birthday' still rankled with him. His interrogation reports provided much useful detail.

6   For information about this mission I scoured 161 Squadron's *Pilot Operation Reports*, its *Diary of Operations* and its *Operational Record Books – AIR20/8456, AIR20/8460, AIR 27/1056*.

7   While on a secret mission to land Czech agents in Czechoslovakia during Operation Iridium, a combined Czech Military/British SIS affair, Flight Lieutenant Prior, (Distinguished Flying Medal), and his crew were shot down over Munich in their Halifax bomber and killed on 14 March 1943. [See *Agents by Moonlight* by Freddie Clark (1999)].

8   As it turned out, it was a wise decision. When checking the operational records, some fifty-five years after the event, I discovered that the third package, containing medical supplies and spare clothing, had not been loaded on to the aircraft

9   Staggs was interrogated twice on his return to England: this is from the first interview, on 14 October 1944. The second was on 3 January 1945.

Chapter 8

Foundation

'The finger that turns the dial rules the air'.
Will Durant

On the Friday morning the two agents slept late, knowing that they were likely to need all their reserves of energy in the weeks that lay ahead. While there was nothing Michael could do immediately, he urged his companion to get in touch with London straight away. Staggs tried again and again without success, and suggested that the most likely reason was the impossibility of positioning the long aerial so that it was clear of interference from the neighbouring building. Michael told Staggs to strip down the set, in case there was a malfunction somewhere, which he did, and at seven in the evening he told Staggs to have another go: this met with equal lack of success. They lapsed into silence until Michael, possibly bored with inactivity and in need of excitement, suggested they went out for few drinks to celebrate their arrival. Aware that they were directly breaching the instructions given to them, they slipped quietly out of the house and spent the evening moving from bar to club, returning to their respective lodgings just before the curfew, considerably the worse for wear but delighted to find that their language fluency and awareness of French life had not been impaired by their sojourn in England.

The next day followed a similar pattern to the first. Michael clambered out of the window to take the aerial higher, but three short bursts of transmission bought no response. Staggs now suggested that the radio set might have been damaged either during the parachute drop, or during the subsequent hike across country, and should be examined by an expert.

In the afternoon de Bizien bought news of Biéler. The doctor had confirmed serious damage to the spine, and there was no question of his moving on in the foreseeable future; he would have to remain at the Monnets' until he regained his mobility, a convalescence likely to last two or three months. She also told Michael that the next day he would be collected for a meeting with Suttill and a representative from CARTE, to discuss the implications of Biéler's incapacity and agree the next steps. Michael told her of their problems with the radio and asked her to see if

Suttill could help: he was keen to confirm their safe arrival and obtain further instructions and details about possible supply drops. She promised to pass the message on. [1]

When she had left, Michael instructed Staggs to stay in his flat while he himself crossed the city to the address given to him by Pierre Séailles, his friend from Mauzac. There, after introducing himself and explaining the relationship, he learned from Séailles's father that his son was still in the camp. Over coffee the elder Séailles listened intently as Michael told of the events before, during and after his own internment in Mauzac, but seemed, understandably, to be a little suspicious and sceptical of this man who had arrived out of the blue. However, Michael mischievously told Staggs that Séailles's sister, Simone, appeared to have no such reservations. Later, Staggs recalled Michael saying she was instantly attracted to the *'handsome man with gently waved hair, bright chestnut-dark eyes and thin moustache, who showed himself to be an agreeable and sparkling conversationalist, completely fluent and at home in her language'*. Michael remembered Séailles telling him that the resistance was a family affair for the Séailles family – Pierre's brother Jean was also an active member – so Michael felt confident enough to explain his mission and was rewarded when Simone responded by immediately offering her services. He asked her a few questions before assuring her that he would send for her as soon as his organization was in place and circumstances permitted. Staggs was uncomfortable with this, feeling that he had taken an unnecessary risk. [2]

Michael and Staggs went out again that evening but Staggs was left sitting at a table on his own while Michael chatted and bought drinks for a score of young women who, Staggs saw, were unimpressed by his gambling instincts and drifted away once his cash began to dwindle. It was only when he sobered up the next morning that Michael realized just how stupid and irresponsible he had been in hazarding the funds given to him by SOE, but it was typical of his impulsive and impatient nature. Still, they appeared to have got away with it.

The following afternoon de Bizien took Michael to the PROSPER letterbox and safe house at 38, Avenue de Souffren, home of the Tambour sisters, Germaine and Madeleine, both also couriers. There she introduced him to Suttill, who welcomed him and gave him a brief rundown on the current situation with his circuit, before filling him in on CARTE. This was both the name of the organization and the code name of André Girard, an active opponent of Adolf Hitler, Marshal Philippe Pétain and the whole separatist Vichy structure. After the fall of France, he had set out to recruit a group of like-minded men to fight for its reunification. A persuasive talker and administrator, he had met with considerable success, establishing contacts all over Vichy France, and he was now looking to extend operations into the occupied territories. With an eye on the eventual invasion, and the hope that a fully trained 'Army of the Liberation' would be in place to rise up and fight as soon as the Allies landed, SOE were interested in aiding and supporting the energetic Girard as far as possible.

Suttill said he was about to meet André Heyermans, CARTE's group leader for the north of France and Belgium, and his assistant, Pierre Geelen, both currently on a mission to find drop zones and landing strips in the north, and he thought it would be useful if Michael sat in. The main object for discussion would be what to do about Biéler, whose original orders had been twofold: first, to act as SOE representative with and adviser to the CARTE organization in the Lille district and second, to provide formal liaison between CARTE and the nascent FARMER. Heyermans was aware of the first but not the second, and Suttill explained that CARTE had no need yet to know anything about Michael or his mission, so he would be presented simply as 'a colleague'. He asked him to say nothing, so, while the other three sat down over coffee to review the situation, Michael stood by the window, ignored by the visitors, who assumed he was a bodyguard. The outcome of the meeting was that the next three months would be important for CARTE's development and as *Guy* [Biéler] would be unable to provide any instruction during that time, his presence in the region was redundant. Heyermans went on to say that he understood another agent was to be sent into Lille, so there would be no point in *Guy* being there too. He suggested that, once he had recovered, a suitable area of operations for him might be the area around St Quentin, a strategically important centre for railway and canal communications to the south-east of Lille. After this, they shook hands and parted. [3]

The two British officers then discussed FARMER. Suttill confessed to having little up-to-date information about the situation in Lille and was unable to suggest any likely contacts. They agreed that Biéler's injury did not affect Michael's own mission and that he should proceed to Lille as planned, making his own arrangements with CARTE whenever they became operational in the north. PROSPER and FARMER would keep in touch via Andrée Borrel until Michael had set up his own couriers. Suttill had been told of his problems with the radio and suggested he send messages though his own WT, Gilbert Norman, while Staggs was finding his feet. He said he was expecting a second operator to arrive during December. Norman had given him the name of Julien Chapelet, a contact in St Erme who had a workshop in the basement of his home and could help Staggs dismantle and examine the set. Suttill suggested that Michael and Staggs should set off for St Erme first thing in the morning, leaving the radio behind. De Bizien, who knew Chapelet well, would telephone ahead and bring the set to them the following day, since women travelling alone with luggage were less likely to be stopped and searched. He ended by urging Michael to keep a low profile and conserve his resources (which led him to suspect that his compatriot might be aware of his evening activities, although no direct reference was made to them). The two men parted on the best of terms.

After discussing all of this Michael and Staggs agreed that Biéler's injury in no way affected their own plans, since he had been assigned a separate mission. Nevertheless they would need to stay in touch, and a courier would have to be found to act as liaison. They discussed their next tasks: Michael's to recruit volunteers for the FARMER circuit and Staggs' to set up a secure radio link with London.

Michael's plan was to get in touch with the three 'Pierres' – Bloch in l'Aisne, Séailles in Paris, and Duval in Abbeville. Staggs thought this was reasonable but he was less happy about his idea of seeking out his contacts from his BEF days, particularly when he learnt that one of them was an attractive young woman. He strongly advised against this course of action. He had seen enough of Michael's penchant for pretty faces to give him cause for concern that his organizer might embark on some indiscreet liaison that would jeopardize their mission. As usual, Michael ignored him.

In the morning, on de Bizien's instructions, they caught a train for St Erme that passed through the small town of Tergnier, where, by arrangement, Chapelet would meet them and they would change trains. The reason for this, Chapelet explained when he passed them their tickets, was that the through trains were always 'controlled' at Tergnier, whereas local trains from Tergnier to St Erme were not. De Bizien arrived the next day by the same route, dressed in her nurse's uniform, with the radio masquerading as her own equipment in an attaché case.

They stayed at St Erme for the best part of a fortnight, during which time Staggs and Chapelet made repeated unsuccessful attempts to contact London. This was in spite of stripping the set down numerous times and occasionally working through the night when it looked as if there might be a breakthrough. Staggs came to the conclusion that he must have been given the wrong codes, whereas his host was of the opinion that the wrong crystals had been fitted. Neither explanation appeared to satisfy Michael, who asked them towards the end of December exactly what they had been doing for the past ten days, causing Staggs to respond angrily. The next morning Michael took himself to Lille, telling Staggs to stay put until he sent for him.

Arriving in Lille with no immediate contacts or accommodation, his first thought was to call on his old flame from 1940, Marie-Jeanne Bouchez, whose home was in Rue des Jardins, a stone's throw from the station. Depositing his suitcase in the left luggage facility, he called her number on the telephone, hoping that she would answer, in which case they could arrange to meet up and she might be able to recommend somewhere to stay, and, possibly, even provide some useful contacts. To his dismay her father answered the telephone and, after his initial surprise at hearing in the middle of wartime Lille the voice of a man he had last seen two years earlier in the uniform of a British warrant officer, he recovered quickly, explaining that his daughter was not in, but would, he felt sure, be delighted to see him. He asked him to ring back in an hour. This he did, from a different call box, and Bouchez said he would take Marie-Jeanne to the *Au Grillon* café in Rue des Arts, which Michael knew was close to both the Bouchez home and the station. They would meet him there at half past two, and Bouchez said he felt sure Michael would understand that he wanted to be there as chaperone.

He was disappointed and at the same time wary. Given their previous relationship, he could think of no reason why Bouchez should be so obliging: he had made it perfectly clear that he did not want him anywhere near his daughter. After killing time in some local bars Michael made his way cautiously along Boulevard Carnot, which joined Rue des Arts near its junction with Rue des Jardins. He was about to turn the corner into the street at around seven o'clock when he was almost knocked over by two locals hurrying by. They gestured emphatically at him not to proceed further, indicating that they had spotted a surveillance vehicle parked in a side road at the other end of the avenue. Michael felt this was unlikely to be a coincidence, and assumed that Bouchez had informed the authorities that he had been contacted by an English soldier at large. He reversed direction and left the area, confident that the police, or whichever branch of the security forces was involved, would be unlikely to waste further time and manpower searching for him in Lille, particularly since the only description Bouchez could give was of a soldier he had last seen in 1940. [4]

His first priority was to obtain shelter. Trusting luck and his instincts, he set about the task of finding someone to confide in who would be sympathetic to his cause. This was asking and expecting much, but nevertheless, he wandered around the cafés and bars near the station, buying drinks and chatting up likely-looking customers. He knew he was taking a risk but felt he had no alternative: he could not at this stage expect people to come to him. Eventually he arrived at *Au Poker*, a gambling bar in Rue Gustave Delory, where they were advertising rooms for the night, and he decided to call it a day. He joined a number of different tables where various card games were in progress for modest stakes. He had some early success, sufficient to keep him through the evening, and ended up with a group of three men with whom he hit it off very well. After the cards were pushed away, they carried on chatting and drinking until two of them left, full of apologies and cheery handshakes. The last man leant across and said quietly that he had heard him enquiring about rooms, adding that all of the bars and clubs in the centre of town, particularly those near the station, received regular early-morning visits from the police, who not only checked the register but asked to see all the papers of every guest. Seeing Michael's reaction he stood and suggested that he come home with him for the night, waving away his polite protests and saying that his wife went to bed early, but he himself liked to stay up, and he would be glad of some company and perhaps another few hands of cards.

With such casual simplicity and almost foolhardy trust was the foundation laid for the relationship between Michael and Victor Emmanuel Lemercier, the man who was to become the first of his most energetic and loyal lieutenants. During the half hour walk through the deserted streets, Michael confided that he was a British officer looking for shelter, which produced no reaction in his companion beyond a satisfied nod of the head, as if his suspicions had been confirmed. Lemercier then told his own story.

During the 'phoney war' Lemercier had been called up and sent to the Belgium frontier, where, in May 1940, he was captured and transported to prison in Germany – a period he recalled with fierce anger and contempt for his treatment, thus echoing the stories told to Michael by his own father. Determined to get out, he told how, with the help of some willing accomplices within the hospital, he dosed himself on medicines that induced a raging fever, so severe that he feared in his few coherent moments that he had overdone it. But his plan was successful. Believing him to be seriously ill, the Germans released him and arranged for his repatriation, with the result that a year after the beginning of his captivity his wife, Eliane, who had remained in Paris, received a telegram giving news of her husband's return. After a brief recuperation they decided to go to Lille with the intention of making their way to Brussels, where they had grown up and met. However, because of their French nationality they were refused permission to cross the border, and they subsequently set up home in Lille's Rue Corneille, where Lemercier established a modest book distribution business.

He introduced Michael to his wife by saying they had been in prison together and giving him the name and title that would later reverberate around Lille: *Voici le Capitaine Michel*. Listening to Michael's genuine stories of his own imprisonment, recounted in impeccable French, Eliane – a lively, chuckling brunette with sparkling eyes, the antithesis of her tall, dark-haired, lean and slightly gaunt husband – had no reason to doubt her husband's story. After she had retired to bed, Lemercier produced a bottle of brandy and the two men sat talking well into the night about the state of France.

Chapter notes

1   Gervase Cowell kindly passed me a copy of a letter sent to him in 1989, when he was custodian of the SOE archives. It was by French researcher Jenan Denis, a former member of the French Intelligence Agency (*Service Renseignements*), *SR/AIR P3/AV*, asking for information on Christiane de Bizien. As well as providing supporting information, it enclosed a scathing report prepared by de Bizien about Michael, his arrival and subsequent activities (hereafter 'the de Bizien report').

2   The events in this chapter have again been reconstructed from conversations with Arthur Staggs, his interrogations and reference to the de Bizien report. Useful additional background was supplied by Suttill's son, Francis, and during my conversations with Séailles. Eliane Lemercier was very forthcoming about Michael's meeting with her husband and his arrival in her home.

3   In an e-mail to me in January 2012, Francis Suttill referred to 'an anonymous report (*HS 9/1430/6*) which includes an extract from my father's first (now missing) report' about this meeting.

4   Marie-Jeanne later told my mother, Yvonne Pachy, that she knew nothing about Michael's attempt to contact her.

Chapter 9

Interlude

'We are to learn about fear, not how to escape from it.'
Jiddu Krishnamurti

By the end of 1942 there was no longer 'one France', nor was there a 'typical Frenchman'. After two years of occupation the people in the north were split into various factions. There were those who welcomed the Germans as friends and saw them as bringing stability to the country, the price for which was some irritating restrictions that would disappear once the Allies made peace. This faction in turn was split into those who actively collaborated and those who simply did nothing, but carried on with life as if the war had never happened. In both of these cases there would be informers, who lost no opportunity to denounce and report anyone, even their own families and friends, who might be doing anything that could disrupt their quiet life and bring reprisals and retributions. Those who resented the German presence were further fragmented. Some exercised purely nominal and passive resistance by flouting authority or regulations without actually hazarding themselves. Others wanted to do something positive, short of actual fighting, so spent their time printing and circulating anti-Nazi propaganda. There were those who were more aggressively inclined and carried out minor acts of sabotage while a few declared open war on the Germans and took to the hills (few around industrial Lille). Some risked deportation, imprisonment and death by opening their homes as places of refuge for Allied soldiers and airmen, acting as couriers to guide them from one safe house to another and thence to Spain or the French coast. All of these latter groups were waiting for liberation in the form of an Allied invasion, which they had expected in 1942 and felt must surely come in 1943.

Lille and the Pas de Calais as a whole were now administered from Brussels, and the occupation had turned law and order upside down, placing citizen against citizen. Before the war restrictions on personal liberty were not easily enforced, as the majority of people resented them. The average Frenchman did not often break the law and in those days a man with a police record was viewed with disapproval. Now he was regarded as a patriotic Frenchman and the stigma attached to a term of imprisonment – except for venal offences such as murder and rape – had vanished. This attitude extended to black marketeers, since without the black market the French people could not live. Consequently avoidance and bypassing of food regulations were considered not only desirable but necessary from two aspects. It enabled one to survive, and, at the same time, prevented those items falling into the hands of the Germans, who were also not averse to turning a blind eye and even offering protection to obtain luxuries for themselves and their women. On the downside, many people in the countryside had earned the resentment of people in the towns because they took advantage of their position to demand exorbitant sums for their produce. Those who were in a position to procure and distribute goods that were otherwise unavailable, or in very short supply, were seen as men risking their safety to provide an essential service, and it was accepted almost without question that they should receive some benefit in the form of a small profit on the transactions. [1]

After breakfast on the morning after Michael's arrival, when Eliane had left the house, Lemercier admitted that he was active in 'buying and selling', and specialized in trading with the various German barracks in and around the city. He showed Michael – and subsequently Staggs – samples of his wares from a small stock of cans and packets of food, coffee, sugar, soap, stockings, cosmetics and even medical supplies bearing the insignia of the *Wehrmacht*. This was, he explained, merely his working stock, and he promised to take Michael to see a cousin who lived in a caravan in the Raismes forest, where the bulk of the illegal goods was stored.

In disclosing the information Lemercier had clearly taken a calculated gamble that his visitor was who he said he was, and not an undercover agent of some kind. Michael decided to reciprocate, and outlined the nature of his mission, realizing how important and useful this ex-soldier and itinerant trader might be, with his established business credentials, travel permits, access to a vehicle and petrol, and a wide range of contacts. He put this to him and suggested that he might be able to fulfil a vital role in identifying and enlisting potential members of the new resistance circuit. Lemercier there and then agreed to join Michael as his first recruit, assuring him that he knew of many local sympathizers who were desperate to hit the Germans, but lacked the leadership, organization and supplies to do anything. They shook hands, agreed that Lemercier should adopt the field name *Manu,* then went on to discuss the prospects for a successful circuit based in Lille, deciding that it was a natural recruiting ground.

When Eliane returned, Lemercier told her that he and Michael would be working together, whereupon she promptly instructed her visitor to fetch his suitcase from the station and become their lodger. Reluctant to put his hosts at unnecessary risk, he took Lemercier to one side and said that Eliane had a right to know his real purpose in Lille and should be given the chance to reconsider. Lemercier agreed, and Michael explained to Eliane that if he was betrayed or arrested and the Germans came to the house, she too would be arrested, and he felt it only fair to warn her of the dangers. Any concerns he might have had that she would ask him to leave were allayed instantly when she offered her services as his secretary, an offer he accepted. She also agreed to monitor the overseas transmissions of the BBC each evening, by means of a large radio receiver that Lemercier produced from his cellar. It was, he explained, a highly temperamental piece of equipment with a mind of its own – sometimes it worked, sometimes it did not: or, as the locals put it, *teuf ou teuf pas*. Perhaps unkindly, *Teuf-Teuf* became the name used jocularly to refer to Staggs.

In finding the Lemerciers Michael had been lucky beyond all reasonable expectation, and, on their assurance that they would be able to find accommodation for Staggs, he sent a brief note to St Erme, instructing his operator to come to Lille, and enclosing a contact address. At the same time he sent a postcard, signed *Michel*, to Chapelet, thanking him for his hospitality. [2]

Two days later Staggs arrived, but almost immediately moved out of the rooms that had been found for him, because the landlady asked constant questions and was clearly suspicious about her guest. Eliane arranged for him to stay in one of the rooms in the top floor of her home, which had been let to an amiable and unsuspecting friend, Marthe Depoortere. The following day de Bizien arrived with the transmitter. It was a visit that stayed in her memory and one she recorded with strong feelings of disapproval:

'Albert [Staggs] *is correct, serious and unsuited to his job.* Michel [Michael] *drinks. In the space of six weeks he has already squandered all the funds and in Lille has fallen in with some suspect characters, including a certain Mann* [sic] *(Lemercier, a printer) who appears to be blackmailing him.* Albert *gives him lists of the people who have sheltered and helped him. He even entrusts the keys to my apartment, which I have left with him in case something goes wrong, to this Mann who gets into my home in my absence.'*

Nothing further was heard in respect of the speculation and questions that might have been prompted by these remarks – of which the occupants of the house in Rue Corneille were presumably unaware. She went on to comment:

'I put my boss, whom I know as* François [Suttill], *in the picture about the behaviour of this agent. By his own admission nothing has been done either in the way of operation control or punishment.'*

On the evening of Staggs' arrival, Michael sat down with him and Lemercier and brought his operator up-to-date with everything that had happened since he had left St Erme, before laying out their immediate tasks. Staggs would continue to try to make contact with London, Lemercier would begin his recruitment programme, and he would go to Paris to give Suttill his new contact address and ask for an urgent message to be sent to London, confirming his arrival in Lille and asking for dates for his first supply drops. Staggs suggested that Michael ask if his radio set could be used for PROSPER'S next transmission since, if successful, it would confirm location or codes was the probable source of the problem rather than malfunction.

Suttill was not at the safe house when Michael arrived, but Norman said he had already reported the arrival of the three men in Paris and given details of Biéler's incapacity. The suggestion of using Staggs' radio was turned down as being too risky and likely to compromise the Paris circuit's own communications: the German direction-finding trucks were constantly on the streets, and transmissions were, of necessity, becoming shorter and shorter. Norman regretted that there was nothing he could do other than recommend that Michael should not discount the possibility that they had not found the right location and atmospherics for a solid connection.

Disappointed at his fruitless journey, he was just leaving when Suttill returned and immediately supported Norman's decision. He depressed Michael further by giving him the news that, shortly after leaving the meeting that Sunday in Paris, CARTE's Heyermans had been arrested by the police in a routine stop and search operation. Geelen, who had been behind him in the queue at the checkpoint, was trying to find out where he had been taken but thought that it had been a matter of a minor discrepancy in a travel permit, a frequent occurrence in Paris and something that could usually be resolved within a few days. The police had almost certainly been on the lookout for *réfractaires**, not insurgents, and Heyermans' employment papers were genuine and impeccable. Nothing further had been heard.

Arriving back in Lille that evening, Michael found that Lemercier had gone away for a couple of days, and Staggs had had no success with his transmissions. He ordered him to keep trying and told him of his discussion with Norman. Staggs wholeheartedly supported the idea that the problem might be one of location, which enabled Michael, who was unconvinced, to propose sending Staggs off each day to cycle around the countryside with his set, broken into easily portable components, to try to find somewhere suitable. This suggestion, possibly borne out of his frustration and impatience, was rejected as far too dangerous by Staggs, who saw it as yet another example of Michael's careless thinking.

---

* Réfractaires – draft dodgers, in this case French civilians who refused to be sent to work in Germany

Nevertheless he insisted, and for several days Staggs set off on his bicycle to locations suggested by Michael, but still without success. As a result their relationship deteriorated further. This is summed up in Staggs' first interrogation report:

'Further evidence of the bad relations existing between source and SYLVESTRE *at this time is contained in his statement that he had endeavoured to find suitable houses for future W/T transmission, but had not been allowed to go to those he wanted, because* SYLVESTRE *insisted he work only where he,* SYLVESTRE, *thought fit.'*

In the meantime Lemercier had returned, and his news was encouraging. He had already recruited one of his uncles and his brother-in-law, who in his turn brought in a young labourer, Lucien Delacroix. Under the field name of *Lulu,* Delacroix became Michael's constant shadow and personal bodyguard, when he was not employed on specific missions for the circuit.

On 4 January a message arrived for Michael from Norman. De Bizien had reported – but evidently had not informed Michael – that Chapelet had confirmed receipt of his postcard and told her that he had found an expert radio and signals technician in Sissonne. He was Michel Lebas, who was far more qualified than Chapelet himself and would be well worth a visit. Norman suggested that Staggs went back in two days' time, when de Bizien would again be available to take the transmitter. When Michael showed this to Staggs, the latter said he would leave early the next morning and carry the set himself. This bought to an end Staggs' attempts to transmit from Lille.

That same evening Michael announced his intention of going to Gondecourt to make contact with Jeanne Pachy, telling Staggs and Lemercier of his conversations with her in 1940 and of her suggestion that she knew local people who might be willing to help the British. Staggs had been critical of Michael when he heard of the Bouchez incident, and thought he would be inviting trouble if he tried once again to resurrect a link from two years ago. He said he had noticed that the loyalties of French citizens seemed to change dramatically according to their circumstances and what they thought was in their best interests. Lemercier reacted angrily to this, while recognizing the possible risk to Michael. He informed Staggs curtly that he would personally go to Gondecourt and talk to the 'untrustworthy French people' there. This mollified Staggs a little, but these two episodes no doubt contributed to the following observation by Staggs' interrogator:

'It is interesting to note that here source gave further evidence of the friction existing between himself and SYLVESTRE *by saying that he did not like or trust LE MERCIER, but that when he aired his*

opinions to SYLVESTRE, *the reply was that he,* SYLVESTRE, *trusted LE MERCIER a great deal further than he would source.'*

The departure of Staggs for St Erme reduced the tension in the house, and Michael sat down with Eliane and her husband to outline his thoughts for his circuit, informing them that he wanted it to operate as closely as possible on professional military lines, while taking due account of the need for flexibility and the patriotic fervour of his men. To this end he wanted to ensure that every single person who joined up signed an oath of allegiance and had his duties and responsibilities clearly defined. This was the oath in its basic format – some groups later added additional clauses:

'I swear never to reveal to anyone the names of members of our organization and to keep to myself all information that comes to my knowledge. I swear to hold myself day and night at the disposal of the Allied armies. I swear faithfully to obey at all times and in all circumstances the leaders whom I have voluntarily accepted. All under pain of death for betrayal. So help me God.'[3]

Not content with this, Michael insisted – as he had done with Eliane – that every man and woman should be made aware of the risks facing them. After much discussion he agreed the wording of a leaflet spelling out basic guidelines for security. Although a lengthy document, it bears reproduction here as an illustration of his meticulous planning and attention to detail. The final three instructions are particularly significant in the light of subsequent events.

1   Avoid causing any trouble in public places.
2   In the area around Lille there are two hundred women under instructions from the German authorities to strike up conversations and listen to everything that is said. Be on your guard.
3   Don't make problems for your colleagues, no matter how annoying you find them.
4   You will be warned in good time when volunteers are required.
5   You will be informed about your objective. It is your duty to look at this and consider the best possible ways of carrying it out.
6   You will be provided with weapons and equipment. But you must think about possible ways of fulfilling your mission without using explosives.
7   You will be shown how to handle your weapons and use explosives.
8   We ask you to help the wife and children of any member of the

association in the case of their arrest. This eventuality should not arise if you are discreet and avoid carrying compromising items.

9　You will almost certainly be operating at night and therefore the risk of capture is relatively low. Remember that you are on your home ground and the enemy is on unfamiliar ground. This and the element of surprise will be your strengths.

10　Surprise is an essential element and the determination with which you carry out your mission is another vital factor for success.

11　Be patient. Patience will bring its own rewards.

12　Each objective will be defined very precisely and you need to remember that its achievement is much more important than putting down a few German soldiers.

13　Be cautious. Caution does not indicate a lack of courage.

14　When you are carrying out an attack be brave and proud to have the chance of raising the French flag. Be assured that your behaviour and your sacrifices will be recognized and when victory comes you will march alongside the victorious French armies. You will be able to say: 'I was there!'

15　Don't try to find out for your own information anything beyond what is strictly necessary to enable you to fulfil your mission (for instance the identity of your leaders, your comrades, intelligence etc.).

16　Refuse to listen to any confidences imparted by a comrade and draw your leader's attention to such indiscretions. This is vital for collective security.

17　Anyone who without good reason gets to know too many of our members or too much about our organization will be a danger to us all.

Eliane worked night after night typing up these documents, and it became her responsibility to ensure that copies were given to each recruit and that the signed copies of the oath were returned. But Michael's demands did not end there: she also had to maintain a typed list of all members. Most would be identified by a letter and a number, but in many cases there might be a name – a diminutive or code name – beneath which might appear various other names that would help to identify them, but never their physical appearance and very rarely their real name – thus *Pierrot*, *Gaston* or *Gabriel* for Séailles, *F.10* for Arthur Malfait, *K.10* for Marcel Fertein, *R.10* for Georges Bayart, *L.L.3* for Jean Chieux, *A.2* Julien Gerekens.[4]

Given Michael's drive and organizational skills, alongside Lemercier's local knowledge and enthusiasm, it was no surprise that recruitment proceeded at a brisk pace. Lemercier had a large extended family and had started to bring in friends and former colleagues, including future key people such as Charles Robbe, Lemercier's cousins Arthur Sénéchal and Victor Leblanc, and, through Lemercier's contacts in Brussels, Belgians Maurice Rowies and Georges Melotte. Very soon a pattern was established that would become standard: each principal recruiter acting like a spider whose web expanded progressively outwards by word of mouth. Michael directed Lemercier to focus on professional people who might have good contacts and, possibly, funds to spare, as well as owners of establishments that could serve as bases and refuges for the circuit.

Realizing that he had insufficient local knowledge to do much about recruitment himself, Michael turned his attention to a problem that struck a chord in his heart due to his own experiences: looking after and returning to England the many British soldiers who had been unable to get out of France. The spring tide of the BEF in 1940 and its rapid ebb in the face of the German blitzkrieg had left pockets of stranded soldiers and airmen strewn across France and Belgium. Since Dunkirk, numbers had been augmented by shot-down airmen of many different Allied nationalities, and organized escape lines had been set up, whereby crews could be passed from one safe house to another. To these could be added escaped prisoners who had been taken in by the population, people hunted by the German and French authorities, and men avoiding forced labour. The various arms of the Nazi security services were anxious to identify these networks and close them down, and the consequences for the French partisans who gave their support were dire. The reality of this came home to Michael from an unexpected quarter.

Following Lemercier's reconnaissance visit to Gondecourt, the news he brought back was not encouraging. Jeanne Pachy and her daughter Yvonne had been arrested in October 1941 and imprisoned in Loos for sheltering Allied servicemen, as had Marie-Jeanne Bouchez and her mother in Lille. After serving an initial three months Yvonne had been sentenced to a further six months in Loos, while Jeanne had been condemned to deportation to Ravensbruck concentration camp. Yvonne had been released in May 1942 and was back at the shop, where her grandfather had moved in to look after her.

Michael was saddened by this news and decided he had to do something to help. Learning from Lemercier that there was no sign of any German activity or surveillance in Gondecourt, he asked him to provide some English chocolate and cigarettes, which he parcelled up and posted to Yvonne anonymously, resolving to see her at the earliest opportunity. So it was that one Saturday in mid-January Yvonne opened her door to a stranger, who carefully and deliberately asked her if she was alone, because there was 'someone special' to see her. Her grandfather was out and, still frightened and fearful of being arrested again and taken back to Loos, she was about to close the door hurriedly when another figure appeared behind the stranger and smiled at her. Yvonne recalled:

'Although he had changed his appearance, I recognized him immediately. It was Michael. He asked me if I had received the chocolates. I was at once happy and confused. What was he doing here? I invited him in, while his companion waited outside – later I realized that he was a bodyguard.' [5]

Michael explained that he would not stay long: he just wanted to make sure she was alright, and asked if she wanted to talk about what had happened. Yvonne again:

'I told him that after the British had left and the Germans had won their battles in Belgium and France we were aware that a great many troops had been left behind, and we heard of plans being made to get them back to England. My mother was approached and asked if she was prepared to help, and she immediately agreed. Michael was interested to hear that one of the first British servicemen we helped was a soldier from the Middlesex Regiment, but I never knew his name.

'Over the next few months we sheltered nine different servicemen, including three airmen who had parachuted from their damaged aircraft. I know this because it had always been our custom from before the war to keep a visitor book, in which we asked people who came to stay with us to write some comment. We kept this going, and it was my job to ask all the evaders to say something. I called it my "Golden Book". I don't know if they gave their real names, but they always wrote something nice about me, often flirtatious, such as quoting lines from the song If you were the only girl in the world. *Looking back it was a foolish thing to keep this book.*

'I also used to help out by carrying messages, sometimes into Belgium, or escorting the men on bicycles to a rendezvous point, where someone else would take them from me. My being there helped us to get through checkpoints, because then we were just a crowd of young people on an outing. I never knew where the men had come from or where they went. We weren't the only family in the area helping in this way, but we thought no-one would notice what we were doing.'

An account of some of the Pachy family's activities is provided by Leonard 'Len' Arlington, the soldier from the Middlesex Regiment who had seen Michael in Wattrelos. He had failed to make it to Dunkirk, been captured, escaped in Belgium, then made his way across the frontier back to Gondecourt, where he had made numerous contacts. He was given refuge with local farmers, first at the Dhénin farm then at the Faucomprez farm. In historian Laffin's story of Arlington's wartime experiences in hiding in France we read:

> 'Madame Passy [sic] was eager to meet him. She had been Jeanne Oliger but everybody knew her as Madame Passy and held her in great respect. Len, while on leave in Britain early in 1940, had brought a record for her. She lived over her boutique in Gondecourt and Len met her in the kitchen. He was not easily overawed by personalities but this tall, dignified and aristocratic widow was the type of woman for whom a soldier stood to attention. Graciously she gestured him to be seated and said in a formidable voice: "We, the French people, will never accept the victory of the Nazis... .Can I count on your assistance, should I need it?" "I'll do whatever you want me to do, Madame Passy", Len promised. At that moment he had informally joined the Resistance, though he did not then know it.' [6]

Arlington's commitment was soon put to the test.

> 'One day a courier came to the Dhénin farm with a message that Madame Passy wished to see him... ."We have two escaped prisoners hiding in a gamekeeper's cottage", she said, "and we want you to certify that they are bona fide British." "Is there some doubt, Madame?" Len asked. "There must always be doubt until we prove otherwise. It is up to you to find out if these men are what they say they are." The embryo Resistance already knew that the Germans were infiltrating their own men, posing as evaders and escapers, into the rescue lines.'

All turned out well on this occasion, and Arlington was often asked to provide a similar service. Not all, however, proved to be genuine.

> 'He walked into the Gondecourt boutique to find five German officers in heated argument over prices with her daughter Yvonne. The girl was only sixteen but she handled the situation posed by Len's arrival with great coolness. "Ah, Leonard" she said, "mother is in the kitchen waiting for you." With a shop full of Nazis, Len and Madame Passy sat a few feet away in her kitchen while they discussed Resistance affairs. It was an exquisite occasion and they

both enjoyed it. "One of our group has a man in hiding. He says he is a Royal Air Force pilot who was shot down in Belgium. Will you talk to him and find out if he really is a British pilot?"'

It did not take Arlington long to find out that something was 'not quite right'.

'To Madame Passy he said "This man may not be German but he's in their service and he's dangerous. How can we get rid of him?" "We can arrange that tonight," the grand lady said with quiet finality. "I have a group of men who will take any step necessary to keep our operation secure. We can safely leave the matter in their hands." In effect, Len had pronounced the man's death sentence, and he was never seen again in Gondecourt. Nor was he ever spoken of. He was a casualty in a necessarily ruthless war.'

A week or so later Arlington's suspicions were aroused when a man claiming to be a British intelligence agent arrived in Gondecourt in a bad way, saying that he had been wounded in a shoot-out with the Gestapo. Code-named *Joe*, and using the name Francis Mumme, he had been taken in and cared for by a local family and soon asked to be taken to Arlington, a 'friend from the old days'. Arlington was suspicious and after confronting the man he was convinced that he was a Gestapo agent and told 'Madame Passy'.

'She looked frowningly serious. "Something will have to be done about him then. I'll get our friends together and we'll discuss what can be done."'

The following day she had news for him.

'Her "disposal specialists" had made arrangements for "Joe" to be invited to a banquet in Lille. The invitation was innocent-sounding – some of the town's notables wanted a private opportunity to pass on a message of thanks to London. After the dinner Joe would be given a large sum of money to hand over to the Resistance. Four experienced men would be waiting and, at a given signal, Joe's career as a German agent would end. His grave, said Madame Passy, was even now being prepared in local marshland.'

However, things did not go according to plan, and *Joe* avoided the trap. Raids on the Faucomprez farm in Chemy followed. Arlington managed to escape but the entire Faucomprez family was arrested.

> *'The district was agog with news of the previous night's happenings in Chemy and Gondecourt. It became clear that afternoon that the local Resistance had suffered a disaster. The Germans had broken into Madame Passy's house and arrested her and her daughter.'*

The Faucomprez family was also taken to Loos, where they were sentenced to various terms of imprisonment. This by chance gave Jeanne Pachy, who had not been formally tried but had been sentenced to death as 'a very dangerous person', the opportunity to put in motion the events that would point the finger at her betrayer. Taking her chance when the warder's back was turned she whispered to the youngest of the children, Marcelle Faucomprez:

> *'"I haven't much time," she said, "so listen carefully. Marcelle, I know that you are a patriotic young girl and that I can trust you. When you're freed, go to Madame Delanghe in Gondecourt and tell her that I was betrayed by Henriette Verbeke, whose lover is a Gestapo agent. She will know what to do. Promise me this." This was a heavy responsibility for a young girl. Marcelle gave her promise and she kept it.'* [7]

In the end the arrests of these patriotic families were not the result of methodical intelligence work or penetration by Germans acting as British airmen. The cause was quite simply one of betrayal, as Brendan Murphy related in his book *Turncoat*:

> *'A local woman who worked as a secretary in the Malterie (or Brewery) opposite the house, Henriette Verbeke betrayed them to the Germans as she not only saw people coming and going but knew who the local resisters were. She betrayed them to the notorious Cornelius Verloop. A Dutchman by birth he was a principal agent within the Lille Abwehrstelle the main German counterintelligence outpost in the north of France. His role was to infiltrate himself into early local resistance groups and Escape lines such as the Pat O'Leary Line operating from Lille. Perhaps as many as sixty people mainly women were arrested in well planned and coordinated raids during the night of October 21/22 in Gondecourt and in other villages surrounding Lille and in Lille itself.'*

At Verloop's request Verbeke introduced him to Jeanne Pachy, thus sealing the fate of mother and daughter. Yvonne recalled how plain-clothes men of the *Geheime Feldpolizei* and soldiers of the *Feldgendarmerie* broke into the house :

'That night, at around three o'clock, we were pulled out of bed by German soldiers and security men. They ransacked the house and arrested my mother and myself. They took away my "Golden Book" and stole many items from our home, including money and my gold watch. They locked us up and beat my mother. When I last saw her she was bruised and bleeding, with chains on her wrists and ankles. The last thing she said to me was that when I was released I was to go back to school to finish my education.' [8]

She also recalled, but steadfastly refused to elaborate on, the cruelty of the Polish female guards working for the Germans in Loos prison. Michael told her that he would do all he could to help. He had a vague idea that he might be able to arrange her mother's release in exchange for a promise of information or some other form of collateral, and he asked Yvonne if she would like to meet him after school one day to tell him more about Loos. This she agreed to do, and he said he would contact her again.

The news reinforced Michael's desire to ensure that, as his circuit grew, it should provide more and more support for this essential undercover activity that was being undertaken largely by untrained civilians who were putting their life on the line every day. He felt it was his duty to help and he knew just the man to take charge – his old friend from Mauzac, Pierre Duval.

While in prison Michael had listened attentively to Duval's story. From the time the Germans invaded he had led a highly dangerous and risky existence as a forager, transporter and procurer of black market and stolen goods, particularly petrol, running a fleet of vehicles that criss-crossed borders seemingly at will. He had a small yard and general purpose shop in Abbeville, which served as a storage and distribution depot as well providing cover and being an outlet for his less legitimate activities. He had been picked up a number of times, but on each occasion he had managed to escape or talk his way out, until he finally ended up in Périgueux, where a tribunal had found him guilty of espionage and sent him to Mauzac. Michael recognized and appreciated the ingenious and resourceful ways in which Duval had managed to extricate himself from seemingly impossible situations, and he realized that such experience would be invaluable to future agents. He had told Duval that, when he was released and back in France, he would come for him.

Michael had given Simone Séailles her first mission, which was to find and contact Duval to arrange a meeting at the station in Lille, and Duval responded instantly. Delighted to see him, Michael introduced him to Lemercier and told him of his plans. Duval volunteered his services and was given the job of setting up an escape line to pass people from northern

France into Spain. In addition, he was made responsible for sorting out all the circuit's transport requirements. For a host of good reasons, particularly security, movements would need to be by vehicle. Duval purchased a lorry in Abbeville and set up with a neighbour a coal distribution business that allowed him easy and innocent access to the *zone interdite*.*

Chapter notes
1   From here onwards we have attempted to reconstruct the twelve months of the SYLVESTRE-FARMER circuit under Michael's direction from the valuable and abundant records generously made available by André Coilliot and Danièle Lheureux (see Introduction). To these can be added my own researches, interviews and correspondence with Pierre Séailles, Arthur Staggs, Eliane Lemercier, Stephen Grady and the many others listed under 'Acknowledgements'. And, of course, my countless conversations with my mother. These sources are not referred to again in subsequent chapter notes, unless there is a compelling reason for doing so.
2   Julien Chapelet's son kindly sent me this postcard in 2000 and allowed me to photocopy it.
3   In February 1944 Pierre Séailles added this paragraph: *'For reasons of collective security members of the association must sever any contact they have or might have with members of any other organization. Only the leaders are qualified to make such contacts if they deem it necessary.'*
4   I have in my possession copies of some pages from this register. Although there is considerable detail against each entry – information of use to Michael – it would have been of no help if seized by the security services, because none of the agents was identified by name.
5   These recollections from my mother were not obtained systematically or chronologically. Instead they emerged over a period of fifteen years in fragments as she searched her memory, either at my prompting, or, as frequently happened, things occurred to her spontaneously and prompted her to telephone me. She continued to remember things right up to the date of finishing this book!
6   This and the citations that follow are taken from the book *The Man the Nazis Couldn't Catch,* the story of Len Arlington as told to John Laffin. They speak for themselves, and both my mother and Marcelle Arlington (née Faucomprez) believe them to be correct, if a little over-dramatic.
7   Marcelle was the youngest of the Faucomprez daughters, sentenced to 12 months. She married Len in April 1946.
8   When I visited Gondecourt with my mother we met an elderly lady (name not recorded) who had been her neighbour during the war. She said to Mother that she remembered very distinctly the raid and the German soldiers in their steel helmets and the shiny metal plates on their chests – ie the silver gorgets of the *Feldgendarmerie.*

---

* *Zone interdite* – forbidden zone, of which there were several in occupied France. In this particular case it refers to a 20km coastal strip running from Dunkirk to Hendaye

Chapter 10

Expansion

'In sooth, a goodly company.'
Thomas Ingoldsby

A start had been made, but it was no more than that. Michael had squandered most of SOE's money and, with no resources on which to fall back, the little he had left was barely sufficient to cover the cost of feeding himself and the founder members of the network. He had to ensure its many important financial needs were met to enable it to function effectively as well as provide for the everyday existence of its members and their families. One of the critical guidelines he impressed on his recruiters was the need to be constantly on the lookout for men and women with access to cash or other useful resources. He needed men, money, transport and weapons, but his most urgent requirement was for a secure and fast line of communication with London.

He desperately wanted Staggs to return with good news but was once more disappointed. After talking his way out of an inspection by customs officers on his train journey to St Erme with the set, Staggs had made contact with Lebas, but in his first interrogation report we read:

> *'Source found that, possibly owing to his having been trying to work the set on the mains current, the 22,000 ohms resistance was burnt out, and since similar resistance was not obtainable, they replaced it with one of 25,000 ohms; on testing the set appeared to be in working order, but again source was unsuccessful in making contact with Home Station.'* [1]

Leaving the set with Chapelet, on the chance that Lebas could find other resistors, Staggs returned to Lille and expressed the opinion that the wrong valves must have been fitted in the first place. However, an interesting sidebar arises in the letter from Jenan Denis to Gervase Cowell (see notes to Chapter 8), where he stated:

> *'One of the transmitters STAGGS was unable to get to work was left with Chapelet in St Erme. As a result of his group being cut off from*

SYLVESTRE FARMER after the tragic events within the network, Chapelet and his groups join up again with our sector in LAON (Aisne). On 13 December 1943 one of our WT operators goes to Chapelet's and was in the process of making a successful transmission from the attic when German police entered the ground floor to arrest the owner of the house... . We recover the transmitter which we carry on using up until the liberation.'

Michael was by now resigned to having to communicate, at least in the short term, through PROSPER, where a second radio operator, Jack Agazarian, had arrived to help with the ever-increasing volumes of traffic generated through Paris. Michael had no choice but to find something else for Staggs to do, and each evening the two of them would sit down with the Lemerciers to review progress with recruitment, fundraising and communications. They were joined by other members of the group who might be in the area. By the middle of January this numbered around twenty and brought about the need to find an alternative location for their headquarters.

Clearly, the house in Rue Corneille was neither large enough nor in the right place to serve Michael as somewhere he could hold meetings, receive reports and issue instructions to future members of the circuit. Further, as Staggs repeatedly pointed out, the stream of men constantly coming and going in the quiet residential street would certainly attract unwanted attention before long: even his landlady had commented on it. Michael put this to Lemercier, who began to look around and very quickly directed him to Madeleine Thyrou, owner of the *Aquarium* café near Lille's Place Philippe Lebon. Michael came to an arrangement with her, carefully explaining the nature of his mission and the risks.

He moved in the following day. Thyrou had given him an attic room with access to the roof and the sole use of her downstairs back room for his meetings. This was on the strict condition that he let her join his 'gang', to which Michael agreed, assigning her the code name *Mado*. He now had the ideal headquarters for his nascent network as the premises ran right through the block, having its main entrance in Parvis St Michel and a rear exit from the back room onto Rue de Fleurs. Thus it provided not only an obvious escape route but also an ideal facility for clandestine visitors. To keep these to a minimum and improve security, Michael ordered that only the future sector leaders and group leaders should know where to find him, and then only in circumstances of real need, or if he had summoned them for a meeting. Routine communications both ways would be via couriers and a chain of letterboxes in Lille and in each sector – public places where messages could be left and routinely collected. Lemercier immediately came up with Pierre Demoor and his wife, who ran

Le Petit Tambour café in Rue des Sarrazins, on the side of Place de la Nouvelle Aventure. She was followed by Roger Vanspranghe, proprietor of a café in Rue du Marché, Camille Demagny, proprietress of a café in Place aux Oignons; and Philippe Wagon, the proprietor of *Au Poker*, where it had all begun. Each of these establishments was to play an important part in the life of the circuit. Staggs would soon move in with Demagny, and it was in *Le Petit Tambour* that Michael became attracted to the long blonde hair and fresh-faced looks of local girl Denise Gilman, who was to become his hard-working courier, steadfast companion, lover and confidante.

Now began an intense period of rapid development and growth for the FARMER circuit. Michael was well aware that he needed numbers, but it was also vital that he found men with leadership qualities, who were mentally strong, resilient, energetic, determined and, ideally, with some experience of action. He needed geographical sector leaders for the regions around Lille, and strategic sector leaders for key areas such as transportation, telecommunications, police and local government. He pointed the recruiters towards managers, supervisors and key workers from these organizations, with immediate and impressive results, as six very effective and respected figures arrived: Marcel Fertein, Jean Chieux, Georges Bayart, Jean Velge, Arthur Malfait and Julien Gerekens.

Lemercier led the way, taking Michael, as promised, to the caravan of his cousin, Arthur Beirnaert, in the Raismes forest, some 50 km south-east of Lille, and arranging for him to stay there for a couple of days a week over the next month. Michael was drawn instantly to Lemercier's gypsy-like friend and impressed by the hidden storage arrangements in the caravan. He soon convinced Beirnaert to join the circuit, and the two of them became a highly effective recruitment team. The itinerant trader exploited his long list of contacts in the area to provide introductions that enabled Michael to approach and enlist a large number of willing volunteers, one of whom – fatefully for the circuit – was André Martel, a *réfractaire* who was working as foreman on a neighbouring farm and had been earmarked by Lemercier for parachute reception duties. Through Beirnaert, Michael was able to infiltrate the local FTP* and spread his net eastwards as far afield as Maubeuge and l'Avesnois. Within two months a very active circle was operating in the areas around Lille and Valenciennes. Meanwhile, Lemercier expanded the circuit westwards towards Dunkirk, Bourbourg, Houdain, St Omer, Abbeville and Ypres, finding a rich recruiting ground amongst members of British and French escape lines who had been isolated following arrests in their organization and cut off from their movement.

While in Raismes, Michael was talking to Beirnaert when they were interrupted by the traveller's cousin, Angèle Malfait, on one of her frequent visits to obtain provisions for her family. Well-accustomed to Beirnaert's

---

* FTP: *Francs-tireurs et partisans* – literally 'sharpshooters and partisans' i.e. groups of armed local communist resistors

anonymous visitors and his instruction never to ask questions, she ignored Michael completely and gossiped animatedly with her cousin about where her recent trips around the countryside had taken her and whom she had met, before turning to the topic of the forthcoming marriage of Beirnaert's sister, Marguerite, to Martel. At first Michael listened politely as the two of them talked, then it dawned on him that here was an ideal person to carry messages from one part of the circuit to another; already a familiar sight on her bicycle, her innocent and wholly plausible activities would provide excellent cover. He duly introduced himself and explained his mission, whereupon Angèle promptly offered her services as a courier. She took the oath later that day in the toilets of a café in Raismes, and promised Michael that she would work on her policeman husband Paul, and her nephew Arthur, to persuade them to join too. Arthur, however, was wary of a possible German trap and advised his aunt to discuss the matter with her husband. If he thought the affair to be genuine, Arthur would go along with him. For the time being, however, Paul decided to wait and see.

Marcel Fertein was a petty officer shipwright at the naval aviation base in Cherbourg when war was declared. As the German net closed around them he and five colleagues commandeered a fleet collier and took it to Morocco, where the aviation units were reorganized. Demobilized by the Armistice Commission he returned to Thumesnil, where he became a foreman at a joinery firm, ignoring the call up from the STO* in order to work with the FTP and the OCM** as leader of a group tasked with protecting the firm from harm and helping the advance of British troops in the event of a landing. He kept himself busy by obtaining false papers and equipment for escapers and men like himself desperate to avoid transportation to Germany. A chance remark from an OCM colleague, Henri Verstraete, alerted him to news from one of Lemercier's nephews that his relatives in Lille were sheltering an Englishman and his radio operator, and were looking for Frenchmen to organize armed resistance. Fertein asked Verstraete find out when and how the supposed Englishman could be contacted.

So it was that on the morning of Sunday, 24 January, Verstraete and Fertein met Lemercier and Staggs in *Le Petit Tambour*, Michael being absent from Lille that weekend. Staggs told them that they were looking for people to carry out a war of subversion but was unable to say more, so they met again the following Sunday, this time with Michael. He outlined his plans and his orders from London to set up commandos of saboteurs, form them into groups and hold them ready to go into action when the Allies returned to France. Fertein took the oath immediately and was given the registration number *D.10* (later changed to *K.10*). Michael gave him

---

* STO: *Service de Travail Obligatoire* – compulsory labour service
** OCM: *Mouvement de Résistance Organization Civile et Militaire* – civil and military movement for organized resistance

responsibility for the sectors to the south and east of Lille, and the slim, thin-faced Fertein, with his toothbrush moustache and high forehead, threw himself into this work with great energy. He adopted a brusque, efficient no-nonsense approach that earned him the greatest of respect from those he recruited and he was to become a key figure in the circuit, and the second of Michael's 'inner circle'. By the time the war in France was over he was one of the most wanted men in the country.

At the end of January Fertein went to Steenwerck, near the Belgian border, to see his childhood friend, Jean Chieux, and, with Michael's blessing, told him about the circuit and suggested a meeting. Chieux was a specialist marine turbine engineer and a lieutenant of the reserve. He had been called up, sent home again, remobilized, and given a special posting to the Fives Engineering Company in Lille, tasked with hurrying through the production of turbines for naval vessels. In May 1940, following the events at the front, his boss ordered him to withdraw to Loir-et-Cher, which he never reached. After a series of near encounters with the advancing German forces, and confused meetings with the retreating French, he realized that he would be unable to rejoin his unit, and he headed for Dunkirk on his bicycle. He almost made it, but hearing that the Dunkirk pocket had been closed he decided to return to his home in Serques and move his family to Steenwerck. When the Fives locomotive factory reopened in July he went back to work there, but he found the French defeat hard to take and wanted to do something, without really knowing what. He was delighted when Fertein told him about the circuit, and was introduced to Michael at *Bar Chagnot* in Lille's Place de la Gare. There he was given responsibility for recruiting and organizing groups in the north-west sector, including Bailleul, Armentières, Hazebrouck and St Omer, areas that he knew well. Always smartly dressed with his hair parted immaculately, the bespectacled Chieux looked like a typical city lawyer, but this outward appearance masked a tough, resolute and determined interior that drove him to focus intensely on his objectives. He was also to provide a vital service through his position at the Fives factory.

Georges Bayart, an industrialist, was introduced to Michael by a former employee and was instantly struck by the Englishman's energy, enthusiasm and commitment, as well as being impressed by his organization, structure and the resources. At 60-years-old, Bayart would be the old man of the circuit. Tall, with receding hair, bushy eyebrows and heavy spectacles, he was an imposing figure; the very personification of an energetic captain of industry. He was also universally respected and his experience was highly valued. He had fought in the First World War, been captured and taken to Germany, from where he had escaped. Wounded in the attempt, he reached France with thoughts of returning to the fray, but to his intense disappointment he was declared unfit for the infantry, and with escapees having no right of return to the frontline, he went into a war factory, where he became depressed. After the war the escapees from the north of France made him president of their group, but the injury to his pride stayed with him. He reproached himself for not having done more for his country and this time around he swore to serve it better. He considered himself physically fit and, being of an adventurous nature, he joined the *Volontaires de la Morte*, a body formed in Lille to carry out dangerous, and often desperate, commando operations. He also joined the *Croix du Feu* organization, whose members had all been awarded the medal of that name for frontline service in the First World War and many of whom had now chosen to resist. He told anyone who asked for an explanation that he was fighting to save the honour of his country. France had sworn to carry on the war alongside its allies, and he was a Frenchman. With other members of his family he distributed pamphlets and provided false papers for escapees. However, in November 1941 the group was infiltrated by a German agent; Bayart's son was arrested and then shot while trying to escape. After this incident the organization folded. In spite of his grief, Bayart carried on fighting with the OCM, but when Michael came along he felt instinctively that at long last he was in a position to do something positive to avenge his son and set about finding recruits from the *réfractaires* in his factory as well as from members of his staff. Michael realized the importance of Bayart's knowledge as well as his contacts in industry and commerce, and insisted that he could serve his country best by staying in the background. Although disappointed at being left out of future aggressive actions against the enemy, Bayart nevertheless saw the sense of his decision.

Next to arrive was Jean Velge, another of Lemercier's seemingly endless list of cousins, who lived with his sister in Hoeilaart, in the Flemish province of Brabant in Flanders, where they had run a restaurant together before the war. He worked for a small intelligence group and was associated with Charles and George Melotte, who, together with Velge's boss, were actively involved with the Belgian escape lines and had earlier been recruited by Lemercier. The Melottes would in due course pass on a number of evading airmen to the FARMER circuit on the Belgian/Franco border, from where they would be taken via Arras or Paris to the French/Spanish border, before eventually making their escape over the Pyrenees into Spain. Following the arrest of his boss in late January, Velge knew he would soon be under investigation by the Gestapo, so he promptly crossed the border into France, where he made contact with his cousin, who introduced him to Michael. The latter suggested that he should continue his struggle from within FARMER, and Velge duly accepted the invitation to become his principal liaison officer and adviser in respect of activities and events on the Belgian side of the border. He adopted the field name *Jahncke*, and, when in Lille, he rented a room at the *Aquarium* or stayed with the Lemerciers.

In the meantime Arthur Malfait had been thinking about the conversation he had had with his aunt when in Raismes. A married man of 28 with a child, he had been called up into a fortress infantry regiment, which, in June 1942, came under heavy bombardment near Châtel-sur-Moselle and was quickly surrounded. Malfait spent the night in prison barracks, and the next day decided to report sick. He was put into a local ambulance and tended by French nurses before being taken to hospital in Lunéville, where colluding doctors managed to keep him for a week or so until his bed was needed when severely wounded men began to arrive. Transferred to a prison camp near the front at Epinal, from where men were being despatched to camps across the Rhine, he noticed that the Germans were singling out men who had worked on the railways or in local government offices. Quickly, he falsified his Army record card and became an employee of the 'Bridges and Roads Department'. His card was rejected but he persuaded the officer in charge that it was a genuine, certified page from his Army record, and was allowed to board a train for Paris, from where he made his way to his home in Roubaix. There he found his wife, who had received no news of him since the beginning of the war and did not know if he was alive or dead. Late in 1942, anxious not to put his wife and child at risk, he went to live in Wattrelos with his uncle and aunt, hoping to find some way to get back at the invaders. There he met up with an old friend, Henri Vandesype, who put him in touch with a resistance group in Roubaix that gave him the job of identifying and recording the names of German units as they passed through the town.

By happy coincidence, Michael had returned to Raismes at the end of February 1943 to look at possible sites for future supply drops near Aubry-du-Hainaut. While there he was invited to the Martel-Beirnaert wedding and found himself sitting at the meal table between Angèle Malfait and her husband Paul, a tall, dark-haired man with penetrating blue eyes who, obviously well briefed by his wife, took advantage of the general hubbub to ask Michael questions about the circuit and his plans. Later in the evening Paul led Michael outside and introduced him to Arthur. Both men declared that they wished to join the circuit, and the next day the Malfaits met Michael in a café in Rue du Molinel.

Michael made an instant impression on Arthur:

'Of above average height, all muscle and nerves, with a powerful and sporting bearing, he was a superb specimen of his race. His dark chestnut eyes were bright and intelligent and according to circumstances, tender, strict or decidedly ironical. He had a strong nose with widely dilated nostrils, a massive jaw with firmly set chin,

and a high, clean forehead. He was intelligent and his whole appearance revealed the free and loyal character of a man who, in direct contrast with his adventurous and dangerous way of life, was stamped with an exquisite sentimentalism. His fairish red hair was lightly waved and a thin moustache adorned his lips. He was a handsome and likeable man. His very slight accent, barely detectable even to someone looking out for it, and the occasional use of well-chosen words that told of an advanced French education, made him an attractive and fluent conversationalist. This was the man who was to create and develop the famous SYLVESTRE-FARMER circuit of the French Resistance.'

As he had done with Bayart, Michael persuaded Paul that he would be of greatest value by just staying in his position – in Paul's case with the police in Wattrelos. After listening to Arthur's story Michael carefully set out his goals and described the work needed: sabotage, intelligence, helping shot-down airmen and other specialists to escape. Arthur accepted the conditions and took the oath with his uncle. He would go on to become the circuit's most forceful and successful sector leader and, subsequently, its assiduous historian.

Michael gave Malfait the task of recruiting and setting up groups to the north and east of Lille. He began by appointing leaders from a small resistance group in Wattrelos, through whom he was introduced to Julien Gerekens, an electrical engineer based in the telephone office at Lille's main railway station. As an essential worker in a reserved occupation he was not called up when war broke out, but when France surrendered he was devastated. Like many others, he did what he could to harry and harass the occupation forces by carrying out small acts of sabotage on abandoned equipment and handing out anti-German leaflets. Hearing rumours of an English group operating in the city he jumped at the chance to speak to Malfait, who told him that *Le Capitaine* would come to see him in his office. Gerekens recalled his first meeting with Michael vividly:

'I can see the captain when he came into my office, fair-haired, full of energy, shining intelligent eyes that instantly appraised you and summed you up. With a smile on the corner of his lips he came towards me and, for the first time, I shook the hand of the man who was to become my friend.'

Michael asked him about his activities and what he wanted. Gerekens showed him how, from his first-floor office right in the middle of the station, he could see everything that happened. Furthermore, in his position within the telecommunications service, he had at his fingertips the means of communicating with railwaymen all across the region. Michael appreciated that in the natural course of their everyday movements the railwaymen would be able to establish contacts in every direction, and he recruited Gerekens on the spot, giving him the field name *Jacky*.

This team of sector leaders – both geographic and strategic – provided the foundation for all of FARMER's future operations, and they wasted no time in developing their areas.

Not one to suffer fools gladly, Fertein proved to be a shrewd judge of character and potential. When Verstraete introduced him to Jean Descamps, a baker from Sainghin-en-Weppes, he found in him an able and like-minded lieutenant. Between them they successfully infiltrated and established groups within the PTT* and persuaded leading members of local communist groups to join the circuit and bring their men with them, causing the sector to expand rapidly. Descamps became a prolific recruiter, bringing in key figures such as Edmond Béghin, leader of an informal band of men in the north-eastern and Belgian frontier regions, who had been isolated and cut off from their units. Through his police job with the Central Commissariat in Lille, Descamps had a good relationship with supplies officer Marcel Rogge, a former garage owner from Phalempin, and he asked him to establish a group there, in an area whose natural surroundings were ideal for concealing large numbers of illegals. While he was taking his inspector's examination at the *Sûreté*, Descamps met Louis Coudoux, general secretary of the Central Police Commission, and persuaded him to join, along with a number of senior inspectors and many constables. This important group of police administrators was able to provide priceless information that enabled the circuit to forestall and frustrate the occupation forces and Vichy police in many of their round-ups and arrests.

Chieux recruited his brother, Pierre, and a close friend, Jean Sonneville, as well as bringing in his own wife Jeanne, who then devoted herself to the circuit. They soon established sections within the sector in Armentières and St Jans-Cappel, and recruited an important group of railway workers in Hazebrouck. With the help of Fertein, Chieux broadened his search and embraced the whole of the area west of Lille. He was also to provide a vital service through his position at the Fives locomotive factory.

Malfait began by recruiting leaders from a small resistance group in Wattrelos, including his friend Vandesype and two colleagues, Alfred Vanhecke and Georges Philippot, all of whom were to play major parts in the circuit's activities. Vandesype had been taking advantage of his position as a clerk in the office of the Mayor of Wattrelos to create false identity cards for the numerous English soldiers still in the sector and forged civilian documentation for French prisoners. Within a month Malfait had brought

---

* PTT: *Postes Télécommunications et Téléfusion* – French post office and telecommunications service

in a score of men and was instrumental in setting up and developing the whole of the Roubaix-Tourcoing area and in building up the Arras, Béthune, Aires-sur-la-Lys and St Omer sectors. He had also targeted the customs service, from which he recruited a group of French officers on one side of the border and a Belgian group on the other. The SNCF* was another priority group. Through Vanhecke, Malfait found a number of enthusiastic foremen and supervisors, including Emile Dubocage, a blond giant of a railway policeman from Roubaix. These in turn brought in railway workers from Tourcoing, Wattrelos, Roubaix, Croix, and Wasquehal and from as far afield as Mouscron in Belgium. Through Vanhecke and Dubocage Malfait was able to penetrate SNCF operations in both the Nord and the Pas de Calais.

Recruitment on the railways quickly spread as far as Valenciennes, from where Gerekens brought in a group of men under Jean Liébault who, in just a few weeks, set up a number of sub-groups, including one from the repair shop at Valenciennes station. He also set up groups in the stations at Fives, St-André, La Madeleine and Lille Déliverance, and soon had men at every important railway location across the region and around sixty altogether in his charge. Impressed, Michael issued orders that they should create maximum disruption to German movements, while at all costs doing nothing to endanger the lives of innocent travellers.

So far, the success and speed of recruitment had exceeded his wildest hopes. The circuit had infiltrated the railways, the police, the post office, the customs, the fire services, and many layers and departments of local civil authorities. It had members in every important town and strategic communications location in the north of France, all of whom had been biding their time and waiting for someone like Michael to come along. Enthusiasm and a wild desire to get at the Germans was rampant in all who joined, along with a large degree of impatience, and he was forced to step in to impose order and discipline on what could easily have become chaos.

In setting things down on paper – the oath, the security leaflet and the register – he was taking an incalculable risk and deliberately disregarding SOE's specific instructions. But it convinced his men that they were part of a highly organized operation, and they were proud to have been selected by a British officer to play what they saw to be a leading role in the eventual liberation of France. They considered that their leader's professionalism, experience and skills, coupled with the promised flood of arms from London, set them apart from the largely undisciplined and ill-equipped assortment of other French resistance organizations that were forever squabbling over politics and fighting with each other for supremacy. Michael's men perceived themselves to be an elite force specially recruited by the British high command, and they pressed to be allowed to call their

---

* SNCF: *Société Nationale des Chemins de Fer* – the French railways

organization 'The War Office Group'. Michael relayed their request to London but, understandably, it was refused. He softened the blow by pointing out that all secret organizations operated under code names, and suggested that, as an acceptable subterfuge, they adopted the letters 'WO'. They would know what it meant, but the enemy would not. The Frenchmen accepted this compromise and the letters were adopted with the Cross of Lorraine as the operational name for the circuit. Few were aware of the formal SOE designation SYLVESTRE-FARMER.

Michael felt responsible for them all. He now found himself in the position of chief executive of a large, diverse and far-flung organization, while at the same time sales director, chief planner, finance officer, head of operations, personnel manager and chaplain. Since all his people were volunteers, he felt unable to sanction discipline or dismissal. They needed careful managing to ensure that they concentrated on what mattered, that inter-group rivalries and territorial disputes did not get out of hand, and that everyone who had ideas as to how the circuit should be run, or came forward with constructive suggestions and comments, received a sympathetic hearing from one of his lieutenants before being mildly chastised, encouraged or congratulated according to circumstances. Michael himself was constantly on the move, usually accompanied by his bodyguard Delacroix. He believed that it was safer for him to go to his men than for them to come to him and that it was in everyone's interests that only those who needed to know had any idea where he was.

One of his occasional destinations was Gondecourt. He had not forgotten his promise to Yvonne Pachy, and with the help of two former inmates of Loos who had joined the circuit he planned an expedition to blow the walls of the prison adjoining the women's quarters. At the beginning of March he sent a message to Yvonne asking her to meet him at *Café Delanghe* in Lille's Grand Place at five o'clock in two weeks' time. She was to wait no more than ten minutes, after which, if he had not arrived, she was to get up and go. When he arrived she was already there, but in the meantime he had learned that her mother Jeanne Pachy was no longer in Loos. [2]

Yvonne recalled:

'He said he had put a plan in place to break my mother out of Loos, but he had found out that she had been moved shortly after I was released, in August 1942. He said he would have to think again, but I think he knew it was an impossible situation. I asked him not to do anything that would make things worse for her. He nodded, and said that the arrangements had already been made, the Loos mission was in place, and he would let it go ahead, so that at least some poor souls might have their freedom. With that he stood and left, asking

me to stay for another fifteen minutes in case he was being followed. He told me he would come to Gondecourt again. At that time I believed that he was himself working for an escape line and had come back to Lille for the sole purpose of freeing us and the other prisoners from Gondecourt, as well as Marie-Jeanne and her mother, who had been arrested in Lille at the same time as us. He seemed to have a good idea of who was in the prison, but finding out where people had gone was almost impossible, because of Hitler's Nacht und Nebel *decree.'*[3]

He did let the plan go ahead, in the hope that some of the captives would reach freedom, but, in the event, all of those who broke out were quickly recaptured.

To impress on the men that they were joining a military organization, with a competent and visible leader, Michael insisted that he was always introduced and referred to as *Le Capitaine Michel,* or simply *Le Capitaine.* In the early days he would vet each new recruit personally and on Sunday mornings he – or in his absence, Lemercier – would gather them all together for what he termed his 'church parade', an opportunity to get to know faces and assess potential. As time passed and membership swelled, responsibility for vetting was shared with his lieutenants and the weekly gatherings were abandoned as an unnecessary risk. At the end of its first week the circuit had numbered just half a dozen sympathizers, and from this nucleus it quickly rose to 300 members. By August 1943 this would grow to around 800, covering an area from the Belgium frontier in the north to the departments of the Somme and the Aisne in the south and east. But that was in the future.

Michael had a formidable band of men at his disposal who were ready and eager to get at the Germans. They had come to him on a promise of action and were waiting expectantly. Now it was time for him to deliver. Yet few of them had combat or operational experience, and, if they were to succeed as a hard-hitting force they would have to be trained and given instruction in the sabotage materials and techniques they would need when the time came. For this Michael needed equipment and materials, and to get them he had to find suitable landing sites and have them approved by London.

Fortunately, this was something that could be carried out by men in the course of their innocent and lawful movements around the countryside, without the need for weapons and munitions. He formed and briefed a number of teams and sent them all over the region to look out for sites that could be made suitable for operations. They had to pinpoint the exact location of the field, report on whether it was perfectly flat, whether there were isolated trees or coppices, how far it was to the nearest house, and if there were any German installations in the vicinity, especially anti-aircraft batteries. When the enthusiastic and often wildly optimistic results started to pour in, Michael was faced with a pressing heavy workload. He had to scrutinize every detail of each report very carefully, verify the coordinates on a map, check that the stated dimensions met London's stringent requirements, and then go to see for himself, as a final check. This was something he could not delegate, for the RAF insisted that only a trained serving officer could make such critical assessments. Once satisfied that the conditions had been met, he then had to arrange for details to be passed to London for acceptance or rejection, a time-consuming business involving a succession of couriers to and from Paris.

Chapter notes
1   In fact, London did receive a number of faint transmissions around this time, but they were spasmodic and indecipherable – see Chapter 26.
2   My grandmother Jeanne Pachy was deported to Lübeck-Lauerhof in Germany in July 1943. From there she went to Cottbus and eventually to Ravensbruck. My mother, Yvonne, had to wait another three years for news of her.
3   Issued in December 1941 the *Nacht und Nebel* (Night and Fog) decree was meant to intimidate local populations into submission (and identify any members of the resistance) by denying friends and families of the missing any knowledge of their whereabouts. The prisoners were secretly transported to Germany, vanishing without trace. In 1945, the seized SD records were found to include merely names and the initials NN. Not even the sites of graves were recorded.

Chapter 11

Frustration

'Beneath the strain of expectation.'
Ronald Firbank

So far, the scope of operations had been as defined in Michael's briefing: to prepare for the invasion and avoid local action. This changed when the Germans moved into the previously unoccupied zone in the wake of the Allied landings in north Africa in November 1942. The chiefs of staff issued a new directive to SOE on 22 January, which resulted in F Section being given two main objectives: the sabotage of the German war effort by every means available, and the full support of the CARTE organization for as long as it was justifiable. Targets on which action was called for were allocated to each agent when he was briefed, and reconnoitred by him immediately upon his arrival in the field. The ban on violent action was removed, with the only proviso that sufficient stores should be kept back to deal with reserved railway targets.[1]

Suttill and his men became busy, carrying out sabotage incidents almost daily in the greater Paris area. These included attacks on electricity transformers, railways and oil and alcohol refineries. Michael, who heard about the new instruction on one of his frequent visits to Paris, could himself do nothing to implement the directive, except ensure that his men, growing in numbers daily, were kept busy with the many tasks that had to be fulfilled before FARMER could become an effective fighting force. Preparing for action for when an invasion came had seemed a sensible step, but the event itself was something for an as yet undefined future. Now the change of direction and the prospect of immediate action brought with it a new urgency.

The question of landing fields was paramount and the FARMER men were already working on this. Reception parties had to be set up to mark the dropping zones, recover the supplies under cover of darkness, and hide them until they could be recovered. Transport had to be found to move the heavy consignments, often some considerable distance, because it was clear that the RAF would only accept fields in remote rural areas, well away from established anti-aircraft defences or fighter airfields. However, all the important targets lay in the urban areas around Lille and Valenciennes. They needed to find secure storage locations, which were accessible to those who knew but unlikely to be disturbed by casual visitors or chosen for random searches. Arrangements then had to be made to distribute arms amongst the various groups. Once this was done – and only then – the process of training the men in the use of arms and explosives could begin. To make it all work Michael needed good communication with London, arms, vehicles, fuel, a source of false documentation to provide cover for all the necessary daily movements, and funds to keep the circuit going. It was a daunting list of requirements.

With most of the team busy in their own areas and businesses, the bulk of the early work fell to the tireless Lemercier. He abandoned his book selling, except in so far as it provided him with cover, and gave himself up full time to the circuit, travelling widely, often with Delacroix. He made numerous trips to the outskirts of Paris, where he picked up the few precious weapons that Michael could coax from PROSPER and took them to the *Aquarium.* He also went to Abbeville to make arrangements for the collection of an eclectic range of modest family cars, usually stolen and equipped with false number plates and documentation by the resourceful and inventive Duval. This arrangement served a number of purposes: it took the vehicles away from the area in which they had been purloined, ensured that Duval's premises remained as clean and legitimate as possible, and enabled their use in and around Lille, to where news of their theft would not have been sent and consequently no searches would be implemented.

Lemercier next invoked the aid of Emile Hertault, whom he had recruited at the beginning of the year and who owned a garage in Avenue Boufflers in Lambersart. This he had put at Michael's disposal, along with his own collection of vehicles, and it now proved the ideal location for delivery of the cars from Abbeville and any necessary repainting or touching up. Hertault had 18-year-old apprentice mechanic and driver Jean Woussen working for him, and the two of them saw their first taste of action when they joined Gerekens and Delacroix in a raid on a German fuel dump, staged in response to an urgent demand from Michael for petrol. The French workers and German supervisors were taken by surprise when a truck roared through the gates in the wake of an army tanker and pulled up close to a stock of 200 litre drums; three men leapt down from the vehicle and quickly hauled onboard two drums, before vanishing as quickly as they had come.

The energetic Descamps now brought off another coup, recruiting the commander of the Flanders group of the GMR* that had been formed in Lille. This was Adolphe Herry, a primary school teacher in Boulogne who had been taken prisoner at the age of 40 and sent to a camp in Dinan, from which he escaped. Never able to come to terms with the presence of the

---

* GMR – *Groupes mobiles de réserve* – barrack-based mobile police reserve

Germans, he did whatever he could to annoy them, which resulted in his capture and re-arrest while he was trying to get hold of plans for the fortifications at Cap Gris Nez. He was interrogated and handled roughly for three days, before being released on lack of evidence. He then heard about the formation of special police units, made some enquiries and, although he had no police experience, decided that he could do more to help bring about the liberation of his country if he was on the inside, and joined up. After six months' training he was made commandant in Lille. From that point on he had only one thought in his mind: to make contact with the resistance.

Descamps had targeted the GMR and had already recruited Herry's driver, who arranged for him to meet his boss. After a few tentative approaches he decided to make a direct proposition to Herry, who was delighted to accept. The next day Michael and Fertein met with Descamps and took the tram to Rue de Turenne, where Herry was waiting at the entrance to the barracks courtyard. Introductions were made and they all retired to the commandant's office, where they had a long, detailed discussion. Herry's task was gradually to turn the GMR into a resistance organization, in which he succeeded admirably, and the ongoing relative security of the circuit was due in no small measure to the collaboration of Herry and his colleagues, positioned as they were at the heart of the police system. Herry himself led a difficult double life throughout the occupation that was full of risks. As a serving policeman charged with inflicting the orders of the Vichy government on honest Frenchmen he had to endure their contempt, frequently being spat on and threatened, while at the same time using his position to make GMR resources available to the circuit – particularly vehicles to ferry arms, ammunition and explosives to the various undercover groups.

Michael now had a team of leaders that provided him with the support and encouragement he needed to guide the FARMER circuit through its early days. All of them had previous experience of working within some form of resistance group and had seen action; their courage and determination had been tested, and they had not been found wanting. They oversaw the organization of the men into regional groups, each under a designated leader whose task it was to ensure that members were placed in compartmentalized cells of no more than five people, with each cell unaware of the identity or composition of the others. Apart from Velge, they all lived with their families, and many had full-time jobs. There were no meetings or regular conferences. Casual visitors to headquarters were actively discouraged, and group leaders would come to Michael by appointment only.

The circuit resembled a spider's web, with Michael at the centre and his sector leaders as the anchor points. Malfait to the north and east, Fertein to the south-east, Chieux to the west and Velge in Belgium – along with Bayart, the industrialist, Herry the GMR commandant, and Gerekens the railway and communications supremo. Below these were the individual group leaders and cell leaders. Security was so tight that in more than one case members of the same family had been recruited in different cells and had no idea until after the war that they were each part of FARMER. Along the threads of the web moved the couriers – chiefly Simone Séailles, Angèle Malfait, Pierre Gérard and Denise Gilman. Lemercier, the fixer, and Delacroix, the minder, were based at headquarters, while Eliane Lemercier worked from her home.

There was no stopping Lemercier. He arranged with one of his 'customers', the director of the *Secrétariat des Prisonniers Libérés*, headquarters of the association that looked after released French prisoners of war, to sign him on as a secretary clerk at the *Maison du Prisonnier*, where they promptly had Michael registered as a *'volontaire de famille'*.*
This provided him with an effective cover, giving him legitimate reasons for moving around Lille as well as a perfectly genuine and priceless identity card that took him easily through police checkpoints. In the course of their 'duties' he and Lemercier were able to lay their hands on specimens of all the documents that the *réfractaires* would need in order to avoid the clutches of the STO. To deflect suspicion of their movements even more they both took to wearing the *Francisque* – a Vichy decoration – in their buttonholes and passing themselves off as supporters of Pétain. They disliked doing this because of the animosity they received from members of the public, but it was effective cover.

Lemercier then persuaded two young girls in the rations office at the Town Hall in Lille to pass him their official stamps, which he had copied. He found the documents needed to set up new identities for the *réfractaires,* and safe families to put them with. Descamps came up with vehicle registration documents and stamps from the police administration, as well as copies of various signatures, all of which he passed to Michael. Through a neighbour who worked in the mayor's office in Croi Descamps's brother-in-law obtained some blank mayoral forms that he handed to Fertein. The municipal engineer at the mayor's office in Lille had a card for the Ministry of Waters and Forests which he let Descamps copy.

The more successful and buoyant Lemercier became, the more despondent Michael must have felt about his own lack of achievement. He was well aware that the French character welcomed and relished the prospect of action, provided it was immediate, but became quickly discouraged if action was long deferred. He needed a supply drop, but the RAF had its own problems.

---

* Volunteer responsible for calling on families and processing enquiries about prisoners' wives

In his post-war report Colonel Buckmaster stated:

'Taking the period 1 December 1942 to 28 February 1943: – we were severely handicapped during this period in respect of despatch of personnel and stores to the field, partly owing to bad weather, but chiefly owing to lack of aircraft... . We had regular contacts with five W/T operators and occasional contacts with three others... . Our chief trouble during the three months under review, and indeed for the rest of 1943, was the chronic insufficiency of aircraft and the consequent impossibility of supplying stores, even in small quantities, to certain areas to the north and north-east of France. We were now entering the phase when our organizations in the field were sufficiently virile to make themselves felt both as organizers of subsequent guerrilla action and, more particularly, as the instigators of sabotage on a controlled plan.'[2]

This comment on the RAF, written post-war and with the benefit of hindsight, appears harsh. The attachment of a large part of the blame to the unavailability of aircraft, or, implicitly, to the air chiefs' refusal to make them available, is perhaps an understandable judgment from the viewpoint of SOE. But the truth was that the RAF had been far from idle and its crews were no less frustrated than Michael and his men on the ground. The fact that no supplies reached FARMER in February was due neither to shortage of aircraft nor reluctance to allocate them to supplying agents. The two dedicated support squadrons at Tempsford, nos. 138 and 161, were working flat out. As will be seen, they did try to reach FARMER.

As part of the preparation Michael had to compose a unique message for each landing ground. Occasionally he would ask his men what they would like to hear, and include it in the wording. The location, the message and the date from which he would be ready for operation were sent to London. From then on the men had to listen out each night to messages broadcast by the BBC after the nine o'clock news, in the hope and expectation that one of them would be for FARMER. An initial message would announce an operation planned for a given location, usually during the following night, and, if it was going ahead, a confirmation message would follow the next evening. At the first announcement the designated team would get itself ready, and at the second, it would set off in a vehicle to pick up the goods and take them to a store for onward distribution. As soon as they arrived at the landing ground the men would mark out the landing area with different coloured lights. Then all they could do was wait.

Proposed drop zones suggested by Michael in open countryside between Lille and Valenciennes, and between Arras and Sissonne in the south-east, were accepted, and the RAF drew up detailed instructions for each mission, starting with the period of the February moon. The first of these, code-named FARMER 1, was scheduled to take place between 21 and 27 January, 4km north-west of Valenciennes and 3km north-east of Herin. Five containers were to be dropped during the period between 15 and 21 February between 2200 hrs and 0200 hrs with a fall-back of the nights of 22 to 27 February, between 0000 hrs and 0400 hrs.[3]

On the night of 15 February Flight Lieutenant Austin arrived over the target at 0110 hrs and circled expectantly, looking in vain for marker lights and the long-short-short flashing of the agreed code sign 'D-Dog'. Standing operational instructions were for the aircraft to return to base with the full load if the reception lights were not seen, so after waiting for fifteen minutes he set course for home. A planned second attempt, due to be flown two nights later by Pilot Officer Clow, was cancelled because of heavy cloud across the whole of western Europe, but on the night of 25 February Clow finally took to the air with clear skies all the way to the French coast. This he crossed at 0220 hrs, before setting course for a point east of Arras, from where he planned to swing up to the target. West of Arras he ran into low haze and fog, and by the time he reached the drop zone the ground was completely covered, leaving him no alternative but to head back to England. One final attempt was made twenty-four hours later, the very last night of the operational window, when Pilot Officer Wynne was unable to identify any pinpoints, again because of low cloud, and he too was forced to turn back. Operating instructions were also issued for FARMER 2, calling for six containers to be dropped in fields located 5¼km south-west of Sissonne and 1½km north of Montaigu, during the period between 17 and 26 February. This mission was never executed.

Why no reception team was available for the first mission is a mystery, for there are no records to explain what did or did not happen on the ground, and there are no references anywhere to Michael preparing for drops in February. It is possible that he never received any of the coded signals, but it is clear that an opportunity had been missed; the RAF had certainly tried, but could do nothing more until the next full moon period at the end of March. Malfait had this to say:

'Through a combination of the incompetence of his radio operator and the heavy fog that set in during the winter nights, Trotobas had to wait five long months before he received his first small drop of five containers on 13 April 1943.'

In his report, Buckmaster described the situation in northern France in the following terms:

> *'At 28 February 1943 we had active groups in the following areas: Lille (no direct contact, very few stores) and Paris (two) good W/T contact. The F Section circuits had now got through their period of digging in and, as a result of the permission to go ahead with sabotage sent on 13 November 1942, had an important and steadily increasing number of sabotage jobs to their credit. They had by now ceased to be individual uncoordinated acts of brilliance by daring officers, and had become coordinated organizations with a strict code and strict discipline. The men went out into the field with a feeling of pride in their show. They saw the purport of it, and they could imagine the extent to which it might grow.'*

This may have been true of PROSPER, but as far as FARMER was concerned there had been no actions of any kind, and Michael was forced to turn his attention elsewhere. As well as re-defining the rules of engagement for sabotage, the directive of 22 January had called for support of the CARTE organization and expanded on this under two headings: evacuation of personnel, and delivery of arms and equipment. For the latter, token deliveries were to be continued during the February moon period, but these also failed to take place. The priority for evacuation was first of all Andre Girard, which suggested that SOE were keen to get him back to England for talks as soon as possible. At his initial meeting with Suttill in Paris Michael had agreed to give whatever assistance he could to CARTE, but he had received no contact from the group whatsoever and had no idea where to find them. As a precaution, he went to Abbeville to see how Duval was getting on with his escape line, in case Girard suddenly appeared asking for help.

Duval had been busy, trying to make his routes more secure. He knew conditions on each journey could change rapidly and arranged for people along the route to update him on what was happening each time he passed through. He recruited a friend, Colette Pye, and sent her to St Jean-de- Luz, a fishing village in the Basque region between Biarritz and the Spanish border and one she knew well, and made her responsible for working out ways to cross the frontier. This done, he returned home to begin looking for other suitable locations. At the end of December he installed his wife in a villa at Arcachon, with a view to her gathering information about the sector between Lamothe and Dax. However, the activities of the French police and the *Feldgendarmerie* soon made life too difficult, and the family moved to La Hume in the Gironde. Pye meanwhile had recruited an English-French-Spanish interpreter who lived in St Jean-de-Luz and two other Spanish speakers: they were given the job of finding Spanish border smugglers who could be persuaded to act as guides. A family in St Jean-de-Luz had volunteered to shelter fugitives in their villa, and their son, who lived in Bordeaux, offered to keep Duval updated on the stretch between Angoulême and Lamothe.

In Paris Duval had a team of four supporting him, and with the assistance of FARMER's railwaymen he travelled around freely on the footplate of goods engines, accumulating a wealth of information that would enable him to complete the line, which ran from the Belgium border to the Spanish border, passing through Lille, Paris, Bordeaux and St Jean-de-Luz. After Paris no individual journey would ever be made more than once as for reasons of security different trains and stops would be used. He told Michael that he expected the line to be fully operational by the end of March. Michael gave strict orders that priority was to be given to getting downed airmen back into the war and that all applications had to be approved by him personally. No doubt satisfied that progress was being made in one area at least, he returned to the problems awaiting him in Lille.

Chapter notes
1   Directive *DCDO/415 (HS6/322)*.
2   Extracted from *F Section History,* paragraph 27.
3   For operational plans and reports I have drawn on the *Pilot Operation Reports, Diaries of Operations* and *Operations Record Books* for 138 and 161 squadrons – *AIR20/8256, AIR20/8476* (not all of which are complete).

Chapter 12

Despair

'Do not confuse activity with action.'
F Scott Fitzgerald

During his frequent visits to Paris Michael had been following the process of Biéler's recovery. After Suttill's report of the outcome of the meeting with CARTE, SOE had sent a message recalling the Canadian to London as soon as he was fit to travel, but Biéler refused to go. At that meeting Heyermans had planted the seed of possible operations around St Quentin, and Suttill now followed up on this. He suggested that Biéler go there and take over one of the sub-groups that Suttill himself had set up when he recruited George Darling, a British Army officer who had stayed in France after Dunkirk and was now finding it difficult to coordinate activity in St Quentin as well as run the group he had set up around Trie-Château, where he lived with his girlfriend. Biéler was only too happy to agree, and once approval had come through from London he set off in the middle of March to establish under his codename *Tell*, the MUSICIAN network, based at the home of Eugène Cordellet, one of Darling's friends from his Army days. He was travelling with Simone Séailles, and on the way from Paris he asked her to take him to see *Sylvestre*.

Professor Michael Foot referred to this visit in picturesque terms:

> *'Michael Trotobas...settled in Lille and dived straight into the atmosphere of Graham Greene's* Brighton Rock. *Biéler, visiting him in the spring, found him having a bath in the scullery of the working man's house he was living in, arguing through the steam with some members of a gang of bookies' touts; others of his close acquaintance seemed even less savoury...Trotobas knew what he was up to. For a man in his late twenties, he was unusually worldly wise; he chose to work in circles that understood already the importance of keeping their mouths shut, weighed up the people he met, and soon assembled a strong and secure body of saboteurs, devoted to himself and supported by the least pro-German members of the local French police.'*[1]

PSM Trotobas
Middlesex Regiment
BEF in France 1939.

Mauzac Prison 1941 Trotobas in front centre legs astride.

Auxy-Juranville railway
station where the three
agents made their way to in
the early hours of 19
November 1942.

Bar Mado, first HQ at
No 4 Parvis St Michel,
Lille. Now called *Le
Bel Ouvrage.*

Trotobas in Lille on the day of the christening of his godson, son of Manu and Eliane.

Trotobas French ID photograph.

Trotobas British Military ID Card.

Trotobas in uniform of the
Middlesex Regiment 1939.

Arthur Staggs in Lille.

Arthur and Paul Malfait.

Emmanuel Lemercier
'*Manu*' in Lille.

Francis Suttill leader of PROSPER in Paris
SOE P/F photograph.

Arthur Staggs SOE P/F photograph.

André Dubois *'Hercule'* wireless operator to
several F Section circuits SOE P/F
photograph.

Gustave *'Guy'* Biéler leader of
MUSICIAN in St Quentin SOE P/F
photograph.

Postcard (front and reverse) of Lille signed by Trotobas and sent to Julien Chapelet in St Erme.

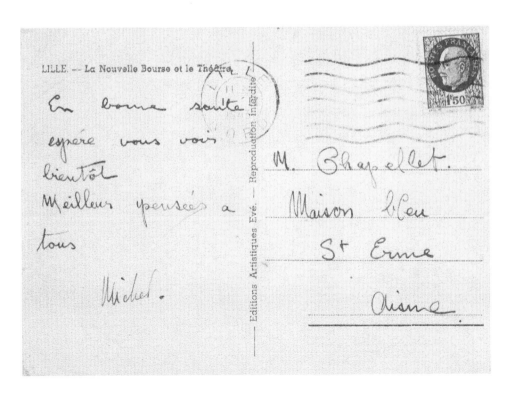

Trotobas with Yvonne
Pachy in Rue National
late 1943.

Yvonne Pachy with
Trotobas and Louis
Cochet late 1943.

Désiré De Becker in Police
uniform at the time of the
Fives raid in July 1943.

Mr and Mrs Désiré De Becker in
Wattrelos 1997.

François William Reeve *'Olivier'* SOE P/F Lille.

Denise Gilman partner of Trotobas.

Home in Arras of Henri Dewispelaere where he and Reeve were arrested.

Pierre
VANESLANDER

Jacky
GEREKENS

Pierre
SERILLES

Arthur
MALFAIT

First memorial in Lille Southern Cemetery when 14,000 French citizens attended 1945.

Stephen Grady (right) officiates at the new housing estate memorial named after Trotobas 1950s.

RÉSIDENCE DU
CAPITAINE MICHEL
SOE W.O. LONDRES
1939 - 1943

Marcel Fertein at one of the post-war memorial services in Lille.

Members of the Middlesex Regiment Association together with French patriots march together at Lille Southern Cemetery 1998.

Yvonne Pachy
schoolgirl.
.

Mr and Mrs
Aimé Binot with
SOE parachute at
their farm at
Ransart.

Stewart Kent presents Mr and Mrs Aimé Binot with an FCO attestation in recognition of their help to SOE and Trotobas 1998.

Pierre Séailles DSO French second-in-command to Trotobas at his home near Paris 1997.

Nick Nicholas outside
No 20 Avenue Belfort in
Lille 2010.

Stewart Kent with
Stephen Grady in
Greece 1997.

Yvonne Baudet née Pachy having just received her Legion d'Honneur from the mayor at the Town Hall of St Quay Portrieux, Brittany 2 March 2015.

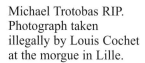

Stephen Grady in Greece with a German grain sack.

Michael Trotobas RIP. Photograph taken illegally by Louis Cochet at the morgue in Lille.

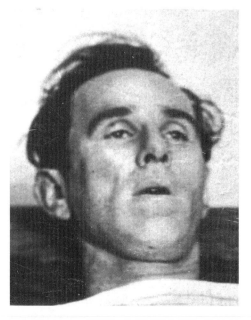

It would have suited Michael to be perceived as a petty criminal, and therefore not worth the time of any serious policeman or investigator. Like all urban organizers, he needed the shady characters of the underworld – forgers who could replicate signatures and official stamps, locksmiths who could break into offices and storerooms, safebreakers who could prise open secure cabinets, burglars who could navigate Lille's darkened streets during the blackout, and toughs who could be relied on to extricate themselves and others from bad situations. They formed a closed community of men used to looking after themselves and each other, naturally wary and suspicious of outsiders and of anyone remotely resembling authority.

The *Aquarium* – known within the circuit as *Mado's* or *Bar Mado* – was his command post and it was here that his leaders came to deliver good or bad news, make their case for a particular operation they favoured, or simply stake a claim for more weapons, supplies or money. The unique atmosphere of the headquarters was graphically described post-war, first by Duval in an interview with author Danièle Lheureux:

> '*To get into the back room you had to show your credentials because Lucien Delacroix would always receive you with gun in hand. There you would meet Velge, Vanspranghe and Delacroix who would let off steam about something or other or complain about lack of arms,* Manu *who needed money, etc etc.*'

Malfait expanded on this at some length:

> '*Strictly speaking the HQ was located behind the bar in a little room with an exit onto the rue de Fleurus. Furnished with cabinets, a wardrobe, a table, several low chairs that served as seats during the day and bunks at night, and a petrol heater, it was crammed with explosives, crates, old salvaged weapons, machine guns, revolvers of every calibre and ammunition. Near the suitcase containing false papers and maps were a transmitter and a wireless.* Michel, Denise Gilman, Lulu,[Delacroix] Velge, Rowies and many others hid there and slept in the rooms, on the benches or even on the ground, as also the many illegal workers and airmen waiting to leave. With the daily comings and goings of the intelligence and liaison agents on occasion the HQ resembled a beehive.*
>
> '*This room gave off a strong sense of terrorism, but in fact none took place there. You would find* Lulu *[Delacroix] or* Jahncke *[Velge] preparing a modest supper on the stove. The background noise masked the secret conversations between Michel and one or other of the inhabitants, each of whom came to him for good or bad news.*

Occasionally a loud thump on the door would interrupt proceedings. Everyone withdrew from the line of sight from the door, which was opened by Lulu *or* Jahncke, *revolver in hand, ready for any eventuality, and then a member of the network would come in. Sometimes the knock would come from the door beside the café and a head would appear, unknown to anyone other than Michel. "Come in!" he would say, indicating that he knew the new arrival and there would be no introductions.'* [2]

It was typical of Michael's leadership, and of his confidence in himself and his men, that the intense activity centred on the headquarters, with agents and escapers coming and going, should take place in broad daylight, right in the centre of Lille and at the very heart of enemy-occupied territory. It was also typical of his leaders that, after the shock of their initial visit, they accepted the situation as perfectly natural, such was their faith and trust that their chief knew what he was doing and that he would always be looking out for their safety. This strategy of hiding in plain view was one that had been tried and tested throughout history, as Michael knew well, and his strict instruction, that no-one was to engage in any overt activity against the Germans until he gave the order, ensured that the security forces had no reason to come looking for saboteurs.

There was nothing more natural than men and women congregating in a bar: café life was an integral part of French society, and the chances of a detailed random search of the premises without some incident to trigger it were remote. The everyday risks of checkpoints had to be accepted: Michael could do nothing about those, and on any routine visits by police a prearranged signal brought all conversation and activity in the back room to a halt. But he applied rigid discipline to ensure his men did nothing to draw attention to the hotel, and he came down hard on any infringement, even if unintended. Although danger was always just around the corner, every member was convinced of the circuit's invincibility because their leader himself clearly believed in it. It was Michael's style to foster self-belief in his followers by openly displaying his own: men who were constantly looking over their shoulder were of no use to him. Yet they were growing impatient, so he took himself off to Paris to try to pressurize Norman into pushing London yet again for news of supplies.

SOE's ambitious programme for March provided for twenty-one men and approximately 1,000 containers to be sent into France. However, owing to unrelenting atrocious weather conditions, only three men were inserted, along with just forty containers, ten of which fell straight into enemy hands. Among the cancelled missions were planned re-runs of FARMER 1 between 11 and 26 March, and of FARMER 2 during the same period. Both were re-scheduled for April. The effect on morale across all the active circuits was significant, as Buckmaster recalled:

'We reported at the end of March that unless during April and May we succeeded in sending stores and money in large quantities to the field, as well as up-to-date directives in writing, we risked seeing the whole fabric crumble and waste away. We suspected the beginning, at that time, of an apathy fed upon the absence of action potentiality which, subsequently, manifested itself surprisingly even as late as just prior to the invasion, and most notably in October 1943. Had we been able to send more stores and thus provide more outlet for hatred of the oppressor, this apathy would have been abated without, we believe, provoking the general insurrection which was to become a bogey of SHAEF* (although not of F Section) before the close of the operation. At 28 March 1943 it could be said in general terms that only the lack of stores on the ground prevented our being able to carry out orders for action over a very great part of France.' [3]

The lack of activity on the ground, which no doubt reminded Michael of the 'phoney war' in 1940, would have given him the opportunity to reflect on resistance in France as a whole, and on the various groups he was likely to encounter. He had been well briefed on this, and in mid-March the situation was summed up in a lengthy SOE memorandum, from which the following extract is pertinent.

'CARTE (Non-political)... . This...is one of the oldest, and in its organization one of the most secure, of the Resistance movements. British officers have spent some time at the headquarters in France, and Carte *himself is now here for consultation; when he returns, we propose to send with him three British officers as a "Board of Control". The special value of* Carte's *system lies in the travelling instructors who go round teaching the members on the lines laid down by us.'* [4]

Michael did not know that Girard was already back in England. Equally SOE was unaware that, as a result of a careless breach of security, the addresses of CARTE members had been found in a briefcase on a train and handed to the *Abwehr*, who had moved swiftly to arrest all those named and effectively close down the organization. Girard himself did not return to France and SOE took its own decision not to support the CARTE organization any longer, on the basis that it had no practical value and was too large and insecure. It was decided to split it up into smaller circuits

---

* SHAEF – Supreme Headquarters Allied Expeditionary Force – the organization set up to direct the invasion

which, it was hoped, would carry out active sabotage. One of the circuits that was to figure prominently in the activities of FARMER was DONKEYMAN, within which radio operator André Dubois provided an independent and virtually freelance transmission service from his base near Tours, operating as a sub-circuit with the code name HERCULE.

After dealing with Free French organizations, the Communists, the Poles, and activities in the former unoccupied zone, the report turns its attention to the groups operating north of the former demarcation line. These included the OCM, of whom it was reported a senior French liaison officer, accompanied by an SOE section officer, was currently in France.[5]

The report made it clear that competition was fierce, not only for active personnel and supporters but also for funds, arms and equipment and Michael would have been concerned that he would lose men to more active groups if his fortunes did not very quickly take a turn for the better. He decided to make a personal tour of his territory, with the twofold aim of raising funds and boosting the morale of his leaders. He was moderately successful in the first, eliciting promises of donations from various quarters, and he received good news from his busy lieutenants.

Fertein, who was recruiting in the south, took him to view the ruins of the First World War Hindenburg Line near Fontaine-les-Croisilles, where both men agreed that the overgrown trenches and rat-infested bunkers would provide excellent storage for arms and supplies. Bayart told him that another good location had been found in the Conservatoire de Lille, in the north of the city. At the gate to the Fives-Lille locomotive works, which was Michael's prime target, Chieux told him he expected to be able to put his hands on detailed plans of the factory before very long, and had recruited a handful of sympathizers from the workforce. Gerekens and Liébault explained to him the vulnerable points of the extensive marshalling yards at Lille-Déliverance; and, during a walk along the towpath of the Roubaix–Tourcoing canal, Malfait showed him where charges could best be placed to sabotage the locks and barge houses.

They took him to see some of their men but his visits did not have the intended effect. When they saw their chief the men were delighted, assuming, as Malfait recorded, that he had come to bring them news of supplies or impending action but there was disappointment in their faces when he told them he had nothing to offer and asked them to continue to keep the faith. The unspoken question in everyone's mind was: when will it happen?

The lack of activity affected everyone, and at the end of March Staggs left Lille to live with his boyhood friend, Claude Bagein, in Roubaix. Staggs was to play no further part in the circuit's activities, except for two occasions when Michael used him as a courier. This could be considered a symbolic departure, heralding the beginning of a new era: after all, spring was just around the corner, and with it came renewal of hope.

Chapter notes
1   Extracted from *SOE in France, Chapter IX: Middle Game: 1943.*
2   Malfait's description of the bar and the two paragraphs that follow are taken from the WO booklet *Le Coup de Main de Fives et Historique du Début du Réseau* (see Introduction).
3   Extracted from *F Section History paragraph 33.*
4   *The function of resistance groups in France* – memorandum by SOE 15 March 1943 *(HS6/322).*
5   The British officer was Wing Commander Yeo-Thomas – see Chapter 21.

Chapter 13

Optimism

'To pluck bright honour from the pale-fac'd moon.'
Henry IV Part I

On 9 April Michael was back in Abbeville with Duval and his team, examining two possible drop zones south of the town, one at Huppy and the other on the outskirts of Pont-Rémy. He approved both and had the coordinates transmitted via Paris the next day. Then, in the evening of 12 April, the long-awaited notification finally came through: *'Michael says "patience"'*. This heralded the long overdue FARMER 1 drop in fields at Aubry-du-Hainaut, near the Raismes forest, west of Valenciennes. The operational instruction gave the period of the drop as between 0000 hrs and 0400 hrs (local time) on the night of the 13/14, and the five-man reception team, which included Martel and his wife, was in place just after 2300 hrs. As instructed they waited patiently for the aircraft to arrive and were prepared to stay on for a further hour after the deadline if necessary. Just after 0215 hrs they heard the sound of engines, and Sénéchal flashed out the DASH-DASH-DOT of the agreed code letter 'D' signal at ten second intervals, which was spotted by Flight Lieutenant Dodkin 500 ft above. After making one precautionary circuit of the area he brought the aircraft in from the north-west, over the forest, and at 0237 hrs dropped five containers, all of which arrived safely in the immediate vicinity of the drop zone.[1]

Michael had arranged to spend the night with Beirnaert, and he heard the aircraft pass overhead. The two of them waited anxiously until shortly after 0400 hrs, when they heard Sénéchal's whistle, and both men helped the reception team to stow the materials temporarily in and around the caravan. They were collected by Lemercier, Delacroix and Velge over the next two days and taken to Robbe's house in Ronchin, a southern suburb of Lille.

A second drop north-west of Arras had been planned for the period of the April moon, but this did not take place. Nevertheless, Michael was pleased and encouraged by the results of the Aubry reception: it had been a copybook operation and a good beginning. He was also encouraged to hear from Duval that, during March, Pye's husband and a companion had inaugurated the escape line, reaching Spain without incident. He felt a sense of relief that at long last they were in a position to do something. He was heartened further when on 7 May Simone Séailles brought her brother to him.

After his release from Mauzac, Pierre Séailles had received a message from his sister that a certain 'Michel' was waiting for him, and had made haste to join him. His arrival heralded an important change in the circuit's leadership and organization, for the next day Michael took him to the Morival factory and introduced him to Bayart. He had made up his mind that these two powerful personalities would be his deputies – Bayart, older and more experienced, and Séailles, younger and more active. To demonstrate the importance of the meeting he took the unprecedented step of introducing the two Frenchmen by their real names: he needed them to have utter confidence and faith in each other and knew it was essential that they had the opportunity to talk about their background, their experiences, their beliefs and their visions for the circuit. It was a calculated gamble because the two men might not have hit it off, with unhappy consequences for their future cooperation, but they took to each other immediately, pledging their absolute commitment to the circuit and its mission.

Michael could now feel confident that, if anything happened to him, the circuit would continue to flourish in preparation for the day that Allied troops would land in France. He explained to Bayart and Séailles how the Buckmaster circuits functioned, and instructed them to get in touch with London, if anything happened to him, and ask for a replacement British officer to be sent. This did not in any way reflect a lack of confidence in them, but simply the political reality that SOE required operations and funds to be under the command and control of a trained British officer. He disclosed to them the code number that would enable London to identify them.

The consequences of Séailles arrival were to prove cataclysmic for Lemercier, who, up to this point, had been tacitly acknowledged as Michael's *de facto* second-in-command. Now he had to make way for Séailles. The decision to replace him was one Michael would not have taken lightly, since *Manu* had done a magnificent job in setting up the circuit, raising funds, finding premises and organizing logistics. However, these were no longer the priority, and Lemercier was not a man for the frontline. The operational experience and skills of Bayart and Séailles made them far better equipped to plan and organize the active resistance that was the circuit's next step.

Michael confided to Séailles that he thought that Lemercier was showing signs of strain and had begun to struggle to keep pace with the circuit's rapid growth. He had also become distracted by concern about his wife Eliane's pregnancy.

When their first child was born on 6 May Lemercier was away on a mission, so Michael, Velge and Denise took it in turns to visit Eliane in the maternity home. When Lemercier returned, the happy parents decided to call their son after Michael and invited their friend to be his godfather, a responsibility that he was happy to accept and promising that, whatever happened, the child's future would be provided for. He attended the baptism on 10 May under his cover name of Michel Rampal.

All of this could only have made his decision to ease Lemercier out even more difficult. While Lemercier appeared to accept the situation with dignity and composure, promising to make himself useful in other ways, Eliane was later to write that he had been hurt badly by Michael's casual pragmatism and felt betrayed by someone to whom he had, literally, entrusted his life and that of his family. Although he gave no outward sign, and in fact soon settled into a secondary role, deep down the hurt remained and it proved to be the first tiny crack in the wall of security and trust that had been built up around the circuit. [2]

Michael now entrusted to Séailles the details of his couriers and letterboxes, explaining that through his sister Simone would come reports from PROSPER and PHYSICIAN. Then he told him how to contact Malfait through his principal letterboxes, and that he would be able to contact Fertein via Bayart. With the collusion of the *préfect*'s wife, Jeanne Chieux arranged for a letterbox within the *prefecture* itself and introduced Michael to a number of key men in *La Voix du Nord** in Flanders, including Pierre Lemaire and his deputy, Jean Sonneville. Fertein acted as liaison between Michael and Lemaire. Working from Lille, Chieux also took care of communications between the various groups and headquarters and was also able to contact Michael through his sister, while maintaining communication with Herry through his wife Jeanne, who went to work with the commandant. Chieux also made his own home available as a letterbox.

Séailles swung into action. At the end of his meeting with Bayart Michael had instructed him to get up to speed with everything that the circuit was currently doing although he was not to take part in any operations for the time being. He tasked him with drawing up a plan of action that could be implemented immediately the Allies landed, and handed over a list of London's priority objectives for destruction, stressing that they were to be put into effect immediately after the landings and not a moment before. Séailles, who adopted the code name *Pierrot*, set about this task energetically, carrying out a careful reconnaissance of the territory in order to familiarize himself with his future targets. Gerekens was assigned to help

---

* *La Voix du Nord*: an underground newspaper founded in Lille in 1941 as the 'resistance organ of French Flanders'. It is still going strong today as a respected daily publication. The name was adopted by Lemaire's group.

him, and he found Séailles busy planning post-invasion attacks, studying all the possibilities and determining the best sequence of events for each objective. Séailles's principal focus was on preserving the supply of electricity throughout the region and preventing wholesale destruction by the retreating Germans of the power stations linking into the central grid.

Under Séailles, intelligence gathering reached new levels. Descamps was able to gain access to signals relating to the German Army's equipment and movements, information he passed on to Verstraete. Each evening Fertein would correlate information received locally with messages received via the BBC. To confirm some of the finer details, more groundwork was necessary, and with the agreement of his boss Descamps temporarily gave up his job to work at this. In May he provided a wealth of information on enemy dispositions and movements, the progress of construction work on fortifications, and the creation and locations of fuel and ammunition dumps. Duval provided intelligence on the airfield at Abbeville and on work being carried out there, both inside and outside its perimeter. From other sources information began to pour in about electrical installations and security in the coastal area from Calais to Boulogne and Dunkirk, as well as details of U-Boat activity, the routeing of German supply trains, and, eventually, launching sites for the V1 rockets. To these could be added up-to-date intelligence on the activities of the river police, sketches and sometimes actual plans of the layout of factories, electricity sub-stations, the location of underground shelters, German headquarters, the German central postal and communications station on the road from Douai to Lesquin, the telephone lines that led into the centre of Lille, the transmitter at Vendeville, the airfield at Lesquin and a host of other useful details. Michael had it in mind to cut off the electricity supplies of Nord-Pas de Calais from the rest of the country, and ordered a plan to be prepared to achieve this with the minimum of damage to the national electricity supply. As a result, layout and connection diagrams for the supplies between the three northern centres and the rest of the national network were stolen and found their way to him. All of this information was collated by Fertein, and, depending on circumstances, transmitted to London or used by the circuit itself.

Séailles also relieved Michael of another pressing worry: how to provide his men with the wide range of documents they would need to cover all their movements and support the various false identities that would enable them to get close to their intended targets. He wanted to set up a centralized and professional supply service that would be able to produce documents with the highest possible levels of authenticity and consistency of quality. Until Séailles arrived he had no idea where he could find someone with the necessary experience to do this, on a more or less full-time basis and under conditions of maximum security.

While in the Army Séailles had learned to create false passes by using paste and special inks that were available commercially for making up restaurant menus. When he left Mauzac he had been given a mimeographed release document, which he presented to the prefecture in Périgueux, and they then issued him with identity papers and ration cards. It struck him at the time that the form might come in handy and he had made a copy. When he was released he presented it to the mayor's office in Châteauroux, where no questions were asked and he was given an official identity card and food coupons. He showed the real and the false documents to Michael, who complimented him on the quality of the forgeries. Séailles immediately set up a bespoke production line, slowly improving his techniques until, eventually, he had a small team capable of churning out authentic false papers and identities on a regular basis. He himself usually used the papers of one or other of the French police groups, and when travelling in a car always had his card giving him permission to carry arms and move around. During the whole of his time in Lille, he never had the slightest difficulty with his identity papers. [3]

It was as a result of this activity that the already uneasy relationship between Séailles and Lemercier became even more strained, as reported during Séailles's interview in January 1945:

> *'As already stated, Informant* [Séailles] *replaced* MANU *as principal lieutenant to* MICHEL. *He told* MICHEL *at this time that he did not like* MANU's *way of working nor the people he was recruiting into the organization. A difficult situation was created by* MANU's *resentment of Informant and* MICHEL's *gradual setting aside of* MANU's *recruits… .Informant suspected that* MANU *was giving certain information to the Germans and, in addition, knew him to be selling to people not in the organization the identity cards which Informant was manufacturing.'*

There is no record of Michael's reaction, but Lemercier himself had told him from the outset how he worked, and his contacts were valuable: he was a trader and was always ready to strike a deal. The luxuries he was able to provide were coveted as much by the occupation forces as by the local population and, by frequently selling back to the Germans in one establishment goods he had previously acquired from another, he provided the circuit with much-needed funds as well as useful information about military personnel and operations. He was constantly sowing favours to be called in at a later date, and the identity cards were almost certainly just another example.

Neither Séailles nor Lemercier played any part in the reception of the second supply drop, which took place exactly one month after the first on the same ground, on a clear, starlit night. The initial message *'The flag is flying over the church'* came through on 12 May, and the next evening Michael himself led the reception party of Delacroix, Rowies, Velge, Woussen, Hertault and René Crampon – one of Vanspranghe's recruits – to the Aubry fields. Dodkin was again the pilot, and arriving over the drop zone at 0245 hrs he quickly spotted Delacroix's flashing DASH-DASH of the code letter 'M'. This time he elected to make his run in from the north, but as he did so was momentarily distracted by a flashing DASH-DOT-DASH ['K'] from outside the forest. One of the parachutes failed to open and the container embedded itself deep in the earth, but the team recovered the remaining four containers, Hertault handling the onward transportation in his own lorry. The first container could not be retrieved, as a result of which the field had to be abandoned as a site for future drops. [4]

However, the method of planning and operation had been proven, and the pattern was established for all future drops. As each consignment arrived Michael arranged for the contents to be distributed among the groups, and instruction would begin the moment they had the bare minimum of equipment. Handbooks on the use and handling of the various weapons came with each consignment, but there were only enough of them for one copy to be given to each sector leader. Eliane Lemercier managed to type up twenty copies and Martel, now living with his wife at Lemercier's, was given the job of distributing them. It was down to the sector leaders to arrange onward distribution by whatever transport could be found, missions that might seem unremarkable were it not for the fact that a German patrol might appear at any time and decide to inspect the contents of the beer barrels, wine casks, and other miscellaneous vessels in which the goods were stowed. Carrying out these missions called for a great deal of sangfroid and resourcefulness, qualities the men of the circuit possessed in abundance, as Malfait found when he opened his front door one day to find Delacroix and Velge there with a broken-down van that they had pushed physically through the Lille-Wattrelos crossing. It contained a cargo of guns and ammunition hidden in six innocent-looking chemical drums bearing the legend 'Civil Defence'.

Sometimes operations simply could not proceed because of bad weather at either end, like the planned FARMER 3 drop near Magnicourt-en-Comte on the night of 21 May, which was aborted because of 'thick haze and drizzle'. It was the only reception party in which Séailles took part, which no doubt explains why he recalled it in such detail.

Alerted by the message *'Michael kisses Henri and Nénette'*, Michael, Séailles and Delacroix hurried round to Hertault's garage in Lambersart, intent on going to the drop zone to help the reception team. The venture was beset with problems: Hertault's old van, a gas burner, refused to start for the best part of an hour, then the party became lost in the darkness and fog, and it was only when they passed through an unmanned sentry post on the outer perimeter of an airfield that Michael realized where they were. Carefully reversing course, they eventually arrived at the drop zone, where the reception team waited for nearly two hours before calling it a night. On their return to Lille they ran into a German checkpoint, from which they managed to extricate themselves with some difficulty.

When recounting this story Séailles provided further insight into Michael's leadership style:

'It's important to recall that Trotobas knew every airfield in the region… .Coming back from a mission at Arras the vehicle passed this same camp, and without saying anything to the men Michel went through the entry gate, waved a vague salute at the sentries, drove on further, taking a good look at the aircraft, then drove out again completely naturally with a smile for the sentries. "See, you don't need to be afraid of these guys."'

Although nothing was received on this occasion, the first two drops had yielded sufficient material for Michael to begin training his men. This was carried out on a cascading basis: Michael and Séailles trained the sector leaders, they then trained their group leaders, who passed it on to their teams. In an abandoned building adjoining his home Chieux set up an arms school, where lessons were given on handling the Sten gun and making explosive charges. The men were shown how to take the gun apart, put it back together again and load it. At the end of each day, under Michael's direction, Bayart and two of his workers, Edgar Galmace and Gaston Doby gave live fire instruction for the younger members at targets positioned on bales of straw inside Bayart's factory, where the noise of the shots was masked by that of the running machinery. They learnt to fire their weapons while lying down, kneeling down, standing up and while running. The lights were then turned off and they had to dismantle and reassemble the guns in the dark.

Bayart provided instruction on how to assemble nail bombs, and, as membership grew, Malfait, Vandesype, Vanhecke and Dubocage did the same. Jean Vandeneeckhoutte provided military training and basic introduction to explosives, including the use of time pencils. These were slender cylinders about the size of a fountain pen with a thin copper tube at one end containing a glass ampoule of copper chloride and a detonator in the middle. When the copper end was pressed hard the glass broke, releasing the acid, which then began to eat away at a steel wire. When this snapped it released a spring-loaded striker, which fired a percussion cap that ignited the plastic explosive. The time delay was determined by the concentration of acid and there were five standard versions, distinguished by coloured strips stuck on the side of the pencils: black indicated ten minutes' delay, red thirty minutes, green six hours, yellow twelve, and blue twenty-four.

The plastic explosive itself had been developed between the wars by Nobel Chemicals Ltd in England, and one of the simplest had the production code 'Nobel 808', usually referred to by the British as simply 808, and by the French as *le plastique*. It was a versatile material, relatively safe to use and handle. Michael's men were shown how nothing happened when it was dropped on the ground, kicked or even had a shot fired into it. It was not dangerous as long as it was kept cool, but when it was heated up it became highly explosive. Cut into any appropriate shape and size it was moulded around the object to be destroyed. Unlike dynamite it was not a cutting explosive as such and was best used for melting sections of railway lines, electricity generators, locomotive pistons and virtually anything else made of steel. Primer, time pencils and detonating cord were all that was needed.

Another useful and easily-assembled device was the clam, a smaller portable version of the limpet mines developed for anti-shipping warfare. It was an explosive charge with a Bakelite casing that could be carried around in pockets or shoulderbags, and was fitted with magnets that could be clamped to any magnet-receptive material and primed. It was an excellent weapon for machinery of all kinds.

Michael laid down a few ground rules. When targeting railways, time should be taken to choose a spot where derailment would cause maximum disruption and take the enemy longer to repair the track and remove the locomotive and trucks. Ideal areas included cuttings, where access for cranes and recovery vehicles would be difficult, and on high ground, from where the rolling stock might run down the side of the hill or mountain and cause more damage. On no account were they to target trains that were specifically for civilians. Where the target was machinery of any kind, particularly in numbers, it was best to destroy the same part or parts on each machine. This would prevent cannibalization of parts from one disabled unit for use in another.

The training and weapons induced a hive of activity in each sector. As soon as the lectures were finished everyone knew that from that point on they were under orders to be ready and available at all times to serve the circuit. Finally, the day came when Michael was able to instruct a selected band of men to go into action, and he arranged a number of minor acts of sabotage to reinforce the training and harden the men for the future operations he was planning. On one exercise he led a group that included Malfait, Dubocage and Vanhecke to the Lille-Baisieux railway line for their 'baptism of fire'. He told them to lay explosives at a certain point on the track and was unimpressed by what he felt to be their initial overcautious and furtive approach, which, he felt would be sure to attract attention rather than allay suspicion. Malfait recalls how Michael then demonstrated the importance of being relaxed and confident, strolling along by the track and whistling cheerfully, hands in pockets, and looking for all the world as if he were going for a walk in the country. When he came back, he reinforced his point, stressing that looking as if they had something to hide was certain to attract attention. If anyone had seen him, well, he was just a man taking some exercise.

In spite of this over-simplification and the obvious need to explain away arms and explosives, the men took his point, and this awareness was to stand them in good stead. After watching them rehearse again, he pronounced himself satisfied. They listened attentively to his directions for laying the charges. They first had to mould a large lump of the 808 around the 'T' of the rail, before sticking a fuse in it and crimping it. The resulting explosion would create a gap of 8 or 9cm, which would be enough to derail a small train, and two charges about half a metre apart would derail a fifty-tonne locomotive. Adding three or four more charges at similar intervals would see off a large heavy military train carrying vehicles. On this occasion they succeeded in derailing the next Baisieux-Rouen train. The next morning, railwaymen reported that 4m of track had been destroyed, causing widespread delays and interruptions to the timetables.

In its monthly report at the beginning of June SOE noted:

> *'Lille group (FARMER). This group, highly individualistic, has now received some stores, but not anything like enough to meet their full requirements. Their choice of landing grounds is restricted by the defences of the neighbourhood, and operations are tricky there. BAKER [Staggs] has still been unable to contact us, owing probably to damage to his set, but a new set should have reached him last moon. Meanwhile contact through BUTCHER [Norman].'*[5]

The circuit's period of inactive adolescence was nearly over and, ready or not, Michael's men had to go into action. He had prepared them as well as he could, both by training and by personal example, and had given them some fine leaders. He had nothing but admiration for their commitment and fervent patriotism, but so far there had been only words: they had yet to be put to the test, and deep in his heart he knew that not all would survive the dangerous months that lay ahead.

It was this that led him to take Malfait to the Crétinier cemetery in Wattrelos, where he stood with head bowed over the graves of his British comrades who had fallen in the campaign of May 1940. He told Malfait about the events of July 1941, when a number of patriots from the Sapin Vert quarter were celebrating Bastille Day with a ceremony at the cemetery. The police commissioner had only been at Wattrelos for a month and knew none of the men personally, but he was concerned enough to start gathering up the various flags and plaques that had been carefully and lovingly laid. His actions incensed the crowd and caused a number of minor skirmishes to break out between the patriots and the policemen. The next day twenty-seven people were arrested by the French police, taken to the commissary at Wattrelos, and then handed over to the Germans, who took them to the *Feldgendarmerie* in Lille. After interrogation they were all condemned and punished with sentences ranging from upwards of five years in the prison at Loos.

Michael had not forgotten these people and their organizers, and he paid quiet tribute to them. A large number of those who took part in the ceremony at the cemetery in Wattrelos would later join the resistance, and several of them came into the FARMER circuit. Malfait was moved visibly by the story and, as Michael had hoped, the tale of the villagers' courage and Michael's homage to them spread rapidly through the circuit, adding a final spur and incentive to the waiting and impatient men. Their moment had come.

Chapter notes

1   In this chapter I have again drawn on 138 Squadron records *(AIR/20/8256 & AIR/20/8476)*.
2   Eliane Lemercier told of her husband's distress in a letter to me in 1998.
3   Séailles was interviewed by Major Hunt (probably from the Special Intelligence Service) in January 1945 *(P/F/20)*. It is a lengthy report with several annexes.
4   The mysterious 'K' signal was never explained.
5   Extracted from *HS6/327*. No replacement transmitter reached Michael. The reference to the 'last moon' must refer to the May drops, and it is possible that the set was in the container that buried itself in the ground on 12 May and was never recovered.

Chapter 14

Fives

'Judicious use of sabotage.'
Thorstein Veblen

In the course of the intensive preparation and training for operations Michael had not forgotten his commitment to help repatriate Allied airmen and soldiers. By the end of May a number of successful transits to Spain had been made via Duval's line, and the story of Irishman Thomas Hutton and his companions provides a vivid illustration of the detailed planning and coordination that was in place.

In mid-April Flight-Sergeant Hutton's Lancaster bomber was hit by flak over Pilsen in Czechoslovakia. A fire broke out, and, mishearing an order because of a fault in the intercom, Hutton bailed out, along with Rudkin, the rear gunner, and McKay, the bombardier. In the event the aircraft arrived safely back at its base, but for these three men their return was to take somewhat longer. Thanks to the cooperation and bravery of an assortment of Belgian farmers, postmen, salesmen, and on one occasion the local priest, they were passed from village to village north-west into the Pas de Calais. Hutton arrived in Wattrelos on the 1 June, where his sojourn at the home belonging to Vandesype sheds some interesting light on the commitment and involvement of the families of the resistance men, and on their often reckless and risky behaviour. Doubtless this is attributable in no small measure to the example set by their leader, and the fact that, by the time of Hutton's journey, the members of 'WO' regarded themselves as near invincible. In Hutton's words:

'Henri [Vandesype] *and his wife Cerealia welcomed me most warmly when I arrived at their home in the rue de la Paix. Their home contained two bedrooms, one large, the other small. Normally they occupied the larger of the two, and their young daughter Rosaline the smaller one. However, they insisted, that I must use their room, and accordingly, they moved into Rosaline's. Henri was a small, insignificant-looking man, but he had a large and generous heart and was quite fearless but somewhat foolhardy; for example, one*

*night when he and I were returning home after a convivial evening
in a café owned by a member of the underground, Henri, for no
apparent reason, produced an automatic pistol out of his pocket and
fired a shot across the canal on our right. It was a stupid and
dangerous action; curfew had started half an hour earlier and we
would have been in trouble for that alone. Fortunately, there were
no German patrols in the vicinity or I might not be writing these
notes. He had taken too much drink! Henri was employed in the local
Town Hall and he used his position to further the progress of the
resistance movement whenever he could. In order to fool the
Germans he wore a Field Marshal Petain lapel badge to indicate
that he was a collaborator. Henri derived pleasure in taking me to
cafés in the evenings to introduce me to trusted friends. They would
come to our table one by one and luck was with us, we were never
stopped for our papers. Cerealia kept a hand grenade in an empty
flowerpot under the downstairs front window, where the path leading
to the front door could be seen. She declared to me that should the*
Boches *come up the drive to the house she would destroy them with
the grenade: a very courageous lady and as dedicated to the
destruction of the hated enemy as her husband. One night when
Henri and I came home from visiting a café Cerealia informed me
that a* Captain Michel *had called and advised that I was to leave at
0800 hrs next day.'* [1]

The next day Michael collected him and took him to the *Aquarium*,
where he met up with Rudkin and two other escapees. The group boarded
a train for Paris, where they were welcomed at the Gare du Nord by Simone
Séailles, who took them to a safe house to rest while they waited for their
connection. That evening they met again at the Gare d'Austerlitz and, after
surviving numerous random security checks, the party followed in
Michael's footsteps, crossing the Pyrenees before moving on to the British
Consulate in Barcelona, then to Gibraltar, from where they left by boat for
Liverpool. When they arrived in England, a prearranged message was sent
via the BBC to confirm their safe arrival. The escape line continued to
operate with a few scares, but no major incidents, until August 1943.

Meanwhile, the railwaymen in Lille were the first to see serious action.
In May they destroyed seven petrol tankers parked in a private siding
between the Lille-Bonnières depot and the sheds at Lille-Déliverance and
from the beginning of June they began to sever coupling pipes and switch
destination labels on carriages. This resulted in hundreds of vehicles
desperately needed by the Germans to simply disappear from the rail
network. More than 200 pieces of equipment were sabotaged as they passed

through the station; they were either destroyed, or vital components were removed from engines, planes and tanks. In Valenciennes Liébault had been recruiting from those around him from the moment he joined the circuit, and, as supplies began to filter through, his team carried out numerous acts of sabotage in the SNCF workshops. They began to place explosives in locomotive exhausts, causing more than a dozen engines to be immobilized for several weeks. They wrecked the engines and controls of two training aircraft left in a siding on a flat freight car and prevented new German cement mixers, which were due to be used on coastal fortifications, from reaching their destination. They also put a number of trains out of service as they passed through the station. Considerable damage was caused by placing time-delayed explosives on the engines of tracked vehicles and light tanks. Fires were started regularly in freight trains carrying linseed oil, straw, coal tyres and equipment requisitioned by the German authorities.

It was a good beginning, but one of the important messages received by Michael that spring related to the SNCF locomotive construction and repair works at Fives, the second largest of its kind in France. The bombing of Germany was intensifying, and the Germans were relying increasingly on the production and maintenance facilities in France and Belgium to maintain their own railway system. The British High Command had ordered the destruction of the Fives factory, which had been attacked four times between October 1942 and January 1943, bombing from a height above 21,000 feet. None of these air raids had produced the required results – partly because the Germans had concentrated the heaviest anti-aircraft defences in northern France on the approaches to Lille, and partly because of the growing discontent among the French people. The factory was located close to the centre of the town, and more damage had been done to the surrounding residential areas than to the works themselves. Civilian casualties were mounting and many hundreds of families had been left homeless. The psychological effect was not helping the Allied cause and German propaganda capitalized on this. The chiefs of staff in London turned to SOE: could its agents in northern France succeed where the bombers had failed?

This was the question put to Michael, who was able to reply almost immediately, since the factory at Fives was on his own target list and he had been studying it for some time. He sent back a message saying he could indeed undertake a sabotage attack on the locomotive works, and was confident of its success. No doubt RAF Bomber Command received this news with some scepticism. An operation of this magnitude required both careful planning and the availability of large quantities of explosives, and Michael was not to be hurried in his preparation. To help him he had Séailles and Chieux, who had worked in the marine division of the factory before the war and again, briefly, in the summer of 1940. While Michael was studying reports on its locomotive production, Chieux provided important information on the general layout of the works and a map, on which he had marked all the key strategic points.

Michael needed more help, but he knew he was unlikely to find it from the workforce. At this time the general climate under the occupation was such that the morale of working men in the urban areas was one tending to defeatism and weary resignation. Everyone feared for their job, and there was little enthusiasm for collaborating with the resistance movement, which was still in its infancy and regarded as an organization of enthusiastic but misguided – and almost certainly doomed – amateurs. The succession of rapid German victories, the relentless Nazi propaganda, and the fate handed out to those who rebelled, were more than enough to terrify and discourage people from anything other than simple compliance and obedience. Michael therefore took what proved to be a fateful decision by persuading Victor Leblanc, one of Lemercier's young cousins, to get him taken on in the factory. His task was to flesh out the information supplied by Chieux, and provide details of the location of suitable specific targets, the guard rosters, the employees, lighting and general security arrangements.

Eventually, as pressure from London increased, Michael decided to have a look inside for himself. Dressed as a factory worker he assumed the role of a slightly stupid new employee being patiently shown the way around by Leblanc. It gave him an opportunity to verify the information he had received and gain first-hand knowledge of the layout, even though he was unable to access the most secure areas. He had to determine where the limited amount of explosives available to him could be used to the greatest effect, and the morning's sightseeing confirmed his belief that the prime targets had to be the large transformers. Although he still lacked detailed drawings of the electrical power grid, he decided to go ahead anyway. To SOE's great relief the message came through: *'We are ready,'* and Michael was ordered to attack immediately. The operation was fixed for Saturday 26 June at 23.00 hrs to take advantage of the weekly plant shutdown. Michael selected men from the Roubaix-Tourcoing sector for this first action, and instructed Arthur Malfait to form a team of committed volunteers made up of genuine policemen and others in police uniform. Paul Malfait suggested six colleagues from Wattrelos – Georges Philipott, Henri Verporte, Alphonse Gaffez, Jean Vanhoutte, Albert Desmarchelier and Désiré De Becker, and arrangements were made quickly: uniforms were obtained, false papers were created, rendezvous points and passwords were agreed, suitable transport was located, and weapons, ammunition and explosives were laid to hand.

Although the lack of direct radio contact with London turned out to be a convenience at this precise point in helping Michael distance himself from his masters' insistent pleas, communications continued to be his biggest headache. From the time of his very first contact with London he had invariably ended his messages with: *'I request another radio operator,'* and, at around midnight on 23 June, his hopes were raised when Lemercier brought to him 24-year-old Lieutenant François William Michael Reeve, introduced under his field name of *Olivier*, and recently arrived from London. Dropped in Touraine on 13 June under the name of *Cardinal*, and carrying 200,000 francs for the circuit, Reeve had been taken in by DONKEYMAN and passed to Dubois in Tours, where he introduced himself under the name on his false documents – Michel Louis Duchesne.

In his report of 16 September 1944 he explained what happened next:

> *'The same evening I got back in touch with* Hercule [Dubois]. *The following day he sent me a message, which arrived some days later. I met with* Hercule *and one of his men in the region of Charge. The following day I left for Lille to get in touch with* Sylvestre *whose contact I would either make at the* Café Poker *or at* the Café Mado *at Place St Michel Lille. I arrived at Lille at about 1030 in the evening...I was given the following address: Manuel Lemercier at the Marche de Wazenne where I went. Colonel* [sic] *Lemercier led me to* Sylvestre *who received me rather badly when he learnt that I was not a wireless operator for he said that it was worth absolutely nothing. What happened next made me realise that this was absolutely true. He introduced me in the* Café Mado, *which was not brilliant, where I met two men called Lucien Delacroix of Lille and Jean Velge, a Belgium subject who had a hotel in the region of Brussels. I handed over the 200,000 francs to* Sylvestre, *a sum of money which he found insufficient and that evening he explained to me the situation which appeared quite confused and that he was going to attack the train factory of Fives in Lille on the following Saturday.'* [2]

No-one could have had any idea of the impact Reeve would have on the circuit, nor of the controversy and division he would create. It would relegate all of the other disagreements, mutual suspicions and antipathies between its members to the status of petty squabbles.

An Anglo-Frenchman with a British passport, Reeve had been employed as a steelworker at Isbergues, in the Pas de Calais region, when the Germans marched in. Immediately he left for Perpignan, where he operated as a delivery driver helping refugees cross the border into Spain, until he was obliged to join them. In England he was recruited by SOE and trained as a saboteur. After leaving the training schools he had been given a detailed briefing on sabotage targets in the north of France, and told to report to *Sylvestre*, the head of the FARMER circuit in Lille, as second-in-command. Like Michael, he had passed through STS 5 at Wanborough Manor then gone on to field training in Scotland, thence to Ringway for parachute training. At Wanborough his escorting officer was Lance Corporal Gordon, whose reports shed interesting light on Reeve's background and evident charisma:

> '[He] *is a man one has greatly to admire. Has obviously lived a hard rough life. Tries very hard in all things, including behaving himself well in surroundings which are strange to him. Will not say how he escaped, on account of others. Has been a smuggler. He has wide experience of the local semi-public figure café life one might expect from a local boxing champion. Seems to be discreet, told me that in café brawls, of which he has considerable knowledge, was never drawn into a fight but always waited for his man outside. Talks French with a strong northern (Lille?) accent.'*

At the end of his preliminary training on 10 March his instructor's report included the following assessments:

> '*Field craft: Does a lot of hard work which achieves very little: lacks the necessary brains and imagination....Explosives and Demolitions: His pet subject on which he has spent a lot of time to good purpose. Confident and capable. Signalling & communications: Hopeless: excused further attempts. Reports: Does not possess the necessary brain power. Map Reading etc.: Slow but has made good progress and if given time can find his way about quite well. No use at Field Sketches etc. Instructor's remarks: A likeable boy who has tried exceptionally hard all through. Although not endowed with all the brains in the world has come on very well and is about the best of this lot.'*

The Course Commandant added:

> '*A genuine, likeable, uneducated tough. Short of grey matter but good as gold and all the right instincts. NCO coup-de-main type and within limitations as good a chap as I have seen here.'*

From Wanborough Reeve went briefly to STS 7 at Winterfold near Cranleigh for further assessment, provided by Lance Corporal Gordon once more:

> *'Not a great deal to add… . Continues to work very hard. On his escape he travelled from N. to South by bicycle, made a living when he arrived by smuggling to and from Spain, in difficult and physically tiring conditions, which required courage, determination and cunning. Is a man who stands on his own feet, and never pretends to be better than he is, socially or any other way. Has been handicapped by a bad chest, which has prevented him doing many things including PT but as he is naturally very powerful and well developed, this does not matter so much in his case. He is very anti-German. Is possessed of a great deal of cunning, he is well balanced and sensible… . Tells me he has many contacts who think as he does and in whom he has complete confidence. He is of a rather suspicious nature and his confidence is not easily given.'*

At STS 23, near Loch Morar, his supervising officer was none other than Michael's old mentor, Corporal – now Lieutenant – Searle, who was clearly taken with him:

> *'Has shown himself well up to standard in training with a particularly sound knowledge of explosives and weapons. Neither organizer nor adjutant he is a very sound man to have in a tight corner. He can be relied upon both to carry out orders and to show initiative. He would perform a lone job, prove an excellent member of a coup de main party or make a good demolition and weapon instructor. As an instructor he has the ability to describe things simply, clearly and concisely, the enthusiasm of his convictions and the knowledge that he would be quite prepared to perform any job which he himself might designate to others. He possesses personal experience of the metal industry.'*

These sentiments were echoed two days later by Lance Corporal Gordon:

> *'He is a self-contained person, rather jealous of his personality, careful in what he says, rather suspicious, yet very forthright. One feels that once he was your friend or you were working with him, one could have the most complete confidence in him and he would not let you down. He looks like a professional assassin, and is a person I like very much and for whom I have the greatest respect.'*

On the completion of Reeve's paramilitary training the course commandant concluded:

'A very good worker who has great physical qualities, and who has done well at all subjects with the exception of signalling at which he is very slow. Has a good knowledge of demolitions and can instruct in this subject competently in clear and simple language.'

Michael of course knew nothing of these character assessments, or how severely they would be tested in the months ahead. The day after Reeve's arrival Michael went through the arrangements for the raid with him, and arranged for him to be equipped with false identity papers and taken to the home of Marcel Dutilleux in Rue Vergniaud, where he would be lodging. He then went to Paris to send details to London of the timing for the Fives raid. He had to get back to Lille the same day to receive the final briefing from Leblanc, but planned to return the next morning to meet Suttill, with whom he had an appointment at eleven-thirty. As he was leaving he was stopped at a barricade and questioned, in what he assumed to be a random search. His cover was good enough to allow him to talk his way out of trouble, but he was worried by what appeared to be a massively increased level of security, and by the large number of French police and German troops on the streets. Such alerts were not uncommon, but the marked presence of officers who were clearly from the SD was unusual and pointed to a special operation being underway. Before setting off for Paris the next morning he took the precaution of telephoning Simone Séailles, who confirmed that roadblocks and checkpoints had been set up all round the inner city, security vehicles were parked at major intersections, and motorcyclists were mounting constant patrols.

The normal arrangement for such contingencies was for any planned meetings to be deferred for forty-eight hours, so Michael decided to go instead to Wattrelos, where Malfait and Reeve were due to brief Malfait's 'policemen'. After explaining the purpose and objectives of the mission and what was expected of each man, Michael left Reeve and Malfait making up clams while he went back to headquarters for a final meeting with Vandesype, Lemercier, Velge and Delacroix.

Leblanc had delivered more sketches and notes of the approaches to the locomotive workshops, but had been unable to gain access to the heavily-watched transformer stations, details that Michael needed desperately but knew he would not get before the raid. He had to hope that he could gather the missing pieces from workers they met as they went along. Otherwise, all was ready. Everyone understood their roles, all the necessary transport had been obtained and rendezvous points had been agreed. Arthur Malfait had prepared the all-important personal identity cards for the leaders: Michael became a Gestapo officer called 'Dulard', a name he chose for himself, Reeve became 'Michael-Reeve Duchêne', while Vandesype, who spoke fluent German and was seen by Michael as a key part of his plan, was transformed into a full-blown *Wehrmacht* engineer colonel – 'Herr Oberst Luwerf'.

On the Saturday afternoon preceding the attack a special courier brought the unwelcome news from Paris that Suttill, along with many others from the PROSPER circuit, had been arrested. Michael decided to say nothing of this to the others for the time being: he needed them focused and concentrating on the operation.[3]

Shortly before nine o'clock that evening Vandesype, Philipott and Malfait met up with Delacroix at the Fives bridge. Michael, Reeve and Lemercier arrived by car an hour later. The bogus policemen, coming in a truck driven by Velge, were due to join them at the boulevard by the factory, but by eleven o'clock no-one had arrived. The silent party exchanged worried glances. It was a hot, sultry evening, and people were leaning out of their windows in an attempt to find a single breath of cool air. The moon was in its final quarter, but provided sufficient light for the men to be clearly visible, and their prolonged inactivity was beginning to puzzle the onlookers. Curious looks were cast in their direction until Michael finally decided that they were becoming conspicuous, and announced that the operation would be postponed for twenty-four hours. At this they all clambered back into Lemercier's car. Fortunately, Malfait insisted they went via the station in Lille, where the team from Wattrelos were due to arrive, and almost immediately their vehicle was seen trundling along in good order and at a fair speed. A small mechanical hitch had brought it to a stop on Boulevard de Roubaix. Reacting swiftly, Michael ordered everyone back.

Shortly afterwards they found themselves once more in the dead-end approach to the factory. Lemercier parked the vehicle in position for a quick getaway. The clams were in the policemen's briefcases. Reeve had packed six additional plastic charges into a suitcase in case they were needed. Delacroix stayed on guard outside, armed with a machine gun, while the others followed Michael towards the little side gate, which they expected to have to break open but, to everyone's surprise, was already ajar. Cautiously they walked in, revolvers and a sub-machine gun at the ready but only to be used as a last resort. Michael had issued strict instructions that the operation was to be carried out with *'finesse'*.

The intelligence provided was incomplete, particularly when it came to the security patrols, and the absence of important details increased the element of risk. Just after eleven-thirty they came across Fagnart, the chief security officer, who was about to leave his hut after completing his turn of duty. Michael shouted a torrent of bewildering orders at him with such urgency and authority that the guard was thrown into a panic and did not know which way to turn. Every time he opened his mouth to ask a question

Michael yelled at him again, telling him to move quickly because there had been a report that saboteurs had got into the factory and they had to be found. This brought quiet smiles to the faces of his men. Fagnart recovered himself and asked if the director had been informed. Michael told him not to be such a damn fool: of course he had, and he was on his way. There then followed a little pantomime, with Paul Malfait, acting as 'interpreter' and ostentatiously pretending to clarify instructions with 'Colonel Luwerf', at the end of which he announced that the terrorists had to be found without delay, or there would be severe repercussions for the guards. At this, Fagnart announced that he would take the men wherever they wanted to go. A nightwatchman arrived, attracted by the noise, and wanted to know what was going on. Michael brandished his Gestapo card and demanded to be taken to the control centre, whereat the watchman saluted nervously and said he would lead them there. Fagnart was about to retreat to the safety of his cabin when Arthur Malfait grabbed hold of him and told him to accompany them.

The party scuttled quickly across the yard, Michael in the lead with the watchman, followed by Reeve, Lemercier, Vandesype, Philippot, Henri Verporte and the two Malfaits, Arthur propelling Fagnart by the arm. When they reached the box the duty electrician, Barbigand, refused to admit them, in spite of their urgent attempts to explain. His orders were to let no-one in without a permit, and there was no way he was going to incur the wrath of his manager and risk losing his job. Unwilling to use force, but conscious of vital seconds ticking away, Michael gestured to the 'Colonel', who, bedecked with Nazi insignia and swastikas, decided to exert his authority and pulled out his revolver. He pointed it menacingly at the dismayed electrician and roared at him to leave. The effect was instantaneous. The man immediately backed away and waved them in, helpfully warning them of the dangers of high-tension transformers and chattering on about correct safety procedures, until Verporte and Malfait took him to one side and started to ask him some worrying questions.

Michael's idea of using deception rather than violence had paid off. Within five minutes he and Reeve had planted their charges and returned to the anteroom, announcing they had found no sign of intruders and asking if there was another transformer room where they might be heading. By now completely convinced, the electrician suggested he take them across Rue Baumann to a second station, where they repeated the process, lamenting the fact that they only had twenty-three charges: there were many other suitable targets to hand.

While this group carried out its mission, Arthur Malfait stationed Gaffez and Vanhoutte at the factory gate and De Becker at the exit from the cellars, instructing them to seize anyone who appeared at the guard hut. Then, with two other men, he ventured into the underground passageways in search of the telephone switchboard. They came across a guard who led them to it willingly, but the watchman there refused to leave his post, pleading that the Germans were in the habit of making frequent telephone checks throughout the night. Paul Malfait resolved the difficulty by pretending to call the Central Police Station and demanding reinforcements to guard the factory. After a particularly anxious quarter of an hour, during which they had no idea how the others were getting on, they went back to the surface, where all the watchmen had been assembled in Fagnart's cabin. At this precise moment, probably because of the temperature in the halls, some charges exploded prematurely. The heavy detonations alarmed the watchmen, who became instantly panic stricken and fearful. Playing his role to perfection the 'Colonel' cursed and lamented that no Germans had been assigned to the protection of such an important facility. He then reassured the watchmen that all was well and that his men had everything under control. Sternly, Paul Malfait advised them not to move from the cabin until the security forces, which were on their way, had finished questioning them. The saboteurs then hurried to the exit, where they collected Delacroix and Arthur Malfait's men. They had been in the factory for a little over half an hour. [4]

The policemen were silent as Lemercier's vehicle hurtled towards Roubaix, where the group split up. The van was garaged at the disused Roubaix Mill, and, in view of the late hour Lemercier decided to spend the night with Paul Malfait, while Michael, Reeve, Vandesype, Delacroix and Arthur Malfait hurried back to the *Aquarium*. As they were crossing the Mont-de-Terre Bridge a series of bright flashes lit up the night sky and they heard the thump of detonations. Aware that the area would soon be crawling with men, they all lengthened their stride and shortly after midnight they were toasting their success at headquarters, delighted with the success of their mission and happy to have put one over on the Germans. The laughing and back-slapping came to an abrupt halt when they heard a sudden and unexpected hammering on the street door. Mindful of the Paris arrests, Michael ordered everyone to take up defensive positions, guns in hand. Delacroix edged to the door and listened; a muted mumbling was heard and he opened the door to admit Velge, whom they had assumed had gone elsewhere for the night. In fact, he had suffered a puncture, and after abandoning the vehicle and seeing Lemercier hurtle past on his way to Roubaix, had jumped into the last *mongy*, the Roubaix-Lille tramway.

Meanwhile, firemen had arrived at the factory five or ten minutes after the 'terrorists' had left; a few minutes after them, German security troops arrived. They found the central control room and the switchboard in

Rue Bauman consumed by flames and important transformers and circuit breakers destroyed. Another 3,000-amp circuit breaker and some scarce raw materials had been damaged. The fires raged until well into the following afternoon, despite the efforts of fire brigades and forced labour units, driven into the collapsing buildings by SS men.

Professor Foot recorded the results:

'Four million litres of oil were destroyed and twenty-two transformers damaged, some of them irreparably; and the works were reported out of action for two months. This was far too optimistic an estimate; a post-war investigation showed that production was never completely stopped, and that after four days it was almost back to normal. Nevertheless the coup provided an example of the kind of demolition that SOE could effect more precisely and more cheaply than could air bombing attacks; the factory was in a heavily built-up area, and to bomb it would probably have cost many scores of French lives.'

The Fives attack marked a significant date for the resistance, but there were repercussions. On the Sunday, road blocks were set up; the factory guards and watchkeepers were interrogated rigorously for several days and shown a selection of clothing and hair styles to help them identify the terrorists. SS troopers rampaged through the working-class districts, rounding up railway workers and seizing their wives and children as hostages and scapegoats; and the German Commandant issued an order threatening to shoot every tenth man employed at the locomotive works as a punishment for what they called 'this abominable terrorist outrage'. In spite of all this, the enemy found no lead to the perpetrators.

In Lille stories began to circulate. The raid had been carried out by a whole army of saboteurs; it was the work of a brigade of Special Policemen; regiments of parachutists had been dropped. The Germans knew otherwise and put up posters offering a reward of 400,000 francs to anyone who could identify the 'terrorists' responsible. Local newspapers carried the story of the 'Fives Strike' and published photographs of the damaged transformers, while accusing the saboteurs of putting innocent Frenchmen out of work. Nobody paid any attention. Several months later, in an attempt to ridicule the Allies, the Germans circulated a number of leaflets asking 'Where are the English, then?' After recovering a number of these Michael had the words: 'Perhaps they were at Fives?' stencilled on the back. He had copies dropped off in various cafés, but the Germans clearly did not appreciate the joke: the reward offered for information jumped from 400,000 francs to 1,000,000. This offer gave the resistants an aura of glamour and prestige that had never previously been attained, and the action revealed beyond any doubt the existence of active partisans in the city.

The strike was a springboard for major organized sabotage operations throughout the summer, but it was also the catalyst for a series of arrests whose shock waves threatened to bring down the entire circuit.

Chapter notes
1   Hutton debriefing report *(AIR/27/167)*.
2   For reasons that will become clear, Reeve was interviewed on three occasions towards the end of 1944 – 16 and 18 September, and 2 October.
3   The lengthy story of the attack on Fives and its immediate aftermath is taken from the *Le Coup de Main de Fives et Historique du Début du Réseau* (see Introduction). This was published post-war by the OFACM (*Organisation Franco-Anglais du Capitaine MICHEL* – see Chapter 25 – and known familiarly as the Amicale). The raid is also covered briefly by Professor Foot in *SOE in France, Chapter IX: Middle Game 1943.*
4   I was personally able to confirm a number of points about the raid with Désiré De Becker when I visited him at his home in Wattrelos in 1999. He produced the gun he had been given by Michael for this mission, a Webley .38 calibre six-shot revolver with a five-inch barrel, which, he said, *'made one hell of a noise'*. It is now in the hands of Wattrelos historian Francis Bohee.

Chapter 15

Arrests

'When our actions do not, our fears do make us traitors.'
Macbeth. IV.ii

SOE had in mind to fulfil the directive issued to it on 20 March. Support for the Russians had become a political imperative as Britain's eastern Allies stepped up their demands for an immediate 'second front' in Europe. While the Allied planners knew that large-scale military action in 1943 was out of the question, it was very much on the cards for 1944, and arming resistance groups and preparing them for the eventual invasion had become a priority. At the same time the British Government was desperate to be seen to be doing something and had, through its directive to SOE, clearly defined its future role:

'You are the authority responsible for coordinating sabotage and other subversive activities including the organization of Resistance Groups, and for providing advice and liaison on all matters in connection with Patriot Forces up to the time of their embodiment into the regular forces.'[1]

Resistance Groups were defined as

'"Organized bodies operating within enemy occupied territory or behind enemy lines" and patriot forces as "any forces which may be embodied in areas liberated by our armies".'

SOE's activities were to be concentrated mainly in support of the general Allied strategy for the war laid down by the Joint Chiefs of Staff. Sabotage of industrial objectives was to be pursued with the utmost vigour; attacks on communications were to be regulated carefully and integrated with other operational plans. The directive ended with the words:

'Sabotage materials and weapons in the hands of Resistance Groups within the enemy's lines are likely to pay a relatively big dividend and could make a large contribution to the enemy's military defeat.'

If he had seen this document, Michael would surely have agreed wholeheartedly with its content. He had received instructions from London to carry out during June, July and August attacks on important targets such as power stations, and to conduct systematic sabotage of communications to make the enemy think that something was about to happen very soon. He was more than happy to oblige, but lacked the means.

The intense security activities Michael had witnessed in Paris on 23 June, which resulted in Suttill and many of his key assistants being pulled in early the following morning, dealt a severe blow to SOE and deprived Michael of his sole source of radio contact with London. Suttill had been recalled to London in May, and on his return had visited Michael in Lille, presumably to pass on instructions. [2]

The seeds of Suttill's downfall had been sown the previous November when he was visited by Heyermans of CARTE, who was arrested in a routine spot check of documents after leaving the meeting. Among his papers had been notes about the meeting held at a safe house – the Tambours' apartment – as a result of which the building had been kept under casual surveillance. It had become the practice for many of PROSPER's agents to congregate there, contrary to all the security training they had received. Increasing numbers of people coming and going alerted the watching Germans, but lack of any positive suspicions led to no action being taken. However, when in early June the Tambours were arrested and interrogated, possibly as a result of betrayal, this, plus Heyermans' notes on the file index, coupled with the reports of high levels of activity in the building, caused the Germans to follow and watch all visitors to the house very closely. As Professor Michael Foot eloquently put it, the agents went there:

'In response to the desire for companionship with people who could share with them the secret of their identity and their mission.'

If the Germans needed any further proof of conspiracy it came when two Canadian agents, who had arrived on 10 June to set up ARCHDEACON in the Ardennes, were arrested on the evening of 23 June while being driven by Pierre Culioli, leader of PROSPER'S sub-circuit in the Cher valley, to catch a train to Paris. Misfortune led them into a German military road block, from which Culioli tried to escape and was shot and wounded. All of them were arrested. Unfortunately, the Canadians had on them messages and documents that included the field names and addresses of Norman and Borrel. This was enough for the Germans, who decided to close in on everyone they had identified so far. Norman and Borrel were arrested on the night of 24 June, and the next morning Suttill was traced to a small hotel in Rue de Mazagran, where he too was apprehended. The chain of arrests that followed effectively decimated the networks in Paris, including Normandy and the Loire. Between 1,000 and 1,500 SOE agents and sub-agents were victims, but clearly at this point the Germans had learnt nothing to direct them to Lille and FARMER.

From Gestapo sources interrogated after the war, Professor Foot suggests that the Germans offered the captured agents the incentive of being treated as military prisoners of war in exchange for information and cooperation in rounding up the remaining members of the circuit. Norman accepted and went over to the Germans, not only revealing details about operations in and around Paris but also providing a full rundown on the whole SOE organization in England, its methods and key personnel. Dressed in civilian clothes, he was seen accompanying German security officers to interview captured agents. His smart, well-dressed appearance and general air of wellbeing, which meant he was evidently on good terms with his captors, doubtless had a significant impact on the morale and will to maintain silence of a number of subsequent arrestees. His radio and codes were captured intact and used by the Germans to good effect to make SOE believe that he was still operational.

Michael was devastated by the news of Suttill: he had come to like and respect his fellow British officer, and valued his opinions and support. He also counted him a personal friend and felt the loss deeply. He knew that he himself had had a lucky escape. In fact, the Germans had acted too hastily: if they had held back on Suttill for one more day they would have snared not one but four of the top SOE organizers in one sweep. In addition to Michael, Suttill had appointments with Claude de Baissac (SCIENTIST) at 10.30 hrs on 24 June, and with France Antelme (BRICKLAYER) at the same time the following day. Both avoided capture at this time. [3]

Michael also realized that it was important to set up another conduit for his communications and inform London of the arrests. The only possibility seemed to be through HERCULE, but he neither knew Dubois nor had he had any personal contact with him. However, Reeve had, having spent time with him after his arrival in France, so Michael despatched him to the Touraine, along with Staggs and Malfait; the latter would be the designated courier between FARMER and HERCULE. Dubois agreed to relay messages for Michael, including the important despatch about Fives, and three letterboxes were set up: one with Dubois' mother in Tours, one to the north at the *Hôtel de la Calandre* in Le Mans, and one at the *Château d'Amboise* to the east. This was far from an ideal solution: to Le Mans from Lille was more than 400km, and it was just under that from Arras. The time and distance involved would not only add to the delay in sending and receiving messages but would also put the couriers at greater risk, hence Michael's decision to entrust this vital link to Malfait.

Michael was desperate for more arms and ammunition and was impatiently waiting for confirmation from London of the various landing grounds he had proposed. He instructed Reeve not to return straight away from the Touraine but to wait for a transmission for FARMER. This Reeve did, sending Malfait and Staggs back to Lille, but when he himself returned the news he brought was not encouraging. The RAF had rejected all of the proposed landing grounds between Seclin and Armentières to the south and west of Lille because of the heavy concentration of flak batteries in the area. Orders were given to investigate possible sites around Arras, and Michael entrusted this to Malfait, who with his aunt Angèle was instrumental in bringing on board another key player.

The area around Arras, 50km from Lille, was largely rural. There were no significant military targets, and no priority had been given to its development as a recruiting centre for the circuit. Now it became of the utmost importance as the location for future supply drops, and the recruitment of local men for reception teams became a matter of urgency.

On the evening of Malfait's return from the Touraine, Angèle told him of a man she knew in Arras where she occasionally went shopping – a young baker who had confided in her his anti-German and pro-British feelings. His name was Henri Dewispelaere. Married with children he lived in Rue Pierre Curie in Arras, while working at his parents' bakery in Rue de Cambrai, just around the corner from the station. Malfait met him with Angèle the next morning. Taking the young man to one side, he explained to him the dangers and the importance of the missions that lay ahead, and straight away Dewispelaere took the oath and asked to meet Michael. The following day Malfait took Michael to him, and both felt that they had found a good future leader when Dewispelaere told them he could already call on around thirty men in Arras and in St Léger, where his wife came from. He also knew of some suitable fields for parachute drops, which he pointed out to Malfait when they went to St Léger together the next day with Dewispelaere's brother-in-law, Georges Bulcourt, who also took the oath, Michael having returned to Lille.

That evening, Malfait received Michael's congratulations as he handed over the details and coordinates of the first two fields. Malfait was so pleased with the speed and successful conclusion of this particular task that he suggested they might reward Dewispelaere – *Henri* as he became known in the circuit – by making the code message for the first St Léger mission '*Congratulations to Henri*'. Michael agreed, and, very taken with this new recruit, ordered Malfait to give him responsibility for recruitment and receptions in the Arras sector: a decision that was to have far-reaching consequences for the circuit. Astutely, Dewispelaere made his first targets the mayors of the local townships and villages, men of great influence in rural France and true leaders of their communities. Three of these were to play significant roles in the events that lay ahead.

Lemercier, meanwhile, pressed on with his own work and, during a visit to the bakery in Arras with Delacroix, Dewispelaere led them into the street, where he announced that he thought he had found an ideal location in which to conceal arms. He walked them to the Arras slaughterhouse and abattoir, which was run by Paul Copin, an old school friend and fellow member of the local Chamber of Commerce. There they were issued with grubby, blood-stained overalls and led through the cold store to a disused back room, from which a trapdoor gave access to a ladder leading down into a vast basement, full of cobwebs, that ran the length of two buildings and had another door, presently sealed up, that led out onto waste ground at the rear. As a hiding place it was near perfect, and Delacroix recognized that if the arms were bundled up like carcasses of meat they could be brought in without attracting undue attention. By the same token, vehicles made to look like trade carriers would be able to load up the goods for onward distribution. It was an exultant and triumphant Lemercier that took the news to Michael and received his congratulations.

On 6 July the circuit suffered its first major disaster when Velge was arrested in Hoeilaart, near Brussels, while carrying out a liaison mission with his sister and the Melottes. The loss of one of his key lieutenants, coming so soon after the capture of Suttill, shocked and saddened Michael. He had forged a close bond with the likeable and industrious Belgian and felt personally responsible, because he had persuaded him to make the trip against Velge's own reservations. Shortly after that, Velge's principal contact in his intelligence group was pulled in for questioning, and, while there was nothing to connect these arrests directly to FARMER, Michael believed they did pose a threat to the security of his headquarters and to the groups in Lille and Wattrelos. Everyone was put on a high state of alert. To be on the safe side, Michael avoided all the places known to Velge, and he did his best to hide his anxiety, insisting on business as usual; but the strain was beginning to tell and he was living in an almost permanent state of exhaustion. In Arras they remained uneasy and apprehensive during the weeks following Velge's arrest, while continuing to search for new men and build up the area. Malfait tried hard not to let his fears be known to the new recruits but every time he went home to Wattrelos, as he usually did twice a week, he expected the worst – as did Dubois due to a series of unrelated local arrests. But Velge did not talk and the work went on.

Michael had earlier given responsibility for the Arras region to Malfait, but he now faced a dilemma. The arrival of Reeve had upset the dynamics of his team. Although they reluctantly accepted the intrusion of this new player into their tightly-knit circle, they found his overbearing and officious manner difficult to deal with, as Séailles commented in his report of 28 October 1944:

> *'Some weeks after OLIVIER arrived in Lille he told me that he was not entirely satisfied with the way that he had been received by Captain MICHEL. I advised Captain MICHEL to try and improve his relationship with his lieutenant. Following this OLIVIER gradually lost my sympathy; in particular I did not appreciate his "matador" mannerisms. In my opinion OLIVIER, although brave and enterprising, lacked the qualities required to do his job.'*

Accepting his friend's judgement, and realizing his genuine concern, Michael took Reeve to one side and explained forcefully that their survival as a circuit depended on everyone pulling together to fulfil their objectives. Yet the atmosphere in Lille continued to worsen until finally Michael had had enough. He saw a way out of the problem by building up to Reeve the new-found importance of the Arras sector and placing him in charge there. Malfait took this in good grace, but he was not happy with the way in which the British officer went about his duties, as recorded in his diary:

> *'From July I had to hand over command of the Arras sector to Olivier who was absolutely delighted, because, while Trotobas was disappointed not to have been sent the radio operator he hoped for, Olivier had been led to expect an independent command and was equally frustrated, but being given the Arras leadership went some way to placating him. He was a well-built man, a keen sportsman, who said little but liked to show off. I thought him not particularly intelligent and frequently caught him out in various elementary tricks and deceits he practised to assert his authority and gain the prestige and respect he felt he deserved. From the very outset he was jealous and resentful of the evident high regard that the Arras men accorded to Trotobas. Olivier they soon perceived as outwardly bold, but lacking true strength of character, as events were to reveal. They felt he was impetuous and dangerously rash; they saw him as boastful and vain.'*[4]

Nevertheless, Malfait arranged for Reeve to stay with the Mayor of St. Léger, Jean Baptiste Miseron, father of Constant. Reeve, Malfait and Dewispelaere then set about looking for suitable drop zones, of which a handful were identified, approved by Michael, and duly passed to London through HERCULE.

The feelings of the men appeared to have been vindicated when Reeve's first demonstration of his authority proved to be somewhat of a fiasco. He informed Michael that he had personally identified and vetted an excellent field near St Léger (actually found and reconnoitred by Malfait), and, on his own initiative he arranged for Dubois to send a message to London, requesting a supply drop during the July moon. The notice was too short for the RAF to incorporate this within their busy schedule, but, according to Malfait, on receipt of the message *'The gods are thirsty'*, Dewispelaere and his brothers-in-law duly went to the designated drop zone and prepared the landing ground. At around 2330 hrs as expected, they heard the synchronized drone of a twin-engine aircraft in the distance. It stayed, circling for half an hour before disappearing. When Michael looked into this he concluded – as his disappointed men had done – that Reeve must have passed on inaccurate coordinates. He ignored Reeve's blustering and protests and ordered that in future each location had to be approved and passed to him by Malfait, and that he would go back to preparing the messages and coordinates himself. This did nothing to improve relationships between the two men. [5]

With fine weather prevailing, Michael was confident that he would receive material during the full moon period between 10 and 25 August. In preparation for the expected drops he ordered Hertault to take his truck to Arras, hand it over to Reeve, and arrange for Woussen to look after it. It was to be used to remove the arms and ammunition from the drop zones as quickly as possible, since news of low-flying aircraft circling at night would certainly reach the Germans rapidly, and they would descend on the scene immediately and search the area. In anticipation of this Malfait had arranged to rent an isolated cottage in Beaurains, located in the middle of fields at the border with Tilloy-les-Mofflaines, and had despatched Angèle to tie up the financial arrangements. Woussen parked the vehicle up at the home of Edmond Verroken, a friend of Dewispelaere, to whose great delight a coded message Malfait had chosen with Michael – *'Congratulations to Henri'* – was received on the evening of 11 August. This sent the baker scurrying to a field belonging to Charles Carlier, between Hénin-sur-Cojeul and St Léger, accompanied by Reeve, Georges Bulcourt and his brother Charles, Constant Miseron, Alexandre Maury, Pierre Ditte, and Albéric Volckaert, a 57-year-old Belgian butcher and horse breeder and another of Dewispelaere's friends.

At around 0100 hrs the waiting men heard the noise of the aircraft overhead. Flying Officer Bell picked up the flashing 'U' and the reception lights, successfully releasing fifteen containers, each containing five canisters. The reception team men wasted no time. As soon as the consignment hit the ground, the men rushed forward to gather up the parachutes and containers, but Dewispelaere waved everyone to stop when Volckaert caught sight of lights moving in the woods at the edge of the field. What happened then was subsequently recounted to Malfait by Dewispelaere:

'Volckaert immediately alerted Miseron, whose job it was to keep away curious onlookers. Urging everyone else to silence, Miseron crept up on the intruder and grabbed him forcefully by the arms, only to realize with dismay that he was not alone. After a brief struggle a well-known voice hissed: "Let me go, you idiot. It's me, Captain Michel. *" Trotobas had come by train from Lille with* Lulu *[Delacroix], bringing their bicycles, but it taken them longer than expected to get to the field, and the chief's initial annoyance turned to amusement when he realized the fright he had caused his men, all of whom then dissolved into quiet laughter.'*

Michael directed the recovery and temporary storage operations. The consignment was split up and hidden in haystacks for the night, in anticipation of its collection the next day by another team that would take it to a safer and more permanent home. This delivery, typical of many, included bicycle tyres, medicines, Sten guns, revolvers, automatic pistols, grenades, incendiary pencils and explosives, including 808 and TNT. Michael's personal package contained chocolate, coffee, tobacco and cigarettes, which he shared out among the men, and also money needed to sustain the everyday existence of the permanent members of the network. Their work done, everyone left the area carrying parachutes and assorted paraphernalia to be hidden in the village.

The following day disaster struck when Lemercier's cousin Leblanc was arrested, along with a group of other young workers from the Fives factory, while handing out pamphlets urging the people of Lille to take passive action against the occupying forces. Following the arrest of Velge, Michael had told Eliane Lemercier that, for her own safety and that of her child, she should get out of Lille, and she went to stay with her aunt, Berthe Galiot, in Olhain, sixteen miles south of Béthune. He had also asked Lemercier to leave the area and go into hiding, and before he left Lemercier had transformed the ground floor of his house into a bookshop and entrusted its management to Martel. Then he had moved in with Fernand Wante, a tobacconist in Roubaix's Rue de Collège, from where he kept an eye on the progress of the bookshop. When Leblanc was arrested Lemercier realized that his house would inevitably be visited by the *Geheime Feldpolizei* (GFP) as a matter of course, and felt he should warn Martel.

Two months earlier, Lemercier, then Michael's acknowledged second-in-command, might have acted instantly. Now, fatally, he hesitated to say anything to Martel without Michael's agreement. Michael however was busy in the Pas de Calais region with the receptions, and although Séailles advised him to send Martel away and leave the area himself, Lemercier ignored the instruction. Relations between the two men were always uneasy and mistrustful, and Lemercier possibly resented being told what to do by the man who had usurped him as Michael's deputy.

After interrogating Leblanc, the Germans established a link between him and Velge. The latter had been transferred from Brussels to the Lille jurisdiction because he had in his possession a false identity card with Lemercier's address, which was where he sometimes stayed when in Lille. Realizing that both Velge and Leblanc were connected to Lemercier, the GFP sent a squad to Rue Corneille, where it discovered Martel and his wife. Although Martel produced a false identity card in the name of André Martin, this was soon established to be a forgery, and it became evident that the Lemerciers had fled. The Martels were duly arrested for being in possession of false papers.

Michael was unaware of these events as he, Delacroix and Woussen, helped by Volckaert, Copin and three men from his group, loaded all of the previous night's supplies and materials into Hertault's truck and took it to Beaurains. From there Constant Miseron and the Bulcourt family took the parachutes and containers by farm cart to Hénin-sur-Cojeul and buried them beneath a mound of manure in a field owned by Ida Edouard, Miseron's aunt. Everything went well, and Michael complimented Malfait on the efficiency and thoroughness of his organization, as well as remarking on the way in which whole families were willing to risk everything to help the cause, bringing in friends and neighbours as necessary. The fact that so many people knew so many little details was a security risk that had to be accepted, but it was one he felt could be contained by ensuring that no group knew more than it needed to carry out its work locally.

A second big drop followed on the night of the 16 August, heralded by the message: *'I want powder and shot'*. This took place in a field found by Georges Bulcourt to the north-east of Bapaume, where Michael himself led the reception team of Woussen and the men from the first drop, minus Delacroix and Volckaert. On the stroke of midnight Flight Lieutenant Perrins bought his Halifax in from the south-west and dropped another fifteen containers. The supplies were concealed for the night in the trees at the mouth of the woods near the landing ground, to be taken the next day to Beaurains. [6]

Morale among the men of Arras improved significantly as the end product of their planning and preparations manifested itself in an impressive array of war equipment. At last, this was tangible evidence of the commitment and support of the British High Command. For his part Michael was satisfied that he now had sufficient material to begin serious operations. More than six tonnes of supplies had been dropped in two operations, a portion of which would go to the Arras group, and the remainder would be taken by truck to the railwaymen in Roubaix-Tourcoing and Lille. The plan was being put into effect when a hammer blow struck.

In Lille, Martel had begun to talk. This was a desperate act of self-survival that defied the accepted code, which was to try to hold out for at least forty-eight hours in order to give others a chance to escape. Velge kept silent under his grievous torture, but not so Martel, who had been involved in many receptions and, ominously, knew all the participants of the Fives raid. After the briefest of interrogations, and without being subjected to any form of torture, he volunteered to help the GFP, and placed himself entirely at the disposal of the Germans, who paid him a monthly salary and gave him a uniform. The Gestapo continued to fund him for four months, during which time he inflicted major damage on FARMER, revealing all he knew of the circuit's organization and structure.

From the information he supplied the Germans now knew all about the existence and activities of *Capitaine Michel*. They were able to identify the author of the Fives raid, his radio operator *Teuf-Teuf* [Staggs], and his key coordinator, Lemercier. A massive hunt began for the three men. Martel was unaware of the recent arrival of Reeve, and because of the cut-outs in place he had had no contact with any of the other lieutenants. Posters were printed asking for information leading to the arrest of *Capitaine Michel*, identified from Martel's description as short, blond with a thin moustache. Squads of special Gestapo agents were set up to track down the various 'WO' groups, and a wave of more than fifty arrests swept through the parachute teams of Valenciennes, Abbeville, Magnicourt, Sissonne and St Erme.

On 13 August Lemercier was heading for the bookshop when he was hailed crossing Rue du Marché by local café-owner Vanspranghe, who told him not to go home because Germans were swarming all over the store and questioning the neighbours. Fearing the worst, Lemercier decided to abandon his refuge in Roubaix too, because he remembered that he had mentioned it to Martel. Desperately needing guidance he went in search of Michael but, unable to find him, he left in the company of the young Belgian, Rowies, to join his wife in Olhain. This proved to be a wise move, because Martel led the Germans straight to Wante's home, where they promised the householder a large sum of money in return for information that would lead them to Lemercier. When Wante protested that he knew nothing, he was taken into custody and beaten, but was released after ten days for lack of evidence.

While Eliane was surprised and delighted to find her husband at her aunt's door, she listened with growing concern as he told her what had happened. He said he intended to go back to Lille the next day to see Michael, but in the evening his mother arrived and told him that the Gestapo had been to her house looking for him. Clearly, there was no question of his returning, so in the morning Eliane and her mother-in-law went to Lille to find Michael, who told them, sadly but calmly, that Martel's arrest signalled the end of the road for Lemercier as a member of the circuit. He told the women to stay under cover in the Pas de Calais, where he would come to see them in two weeks' time, and forbade the mother to return to her home until her son was known to be safe. He warned them that if the Germans decided to follow a line of enquiry through Eliane's family they might soon arrive at the house in Olhain, in which case it was imperative that they found only a young woman who had taken her baby to visit its grandmother. The women should forget everything they had heard and deny all knowledge of the events in Lille. He told them that Lemercier was to move out immediately and stay with Marcel Schynkel, a pastry cook who had been recruited by Michael in Bruay, 10km to the north-west. Eliane would be able to cycle to see him, and Michael, Séailles and Vandesype would call on him from time to time. The women were to remove all traces of his presence in Olhain once he had left.

While many groups were completely annihilated, thanks to the cellular structure and the 'need to know' precautions demanded by Michael the arrests remained focused largely on Lille and on contacts known directly to Martel. The resistance and patriotism of the many martyrs who managed to keep their silence, even under extreme torture, also made a significant contribution to minimising their effects. Michael always knew there would be casualties but he refused to allow his work to be interrupted. The business of the circuit had to continue. Except for Paul and Angèle Malfait, who had had dealings with Martel and were forced to go underground for the sake of the organization, the series of cut-outs ensured that the groups in Wattrelos and Arras remained intact throughout the huge Gestapo sweep. But there were other trials and tribulations in store.

Chapter notes
1 Chiefs of Staff directive 20 March 1943.
2 Speculation continues to this day as to whom Suttill saw in London and what his instructions were. All of the rumours and alleged 'true reports' have been examined and evaluated in great detail by Francis J Suttill in his book *Shadows in the Fog*.
3 The PROSPER arrests and consequences are described in Foot's *SOE in France, Chapter IX: Middle Game: 1943*. But an exhaustive description and penetrating analysis of events, including the Gilbert Norman scenario, is to be found in Francis Suttill's book. His father was executed in Sachsenhausen concentration camp in March 1945.
4 The idea that Reeve might have been given his own circuit was, almost certainly, wishful thinking on his part, since his fitness reports point very clearly in the opposite direction. It suggests that his appointment was entirely logical and appropriate.
5 In fact, RAF records show no FARMER missions during July. It is possible that the aircraft heard was on another mission.
6 The flight details for the supply drops of 11 and 16 August are taken from *138 Squadron Record Book – AIR/27/1068*, and *138 Squadron Operations Report – AIR/27/8299*, respectively.

Chapter 16

Shootings

'All things betray Thee who betrayest me.'
Francis Thompson

Throughout the summer Michael found a refuge from the daily pressures of the circuit in his occasional visits to Gondecourt. Yvonne recalled:

'He seemed to like coming to see me. He was always accompanied by two bodyguards, one of whom remained outside in the car. He never stayed more than half an hour or so, and would usually bring little treats for me. We would just sit and talk, and he met some of my neighbours. He asked me about Loos, but I didn't want to talk about it, it was so horrible. We were locked up in filthy cells full of lice. There was hardly any food, and we were constantly bullied by the Polish warders, who were much harsher than the Germans.

'I introduced him to my brother, Robert, who was now a policeman and lived with our grandparents. Robert was a keen photographer and a good friend of Louis Cochet, a Gondecourt man who used to come to photograph the escapers for their false identity papers. I remember that one evening Robert took photographs of all of us. Michael often wore an English bow tie, which, he said, was his "code", a means of identifying him to strangers he was due to meet. By this time of course it was clear to me that he was working for the resistance, but he never once mentioned it. I asked him on several occasions if I could help by carrying messages for him, but he always said the same thing, that I had done and suffered more for France than any young person of my age could expect, and that he would not allow me to put myself at risk again. He was always very protective towards me.'

They also met on numerous occasions in Lille.

'I had kept my promise to my mother, and enrolled in a commercial studies course at a school in Lille that was right next to the main *railway station. I also stayed on some evenings for First Aid training at the nearby Red Cross school. This was very convenient for me because in those days you could get to Lille from Gondecourt by train, passing through Seclin. The line isn't there now. Michael would usually arrange to have some business at the station, so we would arrange to meet after school, usually in a café; once, I remember, we danced in the Grand Place. Sometimes we would go window shopping. After each meeting he would set the time and place for the next one.*

'Once, when we had arranged to meet at the café at the station, I arrived early and asked one of the railwaymen I had spoken to before if Michael was there. They all knew Michael. On this occasion the man smiled and told me Michael was in the office above the platforms. By now I knew from the Fives posters all around Lille exactly who he was, but I never let on. I thought it would be a nice surprise for him, but when I walked into the room, where he was talking to some railway men, he was furious with me. He told me angrily to go straight to the café and never to do anything like that again. I was putting myself in danger.'

For all of his professed concern, Michael did put her at considerable risk in a situation of his own making.

'We were strolling through an arcade, looking in the shop windows, when I saw some earrings I liked, and told Michael. "Very well," he said, "let's go in and see how much they cost." It was usual in those days for jewellers and tobacconists to lock their shop doors and only open them to customers when they knocked, because of all the thefts that were taking place. When we eventually entered, we found a German officer looking at some necklaces. Now Michael always carried two guns with him, one in his trousers and one in his coat pocket, and to my horror his coat suddenly swung open. Before he could close it again the German turned round and saw the revolver. We all stood very still, and I saw the officer swallow hard. I felt very afraid as Michael pushed me towards the door and told the shop man to open it. The officer started to look around for help. Michael smiled menacingly at him and told him to stay where he was, saying "Just try something, please!" I could see fear in the officer's eyes. Suddenly we were outside and Michael told the shopkeeper to lock the door again and not open it for five minutes. The man nodded, but he too was frightened. We hurried down a side alley and made our way back to the station. Apart from telling me that the officer was a lieutenant

colonel of infantry he didn't say anything about the incident then or later, and we never heard any more about it. But we never went near that jeweller again.'

Over the weeks she noticed a change in Michael.

'He had become more withdrawn and his mind always seemed to be somewhere else when he was talking to me. I suppose I had become a distraction he could have done without, but every time I suggested this he waved the idea away. I knew he liked to drink, smoke and gamble and I used to scold him as if I were his mother. He took it all as a fine joke. I could always tell when he was nervous – he used to smoke almost continuously. He had a strange way of holding a cigarette inside his hand so that only the tip poked through his clenched fingers, and he used to draw on this. The last time I met him in Lille was in the middle of August, by which time his fingers had become almost bright yellow and he had lost weight. I thought he looked ill, but dared not say anything. He never told me I shouldn't come again, but he made no more arrangements. He had a lot on his mind.'

He did indeed. After Velge's arrest and Martel's disclosures Michael carried out a full review of security. He reminded his team time and time again that basic precautions should not be ignored, pointing out how his call to Paris asking Simone to ring him back at a prearranged time and number had saved him personally. He insisted that the use of cut-outs should be enforced and instructed his lieutenants to follow his own practice of never disclosing future plans to anyone who did not absolutely need to know, nor where they lived or where they were going. He announced that it was time for him to move out of the *Aquarium* and close down all operations there. Malfait told him that he had been given an address by Dubois where he, Malfait, was at some point to meet up with a new WT operator. This was nearby at 74 Rue Caumartin, home of recently widowed Simone Chardin, whose husband had been a member of the circuit. She agreed to put Michael up, and on 18 August he and Denise Gilman moved into the first floor of the house. Michael had returned from Arras unwell, suffering from exhaustion and on the verge of a breakdown, and was forced to take to his bed, where he was attended by Doctor Louis Gernez, a friend of the Chardins, who immediately joined the circuit.

While Michael was lying helpless another operation took place to obtain fuel that was almost a carbon copy of Hertault's earlier raid. Michael had insisted that absolute priority was to be given to moving and distributing the material from the supply drops, and to do this he had to have vehicles and fuel. The latter could only come from the enemy, and Malfait had tasked Dubocage, Vanhecke and their colleague Gabriel Royer with stealing petrol hidden in a coal heap at the Tourcoing Depot. This they achieved by openly and brazenly driving up to the stocks in a stolen van, waving greetings to the numerous guards, and chattering noisily to each other. They drew back the tarpaulins, uncovered the fuel drums, then calmly removed 1,600 litres of petrol and 400litres of diesel fuel and loaded it into their vehicle. Vanhecke then approached a number of the guards, waving a sheaf of papers and asking for a signature, only to be told that it was not their responsibility. Vanhecke made a show of protesting, but was told to be on his way. He ambled back to the van and made a show of telling his companions what had happened. This produced shrugs all round, after which the three men climbed into the van and drove off. This haul was more than enough to meet the immediate needs of the circuit.

Transporting the bulky parachute containers was another matter. Michael had told Hertault that, for this purpose, he needed something larger and more substantial than the old gas-fired truck they had used for the Aubry drops. He took the garage-owner to meet a car dealer from Thumesnil, who had been introduced to Michael by Fertein and from whom Michael had negotiated the purchase of a most unusual vehicle. It was a converted Hotchkiss six-wheeler; a type that had been produced between the wars in a number of variants for use by the French military. With a flat half-deck at the rear, it had been intended primarily as a movable platform for light anti-aircraft or machine guns, but it had proved unsuited for this role and been superseded by a half-tracked version. The model that a bemused Hertault now examined was probably unique in Europe, let alone France, and a more conspicuous vehicle it would have been hard to find. Yet, thanks to his love of the bizarre, this was what Michael proposed to use for his clandestine missions. Hertault duly delivered it to Arras. Michael assured the garage owner that the Germans would not even notice it.

Michael's awareness of the effectiveness of hiding things in full view of the enemy, proved absolutely correct. For eight consecutive days Woussen drove the overloaded vehicle between Arras, St Léger, Hénin-sur-Cojeul and Beaurains, as well as making an unauthorised detour to Loos, where he deposited some of the arms, appropriating two revolvers for his own use, and snatched a few hours with his fiancée. During his trips he frequently had to give way to German patrols and convoys, but he was not stopped. However, the relentless travel over bumpy country roads took its toll on the old vehicle until, finally, Woussen rang the Hertaults and obtained their agreement for it to be serviced. He was told to take it to a garage owned by Roland Dacheux, another of Dewispelaere's acquaintances. This

Woussen did on the evening of 19 August, leaving the vehicle in the garage at 137 Rue de Bapaume, opposite the Rex Cinema in Arras. Next door was the *Café Carvalho*, one of Woussen's favourite haunts, where he liked to hang out with Albéric Volckaert smoking English cigarettes taken from the parachuted consignments. Occasionally he would offer these to Madame Carvalho, the proprietress, who had English origins. The distinctive aroma of these cigarettes was obvious to everyone who entered, but the young men were oblivious to the risks they were taking. Fortunately for them, Michael and his lieutenants were unaware of this blatant indiscretion, which typified Woussen's blasé attitude.

In his own mind Woussen identified himself as an indispensable person of utmost importance to the circuit, and this made him careless. After he had left the garage, Dacheux decided to check the vehicle and was startled to find under the driver's seat a loaded revolver that Woussen had forgotten to remove. This worried Dacheux greatly and, with a view to giving himself an alibi in case of trouble, he drove the truck out of the garage and parked it in the street outside the cinema, reasoning that if it were searched he could deny all knowledge of it. Because of the vehicle's unusual design this action might well have increased the likelihood of it attracting unwanted attention. In the event it was neither the English cigarettes nor the Hotchkiss's appearance that sparked off the remorseless and remarkable chain of events that was to bring about the downfall of Woussen, his employers, and many others.

Early in the morning of 20 August, acting on information supplied by Martel, the Hertaults were arrested. Madame Hertault described how, at around one in the morning, they were awakened by a squad of shouting Germans who broke down the door and rampaged through the house, turning everything upside down and chanting the mocking words *'The flag flies over the church'*, the signal that had been transmitted for the Aubry drops. The Hertaults were bundled into a car and subjected to a stream of questions. These revealed such an intimate and detailed knowledge of their activities that it led them to believe there was nothing more they could add. Madame Hertault was accused of having harboured a certain *Capitaine Michel*. Unaware of the facts and shocked by the accuracy of the information presented to them – information she believed only Lemercier knew – all she could think was that Lemercier had been arrested and talked. Fortunately, she kept her head, explaining that the man they were talking about had spoken such excellent French that she was sure he was a Frenchman. When pressed on the subject of the stream of people who came to her premises, she replied that her husband was running a garage, that people would come to enquire about repairs and that they were nothing to do with her. The ruse appeared to succeed because the subject was dropped.

The same day the Gestapo pulled in Vanspranghe, the Demoors, the Dhénins, Robbe and Thyrou. Other arrests followed in Abbeville, then the net spread to the groups in Houdain, Bourbourg, Condé and Vieux-Condé. Martel did his utmost to implicate all the agents he knew, even to the extent of denouncing his own brother-in-law, Beirnaert, whose caravan in Raismes was torn to pieces.

All of Martel's victims were driven to GFP headquarters in Lille for initial questioning and then taken to Loos Prison, where Madame Hertault realized her husband was missing. He had been taken in handcuffs to Woussen's home at his mother's café in Rue de l'Eglise, in Loos, where, finding him gone, the Germans arrested Madame Woussen herself. She was subsequently imprisoned for eight months. A search of the house uncovered no arms but did reveal one empty parachute canister, which in itself was incriminating (the contents had earlier been removed by Delacroix and distributed among the groups in Thumesnil). Hertault made a full confession and was forced to drive the policemen to Dacheux's garage to recover his truck, unable to believe that his mechanic was in any way involved in the affair and insisting that he had no idea where Woussen might be staying.

That morning Dacheux left his garage at around nine-thirty to go into town. When he returned he found it surrounded by a dozen Germans. He was immediately questioned about the truck and declared that he did not personally know the owner, whom he was supposed to meet later that day to talk about repairs. The Germans said they had been told by Dacheux's employees that there had been two men with the truck. Realizing that the line of enquiry would make it impossible for him to keep quiet about such details, Dacheux replied that, as he recalled it, the driver had been a fair-haired young man and he had with him an older man, who was known to Monsieur Portesse, a local coal-merchant who had his vehicle serviced at the garage. Subsequent investigations led the police to Volckaert's address, where they found only his young girlfriend, whom they promptly arrested and locked up for several days.

Dacheux had been forced to go to the police station for the initial enquiries, and as soon as he was released he rushed back to his garage, arriving shortly after midday. There he found a policeman, left behind to watch the truck, interrogating the blond driver, documents in hand. Woussen had returned to retrieve the revolver on the instructions of Reeve, whom he had met at Beaurains, along with Dewispelaere. Reeve, unaware of the arrests and, therefore, of the reason for the surveillance at the garage, issued no instructions to Woussen to take any additional precautions. At this stage the police were doing no more than following a routine line of enquiry into the status of the vehicle and its driver, and all might have been well had Woussen kept his head and simply explained his presence as a mechanic carrying out his employer's instructions to deliver the vehicle for servicing. Instead, when he saw Dacheux come into the garage, he winked at him conspiratorially, which made the guard turn away. Taking advantage of the diversion, Woussen immediately pulled another gun and shot the German in the head at point blank range. Without stopping to recover his false documents he jumped on his bike and pedalled quickly away, leaving the panic stricken Dacheux to pick up the pieces.

Dacheux's wife took it on herself to telephone the police, who arrived with reinforcements and questioned everyone in sight, including her and Octave Robbe, a young mechanic who had been working on the car belonging to Portesse, the merchant who had identified Volckaert. On hearing the shot, Robbe had rushed to the scene but dived for cover when he saw Woussen point the gun at him as he rode away. Portesse was pulled in for questioning, as were a number of innocent passers-by. Dacheux himself was taken once more to GFP headquarters, where he was questioned relentlessly about his every movement, his family, his opinions and his religious beliefs. While this was going on he noticed on the table in the interrogation room the enormous revolver that he had last seen beneath the driver's seat in the truck, and guessed that the police had removed it when they arrived at the garage in the morning. This encouraged him to stick with his original plea of complete ignorance. He even managed to reproach the Germans for their carelessness in leaving only one guard to deal with such a serious matter, of which he, Dacheux, knew absolutely nothing. This prompted the inspector to leap to his feet, seize Dacheux by the shoulders and rage that the last thing they needed was French peasants telling them how to run police business. But it was evident that he had been convinced by Dacheux's posturing because he then let him go.

For the garage folk that was effectively the end of the matter, but during the next few hours confusion reigned. The groups in Arras were unaware of the arrests in Lille and of Michael's change of address, and those in Lille knew nothing of what became known as the 'Rex affair', although it made a deep impression on the people of Arras. The account of events by Dacheux's employees frightened those in the neighbourhood, and they became terrified that they would be subjected to reprisal or hostage taking. These concerns were felt even more greatly amongst those who had had some involvement in the activities of the Arras network. It was a well-known fact that the baker, Dewispelaere, had been seen on numerous occasions coming and going between his own home and those of Verroken and Dacheux, as well as *Café Carvalho* and the cottage in Beaurains. The Germans knew full well that resistance agents were responsible and took no action among the local people, but Hertault himself was given very rough treatment by the policemen, who considered him responsible for the death of their colleague. They took him back to the garage and showed him the body of the dead policeman, and on their return to Lille beat him savagely. [1]

According to Malfait's reconstruction, Woussen had gone back to Beaurains, where he poured out his story to Reeve, who was concerned that the Germans would make a connection. Immediately he instructed Dewispelaere and the two men being sought by the police to get away from the area. Reeve's own recollection, in his first interrogation, differed in one important aspect:

> *'On 21 August I arrived at this abandoned house at about 11.30 and found there* Sylvestre *and* Woochen *[sic: Woussen] all agog and a bit troubled. I asked what had happened.* Sylvestre *told me that Woochen had just killed a Boche in the garage where the lorry had been kept. At that point* Sylvestre *told me to deal with Woochen.'* [2]

Séailles also asserts that Woussen contacted Michael and not Reeve, although his version of the events leading up to the shooting was at variance with Malfait's:

> *'During the August arrests the owner of a garage in which one of the organization's lorries was kept was arrested. The lorry had from then onwards been kept in another garage, the owner of which was also arrested. It would seem that the Germans knew the number of this lorry. This man stated, in interrogation, that the lorry was in the garage in Arras. The Germans therefore searched all garages in Arras and eventually found the lorry, filled with parachute materials, together with a member of the organization called WOOCHEN. The latter shot his way out of the garage and escaped. WOOCHEN contacted MICHEL who hid him in OLIVIER's region.'*

To begin with Dewispelaere and Volckaert took refuge with Charles Roger, Mayor of Gommecourt, while Woussen was sent to St Léger, where he spent the first two nights out of doors in the Mezelle Woods, sustained by food provided by the Miserons. Dewispelaere returned to Arras two days later.

The following morning, Madeleine Thyrou's maid, Paula Leblanc, learnt of her employer's arrest and was desperate to warn someone. It was she who had introduced Michael to Marcel Dutilleux, who, in turn had recruited the Chardins. Not knowing where to find Michael she rushed to tell Dutilleux, who passed the news on to Simone Chardin, who informed Michael. He realized that if Thyrou were forced to talk he would be at great risk because of the Leblanc-Dutilleux-Chardin triangle. Wracked with fever and unable to move, he was desperate to find out what was happening, and told Denise to make enquiries among the friends she knew in the circuit, taking care to avoid places where they used to go and keeping the Chardin address secret. When she reported back to Michael he sent her to find Bayart and Fertein and ask them to find a new headquarters as a matter of urgency. He was confident that *Mado* would not talk, but he felt it wise to sever all previous links and addresses and issued instructions that members of the circuit who were under immediate threat were to go undercover right away. He decided to send Delacroix and Woussen to the Pas de Calais, where they met up with Lemercier in Houdain. Reeve placed Delacroix with the Miserons in St Léger and Woussen with Ida Edouard, who ran a café in Hénin-sur-Cojeul.

After leaving the Chardins, Dutilleux hurried back to his house in Rue Vergniaud to warn Séailles, who was lodging there. Séailles, fearing the worst, assumed that Michael had been arrested at the *Aquarium* and, realizing that the men in Arras needed to be warned urgently, went to see Gerekens at Lille station. He told him that Michael had disappeared, that there had been a number of arrests, and that it was essential that Reeve was informed as soon as possible. Séailles had once visited the letterbox in Arras, a little green-painted café at 1 Rue de Cambrai, run by a patriotic widow, Jeanne Soret, who had been enrolled by Malfait. It was to there that Séailles now directed Gerekens, who had never met Reeve and had no password, so could do no more than introduce himself and ask to see *Olivier* on behalf of *Michel*. All he knew from Séailles was that Michael's deputy was an Englishman. Soret went off to fetch Reeve. [3]

According to Gerekens' account, he waited for half an hour before Reeve came in and sat opposite him, demanding to know what he wanted. Gerekens passed on the message he had been given, whereupon Reeve took out his revolver and placed it on the table, jabbing a finger at his visitor and warning him that if he were lying he would be shot instantly. Gerekens was taken aback for a brief moment, then he recovered, pulled his own gun from his belt and placed it on the table next to Reeve's, commenting that Reeve would not have time to shoot him since he would surely die first. This appeared to take the wind out of Reeve's sails, for he nodded and said he would go to Lille that evening or early the next morning. Gerekens then got up and left. As he was leaving, Soret whispered to him that *Olivier*'s behaviour was typical of the man, and that he often went around calling himself *Michel* and bragging in front of his men, who were a little afraid of him. [4]

Shortly after Gerekens had left him at the station Séailles had called on Bayart, who told him about the arrests, and as a result of Denise's visit, was able to state quite emphatically that Michael was not dead and had definitely not been arrested. As soon as he had heard about the arrests in Lambersart, Michael sent word to Séailles from his sickbed, urging him to go to the garage and stop the truck from returning. Séailles immediately left for Lambersart, where he noticed that the garage doors were shut. He questioned a woman at her window, then took his cycle and, passing close to the doors, saw that they were ajar. While pretending to tie his shoelaces he leant against the doors, which swung open to reveal an armed German hiding behind them. Séailles had the presence of mind to appear to fall off his bike, and rolled along the ground, cursing loudly as he pulled himself up and dusted down his trousers. The guard just waved him on so Séailles remounted and went calmly on his way back to Dutilleux. The two of them rushed to station themselves along the road they expected the vehicle to travel, unaware that it would not be returning. They waited in vain until midnight.

In the meantime Bayart and Fertein had very quickly come up with new headquarters at 20 Boulevard de Belfort, at the junction with Rue Kellerman, near the Porte de Valenciennes. It was the home of Pierre Gérard, an early recruit whom Michael used for local courier activities within Lille itself and who had now left for the countryside. On the afternoon of 21 August, Bayart took Michael there. Learning from experience, Michael became more cautious and ordered that only a handful of responsible people who actually needed to know should be given his new address: these were Reeve, Malfait, Séailles, Fertein, Gerekens and Bayart.

When Malfait returned from his trip to Le Mans, Michael had him brought to the new headquarters, where he introduced him to Bayart – the first meeting of these two key men. Meanwhile, Gerekens had arrived back from Arras and gone to Dutilleux's, where Séailles told him the true story of what had happened to Michael and took him to the new base. Greatly relieved, Gerekens told Michael of his meeting with Reeve and was instructed to go back right away and inform Reeve that *Sylvestre* was alive and still running the circuit.

Reeve's own account of these events is different and less dramatic. Either his memory let him down or the transcriber of the interrogation misheard the description of the 'courier'. As opposed to Reeve hearing the news from Séailles back in Arras, he stated that he went to Lille:

'The following day I went back to Mr Soret's house in Rue Cambrai in Arras and who was a postbox of complete confidence. I found there a courier called Jacquie [Gerekens] *who told me that* Sylvestre *had been arrested and that she must lead me to* Pierrot [Séailles] *that evening. When I arrived at Lille that evening I learnt from* Pierrot *that the news was false. I went along to* Sylvestre's *house*

accompanied by Pierrot. *I found* Sylvestre *ill and laid up in bed and he told me what had happened.'*

By the time Michael was up and about again, his lieutenants were reporting increased security and police presence throughout the city, particularly at the stations where all passengers were subjected to thorough checks and searches by guards with dogs. At the forefront, as always, was the GFP, mainly recruited from police officers who had been assigned to the armed forces. Although officially part of the *Wehrmacht*, its personnel could wear either civilian clothes or uniforms in the course of their duties, and its officers were also entitled to pass through military roadblocks and enter military buildings. The police rank of Inspector was retained alongside the military equivalent of Oberleutnant (Lieutenant) for use by plainclothes officers whose enquiries were concerned primarily with civilians. Because of the activities of FARMER, the GFP now had three separate offices in the region: in Lille, at the corner of Rue de Tenremonde and Boulevard de la Republique, in Valenciennes in Boulevard Pater, while in Arras it had taken over the Hôtel de Commerce in Rue Briquet Taillandier. All three offices reported to Brussels, and each of them was involved in the massive investigations launched in August to find and arrest the leader of the 'WO', his lieutenants, and agents, many of whom were on the run and whose names and pseudonyms they had obtained: *Manu* (Lemercier), *Lulu* (Delacroix), Woussen, *Olivier* (Reeve), *Pierrot* (Séailles), Paul Malfait, and others linked with Volckaert.

In Lille the investigation was coordinated by Major Doyen, and the hunt was spearheaded by Inspectors Lynen and Koltz, who had arrested Martel. These two officers of the GFP worked closely with SS Hauptsturmführer [Captain] Willy Kraus of the SD, who had succeeded so effortlessly in turning Martel. Together they directed Martel's efforts towards his native Valenciennes, in the hope of finding *Capitaine Michel* through the various communist networks they knew him to have in that area. This resulted in more than 200 resistance workers being arrested from the ranks of the FTP and National Front. On 22 August Abbeville was surrounded. Accompanied by Martel the Germans went looking for Duval, but were unsuccessful. The wily trader had moved to Royan and sent away his agents.

Since the security forces now had a detailed description of him, it would be impossible for Michael to travel without being recognized. Yet he could not lead his men from his room, so, capitalizing on the fact that he lost several kilos of weight during his illness and was now much thinner, he decided that he and Denise would change their appearance completely. She had her long blond hair cut short and dyed red, while Michael shaved off his thin moustache, dyed his own hair black, and adopted a slicked-down style in place of the waves that women found so attractive. To complete the transformation, Commandant Herry took Michael to his deputy and instructed him to kit Michael out with a GMR uniform and inspector's identity card, without bothering with the formality of entering his name in the enrolment register.

Now completely unrecognizable, and able to circulate with impunity, Michael returned to the fray and immediately gave his attention to helping Reeve clear up the aftermath of the 'Rex affair' and organizing the urgent removal of the remaining supplies from the cottage at Beaurains.

Chapter notes

1   The account of the arrests and the events in Arras are taken from Malfait's post-war reconstruction based on a meeting with Dewispelaere shortly afterwards as well as interviews with, and personal testimonies from, Madame Hertault, the Dacheux family and all of the parties present in the garage at the time of the shooting.

2   The date discrepancy and the differences between the accounts of Malfait and Reeve, which will continue, are examined in Chapters 26 and 27.

3   There was not necessarily any ulterior motive in *Olivier* using *Michel*: he had arrived and initially introduced himself under the alias of Michel Duchesne.

4   This meeting, as reported by Gerekens, is evidence of the good internal security. Gerekens had not met Reeve, even though the Englishman had been 'second-in-command' of the circuit for three months.

Chapter 17

Movement

'He's the man who delivers the Goods.'
Walt Mason

Michael's disguise as a GMR officer was so perfect and effective that the Germans never suspected for one moment that the quiet and unassuming 'Inspector Michael Lesage' – whom they happily let through road blocks as he went about his business on his motorbike, or met in cafés and at stations – was the very Englishman they were searching for so feverishly. On the other hand, it meant that Michael had to endure the mocking of patriotic French citizens taunting him for being a puppet of the Nazis. While this – clearly spontaneous – reaction from the population only served to reinforce the credibility of his cover, Michael knew that, as a result of the arrests, the enemy had worked out that the parachute drops around Arras were feeding FARMER's operations in Lille and Valenciennes. Additional checks and patrols had been set up and a GFP unit had been established in Arras itself.

Michael's immediate concerns were threefold. First, he had to get his saboteurs armed and into action, and to do this he needed to move the large cache of arms at Beaurains to safety as quickly as possible. Second, he had to find alternative escape routes to pass downed aircrew and evaders through to Spain. Third, he had to ensure the security of the circuit following the arrests and the resulting manhunt. He took the step of sending Delacroix to Reeve, who found him lodgings with the Miserons, where he himself was staying, and gave him the important task of watching the cottage at Beaurains.

Moving the arms away from the cottage presented Michael with a major logistical problem. The wave of arrests had scuppered the plan to use Hertault's vehicle, and, the more thought Michael gave to it, the more certain he became that any form of road transport would inevitably fall foul of the extensive checkpoints that were now in place between Beaurains and Lille. This left him with only one possibility: the weapons would have to go by train. For this he would need the railwaymen and quite a few others besides. After a series of hastily-arranged meetings a plan was hatched whereby men would carry the goods as personal luggage by train as far as the station at Petit Ronchin, from where road vehicles would take it the short distance into Lille via the backstreets.

For the all-important first mission Michael chose Malfait and Gerekens. The two of them took the train to Arras and walked to the cottage at Beaurains, where Delacroix displayed the four tonnes of supplies stacked in every available room. After expressing his admiration for the achievements of the men who had managed to collect and assemble such a formidable arsenal, the ever pragmatic Gerekens voiced his misgivings as to how they were going to move so much material, to which the ever phlegmatic Malfait responded that, since Michael had ordered it, they had better find a way.

After helping the captain's two guinea pigs to load up, Delacroix said he thought that their packages were much too heavy and that they would have difficulty in getting as far as the station. He was silenced by an admonishing finger from Malfait, and could only watch helplessly and anxiously as the men wobbled off on their journey, Malfait struggling with a heavy suitcase, Gerekens staggering under the weight of a large crate bearing a label proclaiming it to be 'Property of the Fives Station Electrical Service'. Shortly before they reached the station at Arras they donned SNCF armbands, which enabled them to enter via a service gate and go directly to their platform, where, with great relief, they put down their burdens and lit cigarettes. To their dismay they were engulfed within minutes by a platoon of German soldiers, and, fearing the worst, they were preparing to flee when Gerekens noticed a sergeant with a clipboard taking a roll call. Realizing that this was just a routine movement of a unit and not an advance guard of pursuers, Malfait saw an opportunity to take advantage of the presence of the troops and invited the NCO to sit on the crate to complete his paperwork. With the offer accepted, Malfait declared to anyone who cared to listen that his spare parts were now completely safe from partisans and other would-be thieves and couldn't be in better hands. This was translated by one of the soldiers and produced a delighted roar of laughter from his companions. When the train drew in the NCO detailed two men to help Gerekens get the crate aboard, while Malfait, with an enquiring look, pointed at the carriage reserved for the troops and received an answering wave for himself and Gerekens to find themselves seats near their luggage. Here they were safe from any random checks of passengers because, following numerous complaints from high-ranking officers, the GFP no longer searched carriages occupied by military personnel. As it happened, the journey was uneventful and, when the train arrived at Petit Ronchin, the Frenchmen moved to get off, whereupon the same two German soldiers leapt to their feet once more and helped them with their packages. There were smiles all round when the two agents of the much-sought *Sylvestre* stood and waved at their new-found friends as the train pulled out of the station, before collapsing with laughter.

Michael had designated Petit Ronchin as the destination in order to avoid the many control points and increased security at Lille itself, and there the two travellers were welcomed by Bayart, whom Gerekens was meeting for the first time. After brief introductions they loaded the arms on to the waiting Thumesnil fire engine, then went to inform Michael of the safe arrival of the first consignment. The next day Bayart ordered part of the consignment to be moved to a store in Rue du Faubourg de Douai in Lille. There, Bayart and Doby divided it into smaller lots, which were then shared out among the local group leaders – typically, a dozen machine guns, two revolvers, and sufficient explosives, incendiaries and fuses each. This was enough for them to start training their men.

Michael listened intently to what Gerekens and Malfait had to say about the trial run, and smiled when they recounted the episode with the Germans. He told them they could not rely on the enemy's sporting assistance and cooperation in the future, but he agreed that the plan had worked. Nevertheless, he ordered that each package should weigh no more than forty kilos, as opposed to the fifty that had been carried by Gerekens and Malfait, and the mass transfer of supplies by this method began. Supervised by Gerekens, in the course of the next two weeks the transportation team, led by Gabriel Royer with ten of his railwaymen from Tourcoing, made more than a dozen trips. At around six each evening, when they knew a consignment was due, Bayart and Edgar Galmace would meet on the Douai road and watch for the train bringing the men with their heavy cases. The supplies in Lille slowly began to build, but Bayart noticed that German soldiers had occupied a small disused fortification, close to the station at Ronchin, and turned it into a barracks. When Michael heard this he saw that the risks of discovery had increased significantly. Even though the occupation of the building was clearly coincidental, and not the result of any security concerns or suspicions on the part of the enemy, each movement had to pass the barracks, and a regular evening parade of men carrying large bundles would, sooner or later, strike someone as suspicious. Reluctantly Michael ordered a halt. Another way would have to be found, and he called a brief council of war.

It was Gerekens who came up with the idea of hiring a commercial delivery vehicle and driver for the ostensible purpose of moving industrial materials and components to the Ets Mory warehouse in Lille's Rue de Maury. The simplicity and boldness of this plan appealed to Michael, and he gave Gerekens the go-ahead. Bayart volunteered to organize the reception parties, and, with Michael's agreement, ordered his men to construct six dozen packing cases. These were despatched to Arras, where Reeve and Dewispelaere took charge of them and arranged for the Arras team to pack into them the remaining two tonnes or so of supplies to await collection.

Gerekens picked his delivery team with great care, selecting André Debruyne from his own men, and a group from Arras consisting of Dubocage, Vanhecke and Charles Lecocq, a controller at the Economic Service of Wasquehal. The latter possessed a trump card in the shape of a permit that allowed him to move freely around the area on his motorbike, and Gerekens sent him ahead of the delivery van, with Vanhecke on his pillion, as an advance guard to look out for any road blocks or other obstacles that might necessitate a change of route. They reached Tilloy without mishap, the cases were loaded swiftly into the van, and the party immediately set off on the return journey – a much riskier trip than the outward leg, since even the most innocent checkpoint could now lead to disaster. Gerekens and his men were deeply conscious of the importance of the mission and stayed quiet and alert, making sure that their concealed weapons were close at hand.

They were greatly relieved when they arrived safely at their destination, which had been changed to the Ets Breton in Rue du Faubourg d'Arras, whose proprietor remained blissfully unaware of its clandestine use. His warehouse manager happened to be Eugène Doby, brother of Gaston, and it was he who supervised the unloading of the crates by Gaston, with help from Bayart and Galmace. When it was complete Galmace produced a pad of delivery notes, wrote out a receipt for 'miscellaneous parts', signed it and handed it to the driver for countersignature. Reassured by this routine and normal procedure the driver scribbled his name, handed back the pad, and drove off, doubtless thankful to be free of the intimidating band of men and their possibly dubious cargo.

This time Michael supervised the allocation of material, and he instructed the group leaders to come to the warehouse to receive their allocation after making their own personal arrangements for its concealment. The remainder was loaded on to two horse-drawn flatbeds. Gerekens and a team took the first flatbed and set off for his hiding places. Part of the consignment, including Sten guns, magazines, 9mm cartridges, revolvers with ammunition, 50kg of plastic explosive, detonators, Bickford cord, cordtex, and time fuses, went to the home of Marcel Bavye, from where the party took the road to Lomme and dropped off rifles, carbines and thousands of cartridges. These went into store at a warehouse in Rue Victor Hugo, where they joined a box of grenades that had been 'recovered' from the Germans in 1940.

Gaston Doby had been introduced to René Vincent, general secretary of the Conservatoire de Lille, and on Bayart's orders had set up three groups in the immediate sector there. The second flatbed, accompanied by Doby and Galmace, went to the Conservatoire, as directed by Bayart, who led the way there on his bicycle. The forty cases were offloaded and taken into the Conservatoire by a small side door. Once the vehicle had been emptied of its valuable cargo, Galmace and the driver went back, while Bayart and Doby stayed to hide the material and prepare for the task of equipping and training the men. At the end of September Fertein distributed material to the groups in Annoeullin and Wavrin and, shortly afterwards, with Michael's permission, drew arms and explosives from the store in Rue de Douai. Béghin took this large amount by horse and cart to give the Baisieux sector its first stocks.

Chieux, meanwhile, was using every method he could think of to get material moved to his own chosen locations – train, motorbikes, vans, horse-drawn carts – and even carrying some in a box strapped to his own bicycle. But his efforts nearly came unstuck when he arrived home one evening from Fives to find a disconsolate neighbour waiting to impart the news that Chieux's wife, Jeanne, was seeing a GMR officer who called at the house regularly while her husband was at work.

What had in fact been happening was one of Herry's men Raymond Petit, dressed in GMR uniform and riding his motorbike, was bringing regular small consignments of supplies to Jeanne, who concealed them in their secret stores. Clearly, since these visits had made the neighbour curious, another method had to be found, and the couple invoked the help of the local postmistress. Thereafter Petit would take small packages to the post office, from where Jeanne would collect them each evening.

Relieved that his logistical difficulties had been overcome, Michael turned his attention to the problem of shifting the increasing number of airmen that had either been rescued by his own men, or had been passed to him by other groups, and were now in temporary hiding places. Even though his circuit was now increasingly under threat and his own safety was compromised, Michael found the question of the Allied airmen constantly running through his mind, and he was determined to do whatever he could to see them returned safely to England. In this, for once, he found a staunch supporter in Reeve, who like Michael had personally benefitted from the sacrifices of those who had set up escape lines earlier in the war.

Foremost among the escape organizations was the PAO line, which had its origins in a line set up in Marseilles late in 1940, when groups of stranded soldiers from Dunkirk and St Valery were helped by French and Belgian civilians, firstly to evade capture – or more often, recapture – by the occupying Germans, and then to travel to the relative safety of the unoccupied zone and thence to Spain. Gondecourt may well have been a link in this chain. In October the line was formally taken over by Edmond Guérisse, a Belgian cavalry officer who had been captured in May 1940 and escaped to England through Dunkirk. He was commissioned into the Royal Navy under the nom de guerre of Lieutenant Commander Patrick Albert O'Leary, and served for a time as an officer on HMS *Fidelity*.[1]

After its sinking he devoted his energy to running the line named from his initials, which became better known as the 'PAO', 'PAT' or 'O'Leary' line. Built around a mixed group of men and women – French, Scots, Jews, Australasians, Greeks and even Germans opposed to Hitler – the line expanded to include the occupied zone and carried more than 600 people to safety. In the winter of 1942/43 the line extended into Brittany but it was soon infiltrated, and a series of arrests in Tours, Toulouse and Marseilles in March, including that of O'Leary himself, virtually finished the line.

Of more local relevance to Michael was the COMÈTE line, which had been set up in 1941 and was based in Brussels, and the BOURGOGNE line, which was established in mid-1943 in Paris. However, neither line had direct links to the resistance nor was particularly anxious to become involved with its members, for fear of jeopardising the security of its own activities. At Michael's suggestion, Reeve discussed the problem with Dewispelaere, who proposed that they contact the OCM, which, with the help of the BOA,* had been making an important contribution to the aims of the French 'government in exile' to provide arms to its own resistance groups so that they could rise up after the invasion. (This was in direct contrast to Churchill's directive to SOE to *'set Europe ablaze'* and inflict maximum damage on the enemy before the invasion.) To facilitate this, SOE had sent a liaison agent into France in December 1942 to organize the BOA teams in the five northern departments, including the Pas de Calais.

The intensive bombing raids on central Germany in April 1943 saw almost daily flights of Anglo-American heavy bombers passing over the area, and it fell to the resistance to recover any downed airmen. The loss of experienced crews was more crucial to the Allies than the loss of equipment, and the OCM/BOA leadership jointly decided to set up its own escape route. The leader of the Lille and Arras sectors of the line was Eugène Dhallendre, assisted by Fernand Lobbedez, Mayor of Arras, who, with his son, had been helping Allied soldiers to escape since 1941. Dhallendre's job and activities as a senior railwayman made him particularly efficient at aiding the passage of evaders by rail. He was also one of the escorts attached to COMÈTE. But the OCM had been infiltrated; in July arrests had begun and the line in the Pas de Calais had collapsed.

Once again it was Dewispelaere who came up with an answer. Among

---

* BOA: *Bureau des Operations Aériennes (Air Operations Office)*, responsible for coordinating air activity on behalf of the Free French forces, including reception and despatch of agents

his customers in Arras was Arthur Richards, a 60-year-old Englishman whom the Germans had left alone, possibly regarding him as a harmless old man. Taking advantage of this Richards had set up his own organization, which he christened 'Richard Coeur de Lion', made up of a dozen or so friends who wanted to help with intelligence and escape activities. He introduced Reeve and Dewispelaere to Berthe Fraser, wife of an interned Scotsman, who ran a small boutique in Rue St Aubert. She too had been arrested in 1941, on suspicion of participation in escape activities, and had been in Loos prison at the same time as Yvonne Pachy, who remembered her. Fraser had been released after a year for lack of evidence. Through the intermediary of the secretary of the town council both Richards and Fraser had had periodic contact with Lobbedez, and when Michael duly contacted them to ask for help they were delighted to have the opportunity to be active once more. Fraser gave Reeve all the assistance she could and carried out his orders faithfully.

She recalled her first meeting with Michael:

> *'They required information concerning troop movements, defence works, fortifications etc., which was to be transmitted to the IS.* They also requested me to find reception grounds for their parachutings, cribs for arms and also to place at their disposal some safe lodgings where they would be able to put any of their men needing shelter from the Gestapo. One of these men – Nenesse – (Volckaert of Arras) who came to London on 1 February 1944 was hidden some weeks in my sister's house (Madame Fournier of Behagnies near Bapaume).'*[2]

Fraser became the letterbox between the BOA and Richards to enable them to communicate with FARMER, and she put Michael and Reeve in touch with a number of other helpers, including Abel Guidet, a veteran of the First World War, in which he had been wounded. He had been Deputy Mayor of Bapaume since 1929, being constantly re-elected unopposed. From the time the Germans marched into France he had applied his energies to doing whatever he could to thwart and frustrate them, while making life under the occupation as comfortable as possible for his own citizens. He decided to do something positive by actively helping in the repatriation of soldiers and airmen of all nationalities who found themselves stranded in his region. Guidet came from an old aristocratic but radical socialist family, and, although she knew of him, Fraser did not know him well enough to approach him about assisting the FARMER circuit to help Allied airmen. However, Dewispelaere managed to pull some strings of his own by arranging an introduction to Guidet through his own friends, the mayors of St Léger and of Gommecourt.

---

* The reference 'IS' presumably relates to Intelligence Service

Guidet had recently received a Russian officer who had escaped from a German concentration camp and found refuge in a farm south of Bapaume, and an English pilot who came down near Bapaume and was taken to Guidet by the owner of the local café. He placed the two officers with his sister-in-law, and tried to contact Dhallendre as usual to arrange their evacuation, unaware that Dhallendre had been arrested. On the same day three downed British airmen were passed to Bapaume resident Henriette Balesi in Arras and she took them to Guidet, with whom she had worked closely for a number of months. She told Guidet of the arrests in Arras and the two of them looked for an alternative means of moving the evaders on, now that the route via Dhallendre was closed to them.

Balesi was a 70-year-old Corsican ex-nurse who had a long history of saving combatants from the Germans. She was an important member of the organization run by Edith Cavell during the First World War, and regarded the current struggle simply a continuation of the previous one. She had retained many of her useful contacts from 1914-18, and, in spite of her age and a painful stomach ulcer, during 1942 and 1943 she acted as a courier for the COMÈTE escape line, covering the routes from Caudry to Arras and from Bapaume to Paris. The COMÈTE organizer in Paris was at this time Jacques de Grelle *(Jerome)*; Balesi had been introduced to him by Dhallendre, but she had no idea how to contact him. By a stroke of good fortune, she was on her way to her small pied-à-terre in Paris when she spotted de Grelle crossing the concourse in the Gare du Nord. Embracing him as an elderly mother might greet her son, she quickly brought him up to date with the arrests, and the need to move on the airmen. He immediately gave her contacts and coordinates for future missions, for which the rendezvous point would be St Laurent's Church in Boulevard de Strasbourg in Paris. Realizing that she was now back in business, she turned around and went to tell Guidet the good news. He took her to meet Reeve, who welcomed her with open arms and gave her the cover name *Madame Blanche* for use within the circuit. Over the next three months Michael's men were able to recover and return ten airmen to England through the Guidet–Balesi combination and the BOURGOGNE and COMÈTE lines.

In September Fertein picked up two American airmen, Lieutenant Scherman and Sergeant Russell, whom he found wandering around Pont-à-Marcq, south of Lille. Michael took them to stay with Descamps, while he made arrangements for them to be found a place in an escape line. He collected them a week later, at about nine o'clock in the evening. The airmen put on civilian clothes and were given false identity cards, before they all set off for Wattignies. Accompanied by Fertein and Lemercier, Michael led them to a safe house in Annoeulin. From there they too managed to get back to England via Spain.

In the Nord Michael recruited couriers from officers of the customs service, who by virtue of their work were well positioned to assist with evasion activities. From the time of the German occupation many of them had been undertaking these kinds of activities spontaneously, either individually or as part of an organized line. New groups were formed in Béghin's sector, and Michael began to contemplate the possibility of using these lines to solve the problem of his own 'loose cannons'.

Chapter notes
1   The former French tramp steamer *Le Rhin* had escaped to Britain after the fall of France and been recommissioned as HMS *Fidelity.*' The French crew was inducted into the Royal Navy and allocated for service with SOE, for whom it carried out a number of missions along the south coast of France.
2   From a report submitted by Berthe Fraser on 7 December 1944.

Chapter 18

Panic

'The atrocious crime of being a young man.'
William Pitt, First Earl of Chatham

Michael was now able to turn his attention to the threats to the circuit posed by those still at large and being actively hunted by the Gestapo, in particular Lemercier, Woussen and Volckaert. At the same time he took comfort from the knowledge that the railwaymen had swung into action and that FARMER had at last begun to inflict real damage on the enemy.

At the beginning of August Gerekens had spotted a flak gun installed on the footplate of one of the carriages of a train in Lille station, guarded by soldiers pacing up and down between the lines. Dressed in his SNCF uniform he slipped onto the track, managed to get close to the gun without attracting attention, and surreptitiously slipped a hand grenade down the barrel. Then he calmly but quickly withdrew. Thirty seconds later the grenade exploded, and from the safe and unsuspected vantage point of his office Gerekens was able to look on and enjoy the spectacle.

In September attacks on German communications began in earnest. On 10 September the remainder of the equipment from the August drops – about four tonnes of arms and ammunition – found its way to Lille, from where it was shared out amongst Fertein, Gerekens and Malfait. The men who had been on the various reception teams were among the first to receive training in the use of the weapons and explosives, and it was not long before the St Léger group was in action. Supervised by Dewispelaere and his cousins, the Bulcourt brothers, it laid explosives on the railway line between Boisleux and Arras. The charges went off at three in the morning of 12 September as a train was passing through. It came to no harm and the 5m of damaged track were repaired within hours, but it was an encouraging start. The next day, despite the attentions of a squad of soldiers assigned to guard the trucks during their stop at Tourcoing, three clams were placed there on linseed oil tanks. These exploded when the train arrived at Douai, causing three 63m^3 tanks to overturn and spill their contents on the ballast.

Michael was reasonably confident that Lemercier was safely out of the way, at least for the immediate future, and Dewispelaere had gone to stay at a farm in Gommecourt, rented from Mayor Roger and managed by Dina Delambre, who then acted as a letterbox between Reeve, Dewispelaere and the mayor. But the future of those involved in the 'Rex affair' was far from secure. The murder of one of their own men in Arras had incensed the police and security forces, and they had thrown considerable resources into tracking down the men involved with the shooting at Dacheux's garage, albeit so far without any success.

The search, helped by some French civil servants who were told they were looking for armed gangsters, was thorough enough to lead them to the Verrokens in Arras and the Rogers in Gommecourt, but these wily organizers had their stories well prepared. Martel had given the police the address of Woussen's fiancée, but it soon became obvious that she knew nothing, and they got no further either with Volckaert's young girlfriend, who had been left completely in the dark about what happened to her lover. She simply said that Albéric had not surfaced anywhere as far as she knew, and he had most probably gone to stay with friends in Belgium, whom she had never met. This lack of progress infuriated and frustrated the High Command of the *Sicherheitspolizei* in Brussels. Deciding that extreme measures were called for, it put up the previously unheard-of sum of 500,000 Belgian francs as a reward for information leading to the arrest of Woussen and Volckaert, and saturated the area with publicity. More than 2,000 posters were plastered on the walls of towns and villages throughout Belgium, the Nord, the Pas de Calais and the Ardennes, and dramatic notices were placed in Belgian and French newspapers, all displaying photographs and full descriptions of the two wanted men.

After two nights spent in the open, Woussen had found shelter with Ida Edouard, Miseron's aunt, who managed a café and was also the clerk at Hénin-sur-Cojeul's post office. Her son, René, had been active with the St Léger Group, and her daughter, Lucienne, a hairdresser, dyed Woussen's blond hair repeatedly until it became jet black. Meanwhile, Volckaert had gone to Mayor Roger for help immediately following the shooting at the garage. He had swiftly passed him on to a friend in Souastre, where further problems arose when Volckaert, cycling through the Adinfer Woods on 13 September, stumbled into a German checkpoint manned by two *Feldgendarmes*. Knowing that he was a wanted man, with papers that would not stand up to serious scrutiny, he decided to fight it out and gunned down the two policemen before escaping on his bike. Unable to return to Souastre, where a German unit had promptly moved in and were conducting enquiries, he turned once more to Mayor Roger, who found him temporary accommodation in Gommecourt.

Although the German publicity campaign brought no immediate results, it had the effect of turning many potentially willing if hesitant supporters against the refugees, significantly reducing their options, exactly as the

Germans hoped. Ida and her daughter were thrown into panic when they were confronted one morning with a large German poster on the wall of the house opposite. It portrayed a picture of the young man who had spent the last month with them and was to be seen drinking regularly in their café or cycling from Hénin-sur-Cojeul to Croisilles or St Léger, where he would meet Delacroix. From that point on, everything changed. Suddenly the nice little brave and amusing lad turned into a dangerous, reckless and unwanted intruder whom nobody wanted to know, and Woussen found himself out in the cold.

Four families with women and young children suddenly felt the chill of danger hanging over their heads. Such a reward was almost certain to lead to anonymous denunciations from ambitious and greedy neighbours, if something were not done right away. As one they took their grievance to Reeve and Dewispelaere, demanding instant action and presenting Michael's lieutenants with a dilemma. Well aware that they would receive no further cooperation of any kind from this important group if they failed to respond to their request, they had no option but to promise that Woussen would leave within a few days. Yet they had no idea where to put him. It was impossible to accommodate him in Arras, where the dangers were even greater, and they had enough on their plate already with Volckaert, who was hiding in fear of his life with Delambre. But the German posters raised their ugly heads there, too, and Roger, conscious of his responsibilities as mayor of his community, insisted that the Belgian leave Gommecourt as quickly and quietly as possible. Shortly afterwards Volckaert was found accommodation at an isolated farm in Coigneux owned by Gaston Bouchez, where he wisely decided to lie low.

Volckaert was a mature man of 57 who felt reasonably at home in the region around Arras, and was perfectly capable of looking after himself, but the situation with Woussen was radically different. Here was a young, impulsive and immature man, little more than a boy, who suddenly found himself at 18 completely on his own. He was unable to contact his fiancée, his mother was in Loos prison, and his father had been arrested and interned for two years in Germany when his name appeared on a list of communists. He was devastated when the people he had depended on and counted as friends suddenly abandoned him and now wanted him as far away from them as possible. In desperation he pleaded with Delacroix to get a message to Michael through Lemercier to tell him about the hopeless situation he now found himself in. He felt sure that his leader would recognize his plight and come to his assistance: after all, they were both hunted men.

In the meantime, Michael and Reeve had reached the conclusion that the only satisfactory solution was to remove their three dangerous fugitives from the country via Guidet's escape line. They told them of their decision and notified the three mayors of St Léger, Gommecourt and Bapaume. While Lemercier and Volckaert, in their respective refuges, awaited the event with calm but eager anticipation, Woussen became more and more nervous and difficult, constantly worrying about the possibility of capture, and heightening the tension and insecurity within the Miseron families. This impacted on Reeve, since he too was staying with the Miserons, and he found himself forced to take their side against the unhappy and nervous Woussen, which only increased the young man's misery. Clearly, this could not go on, and Woussen had to be moved again while the complex arrangements were being made for his escape.

As he always did in times of trouble, Reeve turned once more to the ever reliable Dewispelaere, whom he was wont to flatter on occasion by opening his hands and claiming self-deprecatingly that while he was the brawn, Henri was the brains. But this time even Dewispelaere was stumped for an answer. All his contacts in the area were either interrelated or close friends, and they were well aware of the problem Woussen presented. No-one wanted to know him, the more so since at this precise time Dr Poiteau, who had been instrumental in finding a place for Volckaert, was arrested. The good doctor kept his silence, but this unexpected setback only served to increase the fears of the local people, who began to hide themselves behind locked doors.

The situation was not lost on Woussen, who started to panic and threaten his hosts, saying that if he were caught, many other arrests would follow, and they would be wise to take good care of him. His reasoning was reinforced by a conversation he had with Delacroix on his return from a visit to Bruay, after Lemercier had told Delacroix, quite emphatically, that Woussen should take no notice of the locals, all of whom had sworn their allegiance and knew the risks. They had a duty to ensure Woussen's safety by hiding him, not by chasing him away. He should tell them to stop and think what might happen if he was taken after he had left them: they would shake in their shoes. This was just what Woussen wanted to hear and he became ever more vocal with his threats, to the dismay and concern of his terrified but powerless countrymen.

Throughout this troubled period, despite the arrests and the relentless German searches, FARMER continued to function. For the railwaymen it was business as usual. They worked tirelessly, establishing a highly efficient intelligence gathering and monitoring service that enabled them to feed Michael with important information about the movement of troops and munitions, and the layout and function of power stations and other installations on the rail network. They systematically copied official reports concerning incidents that affected the SNCF in the Nord, which allowed the circuit to gain control of it. Thanks to this knowledge and the specific nature and location of their jobs, they were able quickly to identify sabotage opportunities, and devised methods of attacking enemy rail traffic which became more and more refined and effective as time went on.

On 17 September a Belgian train carrying linseed oil burst into flames at the station in Orchies, and the next morning four trucks were set on fire at Mouscron station. The Germans hit back, swooping on 20 September to round up thirty or so members of *La Voix du Nord* group, thanks to information from a collaborator. As the victims were being led away they were seen by men from the abattoir, who decided they had to recover and remove to safety all the weapons stored in the Conservatoire. That night they put up ladders at the building's gates and carried the heavy packages out via the roof.

The unwitting but deadly game of tit-for-tat continued. On 22 September Fernand Sapin started a fire in a truck carrying linseed oil, and five days later he set fire to three more. In the early hours of 28 September a train from Lille-Déliverance to Le Bourget was derailed. The engine and tender ending up straddling both up and down lines, while thirteen carriages ran into each other and were smashed. These included six coaches containing military equipment, and this section of the track was out of action for several hours. It was one of the most successful attacks so far.

But the Germans had not been idle. On 23 September the remainder of the abattoir men were arrested. When Bayart heard of this he arranged for the compromising weapons to be moved yet again, this time to a garage in Rue de Douai, where the various group leaders were called to collect their allocation. Bayart lent the abattoir men one of his firm's vans to help with the transportation, but on 27 September this vehicle was intercepted while stock was being moved, and it was traced back to Bayart's company. At around two the next afternoon a Gestapo squad turned up at Bayart's home and, not finding him there, carried out a search while they waited for him to return. They were looking for photographs that would help them to identify him, but all they found were some of a 60-year-old man. After interrogating Madame Bayart and her daughters they concluded that someone of that age was unlikely to be the active resistance leader they were looking for, and that it must be his son, Claude, they wanted; but they could find no photographs of him either.

Two officers then left for the Morival factory in Rue Danton. When they arrived there, just before five o'clock, it was Claude Bayart who opened the door to them. Unaware of whom he was, they ordered him to bring Georges Bayart to them. Claude pretended to comply and promptly made off across the roof, leaving his colleagues, including Galmace, to deal with the problem. Galmace was on the run from the STO and had been lodging there for several months; thinking this was a routine police visit, he took the precaution of retrieving his gun, a machine pistol, from under his bed and hiding it in a space under the eaves before going downstairs to join the workmen on the shop floor. There he realized that he should have escaped while he had the opportunity, because he was faced not with the French police but with the Gestapo. He and four other men were pointed out to the Germans by frightened factory workers, arrested, and bundled into two hastily summoned cars. The vehicle with Galmace in diverted via Rue Jean Bart, where Madame Bayart and her daughter were pushed into the back seats in handcuffs. When they arrived at *La Madeleine*, in Rue Francois de Badts, they were all separated. The Bayart women were shown the weapons seized from Bayart's vehicle and told they were to be held as hostages while the search for 'Monsieur Bayart' continued. Around midnight they were taken to Loos prison.

In the meantime Georges Bayart had had a narrow escape. Returning home with Gaston Doby he spotted that the front curtains were tightly drawn, a prearranged family signal warning of trouble. The two men continued walking, discreetly left the area, and hurried to their usual letterbox at *Café Descatoires*. When, shortly after, Bayart was told of the German visit to the factory, the men decided not to go home again. Doby sent a man to warn his family and arranged for them to go into hiding and spend the night with friends. In the course of the evening Bayart learned that his wife and daughter had been arrested. The next morning, after sending a messenger to Lille, he ordered Doby to leave the area and take his family into the countryside.

News of the situation came as another severe blow to Michael. Bayart was the second of his headquarters team for whom he had to find shelter, since Fertein had left his family and his job in July and been accommodated in Camphin-en-Carembault. This time the position was more serious, since, to escape what would certainly be an intense Gestapo manhunt, Bayart would have to leave the region altogether. To begin with he stayed in a property in Anthony belonging to the family, then he moved to hotels previously used by Duval for the escape line. Eventually, a safe place was found for him in Boulevard Murat in Paris. In his exile Bayart joined a number of other men from the north in the same situation, and he had to be content with continuing his work from a distance. Simone Séailles acted as his courier with the Nord.

Throughout the organization's dark period Michael found great delight in and took enormous comfort from the successes of the railwaymen, especially those of Liébault's group. He particularly enjoyed hearing how each morning Liébault would telephone Gerekens and tell him, with heavy irony, that everything was fine and that the *'terrorist bastards'* had been in action again that night, thereby ensuring that his colleague was kept fully in the picture as to what was happening. Michael was so impressed that he asked Gerekens to arrange for him to meet his men. So it was that on 1 October the two men caught the train to Valenciennes. During the trip Gerekens detected for the first time a hint of weariness and despondency in his leader as he talked nostalgically about returning to England when the war was over and settling down. But by the time they arrived, to be warmly welcomed on the platform by Liébault, Michael was his normal, buoyant self once more.

Liébault had laid on a surprise. As he led his visitors towards the Jacob Bridge that ran across the station he asked them to look towards the St Saulve depot and, in particular, platform 16. Following his pointed finger they turned their heads, and were rewarded by the sight and sound of four huge explosions that sent ammunition trucks, tanks and sections of track hurtling into the air. Michael could not contain his delight, and he was deeply touched when Liébault introduced him to some of his team and explained that the 'fireworks' were a small celebration in honour of the Feast of St Michael, which had taken place two days before. Michael congratulated the men, but on the way back to Lille he asked Gerekens to do his best to curb the group's enthusiasm, because he was worried that such devastating activity would unleash reprisal measures that would have dire consequences for all of them. Then, as the excitement and adrenaline left him, he closed his eyes and went to sleep. Gerekens noted with concern the tiredness in his leader's face and his uncharacteristic words of caution.

However, Michael had been fired up by the Valenciennes demonstration and decided that he needed some action. As he later told Malfait, after leaving Gerekens and on his way back to the headquarters in Boulevard de Belfort, he chased a German soldier through the streets, firing his revolver at him because the sight of the uniform had annoyed him. He then turned his thoughts once more to the Fives factory and what he considered to be unfinished business. He had already talked with Séailles about the possibility of mounting a second attack. The first attempt had suffered through lack of sufficient equipment, but things had changed, and he was now convinced that the key to bringing construction to a halt was the destruction of the large overhead cranes. [1]

Meanwhile, stimulated by Michael's visit, Liébault and his team redoubled their efforts. Gerekens passed on Michael's wish that they calm down a little, but it had no effect, and that same night they launched attacks on the engine yards in Valenciennes, resulting in seven locomotives parked inside the turntable being stranded there.

Chapter notes

1 The story of the chase is related in the Amicale booklet (see Notes to Chapter 14) and is similar to another episode, described to me by Pierre Séailles. Michael opened a window in the flat and started firing his gun into the copse opposite, purely to antagonize and frustrate the Germans with the sound of gunshots during the curfew. Having let loose half a dozen shots, he simply closed the window, and by the time the Germans arrived there was nothing to see. Séailles said that this sort of behaviour was *'beyond reckless'*, in that it risked drawing attention to the safe house, but was typical of Michael's tactics from time to time.

Chapter 19

Confrontation

*'Either condemn them en bloc or force them to
repudiate the leaders they adopted.'*
Jean-Paul Sartre

The next morning Michael once again pored over the reports, plans and diagrams that Chieux had provided for the Fives raid, and in the late afternoon he came to a decision: he could not expect his men to put their lives at risk without providing firm leadership and demonstrating that he was with them all the way. He felt the need once more to challenge himself, and resolved to carry out an attack single-handed. He would say nothing to his lieutenants before the event, because, as he told them later, he knew they would try to talk him out of it. Worse, they would almost certainly insist on accompanying him, thereby risking their own lives and endangering the survival of the circuit, which, he was sure, would continue to flourish without him personally but could not survive a mass elimination of its leaders.

He concealed his intentions during a busy day of meetings and, after resting in the early evening, set off at ten o'clock on the short walk across the bridge to Fives. As he turned into the approach avenue, hugging the walls of the buildings, he realized that, while he knew exactly where he needed to go once inside the factory, he had no idea how he was going to gain entry in the first place, and suspected he would need to scale a wall. At this precise moment fate – in the shape of the Royal Air Force – intervened to solve his problem for him. As he looked round for means of entry, the wail of the air raid siren shrieked into the night air, emptying the courtyards, workshops and offices. The numerous guards and armed patrols, which had been on constant alert since the June sabotage, dashed for cover, and the main gates sprang open to let in the emergency services in case of need. Taking advantage of the confusion, Michael slipped inside as the anti-aircraft guns opened up.

Although he had studied the layout very carefully, he was initially disorientated. There was a huge complex of multiple halls and courtyards, each full of equipment, and with the moon barely into its first phase he found it difficult to get his bearings. As he looked around he was conscious that he was losing valuable minutes. When he finally found himself in the engine workshop he saw that the two overhead cranes, which during the day shared the same track, had been stowed as far away from each other as possible, one at each end of the massive hall, presumably as a precaution against damage from bombing. He did not have enough explosive to sabotage them both completely, so he decided to inflict what damage he could by placing charges on each of the electric motors that powered the cranes. He located the steel ladder that provided access to the gantry some 10m from the ground, and, ludicrously (as he realized later, in view of the din from the anti-aircraft batteries), took off his shoes to avoid making any noise, climbed the ladder and hoisted himself on to the service platform. Pushing his satchel ahead of him he cautiously made his way along the framework, laid the charges and set the timers. He was about to climb down and move to the second crane when two night watchmen entered the hall. He froze into the shadows but they had clearly seen or heard something, for they let out a yell before leaving. Knowing they would be bringing help, Michael let himself down as quickly as he could, recovered his shoes, and made his way out of the factory. Just after one o'clock in the morning, two explosions shattered the roof of the workshop, destroyed one crane and distorted the gantry, causing sufficient damage to require lengthy repairs. In spite of his efforts Michael felt disappointed and frustrated: thwarted by the arrival of the patrol, he had once again failed to complete the job, and he resolved to have yet another go at a later date.

Spurred on by the efforts of the railwaymen in Valenciennes, those in Tourcoing swung into action. On 2 October, they started a fire in a truck full of straw; two days later they damaged four wagons carrying linseed oil at Fives-Lille, and on 7 October four more linseed oil wagons went up in smoke. The Germans responded by placing a guard on every locomotive and doubling those at each strategic location – a huge expense of manpower which in itself represented a victory for the saboteurs. The precautions had little effect: on 8 October four more engines were seriously damaged and forty-eight hours later a group led by Liébault completely destroyed the electricity sub-station at St Saulve.

Their next target was the signal box at Ronchin, which controlled direct entry to the St Sauveur railway station that served Paris and Béthune and was reserved exclusively for German military use. It had been damaged during an air raid, since when convoys had been forced to make long detours; these in turn obstructed the traffic from Fives and caused delays in deliveries. Repairs were nearly complete and the box was expected to be back in service on 15 October. Gerekens wanted to stop this happening and, remembering Michael's reservations about further action, went to him for approval to mount an operation. To his surprise he found a completely different man: buoyed by his own activity at Fives (applauded by his lieutenants with a faintly censorial air), Michael was his former positive self, and he told Gerekens to go ahead.

On the morning of 13 October Gerekens carried out a final reconnaissance of the area, noting the positions of the German patrols as they criss-crossed the sector and of the French guards posted to watch the tracks; he also spotted a broken window in the signal box. That afternoon he made up an explosive charge consisting of three blocks of plastic, Bickford cord and an incendiary device, and just before seven o'clock he met up with his friend, Sapin. After a number of minor setbacks they laid their charges later that evening, and had managed to reach the safety of a small copse when a bright flash lit up the night sky, followed by a loud explosion.

The next day at work Gerekens jubilantly copied the official despatch – '*Ronchin signal box destroyed, estimated damage one million francs: beyond economic repair*' – and sent it to Michael, who was absolutely delighted. They were continuing to hit the Germans and were hitting them hard. Two locomotives had to be taken out of service to be cannibalized for spare parts, and the stations and depots at Lille, Fives and St Sauveur were all cut off. The latter was without current for ten days and the damaged turntables and cranes caused serious delays and disruption. Clearly, the hard-won explosives were being put to good use.

Meanwhile, in the Pas de Calais, Lemercier had begun to fret. He had been left to cool his heels for a long time, and he had taken to shuttling back and forth between Schynkel's house in Bruay and his mother-in-law's home in Houdain. At the beginning of September Vandesype had called and told him to be ready to move at any time, and since then he had heard nothing. Frustrated, he had sent a message to Michael via Schynkel, asking what was happening, and had received a reply telling him to be patient and informing him that Michael would be in touch very soon. It came as a complete surprise, therefore, when Lemercier appeared at Malfait's home in Wattrelos on the morning of 14 October. Travelling with papers in the name of 'Jean Murat', he had grown a beard, dyed his hair red, and taken to wearing small spectacles, in the belief that this would make him unrecognizable and enable him to pass along the chain of customs and police officers into Belgium, where he wanted to obtain a rucksack, shoes and various other bits and pieces to take with him to England. His departure, he said, was imminent, and it soon became clear to Malfait that Lemercier felt very bitter at having been shunted to one side and condemned to isolation after all he had done. He found it hard to accept that, in the five months since he had relinquished his position as Michael's number two, the circuit had grown without his involvement and other leaders had risen with it. [1]

In fact, his very necessary departure had come as something of a relief to Michael, who had been forced more and more frequently to step in to resolve the arguments and petty niggles that arose between his old friend and the rest of the team. To his credit, Lemercier accepted without question his leader's rulings in these matters, but he had struggled to cope with the circuit's rapid expansion and the need for responsibilities to be shared round and allocated to others. His frustration came to the fore when he fired a parting shot at Malfait and Vandesype, who had come to join them. He warned them that, while they now had responsibility and power and he was nothing, they needed to remember that the reason he was leaving was to protect them. He followed up by assuring them that their turn would come, and if he were arrested they would have real cause for concern. He then bade them farewell and hoped they would sleep well. With that he left and went back to Bruay, having been ordered by Michael to shave off his beard.

It could be that Lemercier simply wanted to have the last word and threw out some ill-considered remarks, but they were spoken harshly enough for Malfait to take them at face value. Alarmed, he sat down and wrote an urgent report to Michael, urging him to issue a vigorous reprimand to Lemercier for his disloyal and demoralising statements, even if they were just an empty bluff. Malfait was surprised when, a few days later, he visited Michael and found Bayart, Séailles, Reeve and Gerekens discussing the same subject. Having visited other agents, Lemercier had repeated his threat, which Bayart, Séailles and Reeve refused to consider as simply bluff. They were emphatic that the threat was not to be taken lightly and that the former deputy leader was deadly serious. Collectively they saw him now as a potential and highly dangerous traitor, and asked Michael to order his immediate execution.

After thinking it over Michael explained that he was convinced that Lemercier was merely blustering out of frustration, and that a quiet word from himself would see an end to the matter for the short period of time before Lemercier's departure for England. He asked his men to consider that Lemercier was in a desperate position, hunted not because of any harm he had done to the circuit but because of all the good things he had achieved and the damage he had helped to inflict on the German efforts. The thought of setting off for a strange country, to spend the rest of the war inactive and cut off from his family, would put a strain on anyone. Michael demanded loyalty from his subordinates, and insisted that they were entitled to receive loyalty in return. He assured his lieutenants that this was a matter he could, and would, deal with personally, for at the back of his mind would have been the promise he had made to Lemercier's wife Eliane to take care of their son and Michael's godson. He then called the meeting to an end and forced himself to put the matter out of his mind, turning his attention to planning further raids on the German industrial machine. [2]

While the others might have accepted Michael's decision, Reeve left the meeting disgruntled. On his return to Arras he lamented the situation to anyone who would listen, openly criticizing Michael and insisting that in Arras at least there would be positive and decisive leadership, and that he, Reeve, would provide it. He was determined that Woussen would not get off in the same way, and fully intended to make an example of him. Calling Dewispelaere and his three mayors together at the Miserons he declared that, while Michael might not understand the people from the Nord, he most certainly did. Lemercier's story, he stressed, was almost an exact parallel of Woussen's; they needed to take immediate action to stop this treasonable behaviour spreading further and restore people's confidence in the circuit's leadership, as well as ensuring the security and continuity of its operations. He demanded the death penalty for Woussen. [3]

Clearly shaken and subdued by the ferocity of his speech the four men looked uneasily at each other. They were unwilling to give their approval but were conscious of the need for solidarity and obedience to the officer who had been appointed to lead them and make these tough decisions. Eventually Guidet broke the silence. By nature a generous and humane man, he found it incomprehensible that they should be contemplating the murder of an 18-year-old French boy who was simply frightened and had become carried away. He would, he said, look after the lad himself until he could find him a place in the escape line. His outburst was greeted with instant approval and evident relief on the part of his colleagues, and Reeve, faced with unanimous opposition, had no choice but to back down. But he warned Guidet that he would be held responsible if anything went wrong.

Reeve was furious at this second rebuff in the space of a few days, by what he saw as yet another example of Michael's pervasive and damaging influence. He stepped up his campaign to malign him at every opportunity, causing great concern and dismay among some of the men in Arras. Eventually, Dewispelaere raised the issue with Malfait, who, after pressing him for details of what had been said, felt once again that he had no choice but to report the matter to Michael, stressing his concern that, if this situation were allowed to continue, there would be severe repercussions. Malfait described what happened next:

> '*When we went back towards Lille,* Jacky [Gerekens] *shared some thoughts with me that convinced me that he* [Reeve] *had told him similar things and it was the same, I was sure, with Dewispelaere and others. I made my report to* Michel *and remember very well to have said: "I wouldn't like to tell tales and put you up against* Olivier [Reeve]. *But the latter has been bad-mouthing you." I explained as I told him what he said and my suspicions. "If it were only a simple quarrel between two English officers, this would have nothing to do with us. But we are worried, you are leading us and we are risking*

our lives. This could be disastrous if the men notice it. I am asking you to sort it out and I am quite prepared to be a witness against Olivier.*"*

'A few days later, I found the latter at HQ and to my surprise he shook my hand feebly with his head hanging low. After his departure, Michel *commented laconically: "You saw. You understood. I am the leader." Later, finding myself alone with Denise, I asked her if she knew what happened. "Oh yes," she said. "They had it out, and to* Olivier *who had on a previous occasion boasted about being a good boxer,* Michel *suggested a fair contest. I heard then what he had decided when he declared: "The one who knocks out the other will command." Both then withdrew to the waste ground in front of the HQ and after two or three blows* Olivier *found himself on the ground."*

' Our "boxer" didn't know, and we only heard about it 30 years later through Major Smith, who had been his instructor at the Middlesex Regiment, that Michael Trotobas was a fierce competitor in all of his unit's sporting competitions and won all his fights. He had talent, our Michel.*'* [4]

Michael told Malfait that there were no problems between him and Reeve: there had been a simple disagreement, which they had sorted out like gentlemen. Malfait was to tell his men that nothing had changed and that *Le Capitaine* was still in charge. He should stress that Reeve was an honourable man and a fine officer, that Michael had the greatest respect for him as a leader, and that the men should follow and trust him. Malfait left for Roubaix, hopeful that events would now take a turn for the better. However, Michael must have feared privately that he had not heard the last of the Reeve problem. Things could only get worse, for on top of his innate resentment that London had not given him a command of his own, Reeve had now suffered a humiliating defeat at the hands of a man whom he clearly considered unfit to be his leader. Yet the circuit needed him.

The apparent resolution of these areas of discontent came as a relief to all the men. It had become a huge and unwelcome distraction for Michael too, who knew they all needed to do something positive again – and soon. They had grown increasingly concerned at their leaders' preoccupation with personal matters and perceived threats to security, which had caused attention to be taken away from operational planning and preparation. Fortunately, there were no significant developments with the Woussen manhunt during this period, but they were all caught off balance when on 18 October urgent messages were received warning them to be ready for no fewer than three parachute drops the next evening.

Michael had underestimated the effect of the confusion and uncertainty caused in the Pas de Calais by the waves of arrests and their consequences. Constant Miseron's team had been reunited but refused point blank to take any further part in resistance activity until the Woussen threat had been removed. Consequently, when Michael arrived in Arras he found that, through lack of designated organizers, only the St Léger team was anywhere near ready. Furious with his deputies for this failure he decided to supervise arrangements himself, ordering Reeve to take charge of the Gommecourt drop, Delacroix the one at St Léger, and Dewispelaere the one at Ransart. He instructed them to get their teams assembled and hold themselves in readiness to move at any time. But bad weather intervened to make parachuting impossible for forty-eight hours.

To pacify the Miserons, Michael instructed Reeve to take Woussen to Guidet the next morning. The latter had already set wheels in motion, asking Balesi to make the necessary arrangement to have Woussen taken out of the country, but she had been unable to persuade the COMÈTE organizers to accept him. Not one to give in easily she approached the BOURGOGNE network, and, through a process of wheedling, finally succeeded in getting Woussen a place, to her great relief. He, along with two airmen Michael had brought to Arras, was taken by Guidet to Bapaume, and then on to the agreed rendezvous at the St Laurent Church in Paris. From there Woussen went to stay with BOURGOGNE's Madeleine Melot at her apartment in Rue Larrey, until the time for departure came around. By calling in many favours, Guidet had also been able to wangle a place for Lemercier on the convoy after Woussen's, but had no success with Volckaert, who was now under suspicion of killing the two policemen in Adinfer and was regarded as dangerous merchandise by the organizers of the convoys.

The two airmen were Canadians Clarence 'Curly' Motheral and Bill Dumsday, who had been shot down on 30 August and been given shelter at the home of Sonneville, where they stayed for two months while arrangements were made for their onward passage. Here they met the young Stephen Grady, the son of an English father and French mother, who had been living in Nieppe when the Germans arrived in 1940. In a desperate attempt to get away he had cycled to Dunkirk, only to find that the British soldiers wanted nothing to do with him: there was no question of his getting a place on a boat to England when there were a quarter of a million soldiers waiting to be shipped back. Grady was devastated and spent a terrifying summer watching as Hitler's troops seized control of his home town, forcing his father into hiding and leaving the family without any income.

Jules Houcke, the Mayor of Nieppe, knew the family well and stepped in, deciding that, as the young man had French identity papers, he could carry on his father's work as caretaker of the three British cemeteries in Nieppe, and this small income kept the family going. But Grady wanted to do something against the Germans, and his impulsive nature led to his arrest after he scrawled British propaganda on a crashed Messerschmitt fighter. He was put in a cell in Lille for two days without food or water, and told he would be shot. Only after the mayor made a desperate plea for clemency was he released, whereupon Houcke promptly recruited him into *La Voix du Nord* group. Grady's tasks ranged from distributing propaganda leaflets to using his native English to talk to evading airmen to establish if they were genuine or German infiltrators. Sonneville had asked him to vet Motheral and Dumsday. Grady concluded that they were genuine. It was then that he first heard about what was happening in Lille, as he recounted in his book *Gardens of Stone*:

> *'Sonneville offers me a cigarette from a teak-lined silver box. He explains that he is in a Resistance organization called the War Office, or WO, and that sheltering Allied airmen is just a sideline for him. And then he tells me something that makes my eyes widen. The group is run by a young British officer, parachuted into France. A real officer of the British army, right here in our midst. I try, and fail, to look unimpressed. He lights my cigarette. "You haven't heard of your fellow countryman, Captain Michael – or Capitaine Michel, as we call him?" Sonneville studies my face with a disappointed frown. "In a way, it's good that you didn't know, of course. But Capitaine Michel really is someone exceptional. So you will. Before long, everyone will."'*

Michael had found Motheral and Dumsday places in the escape line and Fertein brought them to him. He handed them on to Dewispelaere on 24 October, and after the war Motheral wrote a lively account of their exploits for *La Voix du Nord* newspaper. It provides interesting insight into the glamour and aura of the resistance, as seen through the eyes of the airmen. It also includes another compelling (if, perhaps, somewhat implausible) testimony to the almost legendary status and derring-do of Michael, doubtless brought about and influenced by hugely-embroidered stories told by the various members of the circuit whom the two airmen came across during their stay.

> *'One night we had gone out to take in an arms drop. I had to signal the pilot of the new drop site as the Germans were on to the old site. After stowing away the guns, ammo and explosives, we started home on our bikes. It was after curfew John* [Jean Sonneville]*, Bill, and another Frenchman* [Marcel Fertein] *and I were stopped by three Gestapo and questioned. John gave the signal we used when we were in trouble in our smuggling operations so we both started shooting*

*at the same time. I got two and John the other one. We sent Bill and
the other man to get a shovel while John and I dragged the bodies
through the ditch and into the field where we planted them. John
contacted a British spy in Lille and the next morning Bill and I took
a bus to Lille where we stayed with Captain Michelle [sic] and his
paramour. He was the bravest man I ever met.*

   *'We stayed with them for a couple of days. He took us on a train
to another town where we caught a train to Arras. When we got off
the first train we were walking up the platform when he spotted a
Gestapo officer (who was looking for him). He pulled out his .22
revolver with a silencer and shot him between the eyes. We walked
by the corpse and got on the train for Arras where we had been told
to walk to a certain bridge and stop at a house at the foot of the
bridge. We stayed overnight there and were taken out into the country
to a farm where we spent another night. *[5]

   *'An eighty year old lady who was a Corsican and had nursed with
Edith Cavell acted as guide to Paris but didn't let on we knew her. On
arriving at the Gare du Nord we were told to go to a certain cathedral
where we would be contacted. Simone and another lady contacted us
there and took us on the Metro to go to her place. The train was packed
and after a while Simone told us a Gestapo officer was after us and
was working his way through the crowd. As the train slowed she
pushed the button to open the back door as we jumped out and into
the sewer. I wasn't afraid of the bullets bouncing off the walls but the
rats, bigger than any cat I ever saw, put the fear into me. Simone led
us up one sewer and many others and then told me to climb an iron
ladder and push off a manhole cover. We were in her courtyard. She
hid us out for over a week and put us on a train for Perpingham [sic]
where a Spanish guide was to take us over the mountains to Spain.'* [6]

It perhaps comes as no surprise to read, after these sensational and hair-
raising brushes in their private war with the Gestapo on French soil that,
even when they had crossed the border into Spain, their convoy was
apparently discovered and machine gunned by the Germans, before the two
men were imprisoned by the Spanish and subsequently taken to Gibraltar
for repatriation. [7]

Reeve meanwhile had asked Guidet to provide false papers for Woussen
and Volckaert, and the mayor was happy to oblige. He had the forged
documents made up in Bapaume's Town Hall on genuine cards supplied by
a chemist and part-time artist for whom Guidet had been instrumental in
obtaining an influential position. For the necessary photographs Sophie
Miseron directed Reeve to a family friend who worked in a photographic
shop, was one of the mayor's escape-line helpers, spoke English and had a

fondness for English things and English people. He was able to supply a camera and film, which Reeve used to photograph the two heavily-disguised runaways for the new false identity cards. Everyone then assumed that, given reasonable precautions, the fate of Woussen and Volckaert would be the same as most of the other fugitives – they would hole up somewhere safe and wait for the end of the war, as Paul and Angèle Malfait in Wattrelos had done.

While this was going on, the men from Valenciennes were at it again, setting fire to four more linseed oil wagons and disrupting several convoys in three separate incidents. They set about a hydropneumatic shed at Fives marshalling yard, placing clams and 808 explosive on the compressors and the electric motors. The timers were set for a five-minute delay, allowing the men time to get back to their normal workstations and innocently resume their tasks. Shortly before a quarter to eight they were rewarded by the sound of a series of explosions: the equipment was completely destroyed, and another charge placed in the angle of the walls wrecked the building itself, debris landing on the roof of a sentry box more than 40 yards away. The next evening the same group destroyed a high- tension electrical substation that fed Fives and St Sauveur.

With the departure of Woussen, the inhabitants of Arras, St Léger, Hénin-sur-Cojeul, Gommecourt and Bapaume breathed a sigh of relief that the threat to their safety had been removed. Thankful, they returned to their own dangerous work with renewed confidence and belief. They soon had their reward, for on the evening of 20 October the BBC retransmitted the messages announcing the three drops.

Chapter notes

1   The arrangements were that Delacroix could contact Lemercier at Schynkel's, and Lemercier could also communicate with Michael, Séailles or Vandesype, Wattrelos's Town Hall secretary, all of who visited him at Schynkel's.
2   Michael, was, of course, unable to fulfil his promise to Eliane. I met his godson while visiting her with Arthur Staggs in 1998: perhaps understandably, he was not well-disposed towards Staggs or to the British in general.
3   While Malfait goes into this important scenario in great detail, Reeve himself makes no mention of it in any of his reports.
4   For the same reason, and more understandably, perhaps, Reeve makes no mention of this episode. Personally I struggle with the idea that Michael was prepared to put the leadership on the line in a bout of fisticuffs.
5   Although the essential facts of the escape of Motheral and Dumsday are supported by other accounts, the shooting of a Gestapo officer on a railway station in broad daylight, with all the consequences, repercussions and reprisals that would have followed, is not mentioned by anyone.
6   Article by Clarence 'Curly' Motheral in *La Voix du Nord,* 11 February 1978
7   None of these dramatic events was mentioned during the interrogation of the two men when they arrived back in England on 30 November *(MI9/S/PG1592/1593).*

Chapter 20

Execution

*'How many wolves do we feel on our heels when the
real enemies go in sheepskin by?'*
Malcolm Lowry

For the first of the three drops on 20 October the alert message – '*Josette calls mama Piggy*' – had been conceived by Michael as a tribute to Constant Miseron's wife, Sophie, whose family nickname it was. It was the signal to prepare for a drop at Fontaine-les-Croisilles, in the run up to which Reeve alienated himself further from his men. An American airman, Franck Pessygueil, whose Lightning aircraft had crashed on the outskirts of Eruillers, was picked up by local sympathizers and passed on to Mayor J-B Miseron, shortly before two *gendarmes* from Croisilles came to the farmhouse to talk to the mayor in a routine search for the downed pilot. When they arrived they walked in on the whole reception team, plus the American, who had been dressed as a farm worker and was the only person in the room they had not seen before.

After the usual round of handshakes and backslapping the *gendarmes* asked if the group had seen anything of an Allied airman on the run, at which point Reeve stepped forward, and to the dismay of his team gestured towards Pessygueil and confirmed that he was the man they were looking for. Then, as the policemen moved towards the American, Reeve stepped back and pulled out the revolver he always carried. Pointing it at the two uniformed men he told them they were now faced with an important choice: the wrong decision could cost them their lives. In spite of restraining gestures from the others, he went on to reveal his identity as a British officer and state that the men in the room were all part of his team. They were waiting for a parachute drop of supplies for the resistance and, as loyal Frenchmen, the *gendarmes* had a duty to help them. He was in regular contact with London and if they interfered in any way this information would be passed on, and the result would be their certain execution.

A shocked silence hung over the farmhouse kitchen. The FARMER men looked anxiously at each other, confused and alarmed, while the *gendarmes* stared at Reeve in disbelief. Pessygueil looked at everyone else in turn, bemused and not understanding what was happening. A full minute dragged by before Reeve spoke again. Walking slowly around the room, revolver in hand, he invited the officers to stay and listen to the BBC broadcast that was due shortly. He was able to predict that it would contain a message about 'Madame Cochon', the mayor's sister-in-law, and it would mean that the drop would take place that night. Convinced that Reeve was completely mad and had betrayed the circuit, Constant Miseron, the mayor's son, sunk his head into his hands. Not a word was said by anyone until the message came across the air. The *gendarmes* stood up, looked at each other and nodded. They shook hands with all the Frenchmen and, looking straight through Pessygueil and Reeve as if they were not there, assured their compatriots that no reports of aircraft or parachutes would be passed on to the Germans by any of the local officers. With a brief *'bonne chance'*, they put on their caps and departed.

If Reeve expected this show of bravado to impress his men and repair his image in their eyes he was to be disappointed. They saw it as just another example of his foolhardy and dangerous behaviour, both irresponsible and unnecessary. The mayor had known the two officers for years and felt that they would have cooperated without being threatened at gunpoint, and he was personally incensed by Reeve brandishing a weapon in the kitchen of his home.

Nevertheless, when Flight Sergeant Thomas brought his Halifax in from the east, at just after quarter past two, the men on the ground were still bantering about the reception going ahead *'under police protection'*. The *gendarmerie* could however do nothing about the strong south-easterly winds, and four of the fifteen containers missed the reception area altogether and could not be found in the darkness. The other eleven were hidden in haystacks, before being transported to an underground storeroom that formed part of the Hindenburg fortifications from the First World War, on the outskirts of Fontaine-les-Croisilles. The missing containers were found the next morning by Marcel Dupuis, brother-in-law of the mayor of Fontaine in Chérisy, the village where Delacroix was now billeted at the Michels' farm. He and his group borrowed a tipping cart from a local farmer, Caron, and took the containers to Dupuis's garden, from where they were recovered, and the contents were added to the stock of machine guns, ammunitions, explosives and incendiaries destined for the Béthune sector. Also included was a radio homing transceiver, which Reeve took to Michael, who on the same day also received some much needed funds via Dubois. [1]

The second drop was heralded by the message: *'The Gestapo nicked my shoes'*, another piece of whimsy on Michael's part that recalled the time when his own shoes had been found at the *Aquarium,* during the August arrests, and taken away for examination. The target field, owned by

Delambre, was near Foncquevillers, 18km south-west of Arras. This time Flight Sergeant Watson chose to come in from the south, and once again the high winds caused problems, with only six of the expected fifteen containers recovered. These were hidden in old shell holes and covered with bushes, but were moved quickly when word spread that German military manoeuvres were planned to take place in the very fields where the cache was hidden. They were taken at night to a concealed hideout near the ruins of the water tower in Gommecourt, prior to being shifted to a more permanent home in the abattoir in Arras.

The third message: *'St George's cavalry is on the way'* had been proposed by Malfait following some banter with Michael about English cavalry and German tanks, and it presaged a drop at Ransart in a field owned by Aimé Binot, who, with his son René, formed part of Dewispelaere's reception committee. Flight Sergeant Gopas elected to come in from the west and made a perfect drop. All fifteen containers were recovered and the contents were hidden in beetroot silos.

On 23 October one of Fertein's teams attacked the railway lines in the Don-Sainghin sector; hundreds of wagons were re-routed and sent in directions opposite to those intended. Two days later they attacked the Valenciennes-Anzin electricity company and destroyed or damaged most of the transformers there. At the same time a fire was started in two petrol wagons at Raismes, which engulfed twelve other trucks, and on 27 October two more locomotives were destroyed in Valenciennes. The following morning Sonneville's Le Seau group attacked the bridges over the St Maur canal and at Merville, putting them out of action for two months.

Michael's pleasure at the success of these operations was tempered by the news that his friend Jean Velge had died in Loos on 4 October. Michael declared him a hero of the 'WO' when he learnt of his fate, aware of the tortures that would have been inflicted on him. He had been a loyal and committed member of the circuit, devoted to taking part in missions, recruitment, supply deliveries and sabotage activities. Locked up in solitary confinement in a cell in Loos, with his hands manacled in front of him during the day and behind during the night, he would have suffered horrendous pain and been reduced to little more than a skeleton when he died. Yet, in spite of all the inhuman efforts used to try to break him, he had not given away a single name. It was, or should have been, an inspiring example to others.

On 21 October, the day after the drops, Melot had taken Woussen to the meeting point for his departure to Spain, only to learn that the line had been cut and the operation had been rearranged for a later date, as a result of which she had to keep the young man under her roof for an indefinite period. No-one in Lille or Arras was aware of this: everyone assumed Woussen to be safely on his way. But this delay, and his enforced prolonged stay with the Melots, generated a period full of tension and anxiety on Woussen's part. Furious about the hold-up he took his anger out on his hostess, who was risking her life to protect him. He even raged at her housekeeper, repeating over and over again that if he was captured it would be her fault, and then they would all be in the same boat. So it was with considerable relief when, on 28 October, Melot was able to hand him over to Georges Guillemin and Claude Leclerq, the BOURGOGNE couriers who would be escorting him and nine other Frenchmen to the Spanish border. However Woussen's behaviour on the way to the station made her uneasy: his constant twisting and turning to look around had forced her to tell him to act normally, in case he draw attention to himself and caused their arrest. This warning had little effect and she urged the escorts to keep a close eye on him. She returned home full of misgivings, in spite of Woussen's parting assurance that he would kill himself rather than betray her.

Following the successful October receptions and the departure of Woussen the Arras men were free to concentrate on their main priorities: receiving and distributing arms, passing Allied airmen to the escape lines, and protecting the agents being hunted by the Germans. Michael sent a message to Lemercier, saying that he would come for him in two days' time. On 29 October he wore his GMR uniform to collect him from Bruay and brought him to Lille, where he allowed him to write a last letter to Eliane, in which Lemercier told her of Michael's assurance that he would be safely in England within two weeks. Michael promised his lieutenant that he would ensure personally that Eliane received the letter, and that she would be well looked after. He urged him in the strongest possible terms to lie very low and not let anyone know his identity.

Michael then took Lemercier to meet up with Staggs, whom Michael had called to Lille for the purpose of escorting Lemercier to Arras, no-one else being available for this important, and, in view of Lemercier's threats, delicate mission. Staggs recalled the rendezvous in an interview:

'We met in the café of a hotel in the Grand Place. Trotobas was not there when I arrived, and I berated him for being late when he did turn up with Manu. *Of course, he just told me to mind my own business. He then said I was to take* Manu *to a café in Arras and that he was sending him to England with a message. He asked me if I had a gun, and when I said I had, he told me to give it to him. I refused to hand it over in such a public place, and he took me to the toilets, where he took the revolver from me.* Manu *and I made the journey to Arras on foot and by bicycle. After I left him at the café I never saw him again.'* [2]

From Jeanne Soret's café Reeve took Lemercier to one of Arthur Richards' safe houses.

In a rare moment of unity, Michael and Reeve displayed relief in the knowledge that both of their problems would soon be out of the way – yet it was to be short lived. At the very moment when Lemercier was writing his farewell letter, the BOURGOGNE party had disembarked at St Girons in Ariège, just fifteen miles from the Spanish border, where they were to meet their mountain guides. They had made their way in small groups to the rendezvous point in a café when Guillemin realized that Woussen was not with them. After a hurried search he found him on the pavement outside the station, looking agitated and casting furtive glances around him. Thinking he had simply lost his bearings, Guillemin went up to him quietly and told him to follow. This made Woussen even more agitated, and Guillemin was about to remonstrate with him when an apparently harmless civilian standing nearby suddenly demanded to see their papers. These he pocketed, whereupon armed police appeared and took them to the local office of the SD. There they were accused of being wanted terrorists, planning to escape through Spain, and were taken away to be questioned separately. Guillemin vehemently denied the charges, claiming never to have met Woussen until that moment. His pleas fell on deaf ears and he was taken first to Gestapo headquarters in Toulouse's Rue Meillac then to the city's Prison Saint-Michel, without any opportunity of speaking to Woussen.

From his vantage point at a window table in the café, Leclerq watched the two men being led away, and realized that their mission had been compromised. Quietly and efficiently he shepherded his own little group of fugitives on to the first train back to Paris, where he told Melot about the arrests, although he was unable to satisfy her anxious enquiries about Woussen's fate. The BOURGOGNE leaders began an immediate investigation into what had gone wrong and convoys were suspended.

In the early hours of that morning Guillemin and Woussen were handcuffed and taken to the Gestapo office in Toulouse, where they were once more interrogated separately. Guillemin stuck to his story that he had come to visit relatives and stock up with supplies, but when he was asked if he knew Madame Melot he realized that Woussen had been talking. His expression must have given him away, because he was tortured until he admitted that he had been asked to help some men get to Spain, for an organization about which he knew nothing. He was then taken back to his cell and on the way passed Woussen, who said that he had talked because the Germans had told him that Guillemin himself had confessed to everything – a favourite ploy of the interrogators.

In fact, Woussen had been exposed as soon as the Germans found on him an envelope full of documents he had brought with him to show to

London to establish his credentials although there was nothing that directly linked him to any resistance network. When the questioning continued to focus solely on the escape line, he realized that his arrest had been the result of surveillance of escapers and was not linked to the manhunt back in Lille and Arras. Immediately he saw an opportunity to save his life by confessing to the lesser crime of trying to flee the country, knowing he was one among hundreds with the same desire. He told his interrogators that Guillemin was simply one of the escorts, and that he had been collected from the home of a Madame Melot, whose address he did not know, being a stranger to Paris. He also mentioned Madame Balesi, whom he placed in Bapaume, without giving any more details. This led the Germans to take him back to Paris to try to locate Melot's address, while they held on to Guillemin to extract more information about the escape routes.

In Paris, Melot told Guidet and Balesi of Leclerq's news that Woussen had been seized, and of her concerns that he would confess everything. They agreed that everyone should carry on as normal until they received more information from the BOURGOGNE agent who had been sent down to investigate. Guidet informed Reeve and Dewispelaere, who were shaken. Reeve then rounded on Guidet and told him furiously that if he and his fellow mayors had not been so weak that day in Bapaume, in resisting his proposal to execute Woussen, this latest setback would never have occurred. He finished by reminding Guidet of what would happen to him if Woussen talked, and ordered him to say nothing to anyone else about the arrest, to avoid causing further panic. When Michael was told, he concurred with the decision to do nothing until positive confirmation and more information had been received. Meanwhile there was work to be done.

The next morning an explosion at Raismes set off a violent fire, which destroyed four petrol tankers, five carriages and the two main railway tracks. At the same time an explosion on the Hersaux-Mouscron line caused the front five carriages of a train to leave the tracks and start a fire, which destroyed four petrol tankers and five more carriages. On 30 October, between Landas and Le Rosult, Michael led a party that blew the line as a train passed, sending nine carriages laden with military equipment crashing into the embankment, and blocking the main line for the entire day. These and other successes, frequently spectacular and clearly visible, amounted to no more than pinpricks in the overall resistance to occupation, but they sent out a definite message to the people of the area that underground war had begun against the Nazi military by local soldiers without uniforms. The security forces were well aware that the continuing actions were being fuelled by parachute drops, and by now they knew beyond any doubt that these explosions and fires bore the unmistakable signature of a certain

Capitaine Michel. All they had to do was find him, and the whole organization would come tumbling down.

Two days later, on 2 November, Michael, still elusive in GMR uniform, went to Ransart to supervise the loading of the containers stored in Aimé Binot's beetroot silos. He took an instant liking to the amiable farmer, who was delighted to have the famous leader in his kitchen and plied him with coffee and cognac. So well did they get on, and so comfortable did Michael feel, that he promised to return when he had more time, and he discussed with Binot the possibility of making the remote farm a permanent and secure refuge for himself and Denise, as Aimé's son, René, revealed after the war:

> *'Capitaine Michel came here many times and had coffee at the table where we are now sitting. By mid-October he was very concerned that his flat at Boulevard de Belfort may have been disclosed to the Germans and spoke of setting up a temporary HQ here in the countryside while the heat died down. One of the container drops here contained rubber bicycle tyres. Someone in England had painted over the manufacturer's labels on the tyres but the job was not a good one. As soon as it rained the paint came off exposing the "Made in England" stamps and there were many people in the area who were riding bikes with the new tyres! After the terrible events of late November we expected the Germans but they never came to our farm.'*[3]

He then joined his men to help load the two unwieldy gas-fired vehicles that had been provided by Houcke. Houcke and Fertein had arranged with Michael for the Ransart consignment to be divided between *La Voix du Nord* and the FARMER groups, under Michael's personal supervision. Houcke drove the first truck, accompanied by his brother Marcel, and Sonneville drove the second, with Maurice Leblond as co-driver.

In the back of Sonneville's vehicle, among the turnips to be used to cover the load, was Stephen Grady, who described his first encounter with Michael thus:

> *'We watch in disbelief as a uniformed figure marches towards the first lorry. "What the hell do we do now?" Maurice is already reaching for a turnip. I peer through my fingers at the man advancing upon us. He is even more dangerous than a German: his dark blue uniform marks him out as a member of the Vichy security police... but the policeman climbs up into the first lorry, and Mayor Houcke drives away.'*

They drove into Binot's field, where

> *'Mayor Houcke points in my direction and the Vichy policeman strides purposefully towards me… he is wearing a holstered side arm and a thin smile…a few feet from me he holds out his hand. "Hello,* Iroquois [Grady's code name]*" he says, in English. "Thank you for coming." His accent is as clipped as his slim moustache. "I expect the chaps will have warned you about me. My British code name is* Sylvestre. *But most people call me* Capitaine Michel.*"'* [4]

After the parachute cylinders had been unpacked and loaded onto the trucks, Michael showed Houcke's men how to assemble and fire a Sten gun, before waving the little convoy on its way. While struggling up the Côte St Catherine, a hill just outside Arras, Sonneville's vehicle broke down and Michael left. After carrying out repairs, Sonneville carried on and arrived without further mishap at a farm near Nieppe, where the cargo was unloaded to be distributed a few days later.

Michael subsequently visited the Houcke group in Nieppe, where he instructed the men in small arms fire and the use of 808 explosives, at the conclusion of which he turned to Grady.

> *'Reaching down beside him, he hauls an aluminium drum on his lap and extracts from it two Luger pistols, one of which he hands to me. "Have you ever shot anyone?" I shake my head. "Right, here's the drill. Two shots, no more, no less. One to the stomach, one to the heart. Even if you miss with the second, the first will kill him in the end. And don't look at his face."'* [5]

During this session Michael gave Grady cigarettes, chocolate and tea for his father, saying that he would like to meet him, but doubting that this would happen before the end of the war. Nevertheless, he found time a few days later to go to the Grady home with Sonneville and have a private conversation with Grady's father, after which:

> *'He* [Sonneville] *and the captain slip out into the night. My father closes the back door softly behind them. He looks taller and straighter than he did yesterday. And, for the first time since the Middle Ages, he smiles at me.'*

The following morning, 3 November, events took a sinister and sombre turn with the execution of Lemercier, of which there are conflicting accounts. According to Malfait:

'The day before, having been told of the threats uttered by WOUSSEN at Mme MELOT's, OLIVIER [Reeve], furious and giving way to his impulses, started by shouting soundly at GUIDET, the bearer of bad news and responsible, according to him, for the problems incurred for having opposed the pure and simple execution of the young man: "Not a word to anyone", he added, "otherwise it's the end of our work. Can you see how responsible you are in this matter, if he ever opens his mouth?" He concluded by instinctively putting his hand on his gun that he carried on him at all times.

'Today, OLIVIER makes his decision. This matter has been judged at Lille. He is going to show MICHEL and the others that he has no intention of waiting for further betrayal to take place before he acts. He ordered Henri DEWISPELAERE to go and get MANU [Lemericer] at his landlord's and take him to the isolated house at Beaurains, abandoned since the Rex affair. Then he watched out for their arrival by settling near the window on Mme SORET's café, to whom he cynically declared as he saw them arrive: "Here is the man who hasn't got long to live!" Soon after he followed them and went into the house after them. Then, as MANU's back is turned away, he shoots him down with a bullet in the back of the neck in front of a staggered Henri. It was 15.30.'

Meanwhile, Reeve, in his first report, ascribed responsibility to Michael:

'At the beginning of the month Sylvestre *received connections coming from a woman named Simone who was managing a café at Herseaux in a small village in Belgium. This woman, as well as* Sylvestre, *was in touch with the organization of* Petit Navire *of Brussels. This connection revealed that due to its lack of attention and due to careless conversations in the cafés the person named Emanuel Lemercier had caused the arrest of Jean Velge and of other members of the organization* Petit Navire. Sylvestre *therefore decided to make Lemercier disappear. This was to be done in the abandoned house outside the town of Arras. But* Sylvestre *could not finish his work and he came to find me telling me to search the body of Lemercier and to make him disappear, which I did in the evening of the following day with the help of Henri Dewispelaere and Paul Copin. Everything I found on the body of Lemercier I gave back to* Sylvestre.*'*[6]

Dewispelaere and Copin moved the body to a disused well, into which they threw the corpse and covered it with stones. Afterwards, pale and visibly shaken, they retired to Soret's café for a stiff drink before going their separate ways.

Michael meanwhile was preoccupied with the final stages of planning for another major raid. The Desmet factory in Thumesnil made shortwave radio transmitters and electrical contacts for anti-aircraft tracking systems, and it was high on London's priority list. However, as with Fives, its location right in the centre of town made the risk of excessive civilian casualties from bombing unacceptable. It was a target high on Michael's list too, and he had tasked Gerekens with carrying out detailed reconnaissance and drawing up a feasible plan. Gerekens proposed 10 November for the attack, but Michael wanted to be able to include the attack in the report he was preparing for London, and he instructed him to bring it forward by a week.

On the evening of 3 November Gerekens launched his attack, gaining entry by the simple subterfuge of pretending to have a package for the managing director. After restraining the concierges, charges were laid and hammers were used to smash valuable high-precision equipment in the laboratory, while construction and assembly drawings were removed. To mislead the investigators Gerekens left his 'prisoners' with the impression that he was an English commando, and he watched from an alleyway about 100m from the factory as a loud explosion was followed by flames and sparks shooting into the air. The police, fire brigade and soldiers arrived shortly afterwards.

Before he set off for Arras the next morning, Michael was delighted to hear of the success of the attack and of the Germans' belief that it had been carried out by parachutists, apparently convinced by the concierge's testimony as to the leader's strong English accent and by the lengths of parachute cord used to bind the prisoners. He laughed when told that a radio transmitter, seized in the raid and repacked in an anonymous crate, had been taken to Valenciennes station, where the team had loaded it on to an SNCF trolley, and, donning railway hats, pushed it to a waiting train for Lille, assisted by a couple of German soldiers who cleared a path for them on the platform. Gerekens escorted the consignment to Lille and enlisted the help of a German soldier to take it off the train via the door reserved for German officers. While this pleased Michael enormously, he was less than happy to find that the set could not be made to work.

If Dewispelaere thought he had heard the last of the Lemercier affair he was mistaken. Michael was lodging with him that night, and he, Dewispelaere and Reeve had to endure a non-stop tirade from Dewispelaere's wife Marie, aimed chiefly at Reeve, as she accused him of being idle and living off the back of her husband, to whom he gave all the humble and dirty work that needed doing, and now he had even made him a murderer. It was an uncomfortable meal and she continued with her recriminations as she cleared away the dishes. These were cut short by the sound of a coded knock on the back door, which she opened to admit Denise, who asked instantly what was wrong. When Michael quietly told her about Lemercier she put her hands to her face, burst into tears and ran to Marie, who later recounted how she and Denise had hugged and comforted each other while the men remained silent. Michael sat upright and grim faced, Dewispelaere had his head buried in his hands, and Reeve stared defiantly into space, arms folded, sullen but unrepentant.

Eventually, Michael asked Denise if she had brought any messages from her routine visit to the letterbox in Amboise, a task she had taken over from Malfait. In a halting voice she described how she had found a group of people there who were panic-stricken at the news from Touraine. The little circuit had been penetrated, completely destroyed and all the radios had been seized. Dubois was on the run, but his letterbox at Laudet's safe house in Montrouge was so far intact. He had managed to leave a message there for *Michel*, fixing a meeting for 6 November and suggesting that he brought with him a report and any other correspondence for London, since he expected to be leaving shortly. Denise had picked up that message. Although Michael welcomed the opportunity to get his report to London, this news dealt him another hard blow; he had come to rely on Dubois for his radio transmissions and this latest disaster effectively meant the end yet again of established communications with London. The men discussed the problem long into the night. [7]

Chapter notes

1   The air reports for the three drops are taken respectively from *138 Squadron Operations Report (AIR/27/8300)*, *138 Squadron Record Book (AIR/27/956)*, and *138 Squadron Operations Report (AIR/27/8477)*.

2   This episode was told to me by Arthur Staggs in February 1998.

3   I visited the Binot farm in November 1998 (see Epilogue).

4   Stephen's memory is a little at fault here: Michael had shaved off his moustache in August.

5   In April 1944 Stephen would execute a German officer in a café in exactly this way. He told me about it when I visited him at his home in Cyprus in 1988, and he describes the incident later in his book.

6   The question of responsibility for Lemercier's execution is examined further in Chapter 27.

7   The message from Dubois had actually been intended for Reeve, whom he knew as *Michel*.

Chapter 21

Countdown

'And coming events cast their shadow before.'
Thomas Campbell

While the discussions were taking place in Arras, Malfait and Dubocage, dressed as railway workers, left Wattrelos for Roubaix station, where they hid their bicycles and collected an assortment of explosives. Malfait had learnt that a long train of loaded fuel tanks made the journey from Roubaix to Tourcoing each Thursday night, so later that evening they concealed themselves in the signal box to await its arrival. They were relying on signalman Ernest Dubus to chat to the frequent German patrols that dropped by and dissuade them from coming in. This happened three times, to the discomfort of the two saboteurs stretched out on the floor and clutching their weapons. Midnight came and went with no word from the duty telephonist, Gérard Berquet, who was to warn them when the train was nearing the station. By two-thirty in the morning Malfait had had enough, and he decided that they should place the explosives anyway, on the condition that Dubus would recover them if nothing happened. He had just arrived home, at around three o'clock, when the night sky lit up, and he knew the raid had been successful.

After a short sleep Malfait went to meet up with Michael at the Dewispelaeres' house. He had intended to discuss Reeve's meeting at the Miserons about Woussen, details of which had been given to him by Dewispelaere. However, after hearing the news about Lemercier and Dubois, he decided to leave the matter for another time. Instead, they discussed the possible threat to Malfait as the courier between Michael and Dubois, concluding that, since Dubois himself had no idea of Malfait's real name nor where he lived, the risks were negligible. They went on to discuss future plans, including the vital question of radio communications. The only possibility that presented itself now was for FARMER to work through Gustave *'Guy'* Biéler and his MUSICIAN/TELL operator. From his occasional contacts with Biéler, Michael knew that the Canadian had received his own operator when Yolande Beekman had been inserted by Lysander aircraft on 18 September. During the meeting it was agreed that

Dewispelaere should go to London, and Michael sent Reeve to see Berthe Fraser to find out what arrangements could be made, and to catch up on latest developments.

Malfait left to collect Dubocage and dressed as railwaymen, they went back to the Roubaix later that morning. There they found a Gestapo team taking photographs of the tender, the three cars and ten 63m³ tankers that had been derailed, the seven irreparably damaged tankers, the 300 yards of twisted track, and the scorched and blackened ground ravaged by the intense heat from 300,000 litres of burning petrol. The line was blocked for forty-eight hours. Later that afternoon a train of petrol wagons was derailed and set on fire shortly after passing through Roubaix, with the loss to the Germans of 40,000 litres of fuel. Meanwhile, near Wattrelos, a trainload of spare parts was derailed, and at Allennes-les-Marais 1,300,000 litres of synthetic alcohol went up in flames. In the evening Malfait, who had the bit between his teeth, led a small team to place charges on the track near Hutin on the Orchies-Tourcoing line. Shortly after ten o'clock, an explosion ripped through a military train, derailing fourteen wagons carrying anti-aircraft guns, destroying 200 yards of track and killing a German NCO.

When Reeve returned that evening he was, for a change, the bearer of good news. While at Fraser's he had, by a stroke of good fortune, met Jean-Pierre Deshayes, the BOA officer responsible for coordinating arrangements for the arrival of a Lysander coming to pick up Forest Yeo-Thomas of SOE's RF Section, which worked in collaboration with the BCRA.* He was now on his way back and Deshayes had told Reeve that there would be space for Dewispelaere on the same aircraft. Yeo-Thomas had no objection to a fellow passenger, particularly a Frenchman with up-to-date knowledge of activities in Arras.[1]

For Michael the day had finished on a more optimistic note than the previous one. It now appeared that, with Dubois and Dewispelaere both due to fly out in the near future, there were two excellent opportunities to get information, reports and requests delivered to London. He told Reeve to keep the appointment for 6 November that had been referred to in the message brought by Denise, but only after carrying out extensive surveillance and checks to ensure he was not walking into a trap. This Reeve did, and handed over a report from Michael, before going to meet Biéler to set up an appointment for Michael. He went back to see Dubois again a few days later to give him coordinates Dubois had requested for a suitable landing ground on which to receive an incoming radio operator.

In Reeve's absence Michael responded to a request from Guidet to accompany him to St Léger, where an explosive and potentially dangerous situation had arisen with the Miserons. Malfait joined them in Guidet's car, and during the journey Michael questioned Guidet at great length about the

---

* BCRA: *Bureau Central de Renseignement et d'Action* (Free French Intelligence Service in London)

information he had regarding Woussen's aborted journey to Spain and the uncertainty that still lingered over his arrest. Did they know for sure that the expedition had been a complete failure, or had some of the party managed to get through? Was it possible that Woussen had merely been questioned and not arrested? All Guidet could do was repeat, with a note of optimism, that an investigation was being carried out, and that so far nothing had been confirmed, which he took as a good sign. As far as the meeting with the Miserons was concerned, Michael explained that he had anticipated their possible refusal to undertake any more operations, and had instructed Dewispelaere to look for alternative landing grounds and establish a permanent reception group around Ransart.

They arrived to a hostile reception, which moderated once it was realized that the third member of the party was Malfait, and not Reeve or Dewispelaere. Michael was initially confused when it appeared that the cause of the discontent appeared to be a trivial incident. It involved a dispute between Dewispelaere and Constant Miseron as to which of them should have the leather flying-jacket left behind by Pessygueil on the occasion when Reeve had brandished his revolver at the two *gendarmes* searching for the airman shot down on 18 October. Mayor Miseron explained that Reeve had apparently sided with Dewispelaere and this, coming as it did on top of an announcement by the Edouards family that they had been told they were to be compensated for the expenses incurred in looking after Woussen, was the last straw. The Miserons had demanded compensation for the considerable expenses they themselves had incurred since joining the circuit, but no response was forthcoming from Reeve. This had prompted the mayor to insist on the closure of the arms depot, in order to avoid possible reprisals from the Germans on his villagers and on his family in particular. Reeve had told them that this was completely out of the question, claiming that the depot's address was known to London, and that, if any arms went missing, this would surely incur the death penalty or, at the very least, ensure the Miserons' appearance before a war tribunal at the end of hostilities. To cap it all, Reeve had told them about the execution of Lemercier and used it as a threat and a grim reminder to anyone whose allegiance and loyalty appeared to be waning. Relations with both leaders had deteriorated to such an extent that Reeve had decided to leave St Léger to stay with Dewispelaere in Arras.

Michael listened in silence. He was unwilling to take sides against Reeve, to whom he had entrusted responsibility for operations in the sector, and, as he confided on the homeward journey, had responded quite reasonably, given the seriousness of the situation and the absolute necessity for every member of the circuit to remember his oath and the fact that their fates were all inextricably linked. When Michael finally spoke it was to inform the Miserons that he was thinking of sending Dewispelaere to England with a report, which would include a list of names and addresses of all the French people who had helped the circuit. By stressing their bravery and describing their exploits, it would ensure that after the war a high British distinction would be conferred on those who deserved it most, and this certainly included the Miserons. This was news to Malfait, but it placated and flattered the Miserons, who eagerly undertook to draw up a list for Michael's approval. Michael then attempted to allay their fears further, and ease their feelings of insecurity, by telling them that Woussen had reached the Spanish border, although, as Malfait was well aware, this was mere conjecture. Regarding the Reeve situation, Michael went on to explain that he had every confidence in his fellow officer, but it so happened that he was planning a reorganization that would effectively take Reeve away from the Arras region, for which responsibility would revert to Malfait. This, too, was news to Malfait, but it was clear that by the time he and the others left, the Miserons were feeling somewhat more optimistic, if not entirely convinced.

On the return journey, Guidet congratulated Michael on his handling of the situation, but the three men would have felt less confident if they had known that while they were on the road the Gestapo had raided the house of Woussen's former landlady, Madame Piletta, in Bapaume, where Henriette Balesi had been staying – although there would have been nothing to indicate that this was not just part of the ongoing round-up of collaborators who had sheltered Allied airmen during the time that she had been working with Dhallendre for COMÈTE. After the line had been penetrated by a Nazi agent posing as an English pilot, Balesi had wisely left the town and gone to stay with friends in Achiet.

Michael was in action again that evening when he led a small team back to the Desmet factory. He had learnt that a number of measuring instruments and detectors had escaped destruction, so he had decided to see for himself the damage that had been done and finish the job. After a second lightning raid production came to an immediate halt, with a substantial amount of very expensive and irreplaceable precision process equipment damaged beyond repair.

But there were still more clouds gathering on the Arras horizon. Maintaining the security of the arms depots was becoming increasingly more difficult as fear spread. The most vulnerable of the stores was the one at Gommecourt in the basement of the water tower, to where as many as ten agents came regularly each week from Bapaume and Arras to replenish their own stock. There were also problems at the abattoir at Arras, where Copin, alerted by his concierge to the large number of comings and goings to the arms store, took it on himself to transfer the stocks to the cellar of Pierre Lochu, a window-dresser who lived in Rue Crinchon, about 200m away. The contents of the canisters had been repacked into pork barrels, which Copin laboriously and conscientiously moved by himself, until one of the barrels slipped from his bike and the watching neighbours shouted loudly to each other that it had on it the seal of the slaughterhouse and was clearly black market merchandise.

This was too much for the nervous Lochu, who began to worry more and more about possible comebacks. He insisted that all of the arms should be removed from his house, forcing Copin to spend the next few days moving everything back again. Lochu then protested to Malfait about the behaviour of Reeve. It was bad enough that, on every visit he made to the Lochus, Reeve made a point of showing them his pistol with a silencer, which he referred to as his 'bicycle pump', but after the incident with the barrel he had sent Dewispelaere to see them and tell them about the list of addresses and the threat of execution or war tribunal for all of those who did not cooperate fully. This had resulted in the Lochus taking against Dewispelaere and Reeve, and telling other members of their group of their treatment. This added fuel to the slowly spreading fire of animosity and resentment that was burning in the Arras sector.

Alarmed by what he saw as Reeve's attempts to enforce his dwindling authority and respect by resorting to bullying and threats to already-worried agents, Malfait once more took his concerns to Michael. He pointed out that the services expected from the agents should be voluntary and not impressed by threats. It was, he said, dangerous and foolhardy to make weakened and demoralized men and women do something against their wishes. If any of them were to be arrested, the Gestapo would not hesitate to take advantage by making their victims feel that they had been betrayed by London. Michael told him that he was planning to ask London to have Reeve reassigned, and, reassured, Malfait returned to action.

The swathe of destruction and derailments in the wake of the sabotage on the railways meant plenty of work for the few travelling cranes available, one of which was sent immediately to the area where its route and progress was monitored by the railwaymen. It reached Lille on the morning of 6 November, and in the afternoon it arrived in Roubaix, where even Dubocage, ever willing to try anything, was unable to get anywhere near it. Security was always at very high levels around these valuable machines, with constant patrols during the day and sentries at night guarding a 100m floodlit perimeter. After detailed study and discussion with Gerekens and Dubocage, Michael was forced to conclude that a sabotage attempt was impossible. A full-scale armed assault might succeed, but casualties were bound to be high, and the risks consequently unacceptable; people would certainly be injured, perhaps even killed. Reluctantly he abandoned the idea.

On the morning of 7 November this prime target arrived in Wattrelos, where Malfait, unaware of Michael's concerns, saw an opportunity and decided to attack it. That evening he and Georges Philippot climbed over a barbed-wire fence, crossed a field, and ended up at the gateway to a farm, where they found themselves just 100 yards or so from the siding on which the short engineering train was parked. In pouring rain they crawled on hands and knees to a point where they were just 50 yards from the crane itself, from where they could see it quite clearly and hear the soft whistle of a steam valve. The strong winds were buffeting the rolling stock and Malfait felt sure that the resulting noise, along with that of the rain drumming on the roofs, would hide the sound of their movements. They managed to crawl underneath the wagons, but every attempt to reach the crane itself was thwarted by the frequent armed patrols. With only an hour of darkness remaining, Malfait abandoned the attempt on the crane, but determined that their efforts should not be totally in vain, placed the charges across the carriage axles and gave the signal to fall back. At dawn the charges exploded, slightly damaging the jib wagon and the track. The detonation was heard in Wattrelos, and rumours – later proved to be false – circulated that the crane had been blown up and destroyed. Malfait was disappointed, but he acknowledged that they had been lucky and had also gained some valuable experience, not the least of which was that even the men of FARMER were human and there were limits to what they could expect to achieve.

Michael learnt of the raid the next evening when he returned to Arras after a meeting with Biéler, of which he gave Séailles a full account, as was his custom. Although Séailles lamented in his interrogation report and interviews that Michael never told anyone where he was going, he appreciated the 'need to know' basis for this and the potential security risks if everyone knew Michael's whereabouts. For the same reason, Michael protected the Frenchman by keeping him well away from operations and the day-to-day activities of the circuit, allowing him to focus on the longer-term strategic planning. A consequence of this was that Séailles had no knowledge of events in Arras but was kept fully in the picture by Michael about everything to do with communications with London and developments in SOE's thinking, information that Michael did not share with his other lieutenants unless it affected them directly. [2]

During his meeting with Biéler, Michael gave the Canadian a detailed rundown on the latest happenings with HERCULE and FARMER and explained that he would have to rely on MUSICIAN for his radio communications with London, until he received the long-awaited replacement for Staggs. Biéler promised to see what he could do, and felt that he had no alternative but to caution Michael that, when Reeve had come to see him, he had asked if he, higher in rank than Michael, could intervene to help Reeve obtain his own command. Although annoyed, Michael took this in his stride. He told Biéler of his decision to have Reeve reassigned, and gave him a message for London that would set this in motion. He decided on the spot to limit the potential for further damage by keeping Reeve as far away from Biéler as possible for the immediate future, offering the Canadian a choice between Malfait and Simone Séailles as his permanent go-between. Biéler opted for Simone, who lived in Paris, as he had his own agents and connections there, and knew the city well. The two organizers then agreed that henceforth Michael would use Beekman as his WT, and they arranged for a letterbox in Douai, through which they could communicate with each other. [3]

When he returned to Arras Michael met up with Reeve and told him what he had agreed with Biéler, though not of his own plan to have Reeve reassigned. He ignored the latter's protests that he should be the principal contact with St Quentin, and gave him the responsibility for maintaining regular contact with Dubois, for as long as the radio operator remained in France.

Meanwhile, Yeo-Thomas had arrived in Arras. Fraser duly alerted Reeve, advising him at the same time that there had been a change of plan. Dewispelaere would not now be flying out with Yeo-Thomas, but would leave via another Lysander, scheduled to land at Montcornet in Aisne near the Belgian border. This was a considerable distance away, but the BOA would be arranging transportation to get Dewispelaere there. There was more good news when Reeve met Dubois by prearrangement in Montrouge and learned that not only had another Lysander been promised to pick up Dubois, but this plane would also be bringing Michael's long-awaited radio operator. [4]

Among the FARMER leadership there was now an air of optimism and, for a while, things returned more or less to normal. Nearly six weeks had passed since Woussen had left Hénin-sur-Cojeul, and Reeve, Dewispelaere and Guidet, all of whom had been living in a state of high alert, began to relax. They now believed that Woussen had either got away after all, or he had kept his silence and they would be left alone. The rest of the Arras group, not knowing that Woussen's original departure date had been cancelled, was now convinced that he had made a clean escape and that they were completely in the clear. In Lille, Michael too thought himself safe, but he decided as a precaution to keep on the move and not spend more than a couple of nights in any one place. He sent Denise to live with her mother in the small town of Auchel, twenty-five miles west of Lille.

Michael was now beginning to feel the strain, and he made time to go in the afternoon of Friday 12 November to Gondecourt, to see Yvonne Pachy, who was dismayed by his appearance and general manner.

'I hadn't seen him for some time. He hadn't been really well since August, and by October he had developed pneumonia, which he

typically did his best to cover up, and kept on going. He came for once without his bodyguards and stayed for only a few minutes. He looked gaunt, drawn and clearly very tired. He was not his usual confident self and he alarmed me when he leaned on the counter in the shop and said "This may be the last time I see you. Take care of yourself, and think of me when I'm gone." To my surprise he pulled from his pockets two British hand grenades, showed me how to use them and said. "You keep these, and if the Germans come for you again you may be able to either kill a few or give yourself time to escape, or commit suicide rather than be returned to jail or perhaps a concentration camp." I was dumbfounded but not scared, and I hung the grenades on the back of the front door. Before he left I mocked him by saying "Piff! You're not going to die. You are Michael!" At this he shook his head, kissed my hand and left. Those were my last words to him and I never saw him again.'[5]

On 13 November Malfait introduced Michael to two *gendarmes* who had come to Fontaine-les-Croisilles to ask about the possibility of obtaining arms for their Béthune groups. Michael agreed, and in the afternoon Malfait and Dewispelaere went to the Miserons, where twenty machine guns and large quantities of ammunitions and explosives were handed over and taken away by the *gendarmes*. Malfait noticed that Dewispelaere was particularly talkative, bubbling with excitement, fired up by the news of his impending departure for England and talking about the change of plans. He heard about the Arras arms dumps, the activities of Guidet, the list Dewispelaere had prepared of the addresses of the most important FARMER men and women in the region. All of this was news to Malfait, who said nothing. Yet privately he was appalled that Dewispelaere should be talking so freely, and felt that the sooner the baker was on that plane the better for all concerned. Later that night Malfait took part in a small railway sabotage operation, then returned home to write down for London, at Michael's request, a summary of the most important actions and results that had taken place in and around Arras. This was to add to Michael's own report, which Malfait read, noting that it included information about Michael's enlistment in the GMR, Lemercier's execution, photographs of the sabotage of the Desmet factory, and samples of German and Vichy official seals.

That same evening, a BOURGOGNE liaison agent, Giselle Vauthier, arrived in Bapaume and went to lodge with Guidet, prior to taking four American airmen to Paris to link up with the network. She bought bad news in the shape of confirmation that Woussen had indeed been arrested and was now in Loos Prison. This prompted Guidet to push again for a place on the line for Volckaert, a request that was denied. BOURGOGNE wanted nothing more to do with hunted terrorists after the problems with Woussen, which had seriously jeopardized the security of the escape line. Guidet then rushed to tell Reeve the news about Woussen, and was surprised when he and Dewispelaere were ordered to keep the information to themselves to avoid further panic among the agents. Not even Michael was to be told. Guidet complied, because he did not want to aggravate the already strained relations between Arras and St Léger, and he was unaware, as was everyone else, that the day after he had spoken with Balesi she too had been arrested. Ominously, she had confided to Guidet her belief that Woussen would talk.

Taking part in the Landas raid had whetted Michael's appetite for action, and he was keen to stage another definitive coup. He had his eyes on the power stations and sheds in the strategically important marshalling yards at Lille-Déliverance, and arranged to reconnoitre them with Fertein and Marcel Dumetz, son of the rolling stock foreman Louis Dumetz, during the afternoon of Sunday, 14 November. When the latter arrived at the rendezvous point at the tram stop on Avenue de Dunkerque, he was disconcerted to find with Fertein a man he did not recognize. In such circumstances – if the first contact appeared to be compromised and a trap had been set – the agreed security procedure was for the second man to leave the area immediately. Or, if the parties were too close to do this without arousing suspicion, the second man was to walk on by with no sign of recognition. Dumetz duly crossed the road as if to take a tram in the other direction, when he was hailed by Fertein, who waved him over. To his astonishment Dumetz saw that the unfamiliar, clean-shaven man with dark hair was none other than Michael, who had turned himself into a railwayman and looked every inch the part.

When they arrived at Lille-Déliverance the railway workers who were supposed to guide them were not there, so they went in and walked towards the offices. They were surrounded by Germans coming and going in different directions, completely unaware that, in their midst, they had one of the GFP's most wanted men. They reached the office of Dumetz Senior, and settled down to wait, with Michael using the opportunity to study with great interest and some amusement the detailed official instructions on security measures for countering sabotage and terrorist attacks. They were then taken to the top of the watchtower, from where they had a panoramic view over the entire station and its surroundings. After a few minutes' observation, Michael pointed out his intended targets and outlined his plan, before joining a bunch of workmen who provided cover for a closer scrutiny of the installations. Michael was delighted with the visit and his good humour prompted him during the return journey on the tram to give deliberately misleading directions to a member of the pro-Hitler Rexiste group, immediately distinguishable by his armband. When the unfortunate man got off, a good two miles before the stop he actually needed, the driver and all of the other passengers burst out laughing.

That evening the Lille-St Pol line was cut, causing an emergency squad of railway workers and forced labourers to be rushed to the spot. They worked through the night to get the line back in action for the passage of ammunition trains in the morning. On the following night Béghin and a team of ten men carried out a second attack on the Willems refinery in Douai, following an unsuccessful raid there ten days earlier. They had just placed the charges at the outlet valves at the bottom of the vats when they were surprised by the arrival of a police squad, and a fight broke out, during which Béghin seriously wounded one of the policemen, and the men managed to slip away. Although the explosives malfunctioned and did not set off the hoped for conflagration, the oil caught fire as it ran out through the open sluices. The subsequent heat was such that the metallic roof structure reddened and buckled, the factory and its stock were destroyed, and 375,000 tonnes of oil were lost. Details of his significant success did not reach Béghin himself until much later, because, suspecting that the police had recognized him, he decided not to wait around to find out and fled to Belgium. On the morning of 16 November a squad was sent to find him, and Béghin was sentenced to death in his absence.

Overnight, Dewispelaere had made the long journey to Montcornet. Yeo-Thomas had got away on 15 November from a landing field at Canettemont near Frévent, but Dewispelaere's own departure on the following day had to be aborted when thick fog frustrated the Lysander's attempts to locate the landing field, and the pick up was rearranged for the period of the December moon. Reeve meanwhile had given Dubois the coordinates of the landing field for the radio man's own departure, as well as the text of the alert message and the address of Soret's café as a stopover point while he was waiting.

On 17 November a locomotive in the Lille-Calais line was burnt out, while on the same day the large German vehicle depot in Rue du Chêne-Houpline in Tourcoing came under fire: seventeen large trucks, three cars, and all the petrol and oil supplies were destroyed by the fire, and the garage was wrecked.

On 18 November Guidet called on Melot in Paris, having extracted her address from the unsuspecting Vauthier. Melot was alarmed to see him, the more so when she learned that the mayor had brought Volckaert, who was waiting around the corner in the Metro station, and insisted that she provide shelter for him until his departure. This she declined to do, on the grounds that it presented an unacceptable risk both for herself and for Volckaert, given that Woussen was almost certainly undergoing interrogation and knew all about her safe house. If the Germans came round, the game would be up for all of them. Equally, Guidet did not wish to take the wanted man back to Bapaume, and he pressed Melot to keep him for just a few hours, while he tried to make other arrangements. This request she also refused, but she agreed to take Volckaert to the home of a friend, who subsequently sheltered him.

Her fears were well-founded but her precautions fruitless, as the following morning two Gestapo officers came to the house and carried out a thorough search, without finding anything. At midday they took her to the office in Rue des Saussaies in Paris, where she underwent a long interrogation, spread over five sessions, during which she was frequently brutalized. From the questions she was asked she realized that Woussen must have given the Germans every last detail about her activities while he was staying with her, including her telephone conversations. Her captors even mocked her with an accurate drawing of her apartment that showed exactly where each piece of furniture was located, revealing beyond dispute that Woussen had been there. She denied everything and continued to protest her innocence, hoping to gain sufficient time to warn Guidet, but she was bundled into a car and led away to Fresnes Prison.

The same day, in Montrouge, following interrogations after the penetration of the HERCULE captives, the SD called in force at the house of Laudet, where Dubois had taken refuge. A fierce gunfight ensued, in which Laudet was killed. Dubois shot dead the SS Sturmbannführer in charge and seriously wounded his interpreter, before leaping out of the window and running up the street, only to be cut down and severely wounded by a hail of machine-gun fire. The Germans took him in and nursed him until he was well enough to undergo interrogation. With his arrest the Gestapo took possession of all the documents given to Dubois by Reeve containing vital information about the FARMER circuit. Armed with this information, and with Woussen in custody and talking, they were now well poised to strike at the spider in the centre of the web – the much-sought after *Capitaine Michel*.

Chapter notes

1   Code-named *The White Rabbit* the story of Yeo-Thomas is told in the book of that name by Bruce Marshall, and in Mark Seaman's *Bravest of the Brave: True Story of Wing Commander Tommy Yeo-Thomas - SOE Secret Agent.*

2   It is clear from this and other later developments that Michael continued to regard Séailles as his deputy and successor, despite the presence of Reeve. As will be seen, the continuing insulation of Séailles proved to be an effective and wise precaution.

3   Danièle Lheureux suggests that Michael's idea was to have Reeve reassigned to support Biéler.

4   Dewispelaere had been 'bumped' to allow two 'blown' French agents of SOE's RF Section – Jacqueline Pichard and Madame Virolle – to get to safety with all their luggage.

5   The most likely reason for Michael saying these words is that he anticipated having to go underground in the countryside at some point, the possibility of which he had discussed with the Binots.

Chapter 22

Pressure

'When sorrows come they come not single spies but in battalions.'
Hamlet IV.v

After the explosion of yet more munitions wagons, this time in Audruicq station on 19 November, Michael decided to hand over command of the Lille-Déliverance operations to Gerekens. However, their plan to hit the installations there had to be scrapped when the Germans reinforced their guards with a machine-gun platoon and an armoured car. Nevertheless, the Lille-Déliverance group, which had been as active as the Valenciennes team and had a remarkable record, continued to make its mark. Moving between trains as they stopped at the stations, the railwaymen placed explosives or incendiaries with delayed charges on all passing targets: motor car and aeroplane engines, cement mixers, military materiel, locomotives and trucks carrying linseed, straw, coal or diverse munitions. They caused fires or 'spontaneous' explosions that disconcerted the Germans. There were only a handful of these men, but they proved to be a real headache for the enemy, and on 22 November they carried out a spectacular strike. Taking advantage of a train's stop at Lille-Déliverance they placed time-delayed clams on a number of trucks loaded with ammunition and explosives destined for work on the V1 rocket launch pads. These went off at Le Rosult station and caused explosions in five wagons of melinite, five ammunition trucks, and one truck full of anti-aircraft defence equipment; ten Germans were killed and several hundred wagons were destroyed. Twelve hundred tonnes of clinker and ballast were needed to fill in a crater measuring 80 by 20 yards and 10 yards deep. Nearly 400 workers on the premises were affected, and they spent about two weeks carrying out repairs. Traffic on the Lille-Valenciennes line was disrupted for eight days as a result of what was one of the group's most successful strikes.

Elsewhere, one of Fertein's teams attacked the tracks in the Don-Sainghin sector, causing hundreds of wagons to be re-routed. Chieux's men were not idle either: the Hazebrouck group hampered the traffic and cut the aerial telephone lines and underground cables which ran alongside the tracks, while the Le Seau group again attacked the bridges over the St-Maur canal, and another team destroyed a crane in Armentières.

Michael savoured the results of the actions, which were now taking place almost every day across the sector. The harassed enemy did not know which way to turn, and, to begin with, failed to look for saboteurs among the railwaymen themselves. Inevitably, however, some men were caught in the act and belatedly, the Germans realized their mistake, pouring more and more men into the railway complexes, arresting anyone who moved at night without proper authorization or was found to be away from his assigned work area. Faced with this massive increase in security Michael decided that the time had come to call a halt, and he sent out an order to all units forbidding any further railway actions without his permission. This instruction was not well received and there were rumblings among some of the saboteurs, who, flushed with their successes, were fired up and eager for more. However, with a few exceptions, the underlying wisdom of the decision was accepted.

Michael remained in complete ignorance of the news about Woussen until he went to visit Madeleine Crampon who had been arrested along with her husband René when items from the Aubry drops were found in their house. René was deported but Madeleine was released after a short period in Loos Prison. She met Michael in Rue du Marché on the evening of 22 November, when she told him all about Woussen's presence in Loos and the inhuman ways the investigations had been conducted. Michael was appalled, grasping the significance of the information and the very real threat it posed. The next day he and Malfait went over security in Arras and decided that there was nothing more that could be done, short of everyone going underground, an option that Malfait rejected. If Woussen talked, he talked, and they would have to deal with the consequences, but they felt it was well within their capability to do so, and that Reeve would have a pivotal role to play in damage limitation. Nevertheless, Malfait agreed to move out of his home and move in with his friend Crépin. He then expressed his concern at the number of different people he had seen coming to headquarters and suggested that it might be time for Michael to leave. Michael agreed, and immediately ordered Séailles and Fertein to remove all the weapons and archives from Boulevard de Belfort and take them to Thumesnil. He arranged to visit Reeve the following day in order to put him in the picture and go over everything with him. To be on the safe side, he and Denise would move permanently out of the Belfort flat at some point and find alternative accommodation. He instructed Malfait not to go there again, and to communicate only by letterbox. Malfait voiced his misgivings about Reeve's continuing irrational behaviour and Dewispelaere's feverish and erratic condition, saying point blank that he trusted neither. He asked how he could be kept in the picture if he did not know where to find Michael. Michael slapped him on the back and told him not to worry: he would leave a message telling him how to get to him. His final instruction to Malfait was that he should listen to the BBC at the end of the month, because Michael had arranged a little surprise for him. That evening Malfait moved out of his home and took the first step to going permanently underground.

Meanwhile there was work to be done and later that day Michael, in his GMR uniform, went to see Herry at his office in the GMR barracks to ask for a lorry to be made available for Arras to move weapons on the night of 26 November. This was duly promised. Later that evening Michael was cheered to hear that the Délivrance men had struck at Le Rosult once again, this time causing the total destruction of another trainload of melinite, shells and bombs.

On 24 November Michael went to Arras for his meeting with Reeve, who told him that he had heard about Woussen. He didn't disclose how long he had known but added that, in view of the amount of time that had elapsed, he felt confident that Woussen had not talked and was unlikely to do so. Michael nodded but told him to be on his guard and alert the group leaders, overriding Reeve's objection that this would cause panic. Michael's argument was that, if the worst happened, they deserved the opportunity to be prepared and to be able to make their own emergency plans. They then discussed the operation to remove the stock from Fontaine-les-Croisilles, which was planned for two nights later, and Michael instructed Reeve to make the necessary arrangements.

On his way back to Lille Michael detoured via Bruay to warn Delacroix of the danger from Woussen, asking him to oversee the removal of stock from Fontaine to Lille. Michael spent the night at the home of Simone Chardin in Rue Caumartin, where he had been sheltered during his illness in August.

The next morning, Delacroix called on Dewispelaere to borrow one of the baker's delivery bicycles to transfer a homing transmitter from Lucienne Edouard to Soret's café, where it would stay until he could move it on further. He arranged to spend the night at the Dewispelaeres and informed Reeve that he was moving out of Bruay and was on his way to Albert Michel's farm to pick up some belongings. He passed on Michael's emphatic orders about the arms movement, whereupon Reeve seized on the opportunity to spare himself a potentially embarrassing further encounter with the Mayor of St Léger and his family by ordering Delacroix himself to give Constant Miseron the necessary instructions and agree arrangements for November 26 and 27.

Michael had been going over the plans in his own mind. During his discussions with Séailles they had spent some considerable time on the logistics of getting arms to Portemont, the local head of the Communist

FTP, a risky operation that absolutely depended on having the GMR lorry. Ever thorough, Michael decided to leave nothing to chance and, late in the afternoon of 25 November, he took himself off to see Herry at the barracks, where the arrival of the uniformed 'Michael Lesage' excited no comment. He noticed a great deal of activity, and found that Herry could only spare him a few moments, during which he confirmed that some sort of action was pending, since all of the police and security forces had been placed on a state of high alert. Clearly, a high priority operation was planned and there was now no question of any kind of vehicle being made available. Everyone was waiting for orders. With a strict curfew in place, Michael decided that it was not worth the risk of sending a courier to get a message to the Miserons: it could wait until morning. He met up again with Séailles and together they made their way to the home of Marie-Thérèse Legrain, a relative of Chardin who lived in Rue Jules Guesde in Templemars. There they dined and spent the night going over things once again.

While they were talking, a Gestapo squad, led by Inspector Koltz, forced its way into the Pilettas' house in Bapaume and arrested Madame Piletta and her husband, on the double charge of being involved with the COMÈTE and BOURGOGNE escape lines and being members of the FARMER circuit. They were questioned about *Capitaine Michel* and Henriette Balesi, before being bundled into a car and taken to headquarters.

At about the same time, René Capeau led a team of railwaymen in an attack on the water-softening factory in Achicourt, completely destroying the sluices that fed water to Arras station and sheds. Later that night Dumetz was at the head of a meticulously-planned assault on the distillery in Allennes-les-Marais, destroying 1,520,000 litres of alcohol, a spectacular result that was attributed by the Germans to a ghost band of 'armed parachutists' that were making their lives a misery. This convenient ploy allowed the local commanders to divert attention from their own failings and it was one they employed frequently.

Early on the morning of Friday, 26 November Michael sent a simple *'no flour today'* telegram to Dewispelaere at the Arras bakery. It was the prearranged signal to say an operation had been cancelled or postponed, but gave no other details. Satisfied that he had done all he could, he and Séailles spent the morning moving all the compromising documents and other material out of Boulevard de Belfort to various safe locations in the neighbourhood, anticipating, as a result of Herry's warning, a possible security sweep and extensive house-to-house searches. In the afternoon they returned there to have a final discussion about plans for the next few weeks. Séailles then left, while Michael removed a few remaining items, promising his friend that he would spend the night somewhere else. They agreed to meet at Boulevard de Belfort at eleven the next morning.

Dewispelaere had not seen Michael's telegram. He had been making deliveries to his customers in outlying farms, so that when it arrived, his wife Marie had passed it to Reeve. Although he must have recognized and understood the implications, Reeve chose not to pass the information on to Miseron, perhaps unwilling once again to face a confrontation with him. He also received word from Malfait that GMR units were on the streets of Wattrelos carrying out random searches of pedestrians. However, unaware of Michael's visit to Herry, he assumed it was just another routine operation, and attached no significance to it. Malfait on the other hand, also unaware of Herry's warning, was nevertheless uneasy at what he felt to be an unusually large police presence and stricter than normal scrutiny and questioning. He thought the surveillance had to be a direct response to the recent round of successful sabotages, a suspicion that was confirmed when Dubocage came to see him and told how he had recognized one of the GMR men as his cousin, Raymond Petit, and accused him of being a lackey of the Germans, unaware that Petit himself was also an active member of FARMER. Petit said they had been told that they were out in force to hunt down the railway saboteurs, not knowing that his cousin was one of the leaders. In the course of a brief but heated conversation they each tried to recruit the other until it dawned on them that they were both members. Malfait laughed when he heard this and took heart from the information that the police were not on a specific manhunt aimed at the circuit. He then put it out of his mind to concentrate on getting things ready for an operation against the locks and barges of the Roubaix–Tourcoing canal, which he was to lead in the early hours of the following morning. Fears that the Germans might have got wind of this attack were eased when in mid-afternoon the policemen boarded their vehicles and dispersed.

When Dewispelaere arrived home from his rounds, Reeve told him that the operation had been cancelled, and he suggested they went back to Fraser's to spend the unexpectedly free evening with her and BOA agent Deshayes, who happened to be passing through Arras. Dewispelaere assumed that the Miserons would have been informed of the cancellation and happily whiled away the evening talking about his trip to England, oblivious to the fact that Miseron and his men were making their way to the rendezvous in Fontaine-les-Croisilles. When the agent left Fraser's at just after midnight, Reeve and Dewispelaere went home and retired to bed.

But there was trouble in store. That afternoon a frightened Liébault and his team had burst into Gerekens's office at Lille station and announced that one of their number, Maurice Hayez, had been arrested in Valenciennes three days earlier. This, they felt, was bound to lead the police to them and they asked as one to be allowed to go underground. Gerekens sent a message to Michael, hoping to find him at Boulevard de Belfort. As it happened,

Michael had finished removing the final load of documents at around six-thirty and had gone back to the apartment to tidy up. There he found not only the message from Gerekens, but also the unexpected and, for once, unwelcome, distraction of Denise. Although the rent on the premises had been paid until the end of November, and he planned to use it occasionally for routine update meetings with Fertein, Séailles and Gerekens, the events of the last two days had strengthened his conviction that he should not spend any more nights there, and he had given Denise definite orders not to return. But she was unwell. Shivering, and running a high temperature, she had come back to be with him after a hard day in Paris. After initially berating her for her disobedience, his natural concern took over, and he packed her off to bed. When he heard his landlady, Marcelle Mahieu, return from work at around seven-thirty he called her in and asked her to stay with Denise, explaining that he had been called away and would not be coming back that night. They had supper together before he left to join Gerekens, arriving at around quarter to nine.

Mahieu gave a detailed account of this encounter with Michael in her post-war testimony:

'Michel *left his apartment on Wednesday* [November] *24 1943 at five o'clock. But on Denise Gilman's insistence he came back on Friday 26 November, intending to spend two or three more days at my house.*

'*On Friday I returned from work at seven twenty-five. As I passed* Michel's *flat he opened the door and asked me to come in to take a look at Denise who was suffering. I went in and she was in bed. I reassured them both by saying that the illness would pass. Michel confided in me that he must stay somewhere else and would like to leave Denise in my care. He insisted that I stay for supper as well as Mme Cheveau and he served us all at the table. Michel left at nine. I tided up his flat.* ' [1]

Michael had left to meet Gerekens. Realizing the absolute necessity of getting Liébault and his men out of the area as quickly as possible, he gave them details of Lille hotels where papers were not checked and of the *Hôtel du Point du Jour* in Fives, which belonged to Maurice Debessel, a member of the circuit. When the men had left, somewhat reassured but still very nervous, Michael and Gerekens discussed what to do next. Liébault and his railwaymen were now illegals, and they agreed to try to place them in the Todt Organization* where they felt they would be safe. The Germans would

---

* The Todt Organization (Organization Todt – OT) was the civil and military engineering body responsible for major construction projects throughout Germany and the occupied countries, employing largely slave labour. In 1943 one of its major tasks was construction of anti-invasion fortifications along the 'Atlantic Wall' of France and Belgium

never think of looking for them there, and they would perhaps be able to carry on their work by making bad cement for the Atlantic Wall. Before leaving Michael pointed out that Gerekens was now as much at risk as Liébault and would have to leave his family. They agreed to meet the following morning at eleven-thirty to sort everything out.

Marcelle Mahieu again:

> *'At around nine-thirty there was a knock at the door. I asked Denise what to do and she said that it was alright to open the door. To my surprise it was* Michel. *He told me that he could not find anywhere else for the night. He did not tell me where he had tried and I did not ask. There were a number of addresses where* Michel *would have been welcomed at any hour. Denise should not have returned to the flat from her mother's home but feeling unwell she wanted to be with* Michel. *This placed him in a predicament. Whether he returned because he genuinely could not find a room for the night or the fact that he felt guilty about leaving Denise we will never know. I stayed with them until eleven. Michel was happy and relaxed. He asked me that if he needed to leave in a hurry could he escape through the loft and I confirmed that he could. As I left to return to my apartment he said "If anything happens so be it, sleep soundly, see you tomorrow Marcelle." These were his very last words to me.'* [2]

Michael would have been completely unaware that his message calling off the Fontaine operation had not been passed on, and that, in consequence, Miseron and his men were toiling away in the expectation of a vehicle that would never arrive. The night was cold and dark, with low clouds hiding the moon and stars – perfect conditions for a clandestine operation. The only drawback was the biting, freezing wind, guaranteed to chill the bones of anyone foolish enough to venture out of doors into the bleak winter countryside around Arras. Yet the men soon worked up a sweat as they laboured to dig up the canisters from their hiding place in the trench among the shelters of the old Hindenburg Line. With great difficulty they manoeuvred the heavy items out of the ground and stacked them up by the side of the cart track that ran around the field. By the time they had finished it was ten o'clock. Lucien Delacroix, Constant Miseron, René Edouard, Alexandre Maury, François Ditte, Jules Dumetz, Albert Michel and Charles Bulcourt settled down to wait for the lorry that would take the arms away. The hands of their watches moved slowly round to midnight and there was still no sign of the vehicle. They waited impatiently for another hour, at which point it was clear that their vigil had been in vain, but they were surprised that neither Dewispelaere nor Reeve had come with a message.

Reluctantly Miseron ordered the men to put everything back in place. Wearily they lifted their shovels once more and worked for another two hours, returning to their homes just after three o'clock, exhausted, cold, and bitterly disappointed in their leaders. Thankfully they sank into their beds and slept.

Malfait meanwhile was implementing his plan to attack the waterway network around Roubaix. Although some of the men wanted to cancel the operation in view of the intense police activity in Wattrelos the previous day, he decided to press ahead. During the First World War a grenade thrown into the lock's evacuation system had exploded and caused disruption on the canal and Malfait decided to repeat the experiment. In spite of meticulous planning his two-pronged attacks on the locks at Leers, Sartel and Hutin, and on the tractor garages in Sartel, resulted in the destruction of just one tractor and slight damage to a garage. Nevertheless he had succeeded in blooding more of his men and given them a taste for action.

Fully occupied with the raid, Malfait was oblivious to the events that had begun to unfold in the early hours.

Chapter notes
1   Madame Mahieu's testimony in 1945 will be cited again, and poses some interesting questions in so far as it appears to contradict subsequent attestations by Séailles.
2   Madame Mahieu occupied the top floor of the three-storey, building, and had let the first floor to Michael. Both apartments were accessed via a staircase and landing leading from a side entrance in an adjoining alley.

Chapter 23

Dominoes

'A pact with the devil is a dangerous thing.'
The Legend of Faust

In the wake of Woussen's capture the expectation had been that, if he talked – which he surely would, sooner or later – he would merely disclose fragments of information relating to the escape line, and to Guillemin and Ida Edouard in particular. This, it was hoped, would keep the Germans busy for several weeks following up the information and buy his compatriots some time. The men of the circuit were not disappointed, but eventually young Woussen was broken. After a month of harsh interrogation, during which he was hanged by the feet and beaten, whipped and burned, he gave in when his mother was dragged before him, beaten, and, according to her own post-war testimony, pleaded with him to tell everything. He must have thought, with absolute justification, that he had granted his colleagues enough time to put their own evasion plans into effect, and could not know that they would not use that time to tighten security and disperse all the active resistants. The Germans now had all they needed to clean up the Arras groups and close in on the elusive British officer who led the FARMER circuit, although they still did not know where to find him.

Shortly after midnight on 26 November, Woussen was taken from his cell, given some soup and a change of clothes, and taken before GFP Inspector Lynen, who questioned him further about details of addresses and names. He was then put into a car with a guard. A few minutes later Martel was taken to another car. Lynen got in beside the driver and told Woussen that he was going back to Arras to assist them with identification. They then drove off, followed by four other cars and a busload of soldiers.

The first hammer blow fell at the house in Rue Pierre Curie. Dewispelaere and Reeve were just dropping off to sleep when, at around one-thirty, they were jolted awake by the sound of vehicles in the street and the slamming of car doors. In his interrogation report, Reeve recounts how Dewispelaere heard the noise of vehicles and, peering through the curtains, saw upwards of forty German soldiers outside. He rushed to warn Reeve, then came back and opened the window. Lynen shouted at him to get his wife downstairs to open the door but Reeve told Marie to stall, as he needed time to get downstairs to retrieve his guns. Nevertheless he was unable to do anything because the soldiers pushed Marie in front of them as a shield and he could not fire for fear of hitting her. Within minutes, Reeve and Dewispelaere were handcuffed and lying on the floor of the kitchen, where they were severely beaten and questioned. The briefest of searches uncovered English chocolate and other goods that could only have come from parachute drops, and this was enough to start the troops ransacking the house, looking for weapons, pulling up floorboards, and ejecting the Dewispelaeres' terrified little daughter from her bed.

Through all of this Marie remained defiant, denying that there were arms in the house and that Reeve was an Englishman, and saying she believed him to be a refugee from the STO. Triumphantly, two troopers waved a pair of revolvers, which they had found in the dining room, whereupon the prisoners were taken outside. Reeve, still in his pyjamas, was dragged in front of a vehicle's headlights, where he heard Lynen ask someone who he was and a disembodied voice reply that his name was *'Olivier, deputy to Capitaine Michel'*. This all happened in the space of half an hour, without a single shot being fired. The Germans had in their custody the two key leaders of the area, who were pushed into cars and taken away, leaving Marie to comfort her child and survey the wreckage of her house. Although her door was left wide open, none of her frightened neighbours came to comfort her or offer help; the streets remained deserted and eerily quiet after the convoy had left.

Reeve's story that he held his fire for fear of hitting Marie suggests that he must have been in a position to fire, with gun in hand, from which the conclusion can be drawn that he chose to put his weapon away rather than use it on himself. While he tells essentially the same story in his other two interrogations, Marie's account is somewhat different. She rejects Reeve's claim that the Germans used her as a shield, and is emphatic that he went downstairs not to *get* his guns, but to *hide* them. [1]

The next port of call was a short distance away at the bakery in Rue de Cambrai, where the Germans repeated their performance, this time breaking the door down and ransacking the house. They seized Henri's brother Michel and his father, but Lynen, well-informed as to who was who, ordered his men to release the older man as being of no interest to them. Henri's mother shouted and protested her son's innocence, punching the soldiers and clinging to them as they took Michel to the car, only to be shrugged off and thrown to the ground. Undaunted, she ran after the convoy in her nightdress and followed the men into the GFP headquarters at the *Hôtel de Commerce* in Rue Briquet-Taillandier. There she learned the full extent of her misfortune: both of her sons had been arrested and there was nothing she could do. The guards told her to go home and take care of her husband.

Reeve and Dewispelaere were taken to separate rooms on the first floor, where they were routinely beaten. Lynen then interrogated Reeve, calling Martel into the room as an observer. He quietly but firmly told Reeve that he knew he was an English officer, that he was *Captain Michael*'s second-in-command, and that all the other lieutenants were marked men and would be picked up within a very short space of time. Slowly and deliberately he recited a list of names, watching Reeve carefully to note his reaction: *Manu* [Lemercier], *Lulu* [Delacroix], *Teuf-Teuf* [Staggs] , Malfait.... . He went on to talk about Woussen, Madame Melot, Guidet, and the capture of Dubois. He knew all about the arms drops and the sabotages, and now he needed to know the whereabouts of Michael's henchmen, the ringleaders of the reception teams in the Arras region, and the precise location of the arms dumps. Most of all he wanted to find Michael himself. [2]

In Reeve's own version of events, the nature and repetition of the persistent questions led him to believe that his captors did not know as much about the circuit as he first thought. They asked him continually about *Lulu* and where to find him. His interrogator told him that they knew Delacroix spent Monday and Tuesday nights at the home of the Dewispelaeres and that they knew all the names of the reception parties, which they then proceeded to reel off. When he asked why, if they already knew, they were beating and questioning him, he received the answer that they were checking to see if he was lying, and the beatings began again. He was then led away to a cell, and in the corridor he met Dewispelaere, who was being taken in the other direction. He tried to tell him to admit everything about the receptions, because the Germans already knew, but, according to Reeve, he could only manage to say *'You can talk, they know everything'*, before the guards prevented him from saying anything more.

Malfait offers an alternative version. In this, Reeve protested that he was a man of honour and could not be expected to betray his colleagues: he was a serving military officer who was simply doing his duty and should be treated accordingly. This statement invoked from Lynen the harsh reply that he was an officer who had given orders to his mobsters to sabotage war installations and kill not only brave German soldiers who too were simply doing their duty, but also innocent civilians who had volunteered to help their own people by doing their duty to keep the country's transport system moving and ensure provision of food and other essential supplies. He had trained a band of terrorists, whose actions could only result in reprisals on many more innocent people, and he and the likes of *Capitaine Michel* were nothing but cowards who used thieves and murderers to do their dirty work, then hid themselves amongst them. There was no honour in such 'service' and he was not entitled to any special consideration. However it was his duty as a GFP officer to protect all German military personnel as they went about their work. To do that he would, if necessary, speak with the devil, if it would bring to an end the tragic and unnecessary suffering and loss of lives on both sides. The surest way to achieve that was to track down the misguided 'patriots' and remove all of their weapons as quickly as possible, something that could be brought about either through further bloody confrontation and the deaths of all the resistors and their families, or through peaceful discussion and cooperation. It was, he pointed out, just a matter of time, but Reeve had it in his power to make things easy for himself and his henchmen, or bring down the severest penalties on everyone: in the face of everything the GFP already knew, resistance was surely futile. Lynen then told Reeve that if he instructed his men to turn themselves in, and reveal the location of the arms dumps, they and their families would be spared and Reeve himself would be treated as a prisoner of war under military law and not shot as a terrorist. [3]

Reeve, Dewispelaere and Woussen were questioned over and over again, until, at around three-thirty, a convoy of vehicles swept onto the Hénin-sur-Cojeul road, with Woussen in the lead car. At four, the Germans burst into Ida Edouard's café, where a search uncovered a revolver, a knife and some parachutes. Ida and her children, Lucienne and René, aged 20 and 22, were taken away. At four-thirty the convoy returned to Arras and left immediately, this time with Reeve, for Copin's home in Rue de la Fourche. The house was sacked and Copin was arrested. From there they drove to the Impasse Vasseur, where they arrested Capeau and took him to the *Hôtel de Commerce*.

It had been a fast and efficient operation, clinically executed, and when Lynen and his colleagues reviewed the situation at five-thirty they were stunned at the results they had obtained in so short a time. They now had in their hands Martel, Woussen, Dewispelaere and Reeve, and knew where to find Delacroix. Anxious to keep up the momentum and the advantage of surprise, the two security factions shared out responsibility for the next stages of the operation: the Arras section would follow up with further arrests and the seizure of arms, while Lynen went back to Lille to arrest *Capitaine Michel*. He would not need to search for his hiding place, because Reeve would lead him to it.

In Arras the Germans rapidly exploited the information they had extracted. Once the head of the detachment had his instructions, a bus and two cars set off for Gommecourt, where, at six o'clock, Mayor Roger was taken by surprise, roughly handled and arrested. He tried to defend himself against the accusations made against him, but, without giving him time to see his wife and children, the Germans took him to the water tower where soldiers were already busy removing arms from the stock there and loading them onto a bus. At the same time, Koltz called for Copin to be brought to his office for further interrogation: he needed to know the exact location of all the Arras stores. Copin steadfastly refused to answer his questions, whereupon he was taken to another room and beaten. He continued to deny any knowledge of arms dumps, and eventually the inspector called a halt to the beatings. Realising that valuable time was being wasted, and that they would get nothing by violence, he ordered his men to bring Dewispelaere to him.

Dewispelaere had made up his mind not to disclose any information that would not have been known to Woussen and Reeve. So, while he was forced to admit to some of the parachute drops, he remained silent about the Ransart drop, of which Woussen had no knowledge. Unaware of the arrests of Copin and Roger, he revealed only the names of the group leaders of all the other drops, then he was taken to Copin and told to order him to give up the information needed. Dewispelaere said that Woussen had been arrested and admitted everything, and that he had been arrested along with Reeve, who had chosen not to resist. Copin should disclose the location of the arms dump. Eventually, no doubt broken as much by the belief that his friend, Dewispelaere, had betrayed him as by the savagery of the beatings, Copin gave in and disclosed the information about the cache at the abattoir.

Once more the Germans moved fast. Copin was bundled into a car and taken to the entrance to the slaughterhouse in Rue de Crinchon, where he was seen, surrounded by armed troops, by Renée Lochu. She was aghast that her group leader had been apprehended and feared that the men were coming for her and her husband. They had sheltered fleeing airmen on several occasions and, only two days previously, they had insisted that Copin remove the arms from their cellar. Copin gave no sign of recognition but turned his eyes to the abattoir, and, as the party went in, she realized that he was telling her about the arms, and knew she had to warn Dewispelaere. When the Germans had completed their business and left, she hurried to the bakery where Dewispelaere's mother, distraught and in a state of near collapse, told her about the raid and showed her the ransacked house. Bitterly she lamented the loss of her sons, and told Lochu to go away and leave her alone. She had earlier said the same to Madame Capeau, who had also come to warn them. Faced with events she simply did not understand, she did not realize that the two women had come in the hope of saving her son and others, or that they would be angry at her abrupt dismissal of them and immediately suspect that it was her son that had betrayed Copin. [4]

In St Léger, another party of GFP troops descended at eight-thirty on La Mairie and seized Miseron as he came out of his stable. They accused him of participation in terrorist activities and told him it was in his best interests to cooperate fully in their enquiries. When he hesitated he was taken to the car in which Dewispelaere was sitting. The two men exchanged a few words, after which Miseron led the Germans directly to the barn where the arms were hidden, a location known only to himself, Dewispelaere and Reeve. Since they had got what they wanted, the Germans did not bother going into the house, but as he was being taken away Miseron managed to whisper to his wife that it was Dewispelaere who had betrayed him.

Armed with a list of the St Léger members that had been provided by Woussen, the Germans forced Miseron to lead them to their homes. His neighbour, Alexandre Maury, was immediately arrested, but Charles Bulcourt, his farm manager, managed to escape, while his brother, Georges Bulcourt, avoided capture because he was away on a mission in Arras. Pierre Ditte had sufficient warning to be able to flee, but, fearing reprisals on his elderly father, he stayed and was arrested at nine-thirty. Word of Dewispelaere's supposed treachery spread rapidly and sparked a huge wave of hatred and resentment against his family.

After leaving the Miserons, Dewispelaere was taken to Fontaine-les-Croisilles, where Albert Michel's farm was surrounded. According to the testimony of her mother, Albert's daughter Christiane Michel was preparing to go out but was taken back to the house, where she joined her mother and her nine-year-old sister, Lucienne. Albert, tired after his night of fruitless waiting in the countryside, was found and arrested in his bed. But it was Michael's lieutenant, *Lulu,* that the Germans desperately wanted, and, having been told by both Woussen and Martel that Delacroix had always expressed his determination not to be taken alive, they forced the women at gunpoint to lead the way to his attic room. Halfway up the stairs, they heard a shot: Delacroix had forestalled them and taken his own life. Furious at being thwarted, the Germans shoved aside the screaming women, burst into the room and emptied their machine guns into his prostrate body, before leaving with Albert Michel in custody.

Lucienne Michel later told Malfait that the body of Delacroix lay where it was until the evening, blood flowing freely from his wounds, forming large puddles and seeping through the ceiling and down the walls, where it crusted as it dried and gave a macabre décor to the room. Faced with the silence and inertia of the local authorities, which were stunned and did not dare to do anything, her mother had to intervene to have the body removed. Some days later Delacroix was cremated anonymously in the Fontaine Cemetery, where he stayed until the liberation, visited faithfully by Lucienne, who admired him greatly. For many months after the war no-one wanted to touch the dried blood on the walls, or the marks and holes made by the bullets that went through the floorboard in the attic. Thirty years later, during a visit to Lucienne, her mother told her that every time she went near the attic, which she did as little as possible, she could still feel *Lulu's* presence. He would, she affirmed, always be there. [5]

Malfait expressed his admiration and respect for Delacroix in a succinct and moving eulogy:

> '*Poor LULU with your tragic destiny. Modest son of the people, patriotic and determined worker, you only had your young life at 20 and you sacrificed it for your country. You were heroic to secure our safety. You were exemplary so as to allow the network to carry on its mission. You are the dignified imitator of* Capitaine MICHEL, *you are our pride.*'

Elsewhere, a squad had set off for Bapaume, where, at around eight o'clock, it pulled up outside Mayor Guidet's house. Not finding him there, it went to the Town Hall, to be informed by the concierge that he was at the Arras Prefecture, so it turned round once more. The squad's arrival and departure had been observed by Madame Duhamel, who despatched her son, Paul, to the Prefecture to warn Guidet, recalling with alarm a conversation the previous day when she had learnt from one of her contacts that the Germans were in a state of alert and that a series of arrests in Arras and Bapaume was planned.

Meanwhile, at the Prefecture, Paul had warned Guidet discreetly, begging him to get away while he could. Guidet dismissed his concerns: this was not the first time he had had to face up to the Germans, and he had always been able to send them away satisfied. His sense of duty told him that he must remain in place to continue to protect and serve his town, and, although he had become increasingly worried over the last few days, he had hidden his feelings from those around him. During this time he had seen very little of Reeve – the atmosphere between them had grown very strained after the threats the latter had made – but he knew the British officer remained quietly confident that Woussen would not talk. Guidet himself did not share this confidence. After the ransacking of the Balesi house on 6 November, the confirmation of Woussen's arrest from Melot in Paris two weeks later, and the arrest of Madame Piletta, his contact with COMÈTE, he had felt the net tightening around him and had drawn up a new will. [6]

Leaving the Prefecture, Guidet stepped into the square, where a quick glance told him everything was normal, and he decided to drop into his favourite café. At that precise moment the Germans arrived. Woussen recognized the mayor's car and pointed it out to his escorts, who directed his driver to pull up alongside it. When Guidet emerged and walked towards his car Woussen identified him. The policemen leapt out and seized Guidet, ordering him to accompany them in their car, ignoring the mayor's protests that he had his own vehicle and could easily follow them in it. They pushed him into the car and handcuffed him. Seeing Woussen already there, Guidet must have known that the game was up.

While this drama was being enacted, Dewispelaere had led a party of Germans down the path to the old Hindenburg shelters and the cache of equipment. Consequently, he did not hear the shots fired in the house and was unaware that Delacroix had died honouring his oath. Nor did he know of the action of the mayor, who when ordered to provide the names of ten men, handed over the electoral roll and wrote his own name at the top, mistakenly believing that it was a list of hostages. As it happened, the Germans merely needed labour to dig up the containers from the trenches and load them into the waiting vehicles, and at around ten they left the village with the prisoners and their booty. News soon reached the surrounding areas and the villages, and fear rapidly spread among the other resistants.

Chapter notes
1   Madame Dewispelaere was one of a number of parties interviewed by Major Dumont-Guillemet as part of an official enquiry carried out late in 1944 – see Chapter 27. It would have been strange if Reeve did not have his weapons with him at night.
2   At this time André Martel was still living with his wife Marguerite at Lemercier's house in Rue Corneille. He was deported to Germany at the end of 1943, where he survived the war. On his return to France he was interrogated, before being indicted for treason and executed.
3   Such an offer would not have been unusual. It was made to and accepted by Gilbert Norman, as recounted by Michael Foot in *SOE in France', Chapter IX: Middle Game: 1943.*
4   After the war Malfait interviewed the wives of Copin, Capeau and Lochu. Apparently, they were unanimous in their condemnation of Henri Dewispelaere as a traitor. Local resentment of the Dewispelaere family lasted for many years.
5   I heard the story of the death of Lucien Delacroix from his mother, whom I visited in the company of André Coilliot.
6   Madeleine Melot wrote to Arthur Malfait after the war, when she returned after deportation and imprisonment in Ravensbruck. She also recounted these events to Henriette Balesi, whom Malfait subsequently interviewed.

Chapter 24

Downfall

'And how can man die better than facing fearful odds.'
Thomas B Macaulay

In Lille that Saturday morning everything at Boulevard de Belfort appeared to be normal. Madame Mahieu left the house at six-forty to go to work as usual; Denise had had a comfortable night, and Michael would have been going over in his mind his plans for the various meetings scheduled for the day. Neither heard the GFP vehicles pulling up a short distance away at six forty-five. In the first car Lynen sat beside the driver; in the back was Reeve, whose directions had led the party to the headquarters. Martel and Woussen had also been brought from Arras, the former accompanying the police in the second car, and the latter being taken direct to the GFP's Lille office in Rue de Tenremonde, where Reeve was also taken as soon as the convoy had reached its destination.

Lynen ordered his men to cordon off the immediate area and prepare to enter the building, confident that he was finally on the verge of capturing the notorious *Capitaine Michel*, who had been the bane of his life for so long. He was looking forward to obtaining from him everything he needed to know to close down the entire FARMER circuit. He waited to give the order to strike as his men took up their positions, but events were taken out of his hands. Four doors away in Rue Kellerman a German soldier was preparing to leave to report for guard duty at the *Citadelle*. As he stepped onto the street, clutching his rifle, one of Lynen's men instinctively opened fire and killed him, whereupon Lynen ordered GFP Oberfeldwebel Gottwald to break into the house.

Inside the apartment Michael must have heard the sound of the shots and the pounding of feet on the stairs, because when, after a peremptory knock and a shout of *Police!*, the door to the flat was kicked open and Michael opened fire immediately, killing Gottwald outright and seriously wounding Obergefreiter Bruygeman. The German troops opened up with their machine guns, pouring a hail of bullets into the room, fatally wounding Denise Gilman and cutting Michael to the floor. True to his oath and to his own very nature, Michael Trotobas had gone down fighting, and inflicting maximum damage on his enemies.

Marcelle Mahieu described the scene to Malfait in a personal testimony, which included the harrowing statement:

'Denise Gilman was shot at the bedroom door. I found bloodstains, firstly at the door then the trail she had made, the length of the bed, finally falling behind the door. The Germans put her on the bed where she died half an hour later from loss of blood. According to neighbours she died in agony having been shot in the stomach. Michael was placed in the corner room along the wall: it was there that I found his bloodstains.'

This account of Michael's death is corroborated by a French police report commissioned in 1948 as part of its investigation into alleged war crimes committed by the GFP. [1]

In the silence that followed Lynen had a suspicion that something had gone wrong, for the body on the floor was that of a man in GMR uniform who bore no resemblance to the description of *Capitaine Michel* that had been provided. He ordered Martel to be brought inside and asked him to identify the body. Martel had not seen Michael since he changed his appearance, and, gazing down on the corpse, told Lynen that it was definitely not him. He did, however, identify Denise as Michael's courier and girlfriend. By now Lynen was sufficiently concerned that the Englishman had, after all, escaped his clutches, and he ordered Reeve to be brought back to the scene. Lynen met him outside and accused him of deliberately providing false information, since the raid had only produced a dead GMR officer and a woman associate. Reeve stared at him and muttered that if it was a GMR officer, then it was almost certainly Michael, since this had been his habitual cover for many months. When Lynen took him upstairs to see the body, Reeve could only nod and confirm that it was indeed Michael's body.

Reeve's presence at the scene had been noticed, and this prompted an intensive investigation by Pierre Séailles and Malfait. They attempted to reconstruct events, in order to determine guilt and responsibility for what they saw as the betrayal of *Sylvestre*, an enquiry that resulted in Séailles formally demanding that Reeve be *'degraded and shot for selling out his chief'*. While Reeve admits in his interrogation reports that he took Lynen to the apartment, the point of dispute, which became his defence, was that Michael had told him on 24 November that he would be abandoning the apartment in the next few days. This was something Séailles refuted strongly and this and other charges brought by Séailles will be reviewed later in detail. [2]

During the course of his post-war enquiries, Malfait interviewed a number of people who gave their version of events.

Pierre Gérard, son of the owner of the apartment building, was a FARMER agent and courier who had earlier rented the same apartment from Mahieu, and had since moved to Sainghin. He said he was cycling to work at the Crepelle metal workshops, about 300m from the house, when, at around ten past seven, he saw *Michel's* body on the pavement, his pistol having slipped to the edge of the gutter. One of the bystanders, a former neighbour, urged him to be careful because Michael had been killed. [3]

At around seven-thirty Fertein arrived on his bicycle at the other end of Rue Kellerman. He was bringing provisions for Michael and Denise, as arranged with her the evening before. When he saw the crowd gathered in front of the house, he guessed what had happened and made an immediate U-turn.

Towards eight o'clock Mathilde Chardin was hurrying towards the Chardin Company in Rue Jean Jaurès, where she worked as a secretary. When she reached the bend in the road she was surprised to see that the area was surrounded by Germans, with a small knot of silent onlookers being kept well back. She knew one of the women, who told her that an Englishman had been shot, which filled her with foreboding. Although she did not know Michael's address, there were precious few Englishmen in Lille, and she knew it had to be him.

Mathilde's son, Michel, told Malfait that he heard about the deaths of the 'resistants' on Boulevard de Belfort when he was going to his foundry, also in Rue Jean Jaurès. Curious, he went to have a look. He reported seeing machine guns used by the GFP lying in the middle of the street at the crossroads, and soldiers right on the roof of the nearby Crepelle factory. As he did not know Michael's address, he passed 20 Boulevard de Belfort without realising that it was his leader's current headquarters. It was then nine o'clock. [4]

Gerekens arrived a little late for his ten o'clock appointment with Michael to discuss the problem of Liébault and three others of the group from Valenciennes who were being hunted for acts of sabotage. He saw the pavement littered with glass, and hastily went on by, noticing as he did so that the shutters were closed and a swastika seal had been posted on the front door. He admitted being surprised and relieved that the Germans had done this, and not chosen to set a trap into which he and others might have walked.

At about ten-thirty Pierre Séailles came cycling along with his sister, Simone, for his scheduled meeting with Michael. As soon as he swung into Boulevard de Belfort he noticed the seals on the door of the headquarters and abruptly reversed direction. He instructed Simone to warn Biéler and Bayart, both at the time in Paris, that something had happened, and to ask Bayart to return to Lille. He explained that until he heard from Michael, or received more information, he was taking command of the circuit, in accordance with the captain's explicit orders for such an eventuality. He gave her details of a new letterbox at the home of the Hortents in Thumesnil then set off for the station to warn Gerekens, unaware that the railwayman had already been to the scene.

Gerekens had only just arrived at the station when Séailles came in. They discussed the events of the morning and Séailles told Gerekens to inform Malfait, which he did immediately, sending Dubocage to Wattrelos to ask Malfait to meet him at the safe house in Rue de Tournai in Lille. Malfait, still tired and a little despondent after the failure at the locks during the night, heard the news with disbelief. Gerekens then sent an urgent message to Fertein and, receiving a reply that Fertein would meet him at the Ronchin level crossing, hurried to the rendezvous. He saw Fertein arrive but not stop, signalling instead that Gerekens should follow him, and after half an hour or so, when they had reached a secluded spot, Fertein finally slowed down and the men were able to talk. Fertein was the first to speak, stating sadly but emphatically, before Gerekens could say anything, that Michael had been killed, he having been the first to arrive after the Germans left.

Shortly before the arrival of Séailles and Gerekens, at around nine-thirty, a German police squad had removed the bodies of Michael and Denise from the apartment and sealed the door of the building. Her body was taken to the Medico-Legal Institute, where it was registered as number 236. Her mother, who had been warned of what had happened by Louis Coudoux at the Central Police Station, took refuge with her cousins the Boutins, butchers in La Place des Quatre Chemins in Lille. Three days later she went with Jean Boutin to the mortuary, where she saw the bullet-ridden body of her daughter and demanded to be allowed to take the body away and prepare it for burial. The request was denied.

The body of Michael Trotobas was taken to Calmette Hospital, because Lynen was still not 100 per cent convinced of the dead man's identity. The name on the papers found on the body was that of Robert Lesage, born on 20 May 1914 in Lille, married at Faches-Thumesnil on 15 November 1939 to Hélène Breton of Paris.

In his first report, Séailles echoed Gerekens assessment that they might all have ended up in the GFP net if the Germans had been more conscientious, since they had left no-one to guard the house for twenty-four hours after the arrest. Consequently, he had been able to observe that the house was blown, because of the seal on the door. He suggested that this might have been due to the fact that two separate security services were employed, one for making the arrest and the other for guarding the house.

However, another possible reason for the lax security is the fact that Lynen only stayed on the scene until he had Reeve's identification of the body. Doubtless he would have been both relieved and annoyed: he had wanted to take *Sylvestre* alive, and his death had deprived him of a vital source of information. Keen to find out what had happened in Arras, he promptly returned there, where he heard about the results of the arrests and the raids on the arms stores.

While he was waiting for Bayart to come back from Paris, Séailles urged Dutilleux to move out and find somewhere safe: he, Michael, Reeve and many others had all lodged with them at some point, and the house could no longer be considered secure. He left again almost immediately to meet Gerekens once more. They desperately needed to know the precise facts and circumstances that had led to the raid in Boulevard de Belfort, in order to determine the extent of the disaster. Routine contact with Arras had been suspended for some time as a precaution, and neither man had any inkling of the arrests there. Séailles ordered Gerekens to go to Arras the next morning and make contact with Reeve to establish how things were, while he himself set about picking up the pieces of the day-to-day work of the circuit. He knew Michael had a meeting arranged that evening with Portemont of the FTP, at which he was to hand over the machine guns and ammunition that were to have been brought in on Herry's vehicle. Because he had set up the meeting, Séailles knew the location, a safe house in Place de Strasbourg, and went along to explain what had happened. Portemont, unmoved by the death of Michael, was furious at being let down and insisted on receiving the promised equipment. Séailles knew the importance of keeping the FTP on side and arranged for a local transfer of a few weapons.

Later that evening, Séailles, Malfait, Gerekens and Dubocage met at *Café Descatoires* in Lille, where they were joined by other members of the circuit. Séailles ordered everyone to take immediate precautions: they had to find refuges for all of the men on the run. Séailles had already agreed that Fertein should leave the Nord, and the arrest of Mahieu, who knew him well, put Fertein in even greater danger. He left to go underground in the countryside. Madame Fertein and her son went to her sister in Pérenchies. Séailles went to the home of Louis Hortent, the fallback address given to him by Michael as a letterbox. Hortent was a member of the circuit whom Séailles did not know, but a password provided by Bayart proved to be all that was necessary to establish his credentials, and the Hortents were happy to take him in.

The next morning, Gerekens went to Arras, dressed in his usual SNCF working clothes, and headed for Soret's café, a regular haunt of the railwaymen. There, the presence of four men wearing raincoats and soft hats stood out and struck a warning note. Gerekens settled himself at the bar and ordered a drink, as if he were on his way home from work. Without showing any sign of recognition, Jeanne Soret told him quietly as she poured that Reeve, Dewispelaere and many others had been arrested, and that the Gestapo were everywhere. Gerekens finished his drink, left the café and headed back to Lille, where he made his report to Séailles, who passed on further bad news. Mahieu had been arrested, and a search had begun for Gérard. [5]

Simone Séailles arrived in Paris early in the morning of 29 November and immediately put Bayart in the picture about events. He set off straight away for Lille to help Pierre Séailles get the circuit back together again, and gave up his job once and for all in order to devote himself entirely to this task. Michael's emergency instructions called for Bayart and Séailles to contact SOE in London, but with no radio links of their own they needed to meet with Biéler. Following his discussion with Gerekens and Malfait, Pierre Séailles rejoined Bayart, and after their meeting that evening the two men left for Paris, where Biéler was expecting them. After seeing Bayart, Simone had left a message about Michael's death with Mani Biéler, the major's sister-in-law, courier and letterbox.

Now began a difficult period of waiting. In the absence of Séailles and Bayart, Gerekens maintained a contact between circuit members, and with Malfait in particular. Michael's death, the lack of funds, and the arrests, led some of them to feel deeply discouraged; they had to react, and quickly, to prevent the circuit falling apart. Malfait, typically, believed that the best tonic would be a successful action, and the next evening he led a heavily-armed team to attack the Nouveau-Monde lock. They put the guards out of action and attacked the upper and lower hinges of the lock doors. The result was conclusive: the explosions damaged the door, one race was emptied and the lock was put out of action for three weeks, during which the many immobilised barges caused a large traffic jam. As a result of the sabotage, the guard was reinforced and the banks of the canal were protected by barbed wire. Because of this, but also because of a lack of equipment and the need to reorganize his sector after the many arrests, Malfait was forced to abandon sabotage attacks on the waterways until after D-Day. Poignantly, before setting off, he had heard on the BBC the surprise message Michael had spoken to him about: *'Courage, deliverance is near. Joseph* [Michael] *to F10* [Malfait].*'*

After Michael's body had been removed to Calmette Hospital, Lynen had ordered further checks to be carried out, and he had instructed that the dead man's face should be cleaned up and made as recognizable as possible. Over the next few days each of the captured circuit members held in Loos was taken to the body. With the sole exception of Madeleine Thyrou, who refused to tell the Germans what they wanted to hear, they all confirmed that it was the body of their chief. Only then was Lynen satisfied that they had killed the English officer and resistance organizer he had hunted for so long, and he handed over responsibility to the Office of Administration and returned to Arras to continue the search for those still at large.

On 2 December Michael's body was sent to the Medico-Legal Institute, where it was registered as number 237, labelled *unknown* and said to be *Michel, of 20 Boulevard du Belfort*. After the formal documentation was complete, the GFP Office released the two bodies for burial, with the stipulation that the interments were to be carried out in secrecy, banning any celebration or religious ceremony. Moreover, the grave was to be unmarked, and the attendance of family, friends and the general public was absolutely forbidden. The Germans handed the task of arranging this to the superintendent at the Central Police Station, confident that their instructions would be followed to the letter. But they reckoned without the thirteen policemen based at the station who were members of the circuit, all of whom refused to countenance the idea that their revered captain should be put away in such a manner, and between them came up with a plan. Sergeant Coudoux suggested to his inspector that there was a strong possibility news would leak out and lead to a series of demonstrations along the route to the cemetery and that it would be sensible to take the precaution of arranging for a number of officers to escort the hearse to deter any intervention. Coudoux was instructed to make the necessary arrangements.

He selected his men carefully, and, on the following day, 3 December, the body was put in a pauper's coffin provided by the charity office, and the convoy left the Medico-Legal Institute under an unusually strong police escort for the Lille-Sud Cemetery. The ban on religious service or a priest's presence was circumvented, thanks to the fortuitous arrival of another convoy coming from the Institute. Some confusion arose, whereby Michael's coffin was lowered in the grave meant for the other burial, which was accompanied by a priest. It was only after the latter gave the blessing that the mistake was discovered. Then each body was buried in the correct grave.

Over the next fortnight the slow but relentless tortures continued in Arras, where the arrested and confused agents were confronted and interrogated. Those still at large, without leadership or instructions, were loath to leave their jobs, their families and their homes. Not knowing the exact reasons for the arrests, they did nothing, and during the night of 13 December the Gestapo mopped up what was left of the Arras sector.

Acting on information supplied by Dewispelaere or Copin, the Germans decided to exhume Lemercier's body and make capital out of the execution, linking it to alleged Communist atrocities. On the morning of 17 December the two prisoners were taken under guard to the well of Beaurains' mushroom cave, where Lemercier's body lay, 10m down in the well. A team of firemen was ordered to empty the 'grave' and bring the body to the surface, and the GFP posted formal 'notices' of the finding and recovery of the body of the *'lieutenant of Capitaine Michel'* who had been *'executed by his leader'*.

Two weeks later a four-column spread on the front page of the *Grand Echo* of Friday, 31 December 1943, told the story of how the terrorist Lemercier had been executed by his leader, the English *Capitaine Michel*. *Le Reveil du Nord* and the *Journal de Roubai* ran similar stories and two macabre photographs of the exhumed Lemercier. All three newspapers revealed that his body had been thrown callously to the bottom of a well, without a blessing and eschewing the customary rites of a Christian burial. The incident was portrayed as an example of how the Engish terrorists dealt with collaborators, and likened to the massacre at Katyn. [6]

These articles were intended to cow the population and denigrate the reputation of British officers and resistance leaders, although Malfait described it as *'excellent publicity for the circuit'*. However, the effect on Eliane Lemercier was devastating. She had already read a couple of lines about it in the December 18 edition of the *Echo*, which had been drafted from the official notice. Suspecting a trap, she stayed put. Only a few weeks before, Michael had told her that he believed her husband had arrived in Spain, and since then she had listened to the radio each day, waiting for the message drafted by Michael that would reassure her husband had arrived in England: *Jean Murat safely arrived, sends love to his wife and son, Michael.* On reading the papers Eliane was horrified and could do nothing about it. The Gestapo was looking for her and there was no question of her going to identify the body. She concluded that it was a new trap and decided not to leave her hiding place. Lemercier's body was buried on 21 December 1943 in Arras Cemetery, from where Eliane had it exhumed after the liberation and moved to the little cemetery in Olhain.

Séailles wrote a long and detailed report of events and gave it to Simone, who passed it to Biéler on 10 December. Acting on Biéler's advice, Séailles called a halt to any type of activity by the circuit, in order to give them all time to draw breath and see what the Germans would do next. But the Germans did not make any great effort to pursue their enquiries any further, and there were no more arrests. The circuit was saved. They now had to wait for the arrival of a new organizer and, most of all, for instructions. Séailles, like Bayart, took refuge in Paris, but before leaving he put in place a courier service, so that he could be informed at all times of what was happening in the region. Through the intermediary of Jean Gambier, he put Mathilde Chardin in touch with two letterboxes: one was *Café Déscatoires*; the other was the *Au Poker* in Rue Gustave Delory, where it had all begun thirteen months earlier, when Michael met Lemercier and the seeds of the circuit were sown.

Séailles would in due course reactivate the circuit, but Michael's death affected him deeply. Although they were of opposite dispositions and frequently engaged in heated arguments, there was great friendship and mutual respect. Séailles later spoke of the huge admiration and regard he had for his chief as a leader of men and one who was always ready to show the way by example. He was a man who inspired and attracted the sympathy of everyone who met him. The far-reaching success of the circuit was due first and foremost to the personality of its leader, who was not happy just to give orders but loved to be out on the ground with his men. He relished action and danger, everything about him made that clear. He was fearless and had a high opinion of an officer's worth.

Contrary to what often happened after the death of a leader, Séailles knew he would have to restrain the men, who were only too willing to carry on and finish the work they had begun. He knew, too, that he would be able to count on Michael's surviving lieutenants.

Chapter notes

1   R*eport #10516 prepared on 27/11/43* by the Commissaire Principal – Chef du Service des Renseignements Généraux, Préfecture du Nord.
2   See Chapter 27.
3   The body seen by Gérard was almost certainly that of the German soldier shot down before the apartment was entered.
4   Neither the weapons in the road nor the men on the rooftops have been mentioned in any other reports, and there is no further explanation of this.
5   Madame Mahieu was arrested on 28 November. *Why shouldn't I have trusted a policeman?* was her response to her interrogator. She was tortured and released on 22 February 1944.
6   The Katyn massacre was a series of mass executions of Polish nationals carried out by the NKVD, the Soviet secret police, in April and May 1940. Exposed in 1943, German propaganda made full use of the event as evidence of Russian barbarity.

Chapter 25

Continuum

'And their work continueth…greater than their knowing.'
Rudyard Kipling

The story of the activities of FARMER following the death of Michael to the end of the war in France has been told by Danièle Lheureux in her follow-up books *La Résistance "Action-Buckmaster": Sylvestre-Farmer après le capitaine "Michel"* and *De Sylvestre-Farmer à Libre Résistance – Avec les Séailles*. We shall confine ourselves to the circumstances involving Séailles, Reeve, Malfait and Staggs, in so far as they impact on our story of Michael and the men and women of Arras. All of these four survived the war, and it is appropriate at this point to summarize their roles following the events of November 1943, as well as taking into account an SOE report on the circuit.

We should first, however, record the demise of the MUSICIAN circuit and the downfall of Biéler, who survived Michael for only a few months. Last of the trio of British organizers who achieved so much in the north of France, Biéler was brought down not by betrayal but through poor radio security.

As instructed by London, Yolande Beekman transmitted according to a prearranged schedule, sending messages at specific times and frequencies three times a week. This was standard practice for SOE wireless operators in France, but most would try and set up several sets at different safe houses, switching between them to avoid detection. Operating from a single static radio post greatly increased the chances of being located by the German direction-finding teams, which were known to prowl the streets of major towns and cities across the country. It is not clear why Beekman did not use additional hideouts – perhaps it was difficult to find suitable locations in such a densely populated area, or she might have had technical problems with the wireless sets available.

Michael's death left Biéler with the task of trying to keep London updated on two circuits, but he continued to push on. From his base in St Quentin in northern Aisne he controlled twenty-five teams, scattered over different areas of northern France. They mirrored the achievements of

Michael's men in damaging or destroying gasoline storage tanks, rail lines, bridges, canal locks, and the tractors used to tow barges on the shipping waterways. Their repeated efforts hampered the movement of enemy arms and troops, but the most important job for Biéler was preparation for D-Day. He had set up groups to attack the local rail networks at twenty-five points, while others would ambush German communications across the region and cut telephone wires to Paris. In November his men had sabotaged ten locomotives, and another eleven at Tourcoing before Christmas, but this, inevitably, made the Gestapo more determined than ever to stop him.

He and Beekman spent Christmas Eve at the home of the Bourys, where Beekman was living. Her steadfast and fearless approach had proved invaluable to the MUSICIAN circuit, but her work was putting everyone in jeopardy. German interception of radio signals had become very efficient, and the regular nature of her transmissions was helping to narrow down the area of the source. On Christmas Day she made contact with London as usual, but the following week a direction-finding van was seen passing the house, an ominous sign that the net was closing. She moved her set to the Boury house, but on 12 January Camille Boury noticed a man walking along the street, with his collar turned up and apparently listening to earphones. Beekman's radio signal had been traced to their block. She immediately packed up her set and moved, this time to *Café Moulin Brulé*, an isolated safe house on the north-eastern edge of the city, on the northern bank of the canal. Beekman knew the owners well, and they took her in for the night. But she had been followed, and when Biéler arrived at the café the following morning, 13 January, to discuss where she should go next, two Gestapo men walked in with revolvers drawn and arrested everyone. More than fifty further arrests followed before the end of the week, and the circuit was soon unravelled completely.

Both Beekman and Biéler were tortured, and Yolande was later executed at the Dachau concentration camp in Germany. Biéler put up stubborn resistance throughout his merciless interrogations, refusing to give away the slightest piece of information that might be useful to the enemy, until the exasperated Germans sent him to Flossenburg camp in Bavaria. There, on 5 September 1944, he was executed by firing squad in front of an honour guard, spared the noose by his SS captors out of respect for his courage and defiance.

To return to FARMER, Séailles took over leadership of the circuit following Michael's death, and he was forced to discard the whole of the Pas de Calais organization as well as a large part of that in Lille. Not knowing Michael's method of communication with London, and with Staggs still out of action, he was unable to provide what remained of the circuit with directives, arms or money. It was evident that it could not keep going for long, and that confidence was waning. He made numerous attempts to contact other organizations for the purpose of passing a message to London, eventually contacting ZERO FRANCE, who relayed a message stating that Michael and Reeve had been arrested. London however refused to take up contact with him. Then on 2 December he prepared the lengthy report, which his sister gave to Biéler a few days later. It makes interesting reading, not least because it reveals that Séailles at this time did not know the circumstances of Woussen's arrest, nor who had been arrested in Arras, and that he believed Dewispelaere had left as planned and was currently in England:

'*THE DEATH OF* CAPITAINE MICHEL *(FARMER)*

'*Preliminary Observations: The information given here comes from reliable sources and consists mainly of statements made to third persons in confidence by German authorities in charge of the inquest. They should not, however, be looked upon as indisputable, as it is possible that the Germans have voluntarily furnished false information in order to divert suspicion from the true culprits. With this reservation in mind, the following facts emerge:-*

'*A man called HOUSSEN* [sic]*, a member of the organization (with a price put on his head by the Germans following the discovery of an attack in the Arras region), who was being sent to England a few months ago, was arrested in the Midi on his way to Spain. It would appear that the Germans obtained certain information by this arrest, which led to the discovery of the Arras organization, with which Lieutenant OLIVIER* [Reeve] *was especially connected. At all events, the latter was arrested, probably on 26 or 27 November, in circumstances unknown to date.*

'*On 28* [sic] *November at 7 o'clock in the morning a detachment of* La Police de Sûreté de l'Armée Allemande en Champagne, *arrived at* Capitaine MICHEL's *home in Lille.* MICHEL *was up and ready to go out, dressed in Police uniform. Finding himself confronted by Germans, he immediately knocked down the lieutenant in charge of the detachment. The soldiers retaliated with machine-gun fire. In the ensuing brawl,* Capitaine MICHEL *and a young girl belonging to the organization who was there, were killed, as well as another German soldier. In the vehicle belonging to the German police there was a bound civilian, whom we were assured was Lieutenant OLIVIER. The description, furnished by French witnesses on the spot, confirms this assurance. According to the Germans, this man was the Lieutenant OLIVIER who had led them to MICHEL's home.*

'*In exoneration of Lieutenant OLIVIER it should be noted that it is strange that only* MICHEL *should be implicated by this and the other important addresses given to* OLIVIER *are intact up to the present. Until now, we have not had precise details of the events at Arras, except for the arrests of 27 men whom we were unable to identify. Only* HENRI [Dewispelaere] *the baker at Arras, who was sent to England a short time ago by* MICHEL, *would possibly be able to clarify the position in this sector.*

'It is our duty to pay homage to the memory of Capitaine MICHEL. *He was a courageous and yet cautious chief, prudent and at the same time audacious. He was very much admired and respected by all his French subordinates, from whom he obtained, by his tact and methods of leadership, all that he wished. His body was given up to the French authorities and buried in the Cimetière du Sud at Lille. There is a cross on his grave with the simple inscription* 'Michel'. *Flowers were put there, from his men.*

'*PRESENT POSITION OF THE CIRCUIT*

'*Up to the present the threads of the organization recruited and set going by* Capitaine MICHEL *at Lille and in the department du Nord, remain unbroken and ready for the resumption of activity. Steps were taken at once to see that any information which might be given away by those arrested would not result in further arrests.*

'*It should be understood that for the present the Arras circuit must be considered as non-existent. It would be desirable for someone to replace* Capitaine MICHEL *as soon as possible, as difficulties concerning money and responsibility arise, and we can of course only deal with them temporarily. If his departure should be delayed, it is imperative for us to receive instructions in the meantime, particularly concerning D-Day. In default of other means of communication, we have contacted Captain* GREY... . *He will try to get into direct communication with you as from 20 December (1943).* [1]

'*PRESENT STATUS OF EQUIPMENT*

'*If you wish we will send you a special report on this, but we can give you the following details.*
In a safe place: 2 transmitting sets. 2 sets for communicating with aeroplanes
Probably safe: 1 Rebecca
We have no news of the equipment of the Arras sector, which probably
consists of:
1 Rebecca
1 transmitting set (large, but old model rec'd recently) and a delivery of arms consisting of 10 to 15 containers.'

A few days later Séailles received news that a contact would be given to him, and at the end of March a new organizer arrived. This was Major René Dumont-Guillemet (*Armand*), whose orders required him to contact the remnants of the Lille circuit, with which contact had been lost, and to organize a new Paris circuit (SPIRITUALIST). He reported on his arrival that Séailles had successfully taken command of the FARMER circuit, assisted by Bayart. The WT operator, Staggs, was in hiding and no longer capable of work. The organization was in fairly good condition, but it required cohesion, definite orders and material.

Dumont-Guillemet left Séailles in local command, but canalised all messages through himself and maintained, from Paris, strategical command of operations. With Bayart's help, Séailles started to reorganize FARMER's six main regions. In the south of Lille he was forced to remove Fertein from command, since he feared that he was already blown after Michael's death: it was placed under the command of Dumetz. The east was commanded directly by Bayart, the north was placed under the command of Malfait, and the west under Gerekens. Bailleul was placed under the command of Chieux, and the decimated Pas de Calais region was reconstructed by Guy de Valenciennes. [2]

Séailles was able to contact London through SPIRITUALIST's radio operator. A regular courier service was arranged for messages, involving a GMR motorcyclist reporting to an arranged rendezvous in Paris. Otherwise, there was no contact between the men of the Paris and Lille groups. Owing to the fact that the RAF refused all of the landing grounds put forward by Séailles, arms and materiel had to be received through SPIRITUALIST. When weapons had to be transported from Seine-et-Marne to Lille, Dumont-Guillemet arranged for distribution to take place in a wood beside an unfrequented road close to the ground where the arms were hidden. This way, if the car coming from Lille to collect them was stopped on the way back, all the men could have given away was the spot where they had picked up the arms; by the time the Germans got there nothing would be left to tell them who had delivered the materiel. Inevitably, transport difficulties led to a shortage of materiel, but FARMER was able to attack successfully all of its D-Day targets. The circuit was also tasked with setting up an intelligence cadre of its own purely to gather and collate information about the V weapons.

As well as continuing to lead the men of the Roubaix sector, Malfait subsequently took the place of Bayart, who was gunned down on 10 July 1944 when Germans burst into a café in Pont à Marque where he was holding a meeting with Vandeneeckhoutte and Fertein. When Bayart saw the Germans enter he made a dash for the door to the courtyard, hoping to distract the soldiers long enough for his companions to get away, but was shot before he reached it. Vandeneeckhoutte was arrested and imprisoned in Loos before being deported on the last train to leave for Germany. Fertein did manage to escape, thanks to Bayart's self-sacrifice – another example of Michael's lieutenants honouring their oath.

Malfait came directly under threat when his home in Wattrelos was visited by the GFP on 7 February 1944, in the wake of arrests made during January. They went away empty-handed as he had gone underground and came again ten days before the liberation. Following the capture of several agents, one of them made his torturers smile when he exclaimed: *'We are merely the little fish. Look for the "pike".'* This was a reference to a supposed alias written by the enemy on the back of a photograph of Malfait that was shown to witnesses who were arrested and interrogated about him.

The very real damage suffered by the enemy as a result of Malfait's leadership deserves mention here. As well as being involved in the activities of the circuit in the region, which were considerable, he organized and took part in all kinds of sabotage operations with the men from Roubaix-Tourcoing. They wrecked enemy communications in thirty operations, seven of which were on the Lille-Brussels telephone lines. They attacked road services and destroyed a garage containing twenty vehicles, wounding horses and ruining the tyres of around 700 enemy vehicles with nails scattered on the road. His groups carried out thirteen operations on the waterways, four of which involved direct attacks on locks, and three on the drainage systems. Thus the Roubaix Canal was blocked from the time of the Normandy landings in June 1944 until the liberation. But it was the guerrilla activity against the railways that was most significant. Malfait and the men of FARMER carried out fifty-three separate acts of sabotage, seventeen involving destruction of sections of track, eight of which resulted in trains being derailed. In December 1943 eleven locomotives and their repair facilities were rendered unserviceable by well-placed explosives, causing massive disruption at Tourcoing depot for five months. Further acts of destruction of the railways saw the enemy deprived by fire of 300,000 litres of fuel, 500 tonnes of crops and twelve anti-aircraft guns, while the workings of more than fifty locomotives were ruined by abrasive paste resulting in the loss of 500 days of use. Last, but not least, and this still only in the area of Roubaix-Tourcoing, there were sixteen operations that caused severe damage to factories, pylons, farms, warehouses and procurement facilities. To this can be added the execution of seven 'enemy agents'.

After the war Malfait dedicated himself to piecing together the events surrounding the break up of the circuit and to serving as FARMER's principal public relations officer and archivist. Like Séailles, he is merciless in his attribution of deliberate betrayal to *Olivier*, whom he castigates further for never returning to France to face the relatives of those who, Malfait believes, died as a result of Reeve's actions. His own recollections and the results of his efforts and interviews with survivors, set down in his diary and published by André Coilliot in 1984, has figured large in our subsequent analysis.

In the afternoon of Michael's death Reeve was taken to Loos Prison, where, still in his pyjamas and with chains on his hands and feet, he underwent repeated beatings and interrogations. During his four month stay, he stuck for as long as he could to a story that his name was Bob West. He said he had fought in the BEF and gone through Dunkirk, where he had been wounded in the hand and sent back to England. There he had been told that, as he spoke French, it was his duty to go back to France as a special commando, which he had done, and had reported directly to *Captain Michael*. This story did not hold up for very long; the Germans confronted him with Michael's captured reports and during the course of the interrogations, including one with Gilbert Norman, it became clear that they knew almost everything about FARMER and SOE itself. For the duration of his imprisonment Reeve adopted the stance that he would lay everything where possible on the shoulder of the dead Michael, maintaining that he was not on good terms with him, and insisting that the only other men he knew were those arrested in Arras.

On 7 April 1944 he was taken to Arras, where he was tried and condemned to death by a tribunal, before being confined in Arras Prison to await execution. There he submitted a plea for mercy to the marshal commanding all German forces in France, but nothing came of it. During his time in this prison he was interrogated twice, on each occasion being promised his life in return for disclosing information about the vital D-Day targets mentioned in the reports, as well as more details about the FARMER organization. He refused each time. Late in May he was transferred to the St Gilles Prison in Brussels, where he remained until 2 September, being told first that he was only alive because the Germans expected to make further arrests and he would be wanted for identifications, then, at the end of August, he was told he could expect to be shot as soon as the formal documentation for his execution was received.

By now, the Allies were closing in on Brussels, and Reeve was put into a railway wagon in Brussels station, where he managed to hide himself amongst a group of captured airmen. One of these, Pilot Officer Sweeney, mentioned seeing him in his subsequent report, and described how Reeve's back and chest showed signs of brutal and prolonged beatings. When the train left it only went a short distance before sabotaged track forced it to return to Brussels, where all of the civilian prisoners were released. That evening the train set off once more, but only went about 15km outside Brussels, where the guards abandoned it. At dawn the next morning Reeve made contact with the FFI, the French Forces of the Interior, or resistance, who passed him to the British Intelligence Service, which arranged for his prompt return to England.

During the course of the next few days he wrote two reports and was interrogated twice, but the interrogators found nothing that demonstrated that he had betrayed his leader, or divulged information that led to the arrests of others in the circuit. Not surprisingly, the reports portray a vastly different picture than that provided by Séailles and Malfait. He was returned to his regiment in the rank of lieutenant.

Staggs, as we have seen, went to Roubaix in July 1943 and spent the rest of the year in relative obscurity at the home of his friend, Claude Bagein. They were both taken in by the local police for interrogation in December 1943, following the arrest of Claude's father René and his wife, both members of local resistance groups who were betrayed by a colleague. After searching the house and finding nothing the police took the two men away for questioning, but both stuck to their stories that they had nothing to hide. As a native of Roubaix Staggs was able to take refuge behind his identity of 'Albert Foulon'. They were released for lack of evidence on 12 February 1944, when they decided to split up. After a trip via Arras and Bethune, Staggs settled in the Aire-sur-la-Lys area at the home of another friend from Roubaix.

Colonel Maurice Buckmaster stated that when agents left British soil he gave them, at the most, six months survival in a sector. Michael had defied the odds by surviving for a year. Whether or not he would – could – and, indeed, should – have survived the war and led FARMER through the Allied invasion, had Reeve not led Lynen to him, will never be known. FARMER marched on and continued to distinguish itself, which was testimony to the tight cellular security that allowed all but a handful of agents outside the Arras circle to avoid capture. The railway saboteurs and the teams in Roubaix were hardly touched: only the reception teams in the south were lost.

An interesting and revealing testimony to the circuit by third parties is provided in a report prepared following a fact-finding mission led by Buckmaster in October 1944. Surprisingly, at this late date, it opened:

'Of our organization in Lille we know very little more than that FARMER [Michael] had gone there in 1943, that he had some difficulty in making contacts there, that we had never made direct radio contact with him, and that we had made very small deliveries to him. We then learned that he had been killed, and in consequence we lost touch with and had no knowledge of the organization which he had managed to build. We had heard vaguely that he was held in very high esteem, and that his tomb was covered with flowers every day.

> *'Later, messages began to reach London through indirect channels, and we were able to give SPIRITUALIST the necessary contacts to put us once again in contact with the organization; but by this time the RAF had grown to dislike the North of France, and we were unable to deliver any material.*
>
> *'We had heard reports of considerable activity in the Nord and Pas de Calais, but in view of the circumstances indicated above, we had not dared to hope that our own groups had been responsible for more than a small part in them. Our visit showed how wrong we had been.'*[3]

Arriving in Lille on the evening of Monday, 3 October 1944 the party went to the headquarters of the FFI in Boulevard de la Liberté and noticed the building next door, which was decorated with a large sign bearing the legend *OFACM – Organisation Franco-Anglais du Capitaine MICHEL*. At the head of the group of officers there to welcome them was Séailles, and an immediate problem was identified. The report continued:

> *'In the first place they were immensely proud of the fact that they had always been free from politics and had worked under the War Office (we found later that all their banners bore the letters WO prominently displayed, their cars bore WO numbers, their shoulder flashes were WO – some of them specially made in metal in a Tourcoing factory – and WO was completely uppermost in all their thoughts and actions).* Captain MICHEL – *FARMER – had promised them that they could consider themselves as soldiers of the British Army with corresponding rights and responsibilities. It is evident that SPIRITUALIST had carried out an extremely tactful and efficient job in persuading them that the role of the War Office had ceased with the driving of the Germans out of France, and that the surviving members must make their arrangements for "becoming French". This was, of course, a very obvious disappointment to them, but one which they were persuaded to accept.'*

The main difficulty however lay in the fact that those who had been killed had died confident in the belief that their dependants would receive pensions from the British Government on the British scale. These and other issues, including lack of funds, were discussed, and it was proposed that the organization should be completely affiliated with the FFI.

The next morning the party set off on a tour of inspection of the various groups, taking in visits to Auchel, Aire-sur-la-Lys, and Bailleul, before ending the morning in Lille:

'This was the detachment which, under the command of Lieutenant-Colonel HERRY, had been incorporated as a Company in the Premier Bataillon de Securité. After having been received by the Colonel and a number of high police dignitaries we found the men drawn up in a hollow square, impeccably equipped with uniform, greatcoats and helmets. To the strains of God Save The King, *extremely well if a little fancifully rendered by the Band, the twin flags – sewn together – of France and England were solemnly raised to the top of the flagpole. Then the* Marseillaise, *followed by a withdrawal to a short flight of steps behind the house, which served as dais for the March Past, the Colonel taking the salute, and the troops, with their colours, marching past with great efficiency.'*

After lunch, further detachments were visited at Phalempin and Cysoing, before the party arrived at Malfait's Roubaix sector.

'This was under the command of Captain 'ARTHUR' [Malfait], *one of the most active saboteurs and an old associate of* Captain MICHEL's. *Three companies were drawn up on three sides of a square in front of their château HQ; there was a colour party in the middle and a rank of about 30 officers and men on the fourth side awaiting presentation to the Colonel* [Buckmaster].'

At dinner that evening:

'We dined at the Officers' Mess – a building captured from the Germans, who had used it for the same purpose – with Lieutenant-Colonel HERRY, Commandant SÉAILLES, Captain GEREKENS and one or two others. The gravest of the problems calling for comment was the method of incorporation into the Police Force. The leaders of our own organization were intensely anxious that the spirit of enthusiasm and comradeship of which we had been witnesses, should not be lost; whereas the Army authorities were said to be unwilling to allow existing units to preserve their corporate existence, and insisted on a complete admixture of the various organizations, right down to platoon level. There was apparently also a notable lack of sympathy and tact on the side of the military in the person of the General commanding the region, with whom Lieutenant-Colonel HERRY had already had an unsatisfactory interview. Nevertheless, he agreed to approach him again in an endeavour to secure the formation of another WO Company as part of a second battalion of Security Police then in course of formation.'

Throughout the day they realised that they were faced with the problem of more than 2,000 men who were determined through thick and thin to remain defiantly under the WO banner.

'*Outstanding in all our contacts with the various groups was the evidence of a fervent admiration, amounting almost to worship, of* Captain MICHEL *(FARMER), of a burning desire to continue to rank as part of a British War Office organization, and of the development of an* esprit de corps *which was remarkable. It was in its way a tragedy that part of our mission is to declare the British connection officially ended, although there is no doubt whatever that unofficially it will continue to exist for a very long time to come.*'

A largely unsatisfactory compromise was reached on compensation:

'*It was suggested that the question of British pensions might be met by a one-time payment of Frs. 100,000, in which case the French were prepared to pay this sum. They would also provide Frs. 200,000 for necessitous cases where immediate assistance was necessary. Arrangements for complete affiliation would be proceeded with*'.

Subsequently the party met with a group of leading WO saboteurs:

'*They numbered six or seven, and had all been leading figures in coup de main tasks carried out against the enemy. Two of them, ARTHUR* [Malfait] *and GEREKENS, had been original associates of* Captain MICHEL's. *This talk was at once inspiring and disappointing; inspiring in the actions they had carried out whenever they had materials with which to work, and disappointing in the realization of the immense amount of work which might have been done by our groups in the Lille area, if we had only been able to send the supplies which they so richly deserved.*'

Then, in an unprompted testimony and tribute to the spirit of the WO men:

'*This particular meeting was perhaps notable for one other phenomenon, in itself unimportant, but symptomatic of a phase in Resistance life which is of some importance. As explained above, we were meeting with the "toughs" of the organization, working men of various ages and of humble circumstances. Despite this, ten o'clock had scarcely struck when the first bottle of champagne made its rounds. For these men, champagne and cigars were, if not exactly normal, at least not surprising at that hour of the morning. They were, of course, booty captured from the Germans, and in themselves a symbol of the complete mastery of Resistance in the closing stages of the German occupation. These men had in fact been masters of the region, had tasted the joys and sorrows of active resistance in all its phases, and had been living a life with rewards and penalties on the heroic scale. They are now faced with – what? Either incorporation into a Police Battalion or a descent into the present disorganization of French civilian life. We heard later that a second Police Battalion had been formed, which will preserve a number of them from the second alternative; but the problem is a nationwide one, and is not yet in process of complete solution.'*

They were 'masters of the region', but their time had come and gone. The report concluded on a poignant note:

'During the afternoon of 5 October a visit was paid to the grave of FARMER, still bedecked with flowers.'

Shortly after Michael's death a few of his comrades made a clandestine visit to 20 Boulevard de Belfort to search for anything the Germans might not have uncovered. All they found was his black cat (called '808' after the explosive), which was immediately adopted as the post-war symbol of the SYLVESTRE-FARMER group, and appears on its letter headings and banners, as well as on Michael's memorial. At the end of hostilities in France they arranged for Michael's body to be exhumed from its unmarked pauper's grave in Lille-Sud Cemetery and moved to its current location, where a splendid memorial commemorates his life and those of the many French patriots who gave theirs with him.

The memorial was the scene of a succession of post-war pilgrimages to the cemetery on the anniversary of Michael's death when hundreds of people from both sides of the Channel paid homage and tribute to a heroic leader that the French had made their own. Among the host of former FARMER leaders and activists attending each year, and responsible for the organization of the event, were the Frenchmen Séailles, Malfait and Gerekens. Of the surviving British Officers, Reeve never attended, but Staggs did – once. All have since passed on and we would be content to leave them with Michael to rest in peace, were it not for the fact that while writing this book we became conscious of anomalies and inconsistencies in their accounts of key events and those of other sources, particularly Reeve's. While we are confident that these events did occur we find ourselves unable to verify exactly how they happened or project with certainty the thoughts, motivations and decision-making processes that preceded them. Readers must therefore draw their own conclusions from the post-war testimonies of survivors, and extracts from official reports that provide additional, and sometimes conflicting, insight into important areas such as Michael's personality and leadership, his communication problems, the security of the circuit, the relationships, rivalries and jealousies of key players, the 'Rex affair', the execution of Lemercier, the arrests and interrogations in Arras, and, finally, the death of Michael.

Chapter notes
1   The reference to Captain *Grey* almost certainly refers to Captain *Guy*, which could be either Staggs or Biéler, both of who used the code name *Guy*.
2   Dumont-Guillemet was interviewed by Major Hunt on 12 January 1945 *PRO HS6/571.*
3   These and subsequent extracts are from the *Judex Report 1944 RBP/EJB 16.11.44.*

Chapter 26

Post Mortem

'Truth sits upon the lips of dying men.'
Matthew Arnold

Memories are not infallible. For this reason we have largely followed the versions presented by Malfait via André Coilliot, and Danièle Lheureux. Neither writer took part in the activities of SYLVESTRE-FARMER, nor were their accounts written contemporaneously, but the provenance of their principal sources is impressive. Coilliot has relied almost exclusively on the diary of Malfait and his exhaustive post-war interviews with survivors, and Lheureux on the contributions from hundreds of contemporary witnesses and participants. The most significant of these were, undoubtedly, as she makes clear in the foreword to her own book, the testimonies and archives of Pierre Séailles, Malfait, Gerekens and Chieux, and those confided to her by the families and friends of Bayart, Fertein and Herry.

It appears that these key lieutenants of Michael met each other infrequently, working as they did in different sectors, with responsibilities and duties that seldom overlapped or coincided, and there are no grounds for doubting the substance of what they have to say. However, none went around in 1943 with notepad or Dictaphone. Their reconstruction of events is retrospective, and, without 100 per cent recall or recourse to film or sound archives, they would not have been human had they not been susceptible to a cocktail of failing memory and a desire to extol the heroism and virtue of their colleagues. The picture is further complicated by the fact that they do not always record the same events, simply because their separate areas of responsibility meant that none of them had the full picture at any point in time.

We do not have access to the contemporary records of the German security forces, which would be invaluable. Nor do we have the detailed reports that were given to Dewispelaere and Dubois to be taken to London and were subsequently seized by the Germans on their arrests. Michael left no statements, nor did Lemercier, and Dewispelaere did not return from captivity. We do, however, have access to the British Intelligence Service's debriefing and interrogation reports of Séailles in June 1944 and January 1945, Staggs (October 1944 and January 1945), and Reeve (September

1944), which might be considered dramatic and contentious as well as, undoubtedly, informative. These were, of course, after the event, and the reader may detect more than an occasional hint of self-preservation in some of their statements. Additionally, we have the report prepared in late 1944 by Major Dumont-Guillemet on the results of his investigation into events, and a report prepared in January 1948 by the French commissioner of police responsible for investigating enemy war crimes. Both Séailles and Staggs consented to make themselves available for interview by Stewart Kent. We have also been able to bring in the reports and memories of many of the lesser but important players who appear in the narrative, based on face-to-face discussions with Stewart, correspondence, and a wealth of carefully preserved documents and photographs, freely and generously passed to him with the heartfelt enjoinder to *'please take care and return'.*

It seems from these reports and other testimonies that there were problems between Michael's key lieutenants.

Séailles makes it clear that he had no time for Staggs, and he is utterly dismissive of his capabilities as a radio operator. Commenting on the situation when he joined Michael in Lille:

'Communication with London was extremely difficult owing to the inefficiency of GUY [Staggs] *who never seemed to be able to act as an operator, never making his radio work.'*

When Séailles took over in 1944 he placed Staggs in the Pas de Calais area to work as general recruiter and safe-house organizer:

'[Staggs] *had proved completely useless as a W/T Operator...and was far too nervous and security minded to undertake dangerous work. He might have been far better as a short term organizer for recruiting and establishing the security of a circuit, which would be taken over later by a more active and courageous man'.*

Later in his interrogation he stated that the circuit:

'Was never able to make use of the W/T Operator, who seemed to be incapable of working his set. He was also far too security minded and always found a thousand excuses as to why such-and-such a house would not be possible for transmissions. All W/T messages had to be passed through Armand's [Dumont-Guillemet's] *wireless in Paris.'*

In his own interrogation report of 14 October 1944 we read of Staggs:

> *'When source* [Staggs], *came out of prison, he immediately wrote a letter to Pierre Séailles who had taken over the organizing work after the death of* Sylvestre... . *Some time after receiving source's letter, Pierre Séailles came to see him and said that he was anxious to sever all contact with the source in view of his recent experience with the German Police. Pierre Séailles suggested that source should go to Aire-sur-la-Lys to recruit for the organization there, and to obtain intelligence on flying-bomb sites of which there were many in that area. This source did in fact do, sending such information as he could obtain to Pierre Séailles from whom he was supposed to receive his action orders on D-Day. Source was not very informative about the intelligence he acquired, or upon the extent of his recruiting work in the area, giving the impression that he in fact effected very little in either direction. When the area was overrun by Allied troops, source went to Paris with Séailles...before returning to Lille. He later went to St. Omer where he thought he might do some more work, but found none there.'*

There is some variation to this in his second interrogation on 3 January 1945:

> *'In view of informant Stagg's arrest Séailles wished to have as little to do with him as possible and suggested that he should go the Pas de Calais area and start organizing there. Informant obtained...the address of a contact at Aire-sur-la-Lys and for the remainder of his stay worked with this man in the Pas de Calais.'*

Staggs later recalled events differently. In a letter to Stewart Kent in 2000 he commented:

> *'Séailles had no authority over me. I was considered to be of equal standing. He did not send me to the Pas de Calais. It was through Mme Gilberte Braem who had contacts in the Aire-sur-la-Lys region, where the leader of* France Libre *had been arrested by the Gestapo. I then took over and became* Capitaine Bébert *or* Teuf-Teuf.

In his book, *SOE in France,* Professor Michael Foot summarized the Staggs situation thus:

> *'Staggs turned out unable to make effective contact with base, and was only otherwise useful on occasional odd jobs. In December 1943 Staggs was arrested by the Germans, who never established his connection with SOE and released him within two months; he stayed*

*quietly in the neighbourhood till the allies overran it, secretly
training his neighbours in the techniques of sabotage he knew.'*

Staggs himself insists that he was arrested by the Gestapo and imprisoned
in Loos, but the interrogator made short work of this in his unequivocal
summing up:

*'Source is a man of very low mentality, which may account for a bad
memory. It seems clear that during the period of nearly two years in
which he has been in the field he achieved little or nothing, and he
gives the impression of having been more anxious to stay out of
trouble, than to do anything else. Despite his observations that he
was arrested by the Gestapo, it is perfectly obvious that he was
merely "locked up in the common clink" by the military police'.* [1]

Turning to Lemercier, Séailles was suspicious of him, and Lemercier in turn
was resentful and wary of Séailles. The latter's opinion of Reeve was
succinct:

'Some weeks after OLIVIER *arrived in Lille he told me that he was
not entirely satisfied with the way that he had been received by*
Capitaine MICHEL. *I advised* Capitaine MICHEL *to try and improve
his relationship with his lieutenant. Following this* OLIVIER
*gradually lost my sympathy; in particular I did not appreciate his
'matador' mannerisms. In my opinion* OLIVIER, *although brave and
enterprising, lacked the qualities required to do his job.'*

Of Malfait, and his relationship with him, Séailles has nothing to say, as
prior to Michael's death they had very little contact with each other.

Of Lemercier, Reeve has little to say, other than during his interrogation
when he commented:

'Lemercier was a bad type of man.'

He is even more reticent about Séailles; his sole observation being that
he was *'a confidant of Sylvestre',* and, surprisingly, he has nothing
whatsoever to say about Malfait or Staggs.

Malfait offers no personal judgements or opinions of Séailles, but shares
his conviction that Reeve deliberately betrayed Michael, and holds him
ultimately responsible for the arrests in Arras. Throughout his writing he
generally disparages Reeve's character, methods and loyalty. Of his
appointment to Arras he said:

'Olivier *had been led to expect an independent command and was equally frustrated, but being given the Arras leadership went some way to placating him. He was a well-built man, a keen sportsman, who said little but liked to show off'*.

Following the arrest of Woussen, and Reeve's decision to withhold the information from Michael, Malfait presaged his own account of Reeve's behaviour after his own arrest:

'One could not be more of a hypocrite, nor more base a liar. A man of weak and shallow spirit, he sought to get and keep a command that he wanted at any price so as to deprive MICHEL *of a sector and work that he himself coveted. To appear brave when he really was a coward, he gambled his freedom and that of his men on the throw of a dice. Even then his attitude revealed the seeds of betrayal that were fermenting in his mind. If he is caught he believes it will be easy to get out of it: after all, he is British, soldier of a country still at war with Germany, so he will claim the status of prisoner of war according to the Geneva Convention.'*

Malfait is a fierce defendant of Lemercier and of Dewispelaere, while Reeve himself ventures no personal observations on Lemercier except the passing remark quoted above. Staggs has little to say about anyone, other than grumbling about Michael and making some wild accusations about Lemercier. He claims not to have known Reeve, saying in his first report, when asked about the death of Michael:

'Source added that he later heard that Sylvestre *had been betrayed by* Olivier, *whom source did not know and had never met.'*

Malfait contradicted this, as did Reeve, who in his reports referred to the visit to Dubois:

'Sylvestre ordered me to leave for this address where I knew that I would find HERCULE *[Dubois] so that I may give him certain messages that I carried with me. Arthur Malfait came with me as he had to be the courier between* HERCULE *and* Sylvestre *so that they could recognize him afterwards.* Guy *(Bébert)* [Staggs] Sylvestre's *W/T also came with us to examine the situation with us as for some reason he had not managed to set his receiver. After discussion I sent Malfait and* Guy *back to Lille and waited, as agreed with* Sylvestre, *for the response to the messages.'*

What held the team together was the strength of Michael's personality, and its personal loyalty and commitment to him. The individual reports and various other testimonies bear reading, perhaps as much for what they do not say as for what they do, and for some notable discrepancies, which can be briefly summarized here.

There is no disagreement on the fundamental keystones of the story of the events from the time Séailles joined the circuit in May. He usurped Lemercier as Michael's number two, and was then himself usurped by the arrival of another British officer, Reeve, who was then given command of the Arras region over the head of Malfait. The Fives raid took place, Velge was arrested in an apparently unconnected matter, and Lemercier's cousin Leblanc was subsequently arrested at the Fives gates. Both of these arrests led to Lemercier's address. He had left home but not warned his lodger, Martel, who subsequently turned traitor and sparked off the first wave of arrests. Woussen shot a policeman in Arras, and Volckaert cut down two others shortly afterwards, as a result of which a large price was put on their heads and an intense manhunt began. Woussen was arrested on the Spanish border, and talked, leading to the arrests in Arras and, indirectly, to the death of Michael. Lemercier had been executed in the meantime, in case he too talked.

Here we need to bring in a caveat. As excellent and detailed as Coilliot's documentation of Malfait's chronology is, there is running through it an assumption of inevitability, as if everything stemmed from a single cause – Martel's arrest and subsequent betrayals – which is not really the case. Martel was arrested because Lemercier, who had taken flight at Michael's suggestion, failed to warn Martel in time for him to get away. Martel's treachery did lead the Germans to Hertault and, subsequently, to the garage in Arras, but it did not form part of an unbroken line through to the death of Michael. All the Germans found at Dacheux's garage was the truck. If they had searched it, they would certainly have found Woussen's revolver, but if Woussen had not gone back for it, or had not chosen to shoot down a policeman, the trail to FARMER might well have run cold. Woussen could simply have gone underground, without a price on his head and without the subsequent pressure to get him out of the country. This event was a definitive turning point.

Malfait would have nothing to do with Séailles's doubts about Lemercier and his loyalty:

> 'Manu's *devotion for Michel was indisputable. But he couldn't cope with the development of the network and with the indispensable sharing of responsibilities. It often ended up in arguments that* Michel *would skilfully settle to the detriment of* Manu, *who would bend, which was to his credit.'*

Further confirmation of Lemercier's loyalty and faith in Michael comes in the letter he wrote to Eliane on 29 October, shortly before his expected departure for England:

'This is it this time. I am leaving. Michel *has picked me up. He is taking me tonight to the people who are taking me away. Kiss the boy for me. Tell him his godfather is coming to see him... . Don't worry.* Michel *says that I'll be over there in a fortnight.'*

This was followed by another note in which he added:

'I am leaving either over-ground or by air. Michel *assures me that in 15 days I will be over there. He has promised that you will lack for nothing. He will get* Albert *to bring milk and money every month. He is going to come and see you.'*

Eliane provided further testimony in a report she gave to Malfait in November 1945:

'The day I gave birth to my little Michel (6 May 1943), Manu *had been given charge, by* Michel, *to take a message to Paris and it was* Michel *accompanied by* Jahncke [Jean Velge] *who came to visit me at the maternity of Boulevard Vauban in Lille. He came nearly every day, sometimes with Denise,* Lulu [Delacroix] *or* Mado [Madeleine Thyrou]. *On 10 May 1943 was my son Michel's baptism and* Michel *came as the godfather under the name of* Michel (Joseph) Rampal. *It is then that he told me that whatever happened, the British Government would never forget all the favours done and that his godson would never want for anything (but this stayed, of course, a pious aim which could never be realized).* Manu's [Lemercier's] *trust in* Michel *was big; besides he liked him a lot. "*Michel *was for me more than a friend."'*

Staggs adds fuel to this particular fire during his interrogations. In the first report he says that he lived with Lemercier and his wife in Lille for a while, but neither liked nor trusted Lemercier, and he reported this to Michael. After he moved to Roubaix he kept a distance from Lemercier because of his dislike for the man, and in his second report he stated, in the context of early November (Lemercier was executed on 3 November):

'Another man who was arrested in Lille was Manu. *He had attracted attention to himself by spending too much money and going around*

*in a car, which ran on petrol. As a result of his arrest about eight
people who had looked after letter boxes were also arrested.'*

The report goes on to say that Staggs was of the opinion that Lemercier had
become a traitor because he was later released by the Germans, and Staggs
heard that he had been paid a large sum by them. Possible explanations for
this are that Staggs made this up to protect Reeve, if it ever came out that
he had executed Lemercier (they met up before they were both interviewed
more or less at the same time in London), or that Staggs failed to realize
(or chose not to disclose) that this was in fact the story of Martel, not
Lemercier.

These views of Staggs in respect of Lemercier are strangely at odds with
a statement Staggs made to Stewart Kent during a personal interview that:

'He admired Manu *a great deal and he was more like a brother than
a friend.'*

It was Reeve's version of events, as told to the Germans, that led them
to exhume Lemercier's body and exploit the event by publicising it, in an
attempt to denigrate Michael and warn off the population. Yet it seems
inconceivable that Michael would have authorized the killing of the man
who had supported him so loyally, the man with whom he had been through
so much and the father of his godson. Only three days earlier he had taken
his old friend to Arras and told him he would soon be on his way, urging
him to write those last letters to Eliane. Nor is there any evidence
whatsoever to support Staggs's assertion that Lemercier was arrested by the
Germans and subsequently released. Michael would surely have known,
and, if he had ever suspected Lemercier of treachery, he could easily have
had him dispatched at any time in Lille, Roubaix, the Pas de Calais or
anywhere else. And, if he had any doubts, he would surely not have had
Staggs bring Lemercier to Arras and jeopardize security there. And, by the
same token, Lemercier could have betrayed Michael at any time in the
preceding eleven months but did not do so.

Of the circumstances of Reeve's own arrest, Malfait had this to say:

'As for Lieutenant Olivier, *who used to travel around with three
revolvers on him as well as a poison pill (we used to call him the
"Human Arsenal"), we were most surprised to learn that he
surrendered without using his weapons or resorting to his pill.*

'Happily, OLIVIER's *example was never followed, and the
organization was able to count on a host of heroes, every one worthy
of* Capitaine Michel, *who in spite of hideous physical and mental*

torture, gave away not a single name to the enemy and allowed our organization to continue its task of making itself felt to the Boches. According to the testimony of Madame Dewispelaere, far from using his weapons, OLIVIER *went out of his way to collect them all together and hide them in a suitcase...*OLIVIER *wanted to live. His true nature reappeared. False friend to his leader whose authority he undermined, false hard man who hid his weapons when they were needed, he will be the false brother of his men whom he will betray under the false pretext of saving them from the firing squad... . This was how* OLIVIER *was now: a coward, but he did not want to appear like it in the eyes of those who knew him. Disloyal man, he hid his weakness by advocating the spirit of sacrifice. Why did he surrender? So as Henri's* [Dewispelaere's] *wife would not be killed and his mother arrested? Of course! Why did he have to say where the depots of weapons were? So as to save his French friends from the firing squad! His never-ending tissue of lies and betrayal are far-reaching.'*

Responsibility for the Arras betrayals is laid firmly at the door of Dewispelaere, who was never able to defend himself, having died in captivity.

In all of our analysis, none of the major players appear to have given great weight to the evident truth expressed by Lucienne Edouard in her testimony to Malfait thirty years after the event:

'Why was WOUSSEN, *who denounced us, not executed as* MANU *was? All those miseries would never have happened'.*

As we have seen, Reeve was well aware of the dangers of Woussen talking, and he did his best to have him eliminated while there was still time, only to be thwarted by the triumvirate of mayors. Lucienne might well have been surprised to hear that it was her fellow Frenchmen who vetoed what the British officer had proposed.

The chain of events might still have been broken if Reeve had not led Lynen directly to Boulevard de Belfort. None of the other Arras men who were arrested, including Dewispelaere, knew this address, and the GFP had been searching Lille for months trying to find Michael. Given that he chose not to take the path of resistance, could Reeve have kept silent for forty-eight hours, or did he genuinely believe, as he subsequently reported, that Michael had already moved out? Or, simply put, was Michael betrayed?

Chapter notes

1   The reference here to the military police is possibly misleading. Almost certainly this would have been the French *Milice*, and not a German section, in whose hands Staggs might not have received such sympathetic treatment.

Chapter 27

Inquest

'The memories of men are too frail a thread to hang history from.'
John Still

It is neither our role nor our right to sit in judgement and either condemn or exonerate the actions of brave men whose lives were under threat daily and who were subject to pressures we can barely imagine. All we can do is examine the stories of those who were there and try to apply some objective retrospection.

Shortly after his arrival to take over the circuit in 1944, Major Dumont-Guillemet went to Lille, where he interviewed 'various people who knew both Lieutenant Reeve and *Captain Sylvestre* well' and offered the following comments:

> *'Monsieur Mairen is the father of René Crampon who was arrested by the Gestapo and knew both* Sylvestre *and* Olivier *well. Olivier was a bully. One Sunday he said "it is a pity that I am only lieutenant and that Trotobas is a captain". Sometime later he added "I have three men to bump off, two French and one English."*
>
> *'Madame Vansprache* [Vanspranghe] *is the wife of one of* Captain Sylvestre's *collaborators in the circuit who was arrested and tortured to death without speaking. This woman had a good opinion of* Olivier.
>
> *'Olivier often went to his café* [Monsieur Demoor]. *He was referred to as the Human Arsenal because he always carried two or three guns. We felt that things were not quite right between him and* Sylvestre. *He was jealous and a crafty waster.*
>
> *'Olivier lived in her* [Madame Dutilleux] *house* [in Rue de Vergniaud]. *Her husband was arrested and sent to Germany. Olivier seemed straightforward and liked to assure everyone that he would kill himself rather than be taken alive. When Monsieur Dutilleux was arrested in January the Germans assured him that* Olivier *had stated that he lived with Madame Dutilleux. When she protested, the Germans described exactly, without having seen it, the room*

previously occupied by Olivier. *Only* Sylvestre, Olivier, *Delacroix and Pierre Séailles knew this address.* Sylvestre *was killed.* Delacroix *committed suicide, and Pierre Séailles had also been living there and* Olivier *knew it.* Sylvestre *was not friendly towards* Olivier *who had claimed to be able to do a better job than him.*

'Olivier *also frequented this establishment* [Jeanne Soret's café/letterbox in Rue de Cambrai]. *Olivier and Henri Dewispelaere were arrested first, twenty-seven men followed. No-one escaped or came back from Germany. Eight were shot immediately on 14 December 1943.*

'*Madame Henri Dewispelaere is the woman at whose home* Olivier *was arrested. Her husband was arrested at the same time.* Olivier *was very agitated in the days before their arrest. She does not know why. As for the arrest itself she denies that the Germans had used her as a shield for their own protection as described by* Olivier. Olivier *went down from the first floor to the ground floor not to fight but to hide his weapons. According to Mademoiselle Maresco who spoke to Madame Dewispelaere, her fiancé was in prison with Dewispelaere and* Olivier *had accused the latter.'*

Dumont-Guillemet concluded:

'*I do not consider* Olivier *a traitor but feel that severe sanctions should be taken against him for the following reasons:*

1   *From the various statements it appears that Olivier always rebelled against the authority of his leader, Captain Sylvestre.*
2   *The fact that only two hours elapsed between the arrest of Olivier and the death of Captain Sylvestre: not very long.*
3   *The fact that Olivier had given Captain Sylvestre's address so quickly while saying: "the enquiry will prove that Sylvestre had effectively told me he was moving." Perhaps he salved his conscience with this excuse, since Olivier knew full well that there was a chance that Sylvestre had not yet moved; an outcome that would appease the resentment that Olivier felt towards Sylvestre.*
4   *Olivier was without question the cause of the arrest of Monsieur Dutilleux. I cannot speak for the other twenty-seven men arrested, having been unable to obtain evidence with which to denounce Olivier.*
5   *It is regrettable that Olivier (a British Officer) was the only one in the organization who lacked the strength of character either to commit suicide or to go down fighting.'*

Pierre Séailles did not agree with the conclusion. In an attachment to the report of his interrogation by Major Hunt *(HS6/759)* he added another charge:

> '*It is my belief that* OLIVIER *is the only one of the leaders of our organization who did not know how to die without giving anything away to the enemy.* Captain MICHEL *and* LULU [Delacroix] *died on the field of honour, rather than fall into the enemy's hands, on the 27/28 of November, the first one while defending himself, the second taking his own life. We count five leaders who died as a result of the treatment they had to undergo, without talking, and a score of others of whom we have no news. For my part I can find no excuse for* Lieutenant OLIVIER, *alias the "Human Arsenal" for which the essential quality is courage. However, I owe him my own life because he did not reveal my address until 12 January 1944.*'

Séailles goes on to demand the harshest penalties:

> '*In conclusion, it is ninety-nine per cent certain that* OLIVIER *was a traitor and should be degraded and shot for selling out his chief, being responsible for his death, and giving away the address of people who had harboured him, when other members of the organization allowed themselves to die of hunger rather than talk.*'

Thus, François Reeve stands accused on a number of counts. On the first – that he failed to honour his oath – this is sustainable in that he neither fought it out in that he neither fought it out with his captors and died in the process like Michael, nor did he take his own life like Delacroix, and he did not undergo and withstand prolonged interrogation and torture like Velge and many others – at least not prior to Michael's death. In the eyes of Séailles and Malfait, this was the real betrayal, and it is evident that if Reeve had taken the 'honourable path' he could not have led Lynen to Michael. But these reservations do not of themselves make him a traitor, and it is noticeable that neither of his accusers, nor Marie Dewispelaere, acknowledges the fact that Henri Dewispelaere too was armed and could equally have shot it out if he was so minded. For Reeve to claim that he refused to shoot at the Germans for fear of hitting Dewispelaere's wife and children is plausible, logical and honourable. Indeed this seems to have been precisely what went through the mind of Delacroix when faced with similar circumstances. The option of shooting himself or swallowing his pill does not seem to have occurred to Reeve, and once the fleeting opportunity to do either had come and gone, he was no longer master of his own destiny.

As to his rapid yielding to the German will and cooperating with them, only he would know if his defence – that he believed they already knew everything about the parachute receptions and that he was giving nothing away – was honest, and not simply a ploy to save his own life. Malfait's scenario of Lynen offering to strike a bargain with Reeve during his initial interrogation, whereby he would be treated as a prisoner of war if he cooperated, has no factual support, although, according to Reeve, such an offer was made two days later, after the initial wave of arrests, and he rejected it. This might well have influenced Malfait's projected replay of the interview that took place immediately after Reeve's capture.

On the count that Reeve disclosed the address of Dutilleux, who had harboured him, his claim that the Germans had found the address in Michael's flat seems somewhat tenuous, particularly in the light of Séailles's affirmation that he and Michael had removed all incriminating documents the previous day. It is also hard to understand why, as Madame Dutilleux claims, the Germans had in their possession details of the rooms occupied by Séailles and Reeve, unless one or the other gave it to them.

On the final count – that Reeve betrayed Michael and caused his death – the fact that he took Lynen to Michael's last known address does not justify the statements that he betrayed him, and the post-war focus of Séailles and Malfait on this point seems strange indeed; both had seen copies of Reeve's initial report, and in that he does not deny that he led them to Michael. How far Reeve's insistence that he was ignorant of the fact that Michael might still be at the apartment is a product of his desire to protect himself from the very accusations that were levelled at him will, perhaps, never be known. His defence is that he genuinely believed Michael to have left Boulevard de Belfort, and the assertions made by both of his accusers that Michael had not intended to spend the night there only strengthen, not weaken, Reeve's protest that he did not *knowingly* lead Lynen to Michael. It is interesting to note that neither Séailles nor Malfait, nor indeed Dumont-Guillemet, suggest that it was a *deliberate* betrayal. All the facts point to an unfortunate combination of circumstances and lead to a reasonable conclusion that Michael contributed to his own downfall by deciding to stay one more night there because of his concern for Denise Gilman. We can only assume that it was Denise's frail condition – in his interrogation report of January 1945, Séailles suggests that she was in fact pregnant – as well as the suddenness of events, that stopped him from trying to escape through the roof; a possibility he had discussed with his landlady that very evening, in the knowledge that Denise was there too. Whether he would have had time to do this is questionable.

Perhaps the last words on this subject should be those of the official enquiry into events, as stated in the report of Reeve's interrogation carried out 'in the presence of a representative of MI5' on 10 September 1944, during which Reeve was called to account by those whose position and responsibility made it their due. Under the heading *The object of the source's interrogation* we read:

> *'On the same night that source was arrested, his chief –* SYLVESTRE *– was in a house which he had been using near the Porte de Douai in Lille. He was in company with a mistress. The Germans surrounded the house and a fight ensued in the course of which* SYLVESTRE *and his mistress were both shot dead. It had been suggested that source was responsible for the shooting of* Sylvestre *and the main object of the interrogation was to ascertain whether and how far this suggestion was well-founded. The secondary object of the interrogation was to ascertain whether, while in German hands, source had given away any other of his associates in resistance.'*

Further on, under the heading *Source's opinion as to his conduct*, the report added:

> *'Throughout source made no attempt to deny that he was the direct cause of* SYLVESTRE's *death. He said he would never have taken the Germans to* SYLVESTRE's *house had he not thought that* SYLVESTRE *had already left. It was put to him that, in a matter of life and death, it was taking rather a chance to assume that* SYLVESTRE *had of necessity carried out his expressed design of changing his address. Source did not dispute this, but insisted that he had not acted with any deliberate traitorous intent, and that it was an appalling shock to him when he discovered that* SYLVESTRE *had been killed in the shooting. The interrogating officer's impression was that in saying this source was totally sincere. Throughout his interrogation source produced the impression of a man who was doing his best to tell the truth, concealing nothing and bitterly upset at what had occurred.... . Source felt that he had nothing with which to reproach his conscience although, as above stated, he could not dispute having taken a risk with regard to* SYLVESTRE.'*

Although Reeve claimed that he had *'nothing with which to reproach his conscience'*, it is clear that the Germans were nowhere near finding Michael through their own efforts, and it is telling testimony to his security arrangements that, even after his death, his key lieutenants were able to avoid capture. It is revealing, also, that Lynen and his fellow officers were completely unaware that Michael was posing as a GMR officer, and they only learned this when Reeve told them and identified the body. Only minutes earlier, Martel had told Lynen that the body was not that of Michael.

The concluding paragraph, headed *Impression of the interrogating officer*, reads:

> '*It was felt that source was not a man of great intelligence and was the type who might have allowed himself to be too easily bluffed by the repeated assertions of the Germans that they knew everything. Although not tortured...he was undoubtedly subjected to very severe handling and, during the process, allowed himself to be more easily persuaded by these assertions of the Germans than a man of greater perspicacity and tougher fibre would have been. There is no question of any deliberate disloyalty on his part in the opinion of the interrogating officer, but it cannot be said in his favour that he showed as much consistency and firmness of character when being maltreated by the Germans as has been shown by a great many other agents in similar circumstances.*'

Although he was officially exonerated by his superiors from wilfully causing the death of Michael – a death that we feel was both untimely and avoidable – Reeve never returned to Lille to face his accusers.

Epilogue

*'If there be any virtue, and if there be any praise,
think on these things.'*
Philippians IV.v8

When Yvonne Pachy heard the news of Michael's death, from her brother Robert, she refused to believe it. The only way he could convince her was to use his police identity to smuggle his photographer friend, Louis Cochet, into the mortuary where Michael was lying. Cochet had the necessary equipment to take a good photograph in the dim surroundings. As Robert drew back the shroud Cochet snapped the image of the white, lifeless figure on the litter. He had copies made and gave one to Yvonne. This was the photograph that sparked off the young Stewart's lifelong interest in who it was and why he was 'sleeping'.

But the Germans had not finished with the Pachys. Yvonne had kept in touch with their friends in Belgium, and often went riding or skating with them. When it became clear in the spring of 1944 that the Allied invasion was imminent, she asked if she could stay with them. She did, until they told her that on the Belgium border they were likely to be the middle of the fighting very quickly, and she became frightened. She decided to cycle back to Gondecourt, where a neighbour stopped her just as she was coming into the village and told her not to go home. She was told there were soldiers in her house, which had been raided and ransacked several times. Fearful that they wanted to take her to prison once more, she ran with her bicycle to the nearby woods, where she hid out for two days, until a friend came and told her the Germans had left. She never found out why they had come back at this time, or what they might have been looking for. However the grenades Michael had given her had disappeared.

What is missing from the narrative and the testimonies is any real indication of what Michael was like as an individual human being, as opposed to his efficiency as an organizer and leader. Only Yvonne Pachy offers any real insight, no doubt because she saw him only as a private person meeting an old friend, and she knew nothing of his resistance work. It would too, be interesting to know more about his relationship with Denise Gilman, who has been variously described as 'girlfriend', 'secretary', 'confidante', 'mistress' and 'lover'. The brief reference by Séailles to the fact that she was pregnant when she died is intriguing, but not mentioned anywhere by Malfait. If true, it would give substance to, and help explain, Michael's anxiety about her and his decision to return to the apartment on the fateful night. Had Michael survived to give his own reports about the events we have described, they would have made fascinating reading, and the story of the valiant activities of the resistance in the north of France would have received more timely recognition. As it is, the question as to whether he and the men of Arras were in reality betrayed by their own kind, or were simply the victims of circumstances, will continue to linger. Treachery is rife throughout this story. From the strange affair of *Christophe* and the 'mousetrap' at the Villa des Bois in Marseilles, through the betrayal of the Pachys by a friend and neighbour, Martel's perfidy, the betrayals of Suttill and the PROSPER circuit, those of Dubois and his HERCULE team, and the allegations against Reeve, Woussen, Dewispelaere and Copin.

Had Michael returned, the injustice done to him might never have occurred. Séailles was awarded the *Légion d'Honneur*, the *Croix de Guerre*, the *Médaille de la Résistance*, and the British Distinguished Service Order (DSO). Malfait was awarded the *Légion d'Honneur*, the *Croix de Guerre*, the *Médaille de la Résistance* and the OBE, and Delacroix was awarded a posthumous *Légion d'Honneur*. Biéler's contribution to freedom was recognized with the DSO and the MBE, while Staggs was awarded the 'Freedom of the City of Lille' in 1998. In 2006 he was also awarded the *Légion d'Honneur*, much to the surprise of SOE Historian, Professor Michael Foot, standing next in line to him, who knew the true story. But Michael, a true hero who set up and led a powerful sabotage organization, much feared by the enemy, and sacrificed his own life rather than betray his men, received no recognition from his own country. The French awarded him the *Médaille du Résistance* and even struck a special medal to commemorate him. The citizens of Lille named a street and a new housing estate after him, and on the wall of 20 Boulevard de Belfort there is a commemorative plaque. It reads:

> *'Here fell, in the face of the enemy, on 27 November 1943,*
> *Capitaine Michel*
> *British Officer of the SOE Special Forces*
> *Leader of the French-Anglo Organization*
> *Circuit SYLVESTRE-FARMER ex WO*
> *Acting for Buckmaster London in Occupied France*
> *And his devoted collaborator*
> *Denise Gilman'*

From his own people he received nothing, even though he was put forward for a Victoria Cross. Michael's final heroic act of bravery in the field was not however performed in circumstances that would have facilitated an immediate award in accordance with the provision of the Victoria Cross Warrant, which is:

'Under the eye and command of an admiral or commodore commanding a squadron or detached naval force, or of a general commanding a corps or divisions or brigade on a distinct and detached service.'

But there is in the warrant a provision covering this, which reads:

'Where such act shall not have been performed in sight of a commanding officer aforesaid, then the claimant for the honour shall prove the act to the satisfaction of the captain or officer commanding his ship, or to the officer commanding the regiment to which the claimant belongs, and such captain, or such commanding officer, shall report the same through the usual channel to the admiral or commodore commanding the force employed in the service, or to the officer commanding the forces in the field who shall call for such description and attestation of the act as he may think requisite, and on approval shall recommend the grant of the Decoration.'

Accordingly, a citation was prepared and submitted by someone who knew Michael well from his first mission – his co-conspirator in Mauzac, Jean Le Harivel, who ended the war as an administrator in SOE. Now a captain, he wrote on 15 January 1945 to his superior, Colonel Dodds-Parker, a memo with the subject *'VC Citation'*:

'Please find attached a citation for Captain TROTOBAS for the VC. We [SOE] have not as yet sent in a VC citation, but here is a case of great gallantry and heroism, which we feel should be justly rewarded. I understand from SIS that the case of the VC has cropped up there, and feel that the SOE can but also try to obtain the highest decoration for one of its most courageous officers. If witnesses are required we are in a position to supply them.'

The citation reads:

*'12ᵗʰ January, 1945
'Captain M.A.R. TROTOBAS
'Manchester Regiment, 167302
'Captain Trotobas, a British Officer of French extraction, was one*

of that gallant band who as early as 1941 volunteered for special services in France with the SOE. In this decision he was prompted by his intense desire for action, his patriotism and his unswerving belief that under the leadership of British Officers who understood the French mentality, the French could be brought back into the battle against the enemy in a possibly decisive manner.

'He undertook a first mission as an Organizer of resistance groups in the South-West of France. Here he worked for three months until, in October 1941, he was arrested through a series of misadventures which were in no way attributable to his fault. He spent ten months in the prisons of Périgueux and Mauzac, where his physical sufferings greatly undermined his strength. His one thought was to escape in order to continue the fight, and in July 1942 – thanks to outside complicity – he was able to realise his ambition.

'Repatriated to England in 1942, he settled down without delay to perfecting his knowledge of up-to-date SOE methods and, chafing at any delay, managed to persuade the medical authorities that he was fit for active service work again within a month.

'He left on his second mission on 18 [sic] November 1942 to organize that special hotbed of danger, the industrial North. At this period of the war the enemy were particularly combing this area, which contained very many patriotic elements which could be of great service to the Allied cause. He especially volunteered to work in this area in spite of the fact that his previous conviction rendered him more than ever vulnerable to German investigation. Moreover, the Vichy government had condemned him to death.

'Starting his work with infinite precaution, he built up an organization in Lille and the surrounding area which consisted of ardent patriots whose great desire was to emulate their leader.

'Despite the great difficulty of aerial supply owing to the understandable reluctance of the RAF to go to this flak-ridden area, Trotobas succeeded in equipping his men by the most hazardous of all methods, the bringing by road of stores from a region more approachable to the RAF. The dangers run by him and his associates in securing this material are almost legendary, and after his death in action the magnificent seeds of his labours bore fruit in sabotage and guerrilla action against the enemy upon a scale unsurpassed anywhere else in the country.

'Trotobas did not even have the moral support of a radio link with London. His initiative derived from his own immense reserve powers of enthusiasm and he infected those around him with a sense of his complete capability to deal with any situation which arose to the

extent that the organization became known as the "Organisation Franco-Anglaise du Capitaine Michel" (Michel *being the pseudonym which he used locally).*

'His second-in-command, a French Commandant, and all his men have given indications of their veneration for his memory to a British mission which visited Lille in October 1944 to enquire into the circumstances of his work. Not only was the discipline inspired by Trotobas maintained until the liberation of Lille, but men of his circuit undertook any order which was coupled with his name, regardless of risk and thoughtless of the consequences.*

'This personal loyalty to Trotobas can be accounted for by his excellent judgment and his unfailing gift for appreciating the necessity for an occasional personal example of outstanding courage. His men venerated their leader, but they also venerated the organization for which he stood, and gave evidence of their devotion by the pride in which their banners, their cars and their Headquarters bore the insignia "WO" (War Office). As shoulder badges also they bore the same insignia. The strength of the group on D-Day was about 2,500 men, all animated with the* esprit de corps *which bore the hallmarks of a great leader.*

'Six original members of the group were met and all had outstanding sabotage activity to their credit. Two in particular distinguished themselves by attacking enemy trains and convoys in circumstances of extreme peril.*

'Captain Trotobas met his death on 27 November 1943 at seven am, when a strong force of Gestapo completely surprised him by surrounding his domicile. Trotobas was about to leave the house dressed in the police uniform he habitually wore in the streets of Lille. Although the odds were hopelessly against him, Trotobas, recovering from his surprise, immediately drew his revolver and succeeded in shooting the commanding officer. The accompanying soldiers replied with sub-machine gun fire, and called on him to surrender, but Trotobas continued to fire until his ammunition was exhausted, and accounted for at least three of them, before himself being killed outright by a burst of machine-gun fire in the chest and head.*

'From a French-Canadian officer, Major G. Biéler, we have the following testimonial: "It is our duty to pay homage to the memory of Capt. Trotobas. He was a courageous and yet cautious chief, prudent and the same time audacious. He was very much admired and respected by all his French subordinates, from whom he obtained, by his tact and methods of leadership, all that he wished."*

'From a French Commandant, Arthur Malfait, who took over the* command of the OFACM in Lille, we have the following: *"The death of Capt. Trotobas, our highly venerated chief, was a catastrophe for us: but it was also an example. In spite of tremendous difficulties we continued the struggle, but we do not forget that it was the spirit which he succeeded in instilling into us in his lifetime which kept us in the fight after his death."*

'It was entirely due to Trotobas that the spirit of resistance in this vital corner of France took its being and flourished until the liberation of the country justified the heroism of those who so unsparingly contributed to its success.

'We recommend him for the VC.'

Although containing some inaccuracies, the citation is comprehensive. But it was not taken up. The recommendation noted in pencil on the memo and the citation was simply for a *'Posthumous Mention'*, but even this failed to materialise, as Professor Foot records in his book *SOE: The Special Operations Executive 1940-4'*, with yet another comment on Michael's almost heroic and epic stature:

'Going for a drive with him, one of his friends said years later, was like living through a chapter of the Iliad. He was put in for a Victoria Cross, which was refused, as there was nobody senior to himself present to report on what he had done under fire, as the VC warrant requires. In the end, his name fell off the list even of those who were to get a posthumous mention in dispatches, and his parents were left for years to believe he had come to a shady end.'

The last word on this poignant subject belongs with Jean Le Harivel. In a letter to Stewart Kent in December 2000, Michael's Mauzac companion wrote:

'Your question about the VC hurt me. Because one of my last jobs at Baker Street was to write up citations and I spent a long time writing up one for a VC. But it did not succeed, and nobody bothered to propose another one, say for a DSO. What a pity. There was no objection to giving him a medal. It was bad luck nobody took the trouble to try once again. It upset me because he deserved one more than many others who were less brave than Trotobas.'

In the late 1990s Stewart was present at the annual remembrance ceremony in Lille for Michael, one of many he personally attended. He recalled:

'*A sombre, dignified procession of soldiers and civilians, preceded by the Resistance, Regimental and British Legion flags, slowly makes its way through the streets of Lille to the Southern Cemetery, as it has done every year since 1944, when more than 14,000 were present to pay homage. With each subsequent anniversary, the number has dwindled, but even today, nearly four decades later, more than 200 soldiers and civilians are here, including veterans and former members of the resistance as well as veterans of the Middlesex Regiment and other British units. There are many medals, conspicuous among which is* La Croix du Capitaine Michel*, worn with pride by his "*compagnons*". Led by a dignified civilian hoisting a furled umbrella, the procession moves up the long drive to an imposing monument on which appears the symbol of a black cat and poignant reminders of coded messages sent over the airwaves long ago to a darkened France. At the base of the monument stands a headstone bearing the unusual design of two regimental badges. From there the procession marches to the British military cemetery, where, at the Cross of Honour, the* Last Post *and* Reveille *are sounded.*'

On a cold winter afternoon in 1996, Stewart looked at a faded posy of flowers, placed in remembrance by an unknown hand behind a small, rusting plaque on the wall of a smart butcher's shop in Gondecourt. Originally erected in the name of Jeanne Pachy, Yvonne had it changed to show her mother's maiden name. The inscription reads:

'*In memory of Mademoiselle Jeanne Oliger, who was arrested by the Germans and executed in the gas chambers at Ravensbruck concentration camp.*'

On the wall of a small office in the *Hôtel de Ville* was a photograph in a plain dark frame of Jeanne Oliger dressed in striped prison uniform. She is weak and drawn from a bout of pneumonia, but her dark eyes stare defiantly past the lens of the camera, expressing utter contempt for her captors. There was no inscription.

Late in 1998 Stewart visited the farm at Ransart and met Aimé Binot's son, René, and his wife, who told him:

'*The people in the village had accused us of being black marketeers because of all the coming and going of* Michel's *trucks in the dead of night. In response to this, when the Germans had left the area we draped the container parachutes all around the farm buildings.*'

To Stewart's amazement, René produced an SOE container parachute in mint condition from his loft, where it had lain untouched for more than fifty years, and presented it to him. Stewart still has the parachute silk, and he will never forget the experience of being with the Binots, sitting in the very chair that Michael had used. Learning that the Binots had never been recognized for their help to Michael and SOE, Stewart arranged for an 'Attestation of Thanks' to be drawn up by the Foreign and Commonwealth Office in London, which he proudly delivered to René the following spring.

In the United States National Archives there is a file of records relating to *'French men and women who may have assisted American Airmen in France during World War II'*. In it is copy of a French questionnaire completed in respect of Yvonne Pachy, *'Daughter of Deportee Deceased'*. Attached is a schedule of names and awards. This includes the stark entry:

HELPER'S NAME	HELPER'S ADDRESS	AWARD GRADE PROPOSED	CERTIFICATE NUMBER	COMPENSATION PAID	CCLAIM No.	REMARKS
PACHY, Mme & Mlle Yvonne	Rue Nationale Gondecourt	5	16288	15,750 fcs	P7415	Imprisoned. Mme deported and dead
		5	31569			

(Grade 5 is *'For the majority of "helpers" such as those who came to the aid of one escapee, who received a flyer shortly after landing, or helped six to seven men for short periods'*.)

In June 2014 Yvonne Baudet, née Pachy, was visited by two *gendarmes* at her home in Brittany. They informed her, with some pride, that she had been proposed for the *Légion d'Honneur*. As she was naturally distrustful of policemen in uniform, to their astonishment she invited them to leave her house, saying that she had not sought any recognition in 1945 and wanted none now. Fortunately, her son Stewart persuaded her otherwise, urging her to accept the award not only on behalf of herself but also on behalf of her mother who had perished in Germany, and of future family generations, through her children and grandchildren. In due course she received an official letter through the *Office National des Anciens Combattants et Victimes de Guerre* to confirm her award. Stewart was able to send a dossier of more than fifty documents relating to what Yvonne had done during the war. Of most significance was a letter of 5 April 2013, with attachments, from Eric Vanslander of the National Archives in America. Mr Vanslander had managed to find reference to Stewart's mother and grandmother in a file entitled *'Records of the ETO, US Army Awards Branch "French Helper", file references 5682722/UD193/458/1127'*. This was quite a discovery for both Stewart and Yvonne, coming almost seventy years after the events themselves, as it was the first time that they had official confirmation of the names of the soldiers and airmen that had been assisted by the mother and daughter. On Monday, 2 March 2015 the ceremony for the investiture of the *Légion d'Honneur* took place at the local Town Hall, with the mayor and other dignitaries, family and friends in attendance. As is customary, the medal was pinned on Yvonne's jacket by a current holder of the award, in this case ninety-two-year-old veteran and survivor of Dachau concentration camp, Bernard Lechaux, who was pleased to fulfil this solemn duty.

Marie-Jeanne Bouchez, who during the war adopted the style 'Mary-Jane', spent seven months in prison. Her mother, Madame Louise Marie Bouchez (née Vandervliet), was also arrested and deported to Ravensbruck prison camp. To ensure that her friend did not go alone, Jeanne Pachy pushed herself into the same transportation, and they died within days of each other in April 1945.

A cruel counterpoint to these deaths is that their betrayers survived. In a bizarre twist, Henriette Verbeke, who had been instrumental in the Gondecourt betrayals, was arrested by the Gestapo and imprisoned in Loos for a short time, which was almost certainly a German ploy to give her credibility for future work amongst the French. Abandoned by Verloop, who had no further use for her, once released, she tried to take revenge by betraying him to a man she believed to be an English agent. However, he was in fact a double agent, and she found herself back once more in Loos. Verloop took pity on her and arranged for her second release. She was arrested again by the French in September 1944, tried and condemned to death, national disgrace and confiscation of all her property. This sentence was subsequently commuted to life imprisonment, and later to twenty years. Finally freed in 1963, she died in 1974. Verloop was arrested by the British in October 1944 and recommended for execution, but after being interrogated by MI5, in circumstances that are unclear, he was released to the Dutch authorities, and was never brought to trial.

Yvonne Pachy never forgave Verbeke and even today finds her actions hard to understand:

> *'I never knew until after the liberation when Marcelle* [Arlington, née Faucomprez] *was released that we had been betrayed by someone my mother knew and had looked on as a friend for years; a neighbour who had been spying on us from just across the road and who came frequently into our home even when she was working for the Gestapo. It is contemptible that one Frenchwoman should betray another and condemn her to death.'*

Because she never returned from Ravensbruck, Jeanne Pachy did not receive the honours and recognition granted to other local members of the resistance who survived. A street in Gondecourt is named after her, but her name did not even appear on the war memorial. In recent years the Mayor of Gondecourt, and the town's hard-working and diligent Heritage [*Patrimoine*] Association, have laboured long and hard in the face of complicated bureaucracy to correct this omission, for which a ministerial decree was necessary. After preparing detailed dossiers and presenting them in Paris, in the form of a petition to the Department of Veterans Affairs and War Victims, they succeeded in obtaining this decree.

On November 11 2012, Armistice Day, a simple ceremony took place at the cemetery in Gondecourt, after a solemn march through the streets of the town. It was recorded by the newspaper *La Voix du Nord*, famous for its part in the resistance in Lille and still going strong today. It is a fitting point on which to end our story. The article reads:

> *'Two new commemorative plaques were unveiled at the War Memorial during the November 11 ceremony, in the presence of many of the people of Gondecourt. The first plaque is a tribute to those who died in the Algerian War and the fighting in Morocco and Tunisia. The second related to a woman from Gondecourt, Jeanne Pachy-Oliger. This member of the Resistance died in exile, after being deported to Ravensbruck, in May 1945. She had been denounced for hiding English airmen before they were passed on to various safe houses in the area. Arrested in 1941 and condemned to life imprisonment, she was deported to the Ravensbruck concentration camp in Germany, from which she did not return.*
>
> *'At the time of her arrest her daughter, Yvonne Pachy, was still a young teenager. Listening to her own heart, she herself wanted to join the Resistance to follow the example set by her mother. But Captain Trotobas of the BEF, better known as "Captain Michel", talked her out of it in the belief that her family had already paid a heavy price. Long live emotion!*
>
> *'After the war Fred Kent, an RAF veteran, came to France to thank the members of the Resistance who had given aid to his fellow-countrymen. The story would have ended there, if Fred and Yvonne had not met, fallen for each other and got married. She then went with him to Great Britain.*
>
> *'Today, aged 88, she lives in Brittany. Since she was unable to travel to Gondecourt, the honour of unveiling the commemorative plaque fell to her son Stewart Kent, who made a special journey from Cornwall. While a street in the village bears the name of Jeanne*

Oliger, this is the first time that a tribute has been made to her in her married name, Pachy. "It is a very moving moment for my mother and myself," Stewart confessed. After the ceremony, the school children read a number of poems, and planted rose bushes dedicated to "Resurrection" – symbols of peace, remembrance and hope.'

Stewart laid a simple red poppy and then, in the company of Danièle Lheureux, proceeded to the Lille Southern Cemetery, where they paused to lay flowers at the grave of the man whose words and deeds they had jointly done so much to revive.

The simple inscription on the memorial reads:

'The Sylvestre-Farmer Circuit
Of Capitaine Michel –
To their Dead'

Below the memorial are tablets dedicated to individual members of the circuit, including this from Michael's father:

'Captain
M.A.R. TROTOBAS
The Manchester Regiment
27th November 1943 Age 29
In loving memory of my son
Captain Michael
Killed in Action with
the French Resistance'

Testimony

by Danièle Lheureux

Danièle is the recipient of two French literary awards for her works dedicated to the SYLVESTRE-FARMER circuit: the *Prix littéraire Raymond Poincaré* awarded by UNOR, the National Union of Reserve Officers, and the *Prix littéraire de la Résistance* awarded by CAR, the Action Committee of the Resistance.

*   *   *

I first met Stewart Kent some fifteen years ago in the late 1990s when he came to Lille with his mother, Yvonne Baudet. He told me of his desire to write the story of Michael Trotobas from an English perspective including his mother's role during the German occupation. I was all in favour, since Yvonne – Mademoiselle Pachy – had been reluctant to talk about herself and the activities of her relatives in the resistance. After a number of subsequent meetings I realized that Stewart's enthusiasm and knowledge of the Trotobas story was as strong as ever. The later arrival of Nick Nicholas brought fresh inspiration, and he was able to gather together all the elements of Stewart's research in order to start writing the narrative for this book and the story of Michael Trotobas whom Yvonne got to know in September 1939, when he was stationed in Gondecourt (Nord) during his time with the Middlesex Regiment and the British Expeditionary Force.

At the end of November 1942 Captain Trotobas, an agent with SOE's F Section, returned to Lille. A highly charismatic leader, the chief of 'SYLVESTRE-FARMER' soon found himself at the head of a powerful circuit containing more than 800 members, with an escape line, an intelligence gathering service, and numerous parachute reception grounds. He led countless sabotage attacks on all manner of targets. With his extraordinary personal courage and bravery the captain aroused the admiration and devotion of his men. Sadly, sacrifice came when he was at the pinnacle of his success. On 27 November 1943 Trotobas fell in the face of the enemy, gun in hand. His removal did not bring about the end of the circuit: to avenge the death of their leader, his men carried on the battle right up to the liberation.

In January 1985 I uncovered the life of this circuit. Since then I have done everything possible to preserve and pass on the memory of Captain

Michael and his circuit. I am deeply grateful to Stewart and Nick for continuing this homage in England. I know from personal experience the many obstacles they will have had to surmount in order to achieve the splendid results revealed in this book.

Danièle Lheureux

Lille 2015

Acknowledgements

My intention in this book was to tell the story of Michael Trotobas, of whom to the best of my knowledge there are no living relatives. His father, birth mother and stepmother passed away many years ago and he was an only son. Although only a small part of his story, nevertheless my family were inextricably linked with Michael between 1939 and 1943.

The following acknowledgements take this into account. There is no pre-planned order, and I am equally grateful to everyone mentioned, while at the same time I apologise to anyone who has been omitted.

I am extremely grateful to those veterans who are no longer with us but who gave freely of their time through interviews or correspondence to help me: *Maurice Buckmaster, Vera Atkins, Arthur Staggs, Désiré De Becker, Ernest van Maurik, Hugh Verity, Pierre Séailles, Marie J Bouchez, J P Le Harivel, Aimé Binot, Louis Cochet, Tom Roberts, Eliane Lemercier, Tony Brooks and Henry Diacono.*

To *Stephen Grady* now 90 years of age who met Michael Trotobas on three occasions in France. I remember with great fondness my two visits to interview him at his home in northern Greece and his amazing anecdotes of his time with the resistance near Nieppe in the north of France.

I am particularly grateful to *Gervase Cowell* and *Duncan Stuart*, custodians of the SOE Records until their release to the Public Records Office in 2002. To *'Les'*, who introduced me to and sponsored my membership of the Special Forces Club. To authors, historians and researchers alike, *Professor Michael Foot, Danièle LHeureux, André Coilliot, Francis Bohee and Jean Duchateau in France, Marc Vershooris* and *Etienne Verhoyen* in Belgium, *Frans Dekkers* in the Netherlands, *David Harrison* on the SOE Training Schools, and *Arthur Staggs* and *Francis J Suttill* in England. To my very early translators *Frankie Compton, Holly Wilson* and *Helga Kizlink*. To *Cathryn Nicholas*, for her patient proofreading and corrections. To *Simon Cook* for his excellent work on the photographs.

Thanks to the Public Records Office, Imperial War Museum, National Army Museum, *Tom Roberts, Mike Ward* and *Ron Morris* of the Middlesex Regiment Association, the Ministry of Defence Historical Records Section, the World War Two Research Centre in Belgium, *Monica Herzog* of the Ravensbruck Memorial, *Anise Postel-Vinay* and *Marie-Jo Chombart de Lauwe*, both of the Amicale de Ravensbruck. To *Eric Vanslander* of the

National Archives in Washington DC. To the *editor of the North Lane Runner* newsletter in Brighton and the *Principal of the Marist Catholic University School in Dublin*. In particular, to *Jacqueline Biéler* in Canada, daughter of Gustave '*Guy*' Biéler – 'Musician' – who died so bravely in Flossenberg Concentration Camp.

My thanks again to *Mark Seaman* who persuaded me to write about Michael Trotobas in the first instance, and again also to *Nick Nicholas*, without whose help and writing skills this book may never have been written.

To *my dear mother*, who hardly ever spoke about her wartime experiences until she was 70 years of age, and her late husband *Albert Baudet*, resistant and survivor of Buchenwald Concentration Camp. Above all else to *my wife June and our three children*, who have supported me throughout my research and the writing of the book.

Stewart Kent
Penzance 2015

Bibliography

1943: The Victory That Never Was – John Grigg – Penguin 1999
4 Longues Années D'Occupation Vol 2 – André Coilliot – Private Printing 1985
A Life in Secrets – Sarah Helm – Little, Brown 2005
Agents By Moonlight – Freddie Clark – Tempus 1990
Beaulieu – Cyril Cunningham – Leo Cooper 1998
Between Silk and Cyanide – Leo Marks – Harper Collins 1998
Bravest of the Brave – Mark Seaman – Michael O'Mara Books Ltd 1997
Churchill's School for Saboteurs: Station 17 – Bernard O' Connor –
    Amberley Publishing 2013
Chronology of SOE in France – Lieutenant Colonel E G Boxshall – Private
    Publication 1960
France The Dark Years – Julian Jackson – Oxford University Press 2001
Gardens Of Stone – Stephen Grady – Hodder & Stoughton 2013
German Security and Police Soldier – Gordon Williamson – Osprey 2002
Gubbins and SOE – Peter Wilkinson & John Bright Astley – Leo Cooper 1993
Knights Of The Floating Silk – George Langelaan – The Quality Book Club
    1959
Occupation – Ian Ousby – John Murray 1997
Ravensbruck – Jack G Morrison – Markus Wiener 2000
Secret Agent – David Stafford – BBC 2000
Secret War – Nigel West – Hodder & Stoughton 1992
Shadows in the Fog – Francis J Suttill – History Press 2014
Simone et Ses Compagnons – Editions de Minuit 1947
Sisters in The Resistance – Margaret Collins – John Wiley 1995
SOE 1940-1946 – M.R.D. Foot – Pimlico 1999
SOE in France – M.R.D. Foot – HSMO 1966
*La Résistance "Action-Buckmaster" Sylvestre-Farmer Avec le Capitaine
    Michel* – Danièle Lheureux – Le Geai Bleu 2002
The Battle of France 1940 – Philip Warner – Cassel & Co 1990
The Diehards – The Middlesex Regiment – Wolmer White – Hutchinson 1950
The Evaders – Ed Cosgrove – Pocket Books 1970
The French Secret Service – Douglas Porch – Oxford University Press 1997
The German Police – A.J. Munoz – Axis Europa Inc. USA 1997
The Long Silence 1914/18 – Helen McPhail – I.B. Tauris 1999
The Man The Nazis Couldn't Catch – John Laffin – Alan Sutton Publishing 1984
The Secret History of SOE – William Mackenzie – St James Press 2000
Turncoat – Brendan Murphy – Macdonald 1987
We Landed By Moonlight – Hugh Verity – Crecy Publishing 1995
The White Rabbit – Bruce Marshall – Pan Books 1952

Index